Tourism and Everyday Life in the Contemporary City

This book explores the phenomena of the urban everyday and *new urban tourism*. It provides a systematic framework and draws on a mix of theoretical and empirical work to look at the increasing intermingling of 'tourists' and 'residents'.

Tourism and urban everyday life are deeply connected in a mutually constitutive way. Tourism has become a key momentum of urban development and affects cities beyond its economic dimension. Urban everyday life itself can turn into a matter of tourist interest for people searching for experiences off the beaten track. Even living in a city as a resident involves moments, activities and practices which could be labelled as 'touristic'. These observations demonstrate some of the various layers in which urban tourism and everyday city life are intertwined. This book gathers multiple interdisciplinary approaches, a diversity of topics and methodological variety to examine this complex relationship. It presents a systematic framework for the dynamic research field of *new urban tourism* along three dimensions: the extraordinary mundane, encounters and contact zones, and urban co-production.

This book will be of interest to students and researchers across fields such as Tourism and Mobility Studies, Urban Studies, Leisure Studies, Tourism Geography and Tourism Sociology.

Thomas Frisch studied sociology, English and Portuguese, and holds a Master's degree in Sociology from the University of Salzburg. In his PhD thesis he is exploring digital review cultures, their communities, and their consequences for everyday practices. His major academic interests are tourism and media sociology, the sociology of evaluation, slum tourism and urban studies.

Christoph Sommer is completing his PhD in geography at Humboldt-Universität zu Berlin. He co-founded the *Urban Research Group New Urban Tourism* at the Georg Simmel Center for Metropolitan Studies. His main areas of interest include research on urban policy, governance, the anthropology of policy, tourism and new municipalism.

Luise Stoltenberg is completing her PhD in sociology at Universität Hamburg. For her dissertation project, she is studying the online hospitality networks of Couchsurfing and Airbnb with regard to the notion of dwelling. Her research interests include the sociology of everyday life and of digital cultures, as well as mobility and tourism studies.

Natalie Stors is a PhD candidate and research associate at the Department of Leisure and Tourism Geography at Trier University, Germany. In her PhD project she is investigating the motivations for participating in short-term rental practices via Airbnb and the implications of sharing platforms for the construction of tourism space. Her research is dedicated to urban tourism and the sharing economy.

Routledge Studies in Urbanism and the City

This series offers a forum for original and innovative research that engages with key debates and concepts in the field. Titles within the series range from empirical investigations to theoretical engagements, offering international perspectives and multidisciplinary dialogues across the social sciences and humanities, from urban studies, planning, geography, geohumanities, sociology, politics, the arts, cultural studies, philosophy and literature.

For more information about this series, please visit: www.routledge.com/series/RSUC

Tourism and Everyday Life in the Contemporary City

Edited by Thomas Frisch,
Christoph Sommer, Luise Stoltenberg
and Natalie Stors

Routledge
Taylor & Francis Group

LONDON AND NEW YORK

First published 2019 by Routledge

2 Park Square, Milton Park, Abingdon, Oxfordshire OX14 4RN

52 Vanderbilt Avenue, New York, NY 10017

Routledge is an imprint of the Taylor & Francis Group, an informa business

First issued in paperback 2020

British Library Cataloguing-in-Publication Data
A catalogue record for this book is available from the British Library

Library of Congress Cataloging-in-Publication Data
Names: Frisch, Thomas (Sociologist), editor. | Sommer, Christoph (Tourism scholar), editor. | Stoltenberg, Luise, editor. | Stors, Natalie, editor.
Title: Tourism and everyday life in the contemporary city / [edited by Thomas Frisch, Christoph Sommer, Luise Stoltenberg, Natalie Stors].
Description: Abingdon, Oxon ; New York, NY : Routledge, 2019. |
Includes bibliographical references and index.
Identifiers: LCCN 2018050277 | ISBN 9781138580725 (hbk : alk. paper) |
ISBN 9780429507168 (ebk) | ISBN 9780429016486 (mobi/kindle) |
ISBN 9780429016509 (pdf) | ISBN 9780429016493 (epub)
Subjects: LCSH: Tourism–Social aspects. | Cities and towns.
Classification: LCC G155.A1 T58934815 2019 | DDC 306.4/819–dc23
LC record available at https://lccn.loc.gov/2018050277

ISBN: 978-1-138-58072-5 (hbk)
ISBN: 978-0-367-66080-2 (pbk)

Typeset in Times New Roman
by Newgen Publishing UK

Contents

Illustrations

Contributors

Fabian Frenzel is an Associate Professor in Political Economy and Organisation Studies at the University of Leicester, United Kingdom, and a research associate at the University of Johannesburg, South Africa. His research interests concern the intersections of mobility, politics and organisation. He has widely published his research on social movement studies and tourism.

Tim Freytag is a Professor of Human Geography at the Institute of Environmental Social Sciences and Geography, University of Freiburg, Germany. His research foci and teaching interests include urban studies, social and cultural geography, and tourism and mobility studies.

Nils Grube is a PhD candidate and research associate at the Department of Planning Theory and Urban-Regional Policy Analysis at the Institute of Urban and Regional Planning, Berlin University of Technology, Germany. He has also worked as a research associate at the Humboldt-Universität zu Berlin and Goethe University Frankfurt. His PhD project is entitled *Governing touristification – Tourism conflict regulation under postpolitical conditions*.

Markus Kip works as a researcher on urban heritage at the Georg Simmel Center for Metropolitan Studies, Humboldt-Universität zu Berlin, Germany. After studying philosophy and theology, he obtained his PhD in sociology from York University in Toronto, Canada. He is the author of *The Ends of Union Solidarity: Undocumented Labor and German Trade Unions* (2017) and co-editor of *Urban Commons: Moving beyond State and Market,* published in 2015 (Bauwelt Fundamente/Birkhäuser). His main areas of interest include architectural sociology, commons, urban heritage, migration and work, and solidarity.

Clara Sofie Kramer is a PhD candidate and research associate at the Institute of Environmental Social Sciences and Geography, University of Freiburg, Germany. Her research interests are in the field of tourism geography, urban tourism and the production of tourist spaces.

Jonas Larsen is a Professor of Mobility and Urban Studies at Roskilde University, Denmark. He has had a long-standing interest in tourist photography, tourism and mobility studies. More recently, he has also written about cycling, running and urban marathons. He is co-author of *The Tourist Gaze 3.0* (2011, with John Urry). His work has been translated into Chinese (both in China and Taiwan), Japanese, Polish, Czech, Portuguese and Korean (in process), and he is on the editorial board of *Mobilities*, *Tourist Studies* and *Photographies*.

Jessica Parish completed her PhD in Political Science in 2017 at York University in Toronto, Canada. She is currently a visiting scholar at the City Institute, York University. She is employed by Lancaster House Publishing in Toronto, where she works as a research associate and the book reviews editor of the *Canadian Labour and Employment Law Journal*. She is also an associate editor for an open access Palgrave Communications collection entitled *The Geographies of Emotional and Care Labour*. Her core research interest pertains to the social reproduction of urban inequality.

Bas Spierings is an Assistant Professor in Urban Geography at the Department of Human Geography and Spatial Planning at Utrecht University, the Netherlands. His research focuses on the nexus between urban consumption and public space, with specific attention to touristification, retail developments, (cross-border) shopping, walking mobilities and encounters with difference.

Mathis Stock is a Professor of Tourism Geography at the University of Lausanne, Switzerland. His work is about tourist practices in a context of widespread mobilities and cities as tourist places. His main research question asks about the differentiated ways people inhabit mobilities and places.

Bianca Wildish is a graduate of the Urban and Economic Geography Master's programme at Utrecht University, the Netherlands. Her research focuses on place attachment, feeling at home and belonging in the tourism context, and is specifically concerned with the similarities and differences between locals and visitors.

Nora Winsky is a PhD candidate and research associate at the Institute of Environmental Social Sciences and Geography at the University of Freiburg, Germany. She works on tourist practices and related representations in Freiburg and the Black Forest.

Acknowledgements

This book arose out of the conference *Touristified Everyday Life—Mundane Tourism: Current Perspectives on Urban Tourism*, which was held at the Georg Simmel Center for Metropolitan Studies (GSZ) in Berlin in May 2017. Bringing together empirical and theoretical contributions from various disciplines, the conference presented a comprehensive approach for addressing emergent phenomena of urban tourism. Its call for papers drew international attention and received a massive number of submissions. Given this success and the interesting discussions during the event itself, the need for further academic debate and research became obvious. As a result, four members of the initiative team of the conference, Thomas Frisch (University of Hamburg), Christoph Sommer (Humboldt University of Berlin), Luise Stoltenberg (University of Hamburg) and Natalie Stors (Trier University), decided to invite contributions to further continue the debate on *new urban tourism*, and the connectedness of tourism and urban everyday life, in an edited volume.

The four editors are part of an interdisciplinary group of young academics based at the Georg Simmel Center for Metropolitan Studies (GSZ). The *Urban Research Group: 'New Urban Tourism'* was founded in 2015 by Christoph Sommer and Natalie Stors during their doctoral studies to provide a network for PhD students working at the nexus of tourism and urban studies. Since its foundation, the research group has held several meetings every year for scholarly exchange. This ranges from discussing selected publications and relevant research findings to giving constructive feedback on dissertation projects from group members.

It was in this context of efforts to open up the group's debate on recent developments in urban tourism that the aforementioned conference was planned. We would like to express our special thanks to Silke Laux (Berlin Professional School), Nils Grube, Sara Hohmann, Katharina Knaus (all Berlin University of Technology), Christian Samuel Kirschenmann (Bauhaus-Universität Weimar) and Julia Burgold (University of Potsdam), who were part of the conference board. In addition, we particularly would like to acknowledge the support of Professor Ilse Helbrecht, Director of the GSZ, and the funding we received from KOSMOS (a programme which is part of the Excellence Strategy at HU Berlin) for making the conference possible.

Due to the various steps that need to be taken before a book can be published, such a project can turn into a lengthy challenge. We thank Ruth Anderson and Faye Leerink at Routledge for supporting us during the entire publication process and assisting us with any questions that arose.

Without the enormous response for the conference, this book would not have been possible. Therefore, we would like to express thanks to everyone who participated in the event and helped to turn it into such a fruitful and productive meeting. Finally, we wish to thank each author who drafted, revised and edited a chapter for this book for their inspiring contributions and their patient and professional cooperation during the review process.

1 Tourism and everyday life in the contemporary city

An introduction

Natalie Stors, Luise Stoltenberg,
Christoph Sommer and Thomas Frisch

The entanglement of urban tourism with everyday city life

Tourism and urban everyday life are deeply connected in a mutually constitutive way. On the one hand, this seems quite obvious, as tourism's effect on the everyday life of local communities has been a topic for tourism research since its very beginnings (e.g., Sharpley 2014, Jurowski *et al.* 1997, Smith 1989, Cohen 1988). On the other hand, the rather restricted idea of cities as 'destinations' inhabited by locals and visited by tourists is an established and persistent one. As such, thinking about tourism beyond "a series of discrete, localized events consisting of 'travel, arrival, activity, purchase and departure'" (Franklin and Crang 2001, p. 6), is still a pressing and promising endeavour for both urban and tourism studies. In order to shed more light on the manifold dimensions of the deeply interrelated connection between urban tourism and city life, this section looks at four aspects of this connection.

First of all, urban tourism affects cities in an often subtle, yet pervasive manner. As a result, the profound ways in which tourism shapes contemporary cities can prove hard to pinpoint. This shaping not only takes place at crowded sights, famous museums and designated neighbourhoods, but pervades the city as a whole. It is worth considering, for instance, the extent to which tourism-related urban economies structure the everyday work of many residents (Spirou 2011, Veijola 2010, Tufts 2006); how urban infrastructures respond profoundly to demands from visitors from far and wide (Law 2002, Le-Klähn and Hall 2015); and even how the daily repetition of activities, structured patterns and rhythms organize the look and feel of major sights (Edensor 1998, 2001). These examples clearly support the argument that "tourist activities are not *so* separate from the places that are visited" (Sheller and Urry 2004, p. 5, emphasis added), but, in fact, are deeply entangled with urban everyday realities. As an inherent part of the city, they are, of course, not solely restricted to use by visitors. In fact, "[t]ourists tend to share their experiences in cities with local consumers and the anonymity of cities means that it can be hard, and in most cases unnecessary, to differentiate the visitor from the rest" (Wearing and Foley 2017, p. 99). Consequently, it seems inaccurate to hold on to concepts which understand city tourism and urban everyday life as two spheres isolated from each other.

Second, urban everyday life itself can turn into a matter of tourist interest. Thriving on the rich variety of city life, urban tourism attracts many people for a broad range of reasons (Ashworth and Page 2011, Hayllar *et al.* 2008). One strong motivation has always been the desire to gain insight into the everyday life of a visited destination (e.g., Maitland and Newman 2009a, Maitland 2013, MacCannell 1976, Frisch 2012)—to experience the 'real' Tokyo, San Francisco, Rio de Janeiro or Barcelona. This desire builds on the idea that there is a hidden life happening in cities—hidden insofar as it is difficult for short-term visitors to access. This phenomenon has been referred to as 'off the beaten track tourism' in scholarly discourse (e.g., Maitland and Newman 2009b, Maitland 2010, Füller and Michel 2014, Matoga and Pawłowska 2018). However, the appeal of the ordinary, of day-to-day rhythms and normality, is not a novelty in urban tourism at all. What is new though, is that "the current quantitative dimension puts the phenomenon on the agenda of urban and tourism geographies again" (Dirksmeier and Helbrecht 2015, p. 276). This new extent of tourism, focusing on urban everyday life, calls for the elaboration of adequate theoretical conceptualisations as well as a solid analytical framework.

Third, living in a city as a resident also involves moments, activities and practices which have a 'touristic component' (Cohen 1974, see also Diaz-Soria 2017). Especially after moving to a new city, the period of settling in shows striking similarities to what visitors usually do. In order to explore their neighbourhood and get a feeling for its 'vibe', newcomers might consult travel guides for recommendations on bars and restaurants, join a city walking tour, or visit famous sights and attractions. However, this is not only restricted to newcomers. Discovering hang-out spots, lingering at urban beaches, showing friends and family around, visiting 'exotic' street food festivals, joining a guided tour—all of these activities are somehow informed by tourism (e.g., Gale 2009, Shani and Uriely 2012, Diaz-Soria 2017, Dimitrovski and Vallbona 2018). Their effects on cities are in no way marginal, and support the production and shaping of places for urban adventure and entertainment. As a result, it is possible to argue that residents themselves occasionally switch to 'touristic' mode without even leaving the confines of their own city (see also Richards 2017).

The fourth aspect runs transversely to the three already mentioned, and emphasises the influence of technology on the increasing entanglement of urban tourism with city life. For a long time, urban tourists relied on alternative guidebooks and insider tips from friends, as well as their own spirit of discovery if they wanted to explore remote areas of a city. Nowadays they are empowered by digital technology, nearly ubiquitous internet access and online services. If travellers wish to discover the everyday life of a destination, they can easily gain access to this 'attraction' by using travel apps, review websites and hospitality networks (Germann Molz 2012, Jeacle and Carter

2011, Guttentag 2015). However, such services are used by long-term residents as well. Mapping apps, for instance, help residents and visitors alike to navigate their way through less known parts of the city. Online platforms and their networks offer new possibilities for connecting locals and travellers, and thus open up aspects of urban everyday life for tourism. Whether those services help users to find accommodation, arrange to meet for a shared meal or organise a joint activity, they bring together various people who are interested in exploring a city regardless of their status of residence. Importantly, these online arranged encounters "are not just happening in fixed public or commercial spaces, but also popping up in off-the-beaten-path neighbourhoods and in the private realms of people's homes" (Germann Molz 2014). While this feeds into the desire to experience a city beyond its guidebook recommendations, it also influences the everyday life of residents participating in such online networks.

These observations strikingly demonstrate some of the various layers in which urban tourism and everyday city life are intertwined. They all make the case for a closer examination of this complex relationship, as academic literature has so far dealt with their individual aspects a great deal, but has largely ignored their interrelatedness. In contrast, this volume makes extensive use of the term '*new urban tourism*' (Roche 1992, Füller and Michel 2014) and adapts it in order to provide a systematic framework for a dynamic research field. This work thus takes steps towards the convergence of two disciplines, urban studies and tourism studies, which have been staring at each other for too long without talking (Ashworth 2003, Ashworth and Page 2011), yet it is necessary to discuss this to address the phenomena surrounding *new urban tourism*.

This introduction begins by discussing theoretical points of reference which are valuable for developing this emergent research area. Then we propose three key dimensions that characterise *new urban tourism* and serve as an analytical framework for the chapters of this anthology: the extraordinary mundane, encounters and contact zones, and urban co-production. All of these acknowledge the intimate connection of urban tourism and everyday city life. This is followed by a short description of the chapters included in this volume—each one focusing either theoretically or empirically on phenomena related to the three dimensions. The introduction ends with a critical examination of the anthology's limitations and an outlook on perspectives for future research on *new urban tourism*.

Identifying relevant conceptual points of reference

The aforementioned claims not only exemplify how tourism informs urban everydayness, and vice versa, but also indicate how binary distinctions ('tourist' and 'local', 'visitor' and 'resident', 'work' and 'leisure', 'production' and 'consumption', 'extraordinary' and 'mundane') oversimplify the urban–tourism nexus by setting urban tourism and urban everyday life in opposition to one another. In the following, we briefly describe some valuable concepts which have informed our reflections on *new urban tourism* and lay the ground for the three analytical categories we propose later on. These are the 'de-differentiation' of the established oppositional categories of tourism and everyday life (e.g., Rojek 1993, Baerenholdt *et al.* 2004, Uriely 2005, Larsen 2008); the postulated 'end of tourism' (Lash and Urry 1994); and the concept of 'post-tourism' (Feifer 1985, Urry 1990, Rojek 1993). In addition, we make use of the notion of 'performance' (Larsen 2012, Cohen and Cohen 2017) as a conceptual lens to facilitate the integration of an urban studies perspective into our analysis.

Drawing on opposing categories when researching tourism has a long tradition. In the first version of his seminal contribution *The Tourist Gaze*, John Urry (1990) rendered the binary differentiation between *work* and *leisure* as the starting point for his reflections on a 'sociology of tourism'. According to him, binaries are manifestations of the "separated and regulated spheres of social practice in 'modern' societies" (Urry 1990, p. 2). By operating in distinctions, in particular, the separation between tourism and the everyday, he refers to earlier tourism research which characterised tourism as "a temporary reversal of everyday activities" (Cohen 1979, p. 181). Similarly, Louis Turner and Ash (1975) argued that the temporary distance from mundane, familiar environments allowed tourists to relax from the affordances of their social roles and norms as well as the Fordist modes of production. As Larsen (2008) and Edensor (2007) pointed out, this understanding resulted in a differentiation between 'everydayness' constituting the sphere of "repetition, habitual practices, obligations and reproduction" (Larsen 2008, p. 22) and 'extraordinariness', defining life while being away on vacation.

By critically reflecting on these established notions of tourism in his initial version of *The Tourist Gaze*, Urry was already pointing towards a new, post-modern paradigm in tourism studies, which would come to be understood in terms of processes of de-differentiation (Urry 1990, pp. 84–87). Several researchers have taken on this paradigmatic shift, recognising that tourism itself does not take place outside of people's everyday lives (e.g., Rojek 1993, Lash and Urry 1994, Crouch 1999, McCabe 2002, Baerenholdt *et al.* 2004, Uriely 2005, Hall 2005, White and White 2007, Larsen 2008). They have argued that such a narrow conceptualisation would end up producing "fixed dualisms between the life of tourism and everyday life—extraordinary and ordinary, pleasure and boredom, liminality and rules, exotic others and significant others" (Haldrup and Larsen 2010, p. 20). Larsen (2008) has even prominently called for 'de-exoticizing theory' in order to meet the requirements for researching tourism in light of this de-differentiation. Moreover, the various dimensions of the intertwined relationship between urban tourism and a city's everyday life have already illustrated the limits of operating with theoretical binary categories. Support for the de-differentiation thesis is reflected in the search for more adequate terminologies (Sommer 2018). Attempts to bridge what had previously been considered as antithetical range from the term 'host-guest-time-space-cultures' (Sheller and Urry 2004) to 'city users' (Martinotti 1993) or Toffler's idea of the 'prosumer' expanded into tourism (Pappalepore *et al.* 2014). While Sheller and Urry focused on the co-production of places by visitors and residents alike, Martinotti's notion of 'city users' has emphasised that temporary urban populations are constituted of a broad range of visitors (e.g., expats, business travellers, interns and students). This is also reflected in the concept of 'prosumers', a term that highlights the role of host–guest interactions and the simultaneity of production and consumption in "prosuming creative urban areas" (Pappalepore *et al.* 2014, p. 227). As these examples show, the recognition of de-differentiation processes paved the way for an orientation towards postmodern conceptualisations within tourism studies (Cohen and Cohen 2012, 2017).

While the acknowledgement of theoretical de-differentiation provides a powerful initial starting point for analysing *new urban tourism*, some of its further implications also prove valuable. The paradigm shift from 'differentiation' to 'de-differentiation' prompted Lash and Urry (1994) to postulate the 'end of tourism'. With this claim, they referred to the increasing proliferation of mass media and its effect that "people are tourists most of the time, whether they are literally mobile or only experience simulated mobility through the incredible fluidity of multiple signs and electronic images" (Lash and Urry 1994, p. 259). The 'end of tourism' also implies that the 'tourist gaze' has lost some of its distinctive character as sights, places or landscapes are detached from certain spatialities as well as temporalities and have become increasingly mobile. They travel into people's living rooms, and thus leaving home is no longer necessary "in order to *see* many of the typical objects of the tourist gaze" (Urry and Larsen 2011, p. 113, emphasis in the original). As a result, "'the tourist gaze' is no longer set apart from everyday life" (Larsen 2008, p. 26). At the same time, increasing globalisation and its worldwide digital networks have facilitated a 'touristification of everyday life' (ibid., see also Gale 2009). While the 'end of tourism' offers fruitful impulses for studying tourism's interrelations with everyday activities, it has, of course, not completely occurred—after all, people still travel and continue to leave their home for vacation trips. Nevertheless, the concept is valuable for researching *new urban tourism* insofar as it has introduced the idea that technological innovations infuse everyday life with tourist images and practices. As such, Lash and Urry's (1994) conceptual reflections have pointed to one possible direction of how established oppositional categories can be dissolved.

Another concept emerging from the de-differentiation debate is 'posttourism'. Closely related to the idea of the 'end of tourism', post-tourism also accounts for travel experiences made while being at home (Ritzer and Liska 2004). While the 'end of tourism' emphasises the entanglement of tourism with the everyday, the notion of 'post-tourism' is more concerned with the deconstruction of traditional tourist roles. Feifer (1985) introduced the term in the 1980s in order to account for visitors who are highly self-aware and enjoy a broad variety of tourist experiences. Urry (1990, p. 91) then drew on this perspective and pointed out that post-tourists "are aware of the change and delights in the multitude of choice" and "that tourism is a series of games with multiple texts and no single, authentic experience". In this regard, cities provide great opportunities to take on different roles for 'post-tourists' as they "offer social, cultural, physical and aesthetic stages upon which tourist activity can be played out" (Hayllar *et al.* 2008, p. 7). While earlier work linked 'post-tourism' to the idea that the mediated home makes travelling unnecessary (Urry 1990), later contributions have redefined the concept and argued that advances in electronic media have allowed people to casually take in "flows of global cultural materials all around them" (Franklin and Crang 2001, p. 8) and thus combine corporeal and virtual experiences. As Campbell (2005, p. 200) explains: "Post-tourism [...] contests traditional notions of tourist experience offering more than physical travel including, as it does, desire, imaging and mediation in a much more complex and encompassing mobility."

'Post-tourism', understood as tourists being self-aware and having the multitude of choice, offers some interesting parallels to performance theories in the Goffman tradition. Besides post-tourists' ability to switch roles, the notion of 'performance' helps to explain how tourism and everyday life are intimately connected. Edensor (e.g., 1998, 2009) has noted how habitual per-formative norms (e.g., about how and when to photograph) inform tourist habits and thus breaks with an understanding of tourism as a rupture of everyday practice. Tourist performance "includes unreflexive assumptions and habits but [also] contains moments where norms may be transcended" (Edensor 2001, p. 79). Similarly, the *Tourist Gaze 3.0* (Urry and Larsen 2011) argues in the same direction, seeing tourism as a performed and embodied practice. Following Franklin and Crang (2001, p. 8), tourism performance is a "way of seeing and sensing the world with its own kit of technologies, techniques, and predispositions". On the one hand, the 'tourist gaze' could be understood as part of the everyday perception of residents. On the other hand, the gaze (in its visual, sensual meaning) is directed towards the extra-ordinary mundane that 'new urban tourists' are looking for. In this sense, tourism is "a widespread, protean practice that occurs in mundane settings, everyday routines and home cities as well as in far-flung places" (Edensor 2009, p. 545).

Finally, 'performance' illustrates the 'urban co-production' and limitless-ness of (new) urban tourism places. Because tourist places serve to "organis[e] a multiplicity of intersecting mobilities" (Baerenholdt *et al.* 2004, p. 2), they appear to emerge in dynamic relations rather than to be static entities. Therefore, "[i]t is more profitable to see them as 'in play' in relation to multiple mobilities and varied performances stretching in, through, over and under any apparently distinct locality" (Baerenholdt *et al.* 2004, p. 145).

Considering unbounded tourist places as 'performed' offers scholars a point of reference for urban studies perspectives on *new urban tourism* phe-nomena. By building on a *relational* understanding of urban spaces, *new urban tourism* destinations can be seen not as containers; instead, they materialise where *performed* trans-local processes encounter in a highly condensed way. This approach puts emphasis on an understanding of cities and (urban) space as elaborated by 'post-structuralist geography' (see, e.g., Murdoch 2006 for an overview), and even more explicitly by researchers conceptualising cities in terms of 'urban assemblages' (e.g., Farías and Bender 2010). In this, it is worthwhile to note that Urry's und Larsen's (2001, p. 116) abstract understanding of tourist places as "economically, politically and culturally produced through networked mobilities of capital, persons, objects, signs and information" had already addressed some basic aspects of these perspectives on cities in general. According to Murdoch (2006, p. 19), urban "space is generated by interaction and interrelations"; similarly, Farías and Bender (2010, p. 2) describe the city, ontologically, as a "multiplicity of processes of becoming, affixing socio-technical networks, hybrid collectives and alternative topologies". It is important to note that these abstract approaches explicitly stress that 'urban assemblages' need to be enacted in practice and studied *on the ground*. Therefore, the idea of 'performance'—pivotal in tourism studies and deeply influential in reflection on urban life, e.g., in classics by Simmel, Wirth or Fischer (Helbrecht and Dirksmeier 2013)—seems to be predestined to build bridges between tourism and urban studies. Insofar as 'performance' highlights the idea that actions are not conceivable without taking the stage, décor or props (materialities) into account, this concept can also help to develop approaches regarding the socio-materiality of *new urban tourism* assemblages. Moreover, it is a defining strength of 'performance' to turn towards "those under-researched, mundane moments of togetherness that pattern everyday life" (Bell 2007, p. 19 quoted in Helbrecht and Dirksmeier 2013, p. 294) in cities. This means 'performance' provides a perspective onto what city users—acting as (if) tourists—actually *do* and how these encounters affect urban living together (from hospitality to tourist bashing).

Regarding the diversity of the theoretical concepts which present valuable starting points for approaching *new urban tourism*, technological innovation and digital media are seen as significant enablers in allowing mundane existence to be penetrated by extraordinary experiences and exciting visual impressions (Urry and Larsen 2011, Tussyadiah and Fesenmaier 2009, Uriely 2005). Therefore, *new urban tourism* and its emergent phenomena have to be understood as a de-differentiated collection of performative, embodied and digitally backed practices that structure both navigation through urbanscapes as well as the exploration of them. However, the aforementioned concepts present rather general theoretical considerations. By linking them to city tourism studies as well as urban studies, the next section introduces *new urban tourism* along three analytical dimensions.

Introducing *new urban tourism* along its three key dimensions

The term *new urban tourism* was initially introduced by British sociologist Maurice Roche (1992) during his studies on cultural or sporting mega-events taking place in cities. Even though he specifically links this type of tourism to local structural changes of so-called 'micro-modernization', he identifies large-scale events as the only driving force. Several researchers drew on Roche's approach, analysing events and tourism in general as a strategy for inner-city regeneration (see Judd and Fainstein 1999, Spirou 2011). However, Maitland and Newman (2004) paved the way for a wider understanding of the term, as they started to investigate urban areas that were not purposefully designed to attract visitors but in which "tourism seem[ed] to have grown 'organic-ally'" (ibid., p. 339). They labelled these "new tourism areas" (Maitland 2008, p. 340)—places which held a special appeal for so-called 'off the beaten track tourism' (Maitland and Newman 2009b). Despite being originally concerned with the types of people engaging in tourism to residential areas (Maitland 2010) and their particular motivation (Maitland 2008, Maitland and Newman 2009a), their contributions also provided in-depth insights into the appeal of everyday life for urban visitors. The next time the term *new urban tourism* appeared in scholarly literature, it was used by two German geographers, Füller and Michel (2014), without referring to Roche's work, but extensively building on Maitland's contributions. One reason might be that they defined *new urban tourism* with a much stronger emphasis on urban everyday life, rather than special festivals or events. In their article on tourism in Berlin, they argued that "it is precisely the everydayness and the feel of the 'ordinary' and 'authentic' life of a city that has become an important marker for attraction to visitors" (Füller and Michel 2014, p. 1306). Such a perspective highlights the appeal of a city's day-to-day rhythms—an appeal which is not dependent on mega-events. While these two definitions of *new urban tourism* emphasise these two different aspects in city tourism, this volume suggests a broader approach. For this purpose, we put forward three dimensions along which the emergent phenomena of *new urban tourism* can be analysed and discussed: (a) the extraordinary mundane, (b) encounters and contact zones, and (c) urban co-production.

The extraordinary mundane

Starting from the general observation that urban everyday life and tourism are not two strictly separable spheres, this dimension focuses on moments and situations in which urban everyday life is perceived and produced as an attraction in and of itself. As it has become more complex to define who is a 'local' and who is a 'tourist' (Cohen and Cohen 2017, McCabe 2005), one possible way to approach *new urban tourism* is to pay close attention to conditions which facilitate a transformation of the mundane into an extra-ordinary event. Detecting such temporal, situational tipping points requires a sensible and careful analysis of urban everyday life. In order to unravel its complexity, choosing a starting point is a tough decision—researchers have to decide whether to begin by studying the perception and practices of urbanites or by examining the main driving forces which shape a city. No matter which approach is adopted, both offer valuable insights into the appeal of the urban day-to-day life for various city users.

While it seems relatively easy to think about ordinary everyday situations which might hold some interesting appeal for people who are not used to them, it might be harder to imagine exciting ones for people whose daily routines are made up by precisely those moments. However, in our understanding, *new urban tourism* emphasises that exploring the day-to-day rhythms of a city is not only limited to short-term visitors. City residents can turn into urban explorers "by taking different forms of transport, gazing at the environment from the vantage of different time-worlds [...], and stringing together sequences of monuments, landmarks and events" (Holmes 2001, p. 181). Such activities which can be categorised as 'touristic', if they follow more traditional conceptions, enable moments of being a tourist in one's own city, of 'transgressing boundaries', as Pappalepore *et al.* (2010) have put it. This can be an abrupt and rather unplanned experience, such as discovering an unfamiliar spot or trying out a new activity for the first time, but also the conscious decision of showing friends and family around (Shani and Uriely 2012, Larsen *et al.* 2007). Whether such experiences are spontaneous or not, they clearly highlight the inadequacies and limits of a strict theoretical distinction between tourists and locals. Moreover, the experience of the extraordinary mundane is heavily dependent on actors' motivations as well as their perceptions.

One major driving force that opens up new possibilities for city visitors and its residents alike is digital technology (e.g., Sigala and Gretzel 2018, Munar *et al.* 2013, Germann Molz 2012). With the increasing availability of WiFi at many places throughout metropolises around the world and the widespread use of mobile devices, online services and apps specifically designed for exploring a city are becoming more and more popular. These trends have a fundamental impact on how a city is perceived and produced by its long-term and short-term inhabitants (Zukin *et al.* 2015, Stors and Baltes 2018). In regard to *new urban tourism*, the reason digital technology is so powerful is due to its inclusion of all kinds of users. Even though there are websites, blogs and apps aimed at travellers in particular, their content and services can be accessed and used by everyone interested. At the same time, many online portals and websites often depend on 'user-generated content', thus incorporating their recipients into the designing and shaping of content and services available. Compared to professionally curated content by tourism agencies, this inclusion leads to higher credibility among users (Akehurst 2009, Schmallegger and Carson 2008). Research on how to commercially utilise such content in terms of travel and tourism marketing illustrates that user-generated content in blogs and social media can significantly affect the branding of a destination (e.g., Sigala and Gretzel 2018, Munar 2011). By being available to anyone who is looking for recommendations on cafés, restaurants, activities or places, user-generated content introduces new possibilities on how to experience a city. These possibilities not only facilitate moments of the extraordinary mundane, they also create contact zones where heterogeneous city users can meet and intermingle.

Encounters and contact zones

A key premise for *new urban tourism* is the idea to go 'off the beaten track' (Maitland and Newman 2009b, Maitland 2010, 2008). It holds the promise of experiencing a city like a long-term insider would, to get to know its 'real' everyday life and—this is especially true for anyone with a limited period of stay—to leave the confined space of the 'tourist bubble' (Judd 1999). This desire distinguishes *new urban tourism* from traditional mass tourism and its negative associations, such as ignorance (Pappalepore *et al.* 2014, Freytag 2010, McCabe 2005). By opening up spaces for travellers, visitors, short-term residents and locals, digital technology feeds directly into this desire. Digital technology is the backbone of many *new urban tourism* phenomena. In addition to user-generated content, there are other services which directly connect users with each other for 'off the beaten track' experiences. The most famous sharing economy company, Airbnb (www.airbnb.com), allows its users to rent short-term accommodation from other registered users. The lesser known Eatwith (www.eatwith.com) is an online platform where users can book a home-cooked meal at the private dinner tables of other community members. Finally, through the online hospitality network Couchsurfing (www.couchsurfing.org), travellers can meet with residents and spend time together without any exchange of money involved (Bialski 2012, Germann Molz 2012). All these services put a strong emphasis on offering access to local life—Airbnb even claims to enable its community members to 'live like a local' at their visited destination (Oskam and Boswijk 2016, Guttentag 2015).

New urban tourism encounters do not take place at crowded tourist sights or well-known hotspots. Instead, they can be found in residential neighbourhoods and places not mentioned in classic travel guidebooks. Travellers looking for these experiences rub shoulders with other city users in little cafés and spend the night in private apartments. Sociologist Jennie Germann Molz (2014) has noted that this interesting combination of online and offline connection "invites us to rethink the taken-for-granted-ness of the spatiotemporal configurations of hospitality and encounters with strangers in everyday life". While meeting other city users is an important goal for new urban tourists, such encounters do not necessarily have to be organised and mediated by digital technology. As the example of travel blogs has already illustrated, different people can come together simply by enjoying the same place. Regardless of the circumstances which lead city users to meet, such encounters may be attractive but also hold a subtle potential for conflict. This is due to the joint co-production of the city, which has to be (re)negotiated with each new encounter.

Urban co-production

Discovering a city by focusing specifically at its own distinctive pace, its mundane situations and its residents, has a profound influence on the city itself. In the context of tourism, this influence became most obvious when visitors started to venture into edgy, unpolished, creative areas (Maitland and Newman 2009a, Pappalepore *et al.* 2010, 2014). During their stay, tourists no longer are passive consumers of the environment, but rather active (re)producers of the visited neighbourhood. Again, it has to be stressed that this influence is not only limited to travellers or short-term visitors of a destination. Indeed, everyone who is staying and living in a city takes part in shaping it—no matter how long he or she has been there, and regardless of their actual place of residence. In sum, all kinds of different city users co-produce the urban fabric.

An illustrative example of such a joint production is the previously mentioned and relatively recent appeal of residential neighbourhoods as attractive localities. Maitland and Newman (2009b) studied this transition for popular tourism destinations such as New York or Paris, which they characterised as 'world tourism cities'. Such cities are "multifunctional and polycentric with the capacity to draw visitors off the beaten track and where visitors and other city users may share in the creation of new tourism places" (Maitland and Newman 2009a, p. 12). While city governments are keen to present their cities as destinations worth exploring, bringing together so many heterogeneous actors carries with it constant potential for conflict. As Novy and Colomb (2017) noted in the introduction of their volume *Protest and Resistance in the Tourist City*, this potential is multifaceted and can be found in cities in the Global North and the Global South. They identified tourism as a key element for recent urban political struggles, pointing out that:

> politicization manifests itself in different ways: in some contexts residents and other stakeholders take issue with the growth of tourism as such, as well as the impacts it has on their cities; in others, particular forms and effects of tourism are contested or deplored; and in numerous settings [...] contestations revolve less around tourism itself than around broader processes, policies and forces of urban change perceived to threaten the right to 'stay put', the quality of life or the identity of existing urban populations.
>
> (Novy and Colomb 2017, p. 4)

For *new urban tourism*, this potential for conflict becomes visible in a wide range of urban interventions, such as graffiti or stickers highlighting the problem of tourism in specific neighbourhoods, to large-scale mobilisation against tourism-driven gentrification (Gravari-Barbas and Guinand 2017, Füller and Michel 2014). However, for as much as these criticisms refer to problematic dynamics and processes, they do not put much emphasis on the fact that large parts of the local population themselves also participate in urban leisure activities. They travel from one neighbourhood to another to spend the night in a popular bar or club, thus producing a similar amount of noise and waste to those emerging from visitors. Local people also provide much of the infrastructure used: material infrastructure such as local shops, independent restaurants and, recently, Airbnb apartments. However, they also contribute in an immaterial way to the look and feel of neighbourhoods through processes of urban commoning or just by being around. They co-produce hang-out spots that are marked and marketed as insider tips on online platforms. Through all these practices, these locals actively add to the transformation of their neighbourhoods. Notwithstanding this potential for conflict, *new urban tourism* is not conflictual *per se*. Discovering new places and facets of a neighbourhood, engaging in fleeting encounters with others, and taking part in local life can be a rewarding experience for the city users involved.

With the introduction of *new urban tourism* along these three dimensions, the nexus of urban everyday life and tourism can be theoretically conceptualised and empirically researched in an innovative and adequate way. It meets the demands of studying such multifaceted phenomena and is at the same time defined as a heuristic, yet open concept. Insofar as each dimension discussed here is intimately tied to the others, research on *new urban tourism* necessarily refers to all three of them—albeit with a different degree of emphasis.

Studying an emergent field of research—an outline of the chapters in this book

Over the course of ten chapters, this anthology gathers multiple interdisciplinary approaches, a diversity of topics and a methodological variety in order to unravel the complex de-differentiation processes of urban everyday life and city tourism.

Jonas Larsen (Chapter 2) addresses one dimension of the reciprocal relationship between everyday life and tourism in cities by using a twofold perspective. Focusing on travellers, he argues that their practices while on a trip are deeply infused with habits and everyday social regimens. From the perspective of hosts, he points out that their everyday life rhythms and practices are deeply affected by visitors. The actual consequences of this interrelation are discussed in three vignettes drawing on multiple examples of developments in European cities. The first one highlights how personal interests and relationships shape tourism practices; the second one deals with the impacts of the recent desire for local experiences among travellers; the third vignette elaborates on the practical consequences of residents and visitors sharing a city.

In his contribution, Mathis Stock (Chapter 3) understands tourism, especially urban tourism, as a problematic category for contemporary societies and identifies the need for articulating urban theory and tourism theory more closely together. Drawing on the phenomenological concept of dwelling and practice theory, he proposes thinking of (new urban) tourists as temporal inhabitants of cities with a specific relationship to place. They develop certain spatial competences and a 'spatial capital' which allows them to practise the city as tourists. Contrasting the right to mobility and the right to the city, Stock shows how much of the debate on *new urban tourism* is characterised by conflicting narratives which are nevertheless based on legitimate claims on each side. In his conclusion, he argues for thinking about touristification and urbanisation as interrelated processes on a more general level.

From a political economy perspective, Fabian Frenzel (Chapter 4) investigates processes of attraction-making in residential neighbourhoods and its links to (tourism) gentrification. He applies the concepts of labour and praxis to investigate how residents and tourists themselves co-produce (positive) externalities and thus contribute to the value and appeal of a neighbourhood. Tourists, he argues, are significantly involved in production and valorisation processes of urban areas by being present, by altering the place's visibility, or even by creating infrastructure themselves. Similar to residents, they are involved in practices of commoning that can extend or diminish the quality of life of these neighbourhoods and are far from being irrelevant to the production of profits, which, in turn, are frequently skimmed off by property owners.

In Toronto, Canada, Jessica Parish (Chapter 5) demonstrates how the rise of professionalised self-care facilities can function as a signifier for the ongoing gentrification of an urban neighbourhood. Drawing on empirical research of the neighbourhood of Roncesvalles Village, she is able to show that these emergent 'new wellness industries' not only nurture a growing popularity of the area among visitors; by utilising oriental aesthetics, these places also aim to offer their clients a temporary escape from their familiar urban surroundings. In light of these two aspects, 'new wellness industries' are critically examined as transforming an initial working-class neighbourhood into an urban tourism area as well as representing neoliberal means of self-optimisation.

Natalie Stors (Chapter 6) offers insights into the manifold reasons of Airbnb hosts in Berlin for listing their apartment online. Airbnb is the most popular sharing economy company for short-term rental accommodation, and its success is associated with serious impacts on Berlin's neighbourhoods. Therefore, hosting via Airbnb is regulated by a strict municipal legal framework and has been accompanied by a heated public debate. In a detailed study of Airbnb hosts' reasons for subletting their dwellings, Stors reveals that users are driven by a broad variety of different motives. She emphasises that hosts' mobility practices contribute to the idling spatial capacity rented out, and that their rationales for engaging in short-term rental practices are closely related to their personal living circumstances. Ultimately, subletting via Airbnb turns into individual strategies of actually securing the currently inhabited living space.

Bianca Wildish and Bas Spierings (Chapter 7) address how the dissolution of boundaries between tourists and residents plays out in everyday practices and lived experiences of Airbnb users in residential neighbourhoods in Amsterdam. By empirically building on interviews and mental maps, the chapter applies a novel lens to *new urban tourism* by focusing on familiarisation processes and the feeling of insideness/outsideness. They explore two key aspects of boundary blurring—that of tourists and residents through participating in 'local life' and visiting particular neighbourhood spaces, and that of insiders and outsiders through feelings of belonging and being at home in the neighbourhood. The authors show that guests experience feelings as though they were residents and insiders by familiarisation of and with the physical and social setting of the private Airbnb accommodation, certain service encounter dynamics in semi-public spaces and the development of walking routines in public space.

Luise Stoltenberg and Thomas Frisch (Chapter 8) analyse digitally arranged social eating experiences, using the meal-sharing platform Eatwith as an empirical case. Conceptually, the authors bring together two originally separate research strands, the sociological discourse about commensality and research on food and tourism. On this basis, the chapter draws on content analysis and netnography to examine Eatwith's strategies to brand its services as commensal events enabling experiences of the local. Stoltenberg and Frisch identify three key characteristics of meal-sharing platforms: they frame a rather everyday activity as an exceptional event; they open up private homes for tourists and mobile city users; and they connect people who temporarily share the same geographical location. Finally, the authors suggest considering these characteristics as distinctive qualities of many other *new urban tourism* phenomena.

Clara Kramer, Nora Winsky and Tim Freytag (Chapter 9) introduce the concept of *Muße* (Latin: *otium*) in *new urban tourism* research. They conceptualise the experience of urban *Muße* places, such as parks and museums but also department stores and restaurants, as spatio-temporal sequences that allow visitors to temporarily escape and recover from traditional, often stressful tourist activities. Using the example of Paris, they investigate representations of *Muße* places in travel guides and provide a typology of cultural, extensive, green and culinary places. Afterwards, the authors select a set of places identified in both travel guides and online blogs and analyse how such places operate when being visited by travellers and residents alike. They find that the experience of *Muße* seems to be related to the notion of authenticity, defined by the presence of locals in opposition to tourists—rising visitor numbers might thus be a threat to *Muße* places themselves.

Guided by their interest in tourism as constituent of urban life, Christoph Sommer and Markus Kip (Chapter 10) inquire about what emerges when tourists and other city users rub shoulders. Building empirically on happening-like summertime gatherings at a popular bridge in Berlin, they call for understanding such events (which exist in other cities alike) as 'hangout commons'. In contrast to conventional commons-thinking, the commons here is constituted by a group whose constituency changes significantly every evening with several newcomers arriving, and others leaving the scene. To address this choreography of stability and mobility, the chapter draws on the 'New Mobilities Paradigm' and the concept of 'Performance'. As a result, the authors frame the constitutive potency of tourism-related encounters of highly mobile people, objects, imaginings and immoveable material components as *rhythmic (re-)enactment of temporary socio-material gatherings*.

The ambivalent and controversial figure of the 'tourist' inspired Nils Grube (Chapter 11) to conduct a series of intervening field experiments with the aim of learning more about tourism and its impacts on everyday situations. Based on Goffman's accounts on symbolic interactionism, performative approaches from tourism studies and artistic space projects, he describes the set-up and results of his experiments in the Berlin district of Neukölln, a place known for much anti-tourism criticism. Grube's contribution demonstrates the complexities of the role of the 'tourist' and the necessity to perform it in front of an audience in order to create social reality. The method of intervening field experiments proved an innovative and productive tool, yet also revealed risks and limitations, such as their unpredictable outcome.

Limitations and avenues for future research

The ten chapters featured here indicate that *new urban tourism* is a powerful driving force in shaping urban everyday life. Moreover, when taking into account the fact that urban tourism takes place in countries all over the world (e.g., Spirou 2011, Selby 2004, Law 2002) and that the networks of digital media are almost infinite, *new urban tourism* must also be considered as a worldwide phenomenon. Nevertheless, it is also characterised by a broad diversity of paces and qualities, depending on the individual features of a city. *New urban tourism*, its impacts and effects, change according to various urban destinations. While this heterogeneity is the reason why this emergent phenomenon marks an extremely interesting field of research, it also presents challenges for a uniform definition which can respect and account for its idiosyncratic forms and faces. On this account, the research presented in this volume can only provide insights into the nexus between urban everyday life and tourism in selected Western cities. Future research which focuses on other (non-Western) cities is needed in order to further expand the understanding of *new urban tourism*. This shift in perspective would be promising in several regards. It would enrich knowledge about the various facets of 'distinct ordinariness' of urban day-to-day life in new tourism areas. Then, varying ways of 'seeing like a tourist city' (Sommer and Helbrecht 2017) could be compared, i.e. to analyse administrative problematisations of conflict-prone *new urban tourism* as urban political processes shaping the future of city tourism. Finally, a deeper understanding of the entanglement of the urbanscape with tourism, and its related conflicts, could inform city authorities worldwide trying to govern urban tourism not solely as an economic factor, but as an engine of momentum for urban development. Research on Airbnb, for example, has already indicated how such companies may affect urban everyday life and how the absence of supervision and regulation leads to missing tax revenues as well as broader consequences in terms of gentrification processes and the housing market (e.g., Mermet 2017, Sans and Dominguez 2016, Guttentag 2015). Therefore, the emerging interest in certain neighbourhoods and mundane activities needs to be understood and (at least partially) regulated as a force shaping the urban fabric (Gurran and Phibbs 2017).

Even if a city attracts new urban tourists, not every single one of its neighbourhoods holds the same appeal, and some neighbourhoods offer none at all. In order to attract attention and the desire to explore mundane places, these areas need to become mobile and endowed with meaning (Lash and Urry 1994, Edensor 2000, 2001, 2007). This largely happens by being incorporated into the realm of the digital world—into the online networks of personal travel blogs, sharing economy companies, ratings portals or social media. Such technologies, however, not only reproduce digital representations of physical-material places—they also allow people to encounter, appropriate and perform space in different ways. Thus, technologies are fundamentally part of how people engage with urban space (Dourish 2006). Considering the important role that digital media plays as an agent—turning residential neighbourhoods into *new urban tourism* sites—its function as a mere mediator has to be questioned and analysed in subsequent research (see also Frisch and Stoltenberg 2017). Platforms, such as the ones taken into account in this edited volume, need to be investigated more critically. The companies providing digital infrastructures have serious political power which goes beyond the mere supply of services. Private, market-oriented firms and their users are now engaging in discourses about places to an extent that was not possible a few years ago. While this may hold opportunities for local business owners or actors concerned with community-building or political activism, it may also foster processes of exclusion and inequality for those who do not use such technologies—intentionally (e.g., for reasons of data protection and security) or unintentionally (due to a lack of knowledge or economic capacities). Thus, digital technologies function as enablers for *new urban tourism* phenomena on the one hand; on the other, they may reinforce or create power (a)symmetries (Massey 1993, Dredge and Gyimóthy 2015), particularly with regard to the manifold ways places are perceived and enacted. Thus, future research should contribute to reveal such power (a)symmetries and support technology's transformation into a political force that is beneficial for the city and its users as a whole.

Encounters with others have been identified as one of the key characteristics of *new urban tourism*. Various chapters in this volume highlight the fact that it is not decisive whether or not these encounters are actually happening. Its potentiality, i.e., the mere imagination of a possible meeting with 'locals', is powerful enough to motivate urban explorers' search for a city's everyday life. An illustrative example is the short-term rental platform Airbnb, which advertises its services by emphasising its role as an enabler of (meaningful) social interactions between hosts and guests. In fact, many Airbnb listings have turned out to be apartments that hosts rent out professionally—places they do not live in (Gurran and Phibbs 2017, Sans and Domínguez 2016, Guttentag 2015). Nevertheless, the company dwells on a strong narrative of connecting its users via personal encounters, and it is still the most popular online service for short-term rentals (Stoltenberg and Frisch 2017). In short, it does not matter so much whether new urban tourists interact directly with other city users. Instead, it is vital that they engage in activities or visit places that they *imagine* to be mundane, and which promise an immersion in the local everyday life and a desired togetherness with other city users. Although direct encounters or interactions become possible and may even enhance the experience, they are not fundamental. This potentiality, or even fictitious character, is a powerful driver for *new urban tourism* phenomena. Nevertheless, such encounters are not necessarily based on a mutually shared interest in each other, and can give rise to serious conflicts. These gain particular momentum when people feel negatively affected by other city users (Dirksmeier and Helbrecht 2015), when their feeling of home is disrupted (Pinkster and Boterman 2017) or when affordable living space diminishes (Gravari-Barbas and Guinand 2017).

Finally, this volume also offers some empirical attempts to detail how *new urban tourism* phenomena could be analysed by drawing on the notion of 'performance'. The respective chapters address the need for further detailed (empirical) case studies on the specific performative co-production of the urban, and the performative experience of encounters and the extraordinary mundane. In light of Franklin's (2004, p. 277) call to analyse *how* tourism is *enacted* as "a heterogeneous assemblage 'at large' in the world", one could call for more *new urban tourism* research "on what people and things, people and things together, actually *do*" (ibid., p. 285). This seems to be promising with respect to (at least) two regards. First, the empirical commitment to "follow the actors [and to] forget the contexts" (Farías 2011, p. 367)—as it is postulated in assemblage thinking—could produce interesting novel descriptions of *new urban tourism*. Methodological solutions developed according to this commitment, thereby examining specific performances and their effects, could create insights beyond the typical narratives and stereotypes that are often reproduced by motivational research on types of tourists and their experiences (McCabe 2005). Empirically, it might be promising to pin down which performances produce certain 'geographies of prejudice' and how this occurs (Dirksmeier and Helbrecht 2015); it may also be helpful to focus on the variety of possible outcomes of these encounters, rather than considering performances of tourists and residents only in terms of conflict and opposition (Giovanardi *et al.* 2014). Second, it seems to be promising to systematically and conceptually compare how urban studies and tourism studies respectively elaborate on 'performance'. The differences may spur further developments in conceptual thinking on *new urban tourism*.

With these limitations and avenues for future research in mind, each of the ten chapters included in this volume provides a different analytical perspective on *new urban tourism*. Some of them investigate the various actors' engagement in this multifaceted phenomenon; others reflect on the diversity of its implications and effects on the urban fabric. Together with the dimensions of *new urban tourism* outlined here, these in-depth considerations also exemplify that not each and every moment of urban everyday life has turned into an extraordinary mundane attraction; not every neighbourhood is composed of manifold contact zones; and not every aspect of city life is co-produced with new urban tourists having contributed. Instead, *new urban tourism* relies on a certain mindset of certain people engaging in certain practices, on the imaginaries they have about certain places, and the roles they take on. Therefore, travelling images about places, lifestyles and performances are crucial for endowing ordinary places with extraordinary meaning. This reading of *new urban tourism* also indicates that the various binaries discussed will never fully dissolve. In the future, large numbers of visitors will continue to visit major sights, they will engage in practices such as picture-taking and follow the beaten path that so many have travelled before. Some will reflect upon these practices and their implications more consciously, while others will completely surrender to the experience. There will remain moments and places in which people regard themselves as tourists or residents, there will be some practices more similar to work and others more similar to leisure. Still, a postmodern understanding of *new urban tourism* builds upon these binaries as structures against which more fluid observations can be contested, and acknowledges their uncountable moments of transgression. This edited volume thus demonstrates one approach to identifying and explaining some of these complex elements that generate the entanglement of everyday life with tourism in cities.

References

Akehurst, G., 2009. User generated content: the use of blogs for tourism organisations and tourism consumers. *Service Business*, 3 (1), 51–61.

Ashworth, G., 2003. Urban tourism: still an imbalance in attention? *In*: C. Cooper, ed., *Classic Reviews in Tourism*. Clevedon: Channel View, 143–163.

Ashworth, G. and Page, S., 2011. Urban tourism research: recent progress and current paradox. *Tourism Management*, 32, 1–15.

Baerenholdt, J.O. *et al.*, eds, 2004. *Performing Tourist Places*. Aldershot: Ashgate.

Bialski, P., 2012. *Becoming Intimately Mobile*. Frankfurt am Main: Peter Lang.

Campbell, N., 2005. Producing America. Redefining post-tourism in the global media age. *In*: D. Crouch, R. Jackson and F. Thompson, eds, *The Media and the Tourist Imagination: Converging Cultures*. Abingdon: Routledge, 198–214.

Cohen, E., 1974. Who is a tourist? A conceptual clarification. *The Sociological Review*, 22 (4), 527–555.

Cohen, E., 1979. A phenomenology of tourist experience. *Sociology*, 13, 179–202.

Cohen, E., 1988. Authenticity and commoditization in tourism. *Annals of Tourism Research*, 15, 371–386.

Cohen, E. and Cohen, S.A., 2012. Current sociological theories and issues in tourism. *Annals of Tourism Research*, 39 (4), 2177–2202.

Cohen, S.A. and Cohen, E., 2017. New directions in the sociology of tourism. *Current Issues in Tourism*, 1–20.

Crouch, D., ed., 1999. *Leisure and Tourism Geographies: Practices and Geographical Knowledge*. Abingdon: Routledge.

Diaz-Soria, I., 2017. Being a tourist as a chosen experience in a proximity destination. *Tourism Geographies*, 19 (1), 96–117.

Dimitrovski, D. and Vallbona, M.C., 2018. Urban food markets in the context of a tourist attraction – La Boqueria market in Barcelona, Spain. *Tourism Geographies*, 20 (3), 397–417.

Dirksmeier, P. and Helbrecht, I., 2015. Resident perceptions of new urban tourism: a neglected geography of prejudice. *Geography Compass*, 9 (5), 276–285.

Dourish, P., 2006. Re-space-ing place: "space" and "place" ten years on. *CSCW '06 Proceedings of the 2006 20th Anniversary Conference on Computer Supported Cooperative Work*, 299–308.

Dredge, D. and Gyimóthy, S., 2015. The collaborative economy and tourism: critical perspectives, questionable claims and silenced voices. *Tourism Recreation Research*, 40 (3), 286–302.

Edensor, T., 1998. *Tourists at the Taj: Performance and Meaning at a Symbolic Site*. London: Routledge.

Edensor, T., 2000. Staging tourism: tourists as performers. *Annals of Tourism Research*, 27 (2), 322–344.

Edensor, T., 2001. Performing tourism, staging tourism. (Re)producing tourist space and practice. *Tourist Studies*, 1 (1), 59–81.

Edensor, T., 2007. Mundane mobilities, performances and spaces of tourism. *Social and Cultural Geography*, 8 (2), 199–215.

Edensor, T., 2009. Tourism and performance. *In*: T. Jamal and M. Robinson, eds, *The Sage Handbook of Tourism Studies*. London: SAGE, 543–556.

Farías, I. and Bender, T., 2010. *Urban Assemblages: How Actor-Network Theory Changes Urban Studies*. London: Routledge.

Farías, I., 2011. The politics of urban assemblages. *City: Analysis of Urban Trends, Culture, Theory, Policy, Action*, 15 (3–4), 365–374.

Feifer, M., 1985. *Going Places*. London: Macmillan.

Franklin, A. and Crang, M., 2001. The trouble with tourism and travel theory? *Tourist Studies*, 1 (1), 5–22.

Franklin, A., 2004. Tourism as an ordering: towards a new ontology of tourism. *Tourist Studies*, 4 (3), 277–301.

Freytag, T., 2010. Déjà-vu: tourist practices of repeat visitors in the city of Paris. *Social Geography*, 5, 49–58.

Frisch, T., 2012. Glimpses of another world: the favela as a tourist attraction. *Tourism Geographies*, 14 (2), 320–338.

Frisch, T. and Stoltenberg, L., 2017. Affirmative Superlative und die Macht negativer Bewertungen. Online-Reputation in der Datengesellschaft. *In*: D. Houben and B. Prietl, eds, *Datengesellschaft. Einsichten in die Datafizierung des Sozialen*. Bielefeld: transcript, 85–107.

Füller, H. and Michel, B., 2014. 'Stop being a tourist!' New dynamics of urban tourism in Berlin-Kreuzberg. *International Journal of Urban and Regional Research*, 38 (4), 1304–1318.

Gale, T., 2009. Urban beaches, virtual worlds and 'the end of tourism'. *Mobilities*, 4 (1), 119–138.

Germann Molz, J., 2012. *Travel Connections: Tourism, Technology, and Togetherness in a Mobile World.* Abingdon: Routledge.

Germann Molz, J., 2014. Toward a network hospitality [online]. *First monday*, 19 (3). Available from: http://ojphi.org/ojs/index.php/fm/article/view/4824/3848 [accessed 28 September 2018].

Giovanardi, M., Lucarelli, A. and L'Espoir Decosta, P., 2014. Co-performing tourism places: the "Pink Night" festival. *Annals of Tourism Research*, 44, 102–115.

Gravari-Barbas, M. and Guinand, S., eds, 2017. *Tourism and Gentrification in Contemporary Metropolises. International Perspectives.* Abingdon: Routledge.

Gurran, N. and Phibbs, P., 2017. When tourists move in: how should urban planners respond to Airbnb? *Journal of the American Planning Association*, 83 (1), 80–92.

Guttentag, D., 2015. Airbnb: disruptive innovation and the rise of an informal tourism accommodation sector. *Current Issues in Tourism*, 18 (12), 1192–1217.

Haldrup, M. and Larsen, J., 2010. *Tourism, Performance and the Everyday: Consuming the Orient.* Abingdon: Routledge.

Hall, C.M., 2005. Reconsidering the geography of tourism and contemporary mobility. *Geographical Research*, 43 (3), 125–139.

Hayllar, B., Griffin, T. and Edwards, D., 2008. Urban tourism precincts: engaging with the field. *In:* B. Hayllar, T. Griffin and D. Edwards, eds, *City Spaces – Tourist Places. Urban Tourism Precincts.* Amsterdam: Butterworth-Heinemann, 3–18.

Helbrecht, I. and Dirksmeier, P., 2013. Stadt und Performanz. *In*: H. Mieg and C. Heyl, eds, *Stadt. Ein interdisziplinäres Handbuch.* Stuttgart/Weimar: J.B. Metzler Verlag, 283–298.

Holmes, D., 2001. Monocultures of globalization: touring Australia's Gold Coast. *In*: D. Holmes, ed., *Virtual Globalization. Virtual Spaces/Tourist Spaces.* London: Routledge, 175–191.

Jeacle, I. and Carter, C., 2011. In TripAdvisor we trust: rankings, calculative regimes and abstract systems. *Accounting, Organizations and Society*, 36 (4–5), 293–309.

Judd, D.R., 1999. Constructing the tourist bubble. *In*: D.R. Judd and S.S. Fainstein, eds, *The Tourist City*. New Haven, CT: Yale University Press, 35–53.

Judd, D.R. and Fainstein, S.S., eds, 1999. *The Tourist City*. New Haven, CT: Yale University Press.

Jurowski, C., Uysal, M. and Williams, D.R., 1997. A theoretical analysis of host community resident reactions to tourism. *Journal of Travel Research*, 36 (2), 3–11.

Larsen, J., Urry, J. and Axhausen, K.W., 2007. Networks and tourism: mobile social life. *Annals of Tourism Research*, 34 (1), 244–262.

Larsen, J., 2008. De-exoticizing tourist travel: everyday life and sociality on the move. *Leisure Studies*, 27 (1), 21–34.

Larsen, J., 2012. Performance, space and tourism. *In*: J. Wilson, ed., *The Routledge Handbook of Tourism Geographies.* Abingdon: Routledge, 67–73.

Lash, S. and Urry, J., 1994. *Economies of Signs and Space.* London: SAGE.

Law, C.M., 2002. *Urban Tourism: The Visitor Economy and the Growth of Large Cities.* London: Continuum.

Le-Klähn, D.-T. and Hall, C.M., 2015. Tourist use of public transport at destinations – a review. *Current Issues in Tourism*, 18 (8), 785–803.

MacCannell, D., 1976. *The Tourist. A New Theory of the Leisure Class*. Berkeley, CA: University of California Press.

Maitland, R. and Newman, P., 2009a. Developing world tourism cities. *In*: R. Maitland and P. Newman, eds, *World Tourism Cities. Developing Tourism Off the Beaten Track*. London: Routledge, 1–21.

Maitland, R. and Newman, P., eds, 2009b. *World Tourism Cities. Developing Tourism Off the Beaten Track*. London: Routledge.

Maitland, R. and Newman, P., 2004. Developing metropolitan tourism on the fringe of central London. *International Journal of Tourism Research*, 6 (5), 339–348.

Maitland, R., 2008. Conviviality and everyday life: the appeal of new areas of London for visitors. *International Journal of Tourism Research*, 10 (1), 15–25.

Maitland, R., 2010. Everyday life as a creative experience in cities. *International Journal of Culture, Tourism and Hospitality Research*, 4 (3), 176–185.

Maitland, R., 2013. Backstage behaviour in the global city: tourists and the search for the 'real London'. *Procedia – Social and Behavioral Sciences*, 105 (3), 12–19.

Martinotti, G., 1993. *Metropoli*. Bologna: Il Mulino.

Massey, D., 1993. Power-geometry and a progressive sense of place. *In*: J. Bird, B. Curtis, T. Putnam, G. Robertson and L. Tickner, eds, *Mapping the Futures: Local Cultures, Global Change*. London: Routledge, 60–70.

Matoga, L. and Pawłowska, A., 2018. Off-the-beaten-track tourism: a new trend in the tourism development in historical European cities. A case study of the city of Krakow, Poland. *Current Issues in Tourism*, 21 (14), 1644–1669.

McCabe, S., 2002. The tourist experience and everyday life. *In*: G. Dann, ed., *The Tourist as a Metaphor of the Social World*. Wallingford: CABI, 61–77.

McCabe, S., 2005. 'Who is a tourist?' A critical review. *Tourist Studies*, 5 (1), 85–106.

Mermet, A.-C., 2017. Airbnb and tourism gentrification: critical insights from the exploratory analysis of the 'Airbnb syndrome' in Reykjavík. *In*: M. Gravari-Barbas and S. Guinand, eds, *Tourism and Gentrification in Contemporary Metropolises. International Perspectives*. Abingdon: Routledge, 52–74.

Munar, A.M., 2011. Tourist-created content: rethinking destination branding. *International Journal of Culture, Tourism and Hospitality Research*, 5 (3), 291–305.

Munar, A.M., Gyimothy, S. and Cai, L., eds, 2013. *Tourism Social Media: Transformations in Identity, Community and Culture*. Bingley: Emerald.

Murdoch, J., 2006. *Post-Structuralist Geography*. London: SAGE.

Novy, J. and Colomb, C., 2017. Urban tourism and its discontents. An introduction. *In*: C. Colomb and J. Novy, eds, *Protest and Resistance in the Tourist City*. London: Routledge, 1–30.

Oskam, J. and Boswijk, A., 2016. Airbnb and the future of networked hospitality businesses. *Journal of Tourism Futures*, 2 (1), 22–42.

Pappalepore, I., Maitland, R., and Smith, A., 2010. Exploring urban creativity: visitor experiences of Spitalfields, London. *Tourism, Culture & Communication*, 10, 217–230.

Pappalepore, I., Maitland, R. and Smith, A., 2014. Prosuming creative urban areas. Evidence from east London. *Annals of Tourism Research*, 44, 227–240.

Pinkster, F.M. and Boterman, W.R., 2017. When the spell is broken: gentrification, urban tourism and privileged discontent in the Amsterdam canal district. *Cultural Geographies*, 24 (3), 457–472.

Richards, G., 2017. Tourists in their own city – considering the growth of a phenomenon. *Tourism Today*, 16, 8–16.

Ritzer, G. and Liska, A., 2004. "McDisneyzation" and "post-tourism": complementary perspectives on contemporary tourism. *In*: S. Williams, ed., *Tourism: New Directions and Alternative Tourism*. London: Routledge, 65–82.

Roche, M., 1992. Mega-events and micro-modernization: on the sociology of the new urban tourism. *The British Journal of Sociology*, 43 (4), 563–600.

Rojek, C., 1993. *Ways of Escape: Modern Transformations in Leisure and Travel*. London: Macmillan.

Sans, A.A. and Domínguez, A.Q., 2016. Unravelling Airbnb: urban perspectives from Barcelona. *In:* A.P. Russo and G. Richards, eds, *Reinventing the Local in Tourism: Producing, Consuming and Negotiating Place*. Bristol: Channel View Publications, 209–228.

Schmallegger, D. and Carson, D., 2008. Blogs in tourism: changing approaches to information exchange. *Journal of Vacation Marketing*, 14 (2), 99–110.

Selby, M., 2004. *Understanding Urban Tourism: Image, Culture and Experience*. London: I.B. Tauris.

Shani, A. and Uriely, N., 2012. VFR tourism: the host experience. *Annals of Tourism Research*, 39 (1), 421–440.

Sharpley, R., 2014. Host perceptions of tourism: a review of the research. *Tourism Management*, 42, 37–49.

Sheller, M. and Urry, J., 2004. Places to play, places in play. *In*: M. Sheller and J. Urry, eds, *Tourism Mobilities: Places to Play, Places in Play*. London: Routledge, 1–10.

Sigala, M. and Gretzel, U., eds, 2018. *Advances in Social Media for Travel, Tourism and Hospitality: New Perspectives, Practice and Cases*. Abingdon: Routledge.

Smith, V.L., ed., 1989. *Hosts and Guests: The Anthropology of Tourism*. Philadelphia, PA: University of Pennsylvania Press.

Sommer, C. and Helbrecht, I., 2017. Seeing like a tourist city: how administrative constructions of conflictive urban tourism shape its future. *Journal of Tourism Futures*, 3 (2), 157–170.

Sommer, C., 2018. What begins at the end of urban tourism as we know it? *Europe Now* [online], 3 (5). Available from: www.europenowjournal.org/2018/04/30/what-begins-at-the-end-of-urban-tourism-as-we-know-it/ [accessed 10 August 2018].

Spirou, C., 2011. *Urban Tourism and Urban Change: Cities in a Global Economy*. Abingdon: Routledge.

Stoltenberg, L. and Frisch, T., 2017. "Gemeinschaft" als Unternehmensaufgabe. Konsequenzen der Sharing Economy. *Pop. Kultur und Kritik*, 11, 45–52.

Stors, N. and Baltes, S., 2018. Constructing urban tourism space digitally: a study of Airbnb listings in two Berlin neighborhoods. *Proceedings of the ACM on Human-Computer Interaction*, 2 (CSCW), 166, 1–29.

Tufts, S., 2006. "We make it work": the cultural transformation of hotel workers in the city. *Antipode*, 38 (2), 350–373.

Turner, L. and Ash, J., 1975. *The Golden Hordes*. London: Constable.

Tussyadiah, I.P. and Fesenmaier, D.R., 2009. Mediating tourist experiences: access to places via shared videos. *Annals of Tourism Research*, 36 (1), 24–40.

Uriely, N., 2005. The tourist experience: conceptual developments. *Annals of Tourism Research,* 32 (3), 199–216.

Urry, J., 1990. *The Tourist Gaze. Leisure and Travel in Contemporary Societies*. London: SAGE.

Urry, J. and Larsen, J., 2011. *The Tourist Gaze 3.0.* London: SAGE.

Veijola, S., 2010. Introduction: tourism as work. *Tourist Studies*, 9 (2), 83–87.

Wearing, S.L. and Foley, C., 2017. Understanding the tourist experience of cities. *Annals of Tourism Research*, 65, 97–110.

White, N. and White, P.B., 2007. Home and away: tourists in a connected world. *Annals of Tourism Research*, 34 (1), 88–104.

Zukin, S., Lindeman, S. and Hurson, L., 2015. The omnivore's neighborhood? Online restaurant reviews, race, and gentrification. *Journal of Consumer Culture*, 17 (3), 459–479.

2 Ordinary tourism and extraordinary everyday life

Rethinking tourism and cities

Jonas Larsen

Introduction

Much tourism theory used to define tourism as the antithesis to 'everydayness'. In the first edition of the classical *The Tourist Gaze*, John Urry (1990) famously argued that the main feature of the tourist gaze—and modern tourism more generally—"is a difference between one's normal place of residence/work and the object of the tourist" (1990, p. 11). We are told that tourism "results from a basic binary division between the ordinary/everyday and the extraordinary" and "potential objects of the tourist gaze must be different in some way or other" (ibid.). Therefore, difference fuels the economy of tourism. In this chapter, I unsettle and reverse this claim by arguing that the everyday is not necessarily ordinary and tourism not necessarily extraordinary. My key argument is that tourism practices are actually fuelled by everyday socialities and practices and that tourism has real impacts on the everyday life of hosting cultures. I will unfold these arguments in relation to European cities that are—for better and worse—toured by ever-increasing numbers of tourists.

The urban is relatively little discussed in tourism studies while tourism plays an inferior role in urban studies more broadly (see also Stock, Chapter 3 in this volume). It can be argued that much tourist research used to have an anti-urban bias insofar that tourism was conceived as an escape from alienating and stressful cities into the tranquil countryside or nature (Ashworth and Page 2011). Few urban scholars have taken tourism seriously or noted its growing cultural, social and economic significance for, and impact on, major cities around the world (but see Colomb and Novy 2017, Hayllar *et al.* 2008). Yet there are, of course, exceptions. The existing literature, within tourist studies and urban studies, focuses upon famous must-see sights and environments designed specifically for tourists and other leisure visitors (e.g., Judd and Fainstein 1999, Judd 1999, Urry 1990). While such conventional accounts are not unfounded, they erroneously suggest that tourism is not a normal part of the city and that tourism and everyday life are two different worlds. In this chapter, I rethink this separation by discussing empirical trends, concepts and theories that allow us to understand and reassess the intertwinement of tourism practices and everyday practices, and how locals and tourists live closely together, in cities. In broader perspective, this article argues that tourism ought to play a much more prominent role in urban studies that have been remarkably blind to the ever-increasing economic, social and cultural role of global tourism in shaping the everyday spaces of cities around world.

The article is divided into three vignettes. The first 'de-exoticises' tourism theory by discussing how everyday socialities, distant social relationships and hobbies inform tourism practices and fuel specific forms of tourism. In dialogue with Maitland's work on new forms of urban tourism, the second reflects on *new urban tourism* (Stors *et al.*, Chapter 1 in this volume) and practices that value non-touristic neighbourhoods, non-designed local experiences and private accommodation. In relation to this, the third vignette discusses how we can theorise the 'touristification' of neighbourhoods and encounters between tourists and locals. Here I will also draw upon discussions about encounters between strangers within urban studies.

Vignette 1: everyday sociality and practices

Discussions of everyday socialities and practices were largely absent in early tourism studies where the focus was upon sights and places, and how people experienced them. Conversely, mainstream sociological and geographical studies of everyday practices have not explored how the everyday can be mobilised and performed on the move. This has changed over the last two decades where different 'turns' have inserted the social and everydayness into tourist theory. These turns have 'de-exoticised' tourism theory and connected tourism with broader discussions with sociology and geography (Larsen 2008). This research suggests that everyday routines and habitual dispositions influence tourism performances and that pleasant sociality with loved ones are central to tourism performances. Everyday life is not as a-mobile and localised as often assumed.

The influential 'performance turn' (Edensor 2001, Haldrup and Larsen 2009) has discussed how much tourism is not a liminal activity where everyday routines are fully suspended (e.g., Shields 1991) as habits, obligations, everyday objects and social relations move *with* tourists. Everyday life can be mobilised through social habits, small daily rituals, precious objects, mundane technologies and significant others (Kaaristo and Rhoden 2017, Hall and Holdsworth 2016, Wearing and Foley 2017). It is therefore not rooted in one particular place, such as the home. Our everyday life and practices are therefore part of our baggage and bodily performances when we travel and they frame how we experience and understand 'difference' (see also Grube, Chapter 11 in this volume). As Edensor writes:

> Rather than transcending the mundane, most forms of tourism are fashioned by culturally coded escape attempts. Moreover, although

suffused with notions of escape from normativity, tourists carry quotidian habits and responses with them: they are part of their baggage.

(2001, p. 61)

Elsewhere, he argues that "many tourist endeavours are mundane and informed by an unreflexive sensual awareness, and hence not particular dissimilar to everyday habits and routines" (2006, p. 26; see also Edensor 2007).

This is, in part, because it is uncommon to be a self-contained *flâneur*. The 'performance turn' stresses the communal nature of tourism performances as friends and family members do tourism together, and one's particular family or friends afford some performances more than that of others. This sociality is in part what makes tourism fun but occasionally exasperating (Haldrup and Larsen 2009). In the performance turn-inspired *Tourist Gaze 3.0*, Urry and Larsen make the case that experiences with a given place crucially depend upon who you travel with and how you get along at the moment with that person or group. They suggest that it is easy for loving couples to enjoy 'romantic Paris' but much harder for troubled ones (Urry and Larsen 2011). Individual performances of gazing are not only conditioned by cultural discourses and representations but also by the presence of 'others' and negotiations and interactions with one's 'team members'. They refer to Degen, DeSilvey and Rose's (2008) notion of the 'parental look' that brings out that parents are busy keeping an eye on their children and that children therefore 'influence the rhythms and gazes of their parents'. This also means that parents often "see an attraction through their eyes, with little time for sustained, contemplative 'romantic gazing' often associated with tourism" (Urry and Larsen 2011, p. 198–199).

Everyday sociality does not only inform how people do places, but also why they travel in the first place. The 'performance turn' insists that tourists search for authentic sociability between *themselves* (Wang 1999, p. 364). "Getting away from it all might be an attempt to get it all back to together again", as Löfgren once wrote (1999, p. 269). Indeed, it has been shown that families re-enact such imaginative families through their tourist photography practices (Larsen 2005). Tourism *intensifies* family relations, as they are intermittently 'thrown-together' now that work, childcare, schools, workplaces and leisure activities no longer keep them apart. We may say that tourism brings families together and tourists dream about idyllic family life as much as 'exotic places'. Tourism, it has been suggested, is "a utopian performance where everyday routines, doings and roles hopefully become extraordinary: relaxed, jointed and joyful" (Haldrup and Larsen 2009, p. 29). Of course, there is no guarantee that such transition will actually materialise and a holiday might only aggravate family tensions despite—or perhaps because of—the high expectations.

As discussed by the mobilities paradigm (Urry 2000) and others, everyday sociality also matters in relation to so-called VFR ('visiting friends and relatives') tourism where distant friends and family members travel to visit each other and attend 'obligatory' social events such as weddings and family reunions. As VFR tourism will typically take place in cities and off the beaten track, tourists are for once literally part of everyday places. In contrast to commercialised hospitality, VFR tourism:

> [...] is about being co-present with significant 'faces', being their guests, and receiving their hospitality and perhaps enjoying their knowledge of local culture. It follows that contemporary tourists are often in effect both guests and hosts. Repeated hospitality is offered to people that also have 'open doors' (this might be slightly different with family members), with systems of hospitality involving reciprocity.
>
> (Larsen *et al.* 2006, p. 248)

This highlights how tourism can sustain social ties and visiting and hosting friends and relatives have become more central as many people have dispersed social networks and live 'mobile lives' (Elliott and Urry 2010).

The mobilities paradigm argues that travel is much more central to much contemporary social and economic everyday life than acknowledged by everyday sociologists. While this paradigm does not question that most everyday activities take place locally (as demonstrated by Holloway and Hubbard 2001, Ellegaard and Vilhelmson 2004), it highlights the significance of travel, and occasional sociality to the spatialities of everyday life. Moreover, it claims that it is increasingly difficult and futile to differentiate between tourist activities and other mobile activities (Hannam *et al.* 2014, Larsen *et al.* 2007). Tourism is no longer a bounded activity, and we ought to understand it as a part of a wider set of mobile everyday practices.

John Urry argued that VFR tourism fulfils the human need of being physically co-present with other people. Molotoch and Boden's (1993) idea of 'compulsion to proximity' and Simmel's notion 'sociability' (1997a) inspired Urry. Simmel spoke of 'sociability' to describe situations where people congregated to enjoy 'pure interaction', such as sharing a communal meal (1997b; see also Stoltenberg and Frisch, Chapter 8 in this volume). Urry (2003) invented the notion of 'meetingness' to highlight that co-present interactions were pivotal for producing trust, bonds and pleasures among families and friends. Urry's key argument was that such co-present meetings are crucial and require much travel in mobile societies and that tourism is related to everyday patterns of social life, family and friendship. Tourist travel seems essential for many as it connects far-flung networks within places of much needed co-presence (see also Mason 2004).

Lastly, much tourism is informed by, and is an extension of, everyday practices. Stebbins's (1992) notion of 'serious leisure' is much discussed within leisure studies, 'serious leisure' being concerned with devoted and competitive leisure practitioners. Somewhat similar to the 'performance turn' within tourism studies, there is a focus upon leisure as a form of embodied doing. The concept further insinuates that leisure can be a form of work where people develop competences and a 'career' where they become better and more committed at a specific leisure activity through regular training and by attending specific events. This is in contrast to tourism studies where there are few accounts of tourists as serious, competent and well-prepared agents, or of events that require preparatory training and specialised skills. Careers are associated with work and the world of tourism is one of frivolity, relaxation and easily accessible skills. The 'serious leisure' perspective challenges such understandings of tourism.

While 'serious leisure' is mainly performed at home as part of one's everyday life, devoted practitioners tend to travel to attend attractive events where they can corporeally experience, or participate in, significant events, or experience places of high significance and esteem within their subcultural community. Numerous specialised events and places attract thousands and thousands of serious leisure practitioners that have studied and trained hard as part of their everyday to be well prepared for the occasion. Here we might think of international non-local Manchester United, Liverpool FC or Chelsea FC supporters who routinely watch their football team play on TV at their local bar or private homes (Weed 2007). They intermittently travel to Manchester, Liverpool and London to be physically co-present with like-minded supporters and contribute to stadium atmosphere as any other devoted local supporter (Weed 2010, Reimer 2004). Another example could be EDM/techno tourists visiting iconic dance clubs in Berlin. A globalised music industry and social media allow such international tourists to be experts about German EDM/techno and they feel at home in such clubs (Garcia 2016). Marathons are a third example, as I will now discuss in detail.

Urban marathons are an illustrative example of how 'serious leisure' links the everyday and tourism. Marathons were long associated with serious sport and they only attracted a small group of physically competent practitioners. This changed slowly in the 1970s with the jogging movement that de-sportified running and, instead, associated it with casual leisure, health and an active urban life (Latham 2015). Jogging democratised running and made it available for women and the less fit, portly middle-aged. Yet some joggers began to participate in running events designed specifically for more committed runners and competitive road races slowly began to embrace joggers. For instance, The New York Marathon explicitly designed the event with the jogger in mind. Over the years, there has been a dramatic increase in the numbers of runners (with women now accounting for around 40 per cent of the participants) who have completed a marathon and there are some 5,000 marathons worldwide (Larsen 2018). Some of these attract thousands of national and international leisure runners who habitually combine their passion for running with visiting some of most exciting cities in the world. While tourism is seldom the main attraction of running a marathon, it is nonetheless a critical element of the practice. Many 'serious' marathon runners develop what is known as 'event travel careers' by completing major city marathons in world cities such as Berlin, London, New York, Chicago and Tokyo (Axelsen and Robinson 2009, Green and Jones 2005, Shipway and Jones 2007).

While urban marathons are extraordinarily atmospheric events that are staged in exciting places elsewhere, preparing for them involves much mundane training and most of this daily running takes place locally and as part of one's time-pressured everyday/family life. Without months of sustained and time-consuming training, one will not develop the physiological capacity or the 'embodied mind' to pass through the many pain barriers throughout the race. The spur-of-the-moment body will not be successful in a marathon (Edensor and Larsen 2018).

This vignette has shown how tourism is central to how many displaced people and middle-class people do family life, friendships and hobbies as part of their, what we might term, 'everyday leisure life': evenings, weekends and holidays are part of, and not separate from, people's day-to-day life. Moreover, it discussed how local football fans, clubbers and marathon runners cheer, dance and run with tourists that might be equally devoted and knowledgeable.

Vignette 2: gazing on the everyday off the beaten tracks

This vignette illustrates how ordinary everyday life rather than attractions are intriguing for many experienced Western tourists. However, to understand this we need to rethink MacCannell's notion of authenticity. MacCannell (1976) theorised tourism as an emblematic modern search for vanished authenticity. Nostalgia, understood as mourning for an authentic past, thus emerges as a formative theme of modern tourism and modernity as a whole. Tourism is portrayed as a *side*-product of modernity's dominating logic of inauthenticity: modernity's 'other' that transports alienated people *back* to places of authenticity: "Modern man has been condemned to look elsewhere, everywhere, for his authenticity, to see if he can catch a glimpse of it reflected in the simplicity, poverty, chastity or purity of others" (MacCannell 1976, p. 41). Tourism represents a desire for what modernity destroys and excludes. Tourists are a contemporary pilgrimage that leave their homes to seek authenticity in other places and times. This resonates with the fact that many tourism sights are historical and that tourism agencies and advertising traditionally reduces cities to living museums where the authentic resides in a bygone era. The latter explains why tourists often only encounter 'staged authenticity' and fabricated signs, according to MacCannell. Others will argue that such staged environments can include everything from inner-city hotels to shopping malls, resorts marinas and harbour fronts, and they are said to seduce visitors with an uncanny mix of visual spectacles, postmodern theming and McDonaldised rationality as authenticity (e.g., Judd and Fainstein 1999, Judd 1999, Urry and Larsen 2011). They are often denounced as placeless 'tourist bubbles' where tourists live protected lives that are cut off from the messy and lived urban everyday life: tourists and locals seldom bump into each other. Yet new research suggests that this is changing.

Recent studies (Maitland 2008, 2010, Maitland and Newman 2008, 2014) and others (Bock 2015, Dirksmeier and Helbrecht 2015, Novy 2014,

2016, Pappalepore *et al.* 2014) on so-called *new urban tourism* suggest that MacCannell was right about the power of authenticity in steering the tourist gaze but wrong in maintaining that authenticity necessarily resides in the past and inauthenticity in the present. Maitland (2008, 2010, 2013) shows that some tourists turn their back on London's long-established must-see and 'overrun' historical sights (e.g., Buckingham Palace, Big Ben). *New urban tourism* refers to urban tourism practices that move beyond the long establish tourism precincts and must-see (often historical) sights; they also have a desire to move into, and gaze upon, what Edensor (2006) has called 'contemporary heterogeneous tourist places'.

A major reason for this trend is that flying is historically low-priced and pervasive in the Western world. So many places are within reach quickly and cheaply and many middle-class people have become habituated to mobile leisure lifestyle with frequent weekend trips and holidays abroad. Contemporary tourism is characterised by an increasing 'routinization' (Novy 2016, Urry and Larsen 2011) and 'repeat tourism'. Given that return visitors have probably seen the most famous sights on a previous visit, they are less inclined to do it again and since they have already acquired some local knowledge, they are more motivated to venture off the beaten track. Maitland (2008, p. 19) writes: "Many visitors are now experienced users of cities who want to move beyond traditional tourism precincts; some are frequent visitors and feel a sense of belonging to the places they visit. In London, more than 60% of overseas tourists have visited the city before, often many times." The increase in VFR tourism is also fuelling 'repeat tourism' and *new urban tourism*. When tourists visit friends or kin, they are likely to stay at their place and hang out in their local neighbourhoods. The host will be guide and disposed to present his or her local scene. *New urban tourism* is both a reaction to, and product of, what has become known as 'overtourism', which refers to a situation where attractions and even whole cities are visited beyond their capacity (Koens and Postman 2016). 'Overtourism' may have the effect that experienced tourists avoid the most famous attractions; they know from past experiences or reviews that they will have to queue for hours to see that celebrated painting or building and that too many tourists will ruin the experience. Martin Parr's photos, for instance, effectively illustrate how the 'romantic gazer' drowns in a sea of tourists in front of Mona Lisa. Such viewing conditions will discourage many otherwise interested people.

New urban tourists are bored with traditional sights and fascinated by, and drawn to, contemporary everyday life and local non-touristic neighbourhoods where they can rub shoulders and drink coffee with locals instead of tourists (Sommer and Kip, Chapter 10 in this this volume). They gaze upon ongoing mundane everyday life and vernacular architecture rather than 'staged authenticity': the appeal of the areas lies in the authentic qualities that makes it distinctive as a local place. Maitland argues that:

In these real places, the routines and rhythms of everyday life take on a new significance. Mundane daily routines of shopping, going for a coffee, being at work give meaning to places not dominated by a show put on for visitors [...]. Visitors commented enthusiastically about the pleasure of see[ing] people going about their tasks, observing ordinary Londoners just doing their thing, and people going about their day, as they would. Everyday work routines take on new significance—a glimpse of an office worker at their computer, seen through a window, seems really cool, as part of the real London. Going to the local supermarket feels like an incredible experience, since one can observe local people and what they choose to consume.

(2013, pp. 16–17)

Contemporary everyday life and ordinary landscapes of consumption that are almost exclusively frequented by locals are perceived as interesting and authentic as they are not staged for tourists (Bock 2015). Moreover, it also allows tourists to move beyond gazing by interacting with locals.

This resonates with the 'performance turn' that stresses that tourists do not adhere fully to the tourism industry's standardised scripts but construct their own narratives and find their own ways. To some extent, this also reverberates with other concepts in tourism theory. Mansfeldt (2014) coined 'inbetweeness' to explain the fact that tourists' greatest experiences often happen by chance when people move between sights and do nothing in particular while Richards's (2011) idea of 'creative tourism' highlights that tourists wish to be creative, to be actively involved in local communities and do what locals do.

One example of such creative embodied, creative immersion in local practices is cycling in bike-famous Copenhagen. A 'mobilities' approach to cycling (Larsen 2017) involves understanding cycling as utilitarian transport but also as a specific in-between mode of experiencing cities. I have shown ethnographically that many tourists, who are usually intimidated, or even completely put off by the idea of cycling in their home city, corporeally embrace cycling when they visit the famous pro-cycling city; it is seen the most authentic way of moving about in a city where cycling is perfectly ordinary for locals. Tourists told me that the many bike lanes and abundant cyclists of all ages and shapes made cycling appear and feel so innocuous and easy while many of the bike lanes allow more off-the-beaten-track places to be covered and seen than one does when walking or using public transport. They rejoiced in the fact that the bike gives one the freedom to stop at will and make small detours. Moreover, they reported that they enjoyed the physical and affective sensations of cycling while simultaneously having time to visually consume Copenhagen. We may consider the bike the most authentic way of being a new urban tourist. Therefore, in Copenhagen, the bike plays a significant role in facilitating trips to, and experiences of, local neighbourhoods, as well as authentic experiences of local mobility cultures and practices (see Larsen 2017, for more detail).

The kind of neighbourhoods discussed in the *new urban tourism* literature tend to be newly gentrified 'hipster' (e.g., trendy) areas, such as Marias in Paris (Gravari-Barbas and Guinand 2017), Kreuzberg and Neukölln in Berlin (Dirksmeier and Helbrecht 2015, Füller and Michel 2014), and Shoreditch in London (Maitland 2008). This also means that 'less happening' outlying neighbourhoods are still overlooked, so not all everyday life is of interest. Many tourists, particularly those who are themselves cultural 'gentrifiers' at home, follow the recommendations, and in the footsteps, of the local gentrifiers when they shop or go out in a new city (Gravari-Barbas and Guinand 2017, Cocola-Gant 2018). New urban tourists contribute actively to the cultural gentrification that change the place image and social composition of former out-of-the-way working-class neighbourhoods (Gravari-Barbas and Guinand 2017).

Gentrified hipster neighbourhoods are not authentic in the sense that they are original. Their authenticity stems from their 'hipster quality' (e.g., cultural capital) and resemblance with other hipster neighbourhoods across the world. You will find roughly the same type of *independent* bars, coffee shops, record shops, vintage shops, creative locals, clothing and hairstyles in the neighbourhoods discussed in the *new urban tourism* literature. *New urban tourism* is a reflection of cultural globalisation. This also explains why youngish Western tourists easily feel at home outside enclaves (at least in the Western world) because such neighbourhoods are self-referential. Social media also plays a crucial role here. Numerous music, design and lifestyle magazines, newspapers and blogs venerate the coolness of these neighbourhoods; so do the *Lonely Planet* and various 'hipster' online travel guides. They are now also touristically branded and marketed by city tourist offices (Milne *et al.* 2016, p. 102). For instance, *Wonderful Copenhagen* (the Destination Marketing Organisation for Copenhagen) recently launched a new strategy called 'the end of tourism as we know it' where they argued that the future of urban tourism is all about experiencing what they call 'localhoods' and they further claim 'that locals are the destination' (Wonderful Copenhagen 2017).

Lastly, many new urban tourists opt for private accommodation off the beaten tracks because it is often cheaper and perceived to be more authentic than a generic hotel. This desire for living locally is also stressed by the online short-term rental service Airbnb (www.airbnb.com) itself. The company launched a campaign in 2016 where it mocked the selfie-taking-bus-tour-tourist who 'goes to' and 'tours' Paris. The alternative to being a 'tourist jerk' is supposedly to 'live there', 'to feel at home anywhere in the world' and 'do your local routines' fully immersed in the local culture where you happen to be at this moment. As Airbnb co-founder and CEO, Brian Chesky, said reportedly at the launch:

> The number one reason people choose to travel on Airbnb is they want to live like a local. They don't want to be tourists stuck in long lines, fighting with the crowds to see the same thing as everyone else. Our hosts offer

more than just generic hospitality—they welcome travellers from around the world into their communities. Today is the start of an exciting journey to help people not just go somewhere, but truly live there.

(Diaz 2016)

Airbnb believes that it has not only invented a new tourism *economy* where ordinary people save money while travelling and make money on tourists but also accommodated tourist practices that fulfil demands for living with, and as, locals (see also Wildish and Spierings, Chapter 7 in this volume). This system depends on a generalised trust between strangers and their preference for staying in, and sensing the atmosphere of, an 'ordinary' home (Bialski 2016) in a generally less touristy neighbourhood. This form of monetarised hospitality moves tourism into local neighbourhoods where locals, who used to have no or very little contact with tourists, now intermittently rent out their property for monetary exchange. Airbnb 'hosts' (to use the Airbnb jargon) are not the immobile and poor hosts depicted in much of the literature on 'hosts and guests' in tourism studies (Stors, Chapter 6 in this volume). They are more or less experienced tourists and the revenue from hosting will often finance their vacation (most hosting does not involve face-to-face interaction, unless the host only rents out a room and is therefore often present in the property when the 'guest' is staying). Some tourists, we may say, have become tourism entrepreneurs who earn pocket money from commodifying their property and letting it out to 'strangers' (but digitally 'known' to them through their Airbnb verified profile and user reviews). Studies show that those benefiting from tourism financially are less critical of 'guests' than those who are merely living with tourists (Quinn 2007). All things being equal, we may expect that users of Airbnb are more tolerant of (noisy and annoying) Airbnb tourists than the rest of the population.

This vignette has discussed how urban dwellers realise that their everyday life and neighbourhoods have become an object of the tourist gaze; their next-door neighbour is a potential 'guest' and that they can become hosts too. Many neighbourhoods discussed in the *new urban tourism* literature a decade ago are now more or less *on*, rather than *off*, the beaten track. They are swallowed by the global vortex of global tourism that 'overflows' some cities with—sometimes too—many tourists. In the last vignette, I turn my attention to some of the ways in which cities have become tourist cities and how locals live—sometimes in conflict—with tourists.

Vignette 3: living with tourists

Ashworth and Page (2011, p. 1) once argued that cities "are large multifunctional entities […] into which tourists can be effortlessly absorbed so that they become economically, socially and physically invisible to an extent that is not so in many other tourism spaces. The anonymity of cities means that it can be difficult to differentiate the visitor from the rest." While cities can indeed absorb many tourists, it is clear that tourists are now very visible in, and no longer easily absorbed by, some cities, which is said to be the recent case in Barcelona and Berlin. The urban middle classes are beginning to realise that they are not only tourists but also hosts. This reciprocity of rules defines present-day tourism as most Western urban dwellers are both hosts *and* tourists.

Urban studies have long explored how modern cities force urban inhabitants to live in close proximity with strangers (Simmel 1950). Recent studies have focused upon encounters between ethnic populations and ethnic others, such as migrants and refugees, how we live with difference. Some of these studies examine how otherness and stereotypes are not so much pre-existing as produced in, and through, such face-to-face meetings (Koefoed and Simonsen 2011).

The tourist is a much less discussed 'stranger' in urban studies. Yet within tourist studies, there has been some research into such encounters, especially the negative ones. For instance, what is known as the 'local gaze' and 'mutual gaze' illuminate how hosts may resist superficial, unruly, noisy and gentrifying tourists with poor service, an impervious 'local gaze', and anti-tourism stickers and graffiti (e.g., 'Berlin does not love you') rather than with open arms (Maoz 2006, Russo and Richards 2016, p. 2). Such tourism bashing can lead to 'touristphobia'. For instance, a large banner outside a squatted building in Berlin attacks tourists in vile and bigoted language: 'Why is it called the tourist season when we are not allowed to shoot them.' Such 'encounters' label the tourist as 'other' and out of place (see also Grube, Chapter 11 in this this volume). Because of this inhospitality, many try to hide their identity as tourists (Urry and Larsen 2011). New urban tourists can paradoxically enhance everyday feelings of 'overtourism' as such tourists' demand the right to use and move through locals' everyday spaces and be inquisitive. Indeed, Urry and I (2011, p. 61) suggested that "those tourist practices that involve the observation of physical objects are less intrusive than those that involve observing individuals and groups". Living with intrusive new urban tourists may create feelings of being constantly being gazed upon (Maoz 2006, Quinn 2007) and 'out of place' in one's home and neighbourhood (Wildish and Spierings, Chapter 7 in this volume). Indeed, *Der Tagesspiegel* referred to Berlin as a 'conquered city' (cited in Novy 2014, p. 225), with specific reference to 'Airbnb tourism' that literally means that tourists (i.e., 'strangers') become 'neighbours' for a couple of nights. The days are over when downtown hotels accommodated all tourists, and locals and tourists did not live under the same roof or share the same amenities.

As widely discussed, (Airbnb) tourism is scapegoated for causing undesired gentrification, shortage of affordable long-term rentals, exorbitant property prices, destroying local everyday services and shops, and much more (Cocola-Gant 2018, Füller and Michel 2014, Häussermann and Colomb 2003, Mermet 2017). As Cocola-Gant (2016, p. 7) has discussed, in certain places the Airbnb phenomenon corresponds to "a snowball process […]. It leads to a form of collective displacement never seen in classical gentrification, that is to say, to a substitution of residential life by tourism." Lately, civic movements, municipalities and political parties in Berlin, Barcelona and other places are trying to reclaim their right-to-the-city in the face of aggressive Airbnb tourism.

There are indeed many ambiguities and anomalies in Airbnb's notion of being 'hospitable'. Indeed, research reveals that many 'hosts' are not ordinary people that rent out a few times a year but professional investors and landlords that may exploit, bend or violate the law by renting out residential properties short-term to tourists and not long-term to residents as the former is more profitable (Sans and Domínguez 2016; see also Stors, Chapter 6 in this volume). Airbnb has caused much trouble and opposition in places where its service is 'exploited' by investors and former residential flats suddenly become holiday apartments. For instance, in 2015, Barcelona elected the 'anti-tourism' housing activist Ada Colau as mayor; she believes that "the city is being killed by too many tourists" (Colau 2014). She immediately froze licences for all new hotels and holiday apartments, made restrictions on short-term rentals and proposed a new tourist tax (Novy and Colomb 2017, Burgen 2017). However, the same literature also discuss how urban change is often not simply the outcome of 'tourism' and it is much easier to blame the 'nameless, faceless foreigner' and Airbnb for local problems and economic and social inequalities (Novy and Colomb 2017, p. 15, Stors and Kagermeier 2017). Nonetheless, there is a dire need for political regulation of Airbnb.

Instead of inhospitality, locals may choose to encounter tourists with cordiality, interest or at least civil 'inattention' (Sommer and Kip, Chapter 10 in this volume). But studies of such *positive* urban encounters are largely absent. Many Western urban dwellers are willing to welcome more tourists as they appreciate their cultural, social and economic contribution to their place of residence. This is indeed the case in affluent Copenhagen where, according to one study, 95 per cent of the population is willing to welcome *more* tourists— also in their own neighbourhoods—despite the fact that tourism has increased by some 53 per cent since 2009 (Wonderful Copenhagen 2016). Indeed, Maitland and Newman's (2008) research on tourism in gentrified areas of London found that *new urban tourism* could engender convivial relationships and friendships between like-minded locals and guests and that tourists, according to them, did not destroy as much as they added vibrancy and excitement to the areas (Frenzel, Chapter 4 in this volume). Alternatively, they may question essentialist distinctions between 'locals' and 'tourists' as many international students, second-homeowners, business people, VFR tourists and repeat tourists cannot be unambiguously classified as either tourists or residents, host or guests. Moreover, many so-called 'locals' are born elsewhere and speak foreign languages. Indeed, it may be said that it makes little sense to speak of locals when it comes to world cities as few of the current residents are actually born and raised there.

Finally, the social relations between tourists and locals are determined by the degree to which 'locals' positively embrace the touristifying gentrification of their cities. Gentrification studies highlight that urban preferences of some of the locals overlap with those of some visitors and that both groups appreciate the right sort of cultural neighbourhood gentrification (Cocola-Gant 2018, Gravari-Barbas and Guinand 2017, Marais and Gravari-Barbas 2017). 'Locals'—at least in the rich West—travel to other cities and they have learnt to use and appreciate 'foreign' restaurants, bars, cafes, galleries, parks and squares. They demand a vibrant cultural scene at home as part of their everyday life as well as while being on vacation. This involves acknowledging that tourism enriches one's everyday life. Many restaurants, museums, bars, shops, markets and attractions would struggle financially if *only* locals used them. Seen from this angle, cities would be poorer and less exciting without tourism. Locals increasingly behave " 'as tourists' in their own cities" (Maitland 2013, p. 19, Maitland and Newman 2008, 2014, p. 229) and it therefore makes little sense to point the fingers solely at those 'annoying' tourists.

Conclusion

I have discussed some of the ways in which everyday life permeates tourism consumption by outlining theoretical notions and perspectives that can shed a light on, and conceptualise, what we might call ordinary tourism practices, on the one hand, and extraordinary everyday life, on the other. Much tourism is strikingly ordinary, while everyday life in eventful and multicultural cities is full of extraordinary moments and encounters.

I have shown that tourism is no longer antithetical to routines and everyday life. Discussions of everyday practices, social obligations, networking and non-commercialised hospitality ought to inform current tourism theory. Conversely, all of this also indicates that tourism scholars can make a unique contribution to the literature on practice theory and everyday studies by discussing how modern everyday life is not only performed at home but also on the move and away from home, since practice theory and everyday studies are principally ignorant of tourism (see Larsen 2018).

It is specious to portray tourism as physically or symbolically apart from the rest of the everyday city as tourism now influences urban life and events as never before. This has some positive cultural effects. Tourism partly sustains many of the cultural and shopping facilities that many urban (especially middle-class) dwellers appreciate and use as part of everyday leisure life. Tourism enables cosmopolitan lifestyles and cross-cultural meetings.

Yet the last two vignettes simultaneously also discussed civic discontent in cities where many locals negatively perceive the complex social relations of tourism that are part of broader political economy of city where tourists can be blamed and scapegoated for supposedly undesirable developments. While tourism in Europe may create relative few social conflicts since many 'hosts' will themselves be 'guests' on other occasions, the fact is that 'Airbnb tourism' and *new urban tourism* cause tensions. This is common in cities where tourists invade locals' everyday spaces as tourists outnumber them or the number of tourists has increased dramatically over a short period (Quinn 2007). It is also more common when the host population is experiencing rapid economic and social change, as with gentrification that makes it economically difficult for many low-income families to live in the city. These social relations overlap with class relations, and reinforce already contested processes of gentrification and a lack of affordable housing; yet downright 'touristphobia' also infects them. Therefore, tourists will sometimes be met with reservation and detestation instead of cordiality; encounters between tourists and hosts will reproduce otherness and stereotypes rather than pleasures and cosmopolitanism, no matter how inchoately.

Maybe it is time to 'civilise' host and guests. Hosts need to realise and accept that 'hosting' is central to tourism and that the right to tourism obligates one to be a welcoming host and demonstrates a cosmopolitan attitude. Guests, meanwhile, need to acknowledge that they do not visit a liminal zone or a living museum but a place of everyday life where they need to 'fit in' rather than infuriate locals with obnoxious drunken antics, annoying selfie sticks, noisy trolley suitcases and by supporting landlords who only rent out to tourists. Moreover, it is surely time to build bridges between tourism studies, planning studies and urban studies as tourism increasingly makes and remakes our everyday cities in its own image.

References

Ashworth, G. and Page, S.J., 2011. Urban tourism research: recent progress and current paradoxes. *Tourism Management*, 32 (1), 1–15.

Axelsen, M. and Robinson, R.N., 2009. Race around the world: identifying a research agenda for the distance runner. *Annals of Leisure Research*, 12 (2), 236–257.

Bialski, P., 2016. Authority and authorship: uncovering the socio-technical regimes of peer-to-peer tourism. *In*: R.P. Russo and R. Gregson, eds, *Reinventing the Local in Tourism*. Bristol: Channel View, 35–48.

Bock, K., 2015. The changing nature of city tourism and its possible implications for the future of cities. *European Journal of Futures Research* [online], 3 (20). Available from: http://link.springer.com/article/10.1007/s40309-015-0078-5/fulltext.html. [accessed 31 March 2018].

Burgen, S., 2017. Barcelona cracks down on Airbnb rentals with illegal apartment squads [online]. *The Guardian*. Available from: www.theguardian.com/technology/2017/jun/02/airbnb-faces-crackdown-on-illegal-apartment-rentals-in-barcelona [accessed 7 August 2018].

Cocola-Gant, A.C., 2016. Holiday rentals: the new gentrification battlefront. *Sociological Research Online*, 21 (3), 1–9.

Cocola-Gant A. C., 2018. Tourism gentrification. *In*: L. Lees and M. Phillips, eds, *Handbook of Gentrification Studies*. Cheltenham: Edward Elgar Publishing, 281–293.

Colau, A., 2014. Mass tourism can kill a city – just ask Barcelona's residents [online]. *The Guardian*. Available from: www.theguardian.com/commentisfree/2014/sep/02/mass-tourism-kill-city-barcelona [accessed 7 August 2018].

Colomb, C. and Novy, J., eds, 2017. *Protest and Resistance in the Tourist City*. London: Routledge.

Degen, M., DeSilvey, C. and Rose, G., 2008. Experiencing visualities in designed urban environments: learning from Milton Keynes. *Environment and Planning A*, 40 (8), 1901–1920.

Diaz, A.-C., 2016. Airbnb asks, 'Why vacation somewhere when you can live there?' [online]. *AdAge*. Available from: http://creativity-online.com/work/airbnb-dont-go-there-live-there/46533 [accessed 7 August 2018].

Dirksmeier, P. and Helbrecht, I., 2015. Resident perceptions of new urban tourism: a neglected geography of prejudice. *Geography Compass*, 9 (5), 276–285.

Edensor, T., 2001. Performing tourism, staging tourism: (re) producing tourist space and practice. *Tourist Studies*, 1 (1), 59–81.

Edensor, T., 2006. Sensing tourist places. *In*: C. Minca and T. Oaks, eds, *Travels in Paradox: Remapping Tourism*. Lanham, MD: Rowman & Littlefield, 23–46.

Edensor, T., 2007. Mundane mobilities, performances and spaces of tourism. *Social & Cultural Geography*, 8 (2), 199–215.

Edensor, T. and Larsen, J., 2018. Rhythm analysing marathon running: 'a drama of rhythms'. *Environment and Planning A*, 32: 834–851.

Ellegaard, K. and Vilhelmson, B., 2004. Home as a pocket of local order: everyday activities and the friction of distance. *Geografiska Annaler* Series B, 86 (4), 281–296.

Elliott, A. and Urry, J., 2010. *Mobile Lives*. London: Routledge.

Füller, H. and Michel, B., 2014. 'Stop being a tourist!' New dynamics of urban tourism in Berlin-Kreuzberg. *International Journal of Urban and Regional Research*, 38 (4), 1304–1318.

Garcia, L.M., 2016. Techno-tourism and post-industrial neo-romanticism in Berlin's electronic dance music scenes. *Tourist Studies*, 16 (3), 276–295.

Gravari-Barbas, M. and Guinand, S., eds, 2017. *Tourism and Gentrification in Contemporary Metropolises: International Perspectives*. London: Routledge.

Gravari-Barbas, M., 2017. Super-gentrification and hyper-tourismification in Le Marais, Paris. *In*: M. Gravari-Barbas and S. Guinand, eds, *Tourism and Gentrification in Contemporary Metropolises*. London: Routledge, 313–342.

Green, B.C. and Jones, I., 2005. Serious leisure, social identity and sport tourism. *Sport in Society*, 8 (2), 164–181.

Haldrup, M. and Larsen, J., 2009. *Tourism, Performance and the Everyday: Consuming the Orient*. London: Routledge.

Hall, S.M. and Holdsworth, C., 2016. Family practices, holiday and the everyday. *Mobilities*, 11 (2), 284–302.

Hayllar, B., Griffin, T. and Edwards, D., eds, 2008. *Cityspaces, Tourist Places: Urban Tourism Precincts*. Amsterdam: Butterworth-Heinemann.

Hannam, K., Butler, G. and Paris, C.M., 2014. Developments and key issues in tourism mobilities. *Annals of Tourism Research*, 44, 171–185.

Häusserman, H. and Colomb, C., 2003. The new Berlin: marketing the city of dreams. *In*: L.M. Hoffman, S.S. Fainstein and D.R. Judd, eds, *Cities and Visitors: Regulating People, Markets, and City Space*. New York: Blackwell, 200–218.

Holloway, L. and Hubbard, P., 2001. *People and Place: The Extraordinary Geographies of Everyday Life*. London: Prentice Hall.

Judd, D.R. and Fainstein, S.S. eds, 1999. *The Tourist City*. New Haven, CT: Yale University Press.

Judd, D.R., 1999. Constructing the tourist bubble. *In*: D.R. Judd and S. Fainstein, eds, *The Tourist City*. New Haven, CT: Yale University Press, 35–53.

Kaaristo, M. and Rhoden, S., 2017. Everyday life and water tourism mobilities: mundane aspects of canal travel. *Tourism Geographies*, 19 (1), 78–95.

Koefoed, L. and Simonsen, K., 2011. 'The stranger', the city and the nation: on the possibilities of identification and belonging. *European Urban and Regional Studies*, 18 (4), 343–357.

Koens, K. and Postma, A., 2016. Understanding and managing visitor pressure in urban tourism. A study into the nature and methods used to manage visitor pressure in six major European cities, CELTH, Leeuwarden/Breda/Vlissingen.

Larsen, J., 2005. Families seen sightseeing: performativity of tourist photography. *Space and Culture*, 8 (4), 416–434.

Larsen, J., Axhausen, K.W. and Urry, J., 2006. Geographies of social networks: meetings, travel and communications. *Mobilities*, 1 (2), 261–283.

Larsen, J., Urry, J. and Axhausen, K.W., 2007. Networks and tourism: mobile social life. *Annals of Tourism Research*, 34 (1), 244–262.

Larsen, J., 2008. De-exoticizing tourist travel: everyday life and sociality on the move. *Leisure Studies*, 27 (1), 21–34.

Larsen, J., 2017. Leisure, bicycle mobilities and cities. *In*: J. Rickly, K. Hannam and M. Mostafanezhad, eds, *Tourism and Leisure Mobilities: Politics, Work, and Play*. London: Routledge, 39–53.

Larsen, J., 2018. Running and tourism: a practice approach. *In*: L. James, C. Ren and H. Halkier, eds, *Theories of Practice and Tourism*. London: Routledge, 41–57.

Latham, A., 2015. The history of a habit: jogging as a palliative to sedentariness in 1960s America. *cultural geographies*, 22 (1), 103–126.

Löfgren, O., 1999. *On Holiday: A History of Vacationing*. Berkeley, CA: University of California Press.

MacCannell, D., 1976. *The Tourist: A New Theory of the Leisure Class*. Berkeley, CA: University of California Press.

Mansfeldt, O.K., 2014. The inbetweenness of tourist experiences. PhD thesis, The Royal Danish Academy of Fine Arts, School of Design, Copenhagen.

Maitland, R. and Newman, P., 2008. Visitor–host relationships: conviviality between visitors and host communities. *In*: B. Hayllar, T. Griffin and D. Edwards, eds, *City Spaces, Tourist Places: Urban Tourism Precincts*. London: Routledge, 223–242.

Maitland, R., 2008. Conviviality and everyday life: the appeal of new areas of London for visitors. *International Journal of Tourism Research*, 10 (1), 15–25.

Maitland, R., 2010. Everyday life as a creative experience in cities. *International Journal of Culture, Tourism and Hospitality Research*, 4 (3), 176–185.

Maitland, R., 2013. Backstage behaviour in the global city: tourists and the search for the 'real' London. *Procedia – Social and Behavioral Sciences*, 105, 12–19.

Maitland, R. and Newman, P., eds, 2014. *World Tourism Cities: Developing Tourism Off the Beaten Track*. London: Routledge.

Maoz, D., 2006. The mutual gaze. *Annals of Tourism Research*, 33 (1), 221–239.

Mason, J., 2004. Managing kinship over long distances: the significance of 'the visit'. *Social Policy & Society*, 3 (4), 421–429.

Mermet, A.C., 2017. Airbnb and tourism gentrification: critical insights from the exploratory analysis of the 'Airbnb syndroe' in Reykjavik. *In*: M. Gravari-Barbas and S. Guinand, eds, *Tourism and Gentrification in Contemporary Metropolises*. London: Routledge, 52–74.

Milne, S., Deuchar, C. and Peters, K.B.M., 2016. 'Get local': ICT, tourism and community place making in Auckland, New Zealand. *In*: A.P. Russo and G. Richards, eds, *Reinventing the Local in Tourism*. Bristol: Channel View Publications, 101–116.

Molotoch, H. and Boden, D., 1993. The compulsion to proximity. *In*: R. Friedland and D. Boden, eds, *Now/Here: Space, Time and Modernity*. Berkeley, CA: University of California, 257–286.

Novy, J., 2014. Berlin does not love you. *In*: M. Bernt, B. Grell and A. Holm, eds, *The Berlin Reader: A Compendium on Urban Change and Activism*. Bielefeld: Transcript Verlag, 223–238.

Novy, J., 2016. The selling (out) of Berlin and the de-and re-politicization of urban tourism in Europe's 'capital of cool'. *In*: C. Colomb and J. Novy, eds, *Protest and Resistance in the Tourist City*. London: Routledge, 52–72.

Novy, J. and Colomb, C. 2017. Urban tourism and its discontents. *In*: C. Colomb and J. Novy, eds, *Protest and Resistance in the Tourist City*. London: Routledge, 1–30.

Pappalepore, I., Maitland, R. and Smith, A., 2014. Prosuming creative urban areas. evidence from east London. *Annals of Tourism Research*, 44, 227–240.

Quinn, B., 2007. Performing tourism Venetian residents in focus. *Annals of Tourism Research*, 34 (2), 458–476.

Reimer, B., 2004. For the love of England: Scandinavian football supporters, Manchester United and British popular culture. *In*: D. Andrews, ed., *Manchester United: A Thematic Study*. London: Routledge, 265–277.

Richards, G., 2011. Creativity and tourism: the state of the art. *Annals of Tourism Research*, 38 (4), 1225–1253.

Russo, A.P. and Richards, G., 2016. Introduction. *In*: P.A. Russo and G. Richards, eds, *Reinventing the Local in Tourism: Producing, Consuming and Negotiating Place*. Bristol: Channel View Publications, 1–14.

Sans, A.A. and Domínguez, A.Q., 2016. Unravelling Airbnb: urban perspectives from Barcelona. *In*: P.A. Russo and G. Richards, eds, *Reinventing the Local in Tourism: Producing, Consuming and Negotiating Place*. Bristol: Channel View Publications, 209–228.

Shipway, R. and Jones, I., 2007. Running away from home: understanding visitor experiences and behaviour at sport tourism events. *International Journal of Tourism Research*, 9 (5), 373–383.

Shields, R., 1991. *Places on the Margins: Alternative Geographies of Modernity*. London: Routledge.

Simmel, G., 1950. The metropolis and mental life. *In*: K.H. Wolff, ed., *The Sociology of George Simmel*. New York: The Free Press, 409–424.

Simmel, G., 1997a. The sociology of sociability. *In*: D. Frisby and M. Featherstone, eds, *Simmel on Culture*. London: SAGE, 120–129.

Simmel, G., 1997b. Sociology of the meal. *In*: D. Frisby and M. Featherstone, eds, *Simmel on Culture*. London: SAGE, 130–136.

Stebbins, R.A., 1992. *Amateurs, Professionals, and Serious Leisure*. Montreal and Kingston: McGill–Queen's University Press.

Stors, N. and Kagermeier, A., 2017. The sharing economy and its role in metropolitan tourism. *In*: M. Gravari-Barbas and S. Guinand, eds, *Tourism and Gentrification in Contemporary Metropolises. International Perspectives*. London: Routledge, 181–206.

Urry, J., 1990. *The Tourist Gaze*. London: SAGE.

Urry, J., 2000. *Sociology beyond Society: Mobilities for the 21st Century*. London: Routledge.

Urry, J., 2003. Social networks, travel and talk. *The British Journal of Sociology*, 54 (2), 155–175.

Urry, J. and Larsen, J., 2011. *The Tourist Gaze 3.0*. London: SAGE.

Wang, N., 1999. Rethinking authenticity in tourism experience. *Annals of Tourism Research*, 26 (2), 349–370.

Wearing, S.L. and Foley, C., 2017. Understanding the tourist experience of cities. *Annals of Tourism Research*, 65, 97–107.

Weed, M.E., 2007. The pub as a virtual football fandom venue: an alternative to 'being there'? *Soccer & Society*, 8 (2–3), 399–414.

Weed, M.E., 2010. Sport fans and travel – is 'being there' always important? *Journal of Sport & Tourism*, 15 (2), 103–109.

Wonderful Copenhagen, 2016. *Københavnere i ny undersøgelse: Der er plads til flere turister i byen* [online]. Available from: www.visitcopenhagen.dk/da/wonderful-copenhagen/kobenhavn/kobenhavnere-i-ny-undersogelse-der-er-plads-til-flere-turister-i-byen [accessed 8 August 2018].

Wonderful Copenhagen, 2017. *The end of tourism as we know it* [online]. Available from: http://localhood.wonderfulcopenhagen.dk/ [accessed 7 August 2018].

3 Inhabiting the city as tourists

Issues for urban and tourism theory

Mathis Stock

Introduction

The city as a place for tourists raises issues for urban and tourism theory. There seems to be a new awareness among scholars stemming from urban theory towards the phenomenon of tourism, which has not yet been prominently reflected on from the urban point of view. The contention that "effects of tourism on urban neighbourhoods will be quite difficult to distinguish from general processes of urban change and commodification" (Füller and Michel 2014, p. 1306) exemplifies this new perspective by looking into how tourist practices and urban development intertwine. This awareness contrasts with the affirmation, thirty years ago, by Ashworth (1989, p. 33): "A double neglect has occurred. Those interested in the study of tourism have tended to neglect the urban context in which much of it is set, while those interested in urban studies [...] have been equally neglectful of the importance of the tourist functions in cities." This appropriation of knowledge is indeed necessary, for urban studies and tourism studies have only loosely been articulated for the last 100 years. Hence, there is an opportunity to consider further, not only the relationship between tourism and the city, but more generally the complex relationships between the 'touristic' and the 'urban' on the one hand, and, on the other, the implications for tourism theory and urban theory.

Until now, tourism and urban theory have been evolving on parallel trajectories without much cross-fertilisation. Tourism has been approached by urban theory as 'business as usual' because it was seen as an economic activity that contributes to urban economy in a way similar to other 'basic' activities, lately within a cultural economy (Scott 2004). Only sparsely the specific quality of tourism as cultural and economic reworking of the city has been acknowledged (Judd and Fainstein 1999, Hoffman *et al.* 2003). Conversely, tourism theory has been developing an anti-urban bias because of the very definition of tourism as 'flight from the cities' seen as result of its density and overcrowding (Enzensberger 1958). Commentaries even highlight the apparent paradox of tourists fleeing the density of the city just to regroup in the densities of coastal resorts with all its urban problems (Krippendorf 1977). Textbooks categorise a specific 'urban tourism', distinguished from other forms of tourism (ecotourism, seaside tourism, mountain tourism, rural tourism), interpreted as opposed to the urban (Williams and Shaw 2004). By doing so, tourism theory implies urban qualities and urban values of tourism only come into effect in cities, a claim that neglects the inherent urbanisation processes of every single tourist development and tourist practice. Tourism as an urban practice raises questions beyond traditional reflections on 'urban tourism', but rarely have scholars tried to move beyond the obvious city–tourism nexus.[1] Therefore, it is questionable if the term 'urban tourism' is helpful in this respect, and there is a need to think more generally about the linkage between urbanisation processes and touristification processes.

In this chapter, I propose a discussion and conceptual insights about the conflictual ways tourists inhabit cities. It necessitates a renewed understanding of tourists as temporary inhabitants who mobilise competences and rights, and allow for an account of differentiated ways of practising cities as tourists. It is expected the debate and conceptual renewal will allow a better understanding of how and why metropolises have become major tourism spaces, how tourist activities insert themselves in the cities, and how new conflicts between tourists and residents are crucial yet ambivalent components of contemporary cities.

The contemporary situation is indeed a conflictual one, where on the one hand a set of actors foster an ever more important number of tourists in cities, and on the other hand, anti-tourism movements in cities develop. The growing importance of tourism in metropolises and so-called 'tourist-historic cities' (Ashworth and Tunbridge 1990) is one of the key elements of recent urban development, which could be called a 'recreational turn' of European cities (Stock 2007c). Generally, European cities in the last forty years—from 1980 to 2018—have tripled the production of bed-nights, and thus the overall economic importance for cities.[2] According to Eurostat (2016), cities (towns and suburbs included, only rural areas excluded) in Europe count for 66 per cent of the 2.68 billion bed-nights spent in 2016, i.e., about 1.8 billion bed-nights. Political support at all levels, from the local to the global scale, including the European level, has been key, thus exemplifying the multi-level governance of tourism. For instance, in its charter of global tourism, the World Tourism Organization (UNWTO 2012, p. 48) is pro-urban tourism:

> Tourism is a key resource for cities and local residents. The future development of cities [...] will demand policies that take into account cities' economic, social and environmental stability while at the same time offering the best experience for visitors. [...] Tourism needs the diverse and flexible products a city can offer and cities need tourism to achieve their social and economic objectives.

This significance of the economic activity mirrors the remarkable change of the cultural value assigned to the city. Urbanophobic views on moral grounds have long been pervasive for Western cities (Salomon-Cavin and Marchand 2011) and the recoding of the city as a desirable place for tourists can be seen as a significant cultural change. Today, the symbolic capital of cities is informed by touristic values, and the attraction of cities as tourist places is at its peak. Ironically, this also concerns those cities that have been described as cities in decline throughout the 1990s. Indeed, Harvey (2001, p. 405) conceives of a:

> collective symbolic capital which attaches to names and places like Paris, Athens, New York, Rio de Janeiro, Berlin and Rome is of great import and gives such places great economic advantages relative to, say, Baltimore, Liverpool, Essen, Lille, Glasgow. The problem for these latter places is to raise their quotient of symbolic capital and to increase their mark of distinction to better ground their claims to the uniqueness that yields monopoly rent.

Twenty years on, these places have all made bids for the European Capital of Culture, thus positioning themselves in the global tourism field.[3] It leads to the understanding of the contemporary city as genuinely constituted by tourism, and allows us to rethink the city as a place inhabited by mobile and temporary inhabitants, including tourists. Yet, after at least twenty years of pro-growth policies, tourism is acknowledged as contradictory and ambivalent development for cities, both because of increasing number of tourists and because of the fact tourism is no longer concentrated in traditional central tourist districts, but spreads out in virtually every neighbourhood. A first argument evokes 'congestion' and 'carrying capacity', which are terms of classical tourism theory. The following Eurostat statement relates clearly to Krippendorf's (1977) idea of the 'Landschaftsfresser', i.e., tourists who destroy the very landscape they come to gaze at, and Butler's (1980) decline of tourist areas because of the saturation threshold of a 'carrying capacity':

> However, in keeping with many aspects of urban development, tourism is a paradox, insofar as an increasing number of tourists in some towns and cities has resulted in congestion/saturation which may damage the atmosphere and local culture that made them attractive in the first place [...]. Furthermore, while tourism has the potential to generate income which may be used to redevelop/regenerate urban areas, an influx of tourists can potentially lower the quality of life for local inhabitants, for example, through: higher levels of pollution and congestion; new retail formats replacing traditional commerce; increased prices; or increased noise. Venezia (Italy) and Barcelona (Spain) are two of the most documented examples of such issues.
>
> (Eurostat 2016, p. 138)

A second string of arguments relates to the discussion around *new urban tourism* (Füller and Michel 2014, Stors *et al.*, Chapter 1 in this volume). It concerns the unprecedented link between tourism and the housing market, the touristic gentrification of cities, the appropriation of inhabited space, the spreading of tourist activities in residential neighbourhoods, and thus the conflictual encounter between tourists and residents. We might want to be cautious in approaching it necessarily as 'new' since the quest for authenticity as preferred to pre-formatted tourist attractions is co-constitutive of tourism (MacCannell 1976). The fascination for the 'local' has long been constitutive of tourist practices. It leads nevertheless to new questions: Who has the right to the city? Are spaces appropriated by tourists at the expense to residents? Are residents evicted by tourists? How to regulate tourism in a way the city stays inhabitable for everyone?

This chapter is structured around three sections. The first section outlines the difficulties when approaching *new urban tourism*. I identify the challenge of the statistical categories cities use to quantify tourists, but also the category of 'urban tourism'. Moreover, the link between tourism and the everyday life at the heart of *new urban tourism*, raises interesting questions since new practices and new mobilities arise that are posited within practice theory (Larsen, Chapter 2 in this volume). I shall argue the use of the 'everyday' as the central category in practice theory shadows other theoretical possibilities. The playful and non-routinised character of practices is underestimated. The second section follows on from this central thesis and points out how one specific theoretical framework, that of 'dwelling', can be reformulated in order to better understand the ways tourists practise the city: first, by approaching them as temporary inhabitants of the city; and second, by conceiving them as engaging with the city thanks to spatial competences and spatial capital. The concept of 'dwelling' is used as overall category, related to phenomenological theory, whereas the concepts of inhabiting and inhabitants will allow for the description of various forms of engaging with spatiality. The third section will show how the tourist as inhabitant of the city bears rights to mobility and the city, which lie at the heart of conflicting narratives. A cosmopolitanist view of the freedom of mobility conflicts with the freedom of immobility. As this reflection is part of a larger project to articulate urban and tourism theory, the conclusion expands from the city to other kinds of urbanisation and touristification processes.

Contemporary tourism in question: from extraordinary to ordinary practice?

Tourism is a word applied as moral category because of the conflicting values it conveys: the 'bad' tourist against the 'good' traveller; the 'bad' tourist against the 'good' local; but also the 'good' civilised tourist against the uncivilised 'local' (Urbain 1991, Equipe MIT 2002). The urban conflicts around tourism also translates into a moral struggle, where tourists are categorised as invaders: 'Tourist you are the terrorist', reads a sign in Barcelona. It is therefore a challenging task to understand the changing position of tourists within contemporary societies (see also Grube, Chapter 11 in this volume). Therefore, what does 'tourism' mean in a societal context defined by the pervasiveness of mobility, digitality and urbanity? Has tourism become a routinised everyday practice, in contrast to nineteenth- and twentieth-century tourism regimes? Tourism as practice is not the only element to consider, for it is also a legal, statistical and moral category that affects the ways the 'regime of value' of tourism is constructed.[4]

The pervasiveness of tourism, especially, in the contemporary urban world is a problem for urban studies. Contemporary urban places—be it cities, metropolises, city-regions or resorts—are today co-constituted by tourism. Virtually no place is left without the presence of tourism imaginations, practices, tourists. The 'planetary urbanisation' (Lefebvre 2000) is coupled with the 'planetary touristification', i.e., the globalisation of tourism between 1800 and 2000 (Antonescu and Stock 2014). In this respect, tourism has become literally ordinary because of its pervasiveness that contrasts with earlier patterns of concentration. New practices also challenge the traditional definition of tourism, especially second homes and new leisure mobilities, which expand spatially everyday life to places inaccessible before. For instance, Larsen *et al.* (2007) show how various mobilities related to events that have nothing to do with tourism at first glance (such as visiting a friend, organising a family reunion, wedding parties) have nonetheless touristic dimensions, because of the specific locations chosen and the various touristic activities coupled with family duties. The touristic interpretation of the world is decisive in the transformation of the once separated dedicated practice into a practice that can be interwoven with any kind of practice.

Therefore, new tensions for the definition of tourism arise, which will be considered in the two sections that follow. Tourism as category is challenged by the problem of general mobility and raises the question of specificity of tourism as form of mobility, but also the category of 'urban tourism' is more problematic than it appears *prima facie*. A second element relates to the examination of the theoretical effect of practice theory on tourism studies, which construes tourism as 'everyday' practice.

Tourism as problematic category for late-modern societies

Tourism is a statistical category with many subtleties not easy to grasp (Spode 2016). From an international point of view, the tourist is opposed to the migrant on the basis of the length of stay. Implemented in the 1930s by the International Institute of Statistics, both are seen as mobility, but tourism is seen as a temporary mobility. In order to tackle the highly differentiated contemporary mobilities, statistics is left only with a binary classification—migration/tourism—reductionist in its very conception. A tourist is a person who travels for less than a year for every thinkable purpose—ranging from work to pilgrimage—and who is not a migrant (UNWTO 2016). As a consequence, the global statistics on tourism are flawed: tourism is no longer accounted for as a meaningful practice of leisure elsewhere or 'travel for travel purposes' as developed in tourism theory since the 1940s (Spode 2009,

Darbellay and Stock 2012), but is inflated by the account of people who move for work (ranging from traditional business travel to conferences, meetings, events), for maintaining sociality and family ties, for health reasons or religious purposes. On the other hand, these global statistics do not take into account domestic tourism. A rough estimate would probably apply to the 2015 mark of 1.3 billion international arrivals a ten-fold multiplier in order to be more adequate.

Moreover, cities posit themselves from the point of view of the production of bed-nights, one of the key indicators for global benchmarking, which is pervasively used to position the city within the global field of tourism. There is a need for a critical approach to tourism statistics. For instance, Berlin is proud of its more than 30 million bed-nights in 2017, which is used for marketing purposes; yet, this figure does only refer to commercial accommodations in establishments with more than ten beds, which neglects shared accommodations, smaller pensions, or non-commoditised beds, such as second homes, friends, family. For *new urban tourism* relies heavily on alternative forms of sojourn beyond the strict definition of the tourism market, such as Couchsurfing (www.couchsurfing.com) and home sharing, not accounted for in tourism statistics.[5] It also has the usual shortcomings of counting bed-nights in general, whereas the touristic purpose cannot be traced since hotel rooms can be used for multiple purposes. Since it makes a socio-cultural difference if people go on holiday or work, for family, education, leisure or health issues, the official statistics raise questions of interpretation in the context of anti-tourism movements and benchmarking. Does the quantification of increasing bed-nights really mean increasing tourism or does it rather mean an increase of overall mobility for various individual projects? There is a need to unpack and very carefully acknowledge the limitations of the definitions official statistics use in order to adequately interpret *new urban tourism*.[6]

There is also a theoretical issue for urban theory and for tourism theory raised by the very expression 'urban tourism'. It contributes to the confusion, if used to specify tourism or to distinguish specific geographic milieus. As Ashworth and Page (2011, p. 2) state: "Adding the adjective urban to the noun tourism locates an activity in a spatial context but does not in itself define or delimit that activity." However, even this contention is problematic since 'planetary urbanisation' (Lefebvre 2000, Brenner and Schmid 2014) diffuses the urban pervasively. Could we distinguish 'non-urban' forms of tourism in an age of planetary urbanisation? If 'urban' refers to a specific territorial form called 'city' in contrast to a 'countryside', then the location in a specific spatial context could make sense. Yet, the contemporary urban continuum between hyper-centralised urban quarters in the global city and sparsely urbanised countryside would call for a more careful approach of the urban.[7]

Moreover, tourism is historically identified with an urban culture: urbanites going on holiday is a nineteenth-century phenomenon where urban norms and values are performed (Löfgren 1999). Tourism can be approached as a specific situation, where urban cultures are produced and reproduced. It relates to an 'urban praxis' because of urban norms and values the tourists as urbanites carry with them. Lefebvre (1968, p. 120) states: "Urbanites carry the urban with them although they do not bring urbanity."[8] For example, the national parks movement in the USA from the 1860s on can be interpreted as a tourist gaze performed by the urbanites of the cities of the US East Coast, which aestheticises nature as 'wilderness' to be protected. Likewise, the European Alps have been developed as a 'playground of Europe'—an appellation forged by mountaineer and president of the Alpine Club Leslie Stephen (1871)—for urbanites at least since the beginning of the nineteenth century. The multiple encodings, imaginaries, interpretations of place as exotic from the urban point of view is not only a problem of modernity, but specifically a relationship which Western urbanites engage with the world.[9]

This 'urbanisation of consciousness' (Harvey 1985) plays out in tourism in a specific way as the transfer of urbanity from the metropolises and cities to the resorts (Stock and Lucas 2012). Urbanisation through tourism took place from the 1800s on: seaside resorts and mountain resorts emerged as urban places. Therefore, resorts—not only cities—can be seen as urban environments where tourism unfolds. This is consistent with Lefebvre's (2000) urban theory, where the urban revolution of the industrial city redistributes urbanity[10] on other scales: the urbanisation of the seaside through the building of resorts is one of the examples. Empirically, it can be shown through the urban forms of resorts (architecture, density, services, amenities), for example in Montreux (Switzerland), Brighton (England), Scarborough (England), Atlantic City (USA) and Cannes (France), all of them emerging in the nineteenth century. That is why there is a reworking of tourism and urban theory at stake, which would be able to take into account the touristic dimensions of the urban continuum instead of focusing through the expression 'urban tourism' only on cities. It would also dwell on the urban dimensions of tourism, allowing for an intelligibility of how urban imaginaries, values and practices inform tourism and the urban dimensions of tourist places.

Tourism as 'everyday' activity: the theoretical effect of practice theory

In social science, a 'practice turn' (Schatzki *et al.* 2001) has occurred, underscoring the idea that every single element of human societies is seen as constituted by practice. As Reckwitz (2002, p. 249) explains, practice is "a routinised type of behaviour which consists of several elements, interconnected to one another: forms of bodily activities, forms of mental activities, 'things' and their use, a background knowledge in the form of understanding, knowhow, states of emotion and motivational knowledge". From a theoretical point of view, practice theory and its framing of tourism as routinised behaviour is challenging the concept of tourism as contrary to the everyday world as in the notion 'Gegenwelt' (anti-world) (Hennig 1999) or 'elsewhereland' (Löfgren 1999). Several arguments sustain this challenge: tourist practices necessitate elements of everyday life such as sleeping, eating, caring for children, or the continuity of family life (Franklin and Crang 2001, Crang 2002).[11] Moreover, tourism is seen as a routine where the 'corporeal hexis' of the tourist (i.e., the routines inscribed in the body) can be analysed (Edensor 2000). A step towards 'de-exoticising tourism' (Larsen *et al.* 2007) in the sense of integrating touristic elements into everyday mobilities has been taken. As a theoretical effect, the use of practice theory that defines practice as a set of routinised 'everyday' behaviour construes tourism as an everyday practice, defined by routines, habitus, pre-reflexive action and corporeal *hexis*.

However, this theoretical stance has to be critically reflected: what is gained, what is lost for a congruent interpretation of contemporary tourism when proceeding in that way? First, can we really use the notion of 'habitus' for practices that take place in extra-quotidian spaces and times, and which require a certain amount of preparation? Going on holiday is typically an activity where reading guidebooks, imagining destinations and making reservations prior to the travel occur. There are even models insisting on the three key moments in holiday: before, during and after holidays that all combine the activity of holiday-making (Graburn 2002). Routines and pre-reflexive action are combined with moments of reflexivity and preparation.

Second, the very notion of 'everyday' is to be examined critically, because the lifeworld of late-modern individuals is not only constituted by routinised practices, but also by breaking of routines and the contestation of the programmed activities.[12] They have been called 'deroutinising' practices and occur during leisure time on a 'spectrum of leisure', a continuum ranging from heavily routinised to deroutinising practices (Elias 1986). Holidays are seen as means of allowing a time-space for deroutinised activities like heavy drinking, non-routinised sexual intercourse, specific sports activities and play. The notion of play is particularly posited as distinguished to the everyday. Within a theory of play, Caillois (1958) distinguishes four categories of play—*illynx*, *mimesis*, *agon*, *alea*—which are mobilised within tourism theory as deroutinising activities (see also Equipe MIT 2002). Moreover, we could argue every single element—even basic human activities such as eating, sleeping, drinking, body care, sexuality—is assigned a new 'touristified' sense because of the specific context and situation. The changing context modifies the signification of practice, which bears a truly relational definition of tourism. Pott (2007) makes this clear from a systems theoretical point of view with his claim of a 'code' within tourist practices, which sees elements as 'exciting' in a tourist situation where it would be boring in an everyday situation. For instance, the traffic, noise or hustle of the metropolis is coded as exciting within a touristic situation, whereas it is coded as problematic in an everyday situation.

Therefore, I suggest the concept 'practice' is useful also if including 'non-routinised activities', where habitus formations do not necessarily apply. It would open up Bourdieu-style practice theory and allow for an approach of practices as switching between routinised and deroutinising activities. It would also allow for an incorporation of two distinctive patterns of spatiality, home and away, which contribute to make sense to the practices. Tourism remains therefore framed as non-ordinary practice because of a specific relation to place, where a coding as recreation is combined with the coding of place as 'other place'. In order to take into account this specific spatiality and the productive element of the spatial context, I suggest going even one step further. From a geographical point of view, the 'arts of doing' (Certeau 1980) are identified as coping with space and making do with spatiality (Lussault and Stock 2010). This allows for framing of what people do as tourists as *inhabiting*, i.e., establishing a specific relationship with place. Since tourism is about a specific interpretation and assigning a specific meaning to place, it is distinguished from other ways of inhabiting the city.

Inhabiting the city as a tourist

The 'city' can be approached as inhabited space. The commitment of individuals, and the diverse and multiple ways of practising the city, constitute the qualities of contemporary urban space. "Urban life suggests meetings, the confrontation of differences, reciprocal knowledge and acknowledgement (including ideological and political confrontation) ways of living, 'patterns' which coexist in the city" (Lefebvre 1996, p. 75). Therefore, analysing the city as inhabited space requires the reconstruction of the very differentiated projects people form with the city and the very differentiated ways people inhabit the city. In urban theory, the city is conceived of as specific place because "the city creates a situation where distance between things doesn't exist anymore" (Schmid 2006, p. 167). This means people inhabit the city by taking advantage of this annihilation of distance, since societal diversity is made accessible in *one* place. Tourists are now an integral part of the city as inhabited space. They develop a specific way of inhabiting the city, which co-constitutes the city-space.

In order to understand the city as inhabited space for very differentiated place projects, a theory of dwelling could guide empirical investigations. 'Dwelling' signifies here the overall category, whereas 'inhabiting' points towards the differentiated ways individuals practise places. It aims at an understanding of the ways people inhabit the city touristically, the expression mirroring the German poet Hölderlin's verse, 'poetically Man inhabits the Earth' (2008). Heidegger (2004a, 2004b) took this to define dwelling as 'ways of being on Earth', as relationship to place defined by proximity (*Nähe*) and de-distanciation (*Ent-fernung*).[13] It is used in phenomenological geography in order to think about the attachment to place, and the spatiality of the human being,[14] but also to understand inhabited space (or place) and not abstract space as the object of geographical research. Heidegger did not think of tourists in his theory of dwelling, but an interesting shift in the understanding of current tourist practices could occur if one accepted tourists could be framed as 'inhabitants', that is, as humans developing a specific touristic relationship to places they practise.

There have been attempts to approach tourism as dwelling within a narrow Heideggerian conception where the creation of proximity is central (Obrador 2003). It acknowledges the symbolic appropriation of place by tourists, the constitution of familiarity and insideness by tourists and the inclusion of place as meaningful for tourists (see also Wildish and Spierings, Chapter 7 in this volume). Yet, despite this being a first step, this conception underestimates the very sense of place as distant from everyday life and needing adjustment, not routines and familiarity. The conceptualisation of 'dwelling' as proximity and excluding mobile lifeforms from it does not do justice to forms of inhabiting where mobility is key and needs to be expanded to all forms of individuals' spatiality.[15] The idea of 'dwelling in motion' (Hannam *et al.* 2006) points in this direction by insisting on the different ways mobility is creatively appropriated by individuals. More generally, individuals inhabit in mobile and immobile ways; mobility is just a part and expression of dwelling, but is not opposed to it. Delineating the concept of dwelling as coping with spatiality would allow for the recognition of individual dwelling styles, more or less informed by mobility (Stock 2009). Inhabiting the city would therefore be only one element among a multitude of places and displacements.

'Inhabiting touristically' within individual systems of mobility therefore comes into focus. Touristic practices are approached as one way of inhabiting places and can be framed as specific practices where spatial issues are essential. It allows for a conceptual rearrangement: rather than conceived as 'being' as in traditional phenomenological theory, inhabiting is about 'doing', more precisely as 'make do' with spatiality (Lussault and Stock 2010). I will therefore argue towards the conception of tourists as temporary inhabitants of tourist places, and insist on spatial competences and a 'spatial capital' necessary to practise the city as tourists.

Humans as temporary inhabitants of places

Tourists as temporary inhabitants of cities can be integrated in a larger framework of contemporary geographical conditions. The relatively higher degree of mobility expresses a post-sedentary world where inhabitants are mobile. That leads to a theoretical perspective of dwelling in which the practices of residing or sheltering do not summarise the question of dwelling, but are rather one aspect of it. For example, touristic practices also contribute to the dwelling of individuals through the creation of place-relations, an experience of places and movements, and the coping with specific places (Stock 2015).

Several elements are important for the conception of tourists as temporary inhabitants of the city, thus extending the notion of 'dwelling' to all kinds of meaningful relationships to place. We have to consider contemporary human beings as temporary inhabitants, thus integrating the presence/absence patterns and the mobility component in the analysis. That means individuals practise places temporarily; even the residence is not a permanent home despite legal claims. It would be one step further because Heidegger and much of phenomenological geography develop a perspective of immobile human beings, being attached to one place in an authentic way.[16] In addition, individuals develop specific modes of inhabiting, i.e., specific relationship to place according to the intentionality with which they practise space.[17] Touristic practice can be interpreted as a specific mode of inhabiting, where place is practised through a recreational intentionality, and where place is interpreted as place of otherness (see also Parish, Chapter 5 in this volume). Tourists inhabit cities not as ordinary citizens but informed by a touristic interpretation of the world. If inhabiting means developing a sense of place and a meaningful practice of place, then we can contend late-modern societies develop specific meaningful practices of place where mobilities, and specifically, tourist mobilities are the essential elements.

This argument of tourism as 'mode of inhabiting' would also counter the expression 'tourism at home' with the idea of the 'tourist gaze' as a gaze on the extraordinary and the contrast to everyday situations can apply everywhere, even at home (Jeuring and Haartsen 2016). This would happen through abstraction of the familiar and the construction of the unusual. Against this vision, two points can be posited: it is an illusion to see the resident and the tourist as equivalent category of inhabitants when visiting the city because of a different mastering of the urban space. For the former, the urban space is experienced as a familiar space where different spatial problems (such as orientation, accessibility through transport, knowledge) are mastered. For the latter, the urban space is experienced as a space of otherness, where even the most mundane elements (such as food, drink, public transport, traffic) are elements of excitement (Stoltenberg and Frisch, Chapter 8 in this volume). The occasional gaze on the extraordinary cannot be used as criteria that transforms a resident into a tourist; rather a 'mode of inhabiting' (Stock 2014), i.e., a relationship to place maintained for the duration of the touristic situation, in which otherness is key. *Inhabiting* place in a certain way, i.e., combining the code of recreation with the construction of place as other place, is therefore the essential element in the definition of tourism, not a specific practice like going to a museum or visiting a formerly unknown or less known neighbourhood during a guided tour. The key argument is that familiarity with the city as a whole, where people know the codes, the transport system, the language, the national habitus, the food, you sleep at home, etc., is the primordial relationship to place. Inhabiting a 'here', which contrasts with the 'elsewhere' inhabited by tourists. Therefore, the way of inhabiting the city is different from the way a tourist inhabits the city.

Instead of conceiving the concept of dwelling as a relationship to *one* place—be it the residence, the neighbourhood, or the city—the relationship to *multiple* places and mobilities are to be considered. It opens up the study of individual systems of placement/dis-placement on the one hand, and the relationship with different spatial problems under scrutiny on the other. It could also be an answer to the questions the 'mobilities turn' (Sheller and Urry 2006) raise for social sciences. It argues in favour of unpacking the multiple practices of mobility, but is still in search of a sound theoretical base. Inhabiting defined as coping with spatiality, i.e. the multiple spatial problems such as distance, location, limits, scale, territory raised in the lifeworlds, could lead towards such a perspective. Mobilities would not be seen as opposed to inhabiting, but would be framed as one element of 'dwelling styles'. It would help not to focus on specific types of mobility, but define differentiated individual systems of places and movements, which are more or less informed by mobility.

Towards a 'spatial capital' of mobile inhabitants?

Tourists inhabit the city and in order to do so, they develop specific competences, follow norms and have rights, are equipped with technical instruments and imaginations (Stock 2015). As cities are places of otherness for tourists, the spatial problems the latter face are different from those of residents. Therefore, tourists develop spatial competences and mobilise a specific spatial capital. The work on spatial competences and spatial capital is a distinctive feature of francophone geography. The question of the differential capacities of individuals regarding the control of their spatiality has been theoretically explored by numerous authors (Lévy 1999, Lussault 2007, Lussault and Stock 2010). It is related to Bourdieu's (1994, 2000) model of agency where agents engage their social, economic, cultural, technological capital in order to achieve objectives within a specific social field.

The concept of capital has proven fruitful in addressing the question of accumulation and disposition of capacities individuals put into play, which gives them power over situations and advantages towards other agents. Within geography, Lévy (1999, 2003) develops the idea of a 'spatial capital', understood as the disposition of individuals to engage with spatial problems, especially distance. He defines it as "ensemble of resources accumulated by an actor, which allows him/her taking advantage of the use of the spatial dimension of society, following his/her strategy" (Lévy 2003, p. 124).[18] It includes the control over distance metrics, i.e., mobility and accessibility as a fundamental element, more recently explored as 'mobility capital' by Kaufmann *et al.* (2004); location of residence (in the centre or in the suburbs) or memorised experiences of cities also contribute to differentiating the spatial capital of individuals.

In order to make clear the practice-centred spatialities, I will focus on specific spatial competences of tourists. In geography, despite the practice and performance turn, we still lack studies focusing on the competences and skills related to the spatial problems individuals face when constituting their lifeworld. Particularly necessary are the relational definitions of competences.[19] Michel Lussault (2007) proposes to focus on 'elementary spatial competences' of humans, such as: (1) placement defined as the capacity of occupying the adequate place for an activity; (2) scaling defined as the identification of adequate scales for an activity; (3) mastery of metrics defined as capacity of the use of adequate means of transport; (4) delimitation as capacity of drawing limits according to a situation; (5) crossing defined as the capacity to cross spatial limits and multiple forms of territory; and (6) navigating defined as specific capacity of designing adequate routes. This could be mobilised in order to approach touristic practices. Lucas (2018) translates this idea of elementary spatial competences into a study of tourists' practice of Los Angeles, where the competences of wayfinding, delimitation of tourist spaces, identification of centres and the location of the body are the issue. It opens up a situational understanding of tourist practices, where human actors are tested particularly in relation to space and have to make do with space.[20] It leads to the conclusion tourists mobilise their perceptive, cognitive, linguistic, technological and relational competences. The tourist is conceptualised not as a 'cultural dope' but as an actor with spatial skills, inhabiting the city equipped with the tourist gaze.

This is particularly important for what is called 'repeaters' in city tourism (Freytag 2010) for their knowledge and skills differ from one-time tourists. According to their past experiences of cities, they cope more or less smoothly with centrality, transports, public space.[21] Yet, these capacities of inhabiting the city as tourist are unequal: the elementary spatial competences are seen as expressions of different modalities of spatial capital.

Co-inhabiting: whose right to the city?

The massive inhabitance of cities by tourists raises the question of the right to the city. A city is *per definitionem* a place where multiple forms of inhabiting occurs. In an era where mobility is a key element of so-called 'late-modern' societies, the city is precisely characterised by the various and conflicting projects people engage with the city, be it on a temporary or a more or less permanent basis. In this sense, it is important to focus on the co-inhabiting of the city based on very different practices and intentionalities. In the light of the contemporary conflicts in the city around 'overtourism', social movements claim a 'right to the city', such as in Berlin or Hamburg (Novy and Colomb 2012). It touches on the relationship between residents fighting against appropriation of urban space by tourists. This can be seen as a historical moment because cities have been 'dressed up' for tourists for at least the last 100 years. This movement of touristification has been intensifying since the 1980s as a corollary of deindustrialisation, and even more since the global financial crisis in 2008, as a significant element of the urban economy (Pratt and Hutton 2013). Although tourism and the urban economy have been intertwined for the last 200 years, it is a new phenomenon because the impact on gentrification has been less important.[22] Conflicts relate to the use of short-let holiday apartments (Airbnb style) leading to rising rents and cost of living, but also around the use of public space of dominantly residential neighbourhoods for partying and alcohol misuse, creating noise (Colomb and Novy 2017). In contrast, previous conflicts of tourism in the city were seen as crowding around tourism attractions, and did not have the potential to disrupt residents' way of life.

Do we have conceptual tools in order to understand this problem? Is it the translation of the class struggle into urban space or even a struggle *for place* between tourists and residents?[23] I shall try here to discuss and mobilise the Lefebvrian notion of the 'right to the city' and 'right to centrality' in order to raise the question of the legitimate presence of tourists in the city. Integrated in a theory of production of space, where material and immaterial elements are focused on, it is defined as "a transformed and renewed right to urban life" (Lefebvre 1996, p. 158). The right to the city is designed to further the interests "of the whole society and firstly of all those who *inhabit*" (Lefebvre 1996, p. 158, my emphasis). I shall try here to link the question of inhabiting to that of the right to the city by examining how mobile individuals inhabit the city and claim rights to centrality and mobility.

Inhabiting and the rights to centrality

Lefebvre (1968) uses the concept of inhabiting to designate urban inhabitants in contrast to the citizen of a nation-state. The idea of framing the tourist as inhabitant runs counter to Lefebvre's intentions. First, because tourists are not considered as inhabitants by Lefebvre, inhabitants are only those who reside in the city or the outskirts (*banlieusards*); even the global elite, says Lefebvre (1968), does not inhabit, but floats around the globe. Second, Lefebvre is used in a critical way to oppose the tourism industry, in which are embedded the tourists and to argue in favour of the residents. The right to the city is seen as rights of residents to their own city in order to oppose the governance of the powerful few in a neoliberal city, where gentrification processes go on because of tourism (Novy and Colomb 2012, Colomb and Novy 2017, Gravari-Barbas and Guinand 2017, Frenzel, Chapter 4 and Parish, Chapter 5 in this volume).

The concept of the right to the city is designed by Lefebvre to underline the risk of exclusion of people from the city and encompasses:

> on the one hand, the right of users to make known their ideas on the space and time of their activities in the urban area. It would, however, also cover the right to the use of the centre, a privileged place, instead of being dispersed and stuck into ghettos (for workers, immigrants, the 'marginal' and even for the 'privileged').
>
> (Lefebvre 1996, p. 34)

Commentators rightly point towards the "right to command the whole urban process" (Harvey 2008, p. 28), the power of decision-making on urban development, and the appropriation of urban space for the inhabitants, not only for the elite.

In applying the concept not to the immobile city dweller, but to the mobile contemporary individual who inhabits a multiplicity of places temporarily, inhabiting the city as a tourist is also framed as a legitimate spatial action, and therefore can be seen as a 'right to centrality'. Indeed, where is the (middle-class) tourists' residence situated, which defines one of the elements of their spatial capital? In the city centre or in the peri-central or suburban parts of the urban continuum? Surprisingly, a link between tourism and sub-urbanisation is found in that tourism can be seen as one of the practices of city centres by people living in the suburbs. Because of the high real estate prices in the city centre and the transformation of the city centre into a com-mercial place, the only chance to practise centrality is as a tourist or as a consumer (Knafou 2007). Tourism can therefore be seen as exercising the right to centrality by people who can no longer afford to be residents in the central parts of the city.

For Lefebvre, the urban is "more or less the oeuvre of its citizens" (Lefebvre 1996, p. 117). I suggest correcting this to: inhabited urban space can be seen as the oeuvre of its *inhabitants*! The production of urban space occurs through the practice of all people moving through the city, not only the residents. This 'inhabitance of urban space' (Butler 2007) is the issue when reflecting upon the multiple conflicting actors producing urban space. In particular, public space—as place of the encounter of the Other, i.e., where otherness has to be accepted—is the very place where the city makes sense for tourists. It is a kind of space where the right to the city is exercised.

Inhabiting the city as exercising the right to mobility?

The value of mobility as a positive value of freedom of movement (Cresswell 2006) has to be examined because it legitimises the presence of mobile indi-viduals as tourists in cities. There is a cosmopolitan discourse that sees glo-balisation as global accessibilities and the integration of humankind through (tourism) mobilities. Freedom of movement means no barrier to mobilities and emplacement of people. Interestingly, Anthony Ince (2016) makes a plea for an anarchist theory of mobility in terms of 'autonomy', which is a trans-lation of the question of individual competences and power. Autonomous mobilities in a globalised society, where passports are used reflexively to move, are indeed a 'capacity' informing the agency of the late-modern tourist, the reflexive and autonomous practice of places. Tourists undoubtedly have gained the power to inhabit the city and to exercise a right to the city through their capacity of being mobile.

Yet, the question of the right to mobility can also be specifically framed as a legal framework of mobilities. These 'regimes of mobility' (Glick Schiller and Salazar 2013) show an ambiguous regulation of mobility. The spatial regime we observe nowadays could be labelled as contradictory and unequal, where mobility is possible for some projects and some people and not for others. Migration is today evaluated as problematic and heavily enforced. We observe a strengthening of national borders, whereas tourism is seen as a desirable mobility for economic and political stakeholders and for tourists themselves. For instance, the Universal Declaration of Human Rights, adopted by the UN General Assembly in 1946, whose article 13 states the right for a citizen to freedom of movement within borders, to leave and to return to his/her country. Within the European Union, residents are guaranteed the right to freely move within the EU's internal borders. The *European Parliament and Council Directive 2004/38/EC* of 29 April 2004 establishes migration and free choice of residency of EU citizens. UNWTO insists in its 'global code of ethics' a 'right to tourism' for everyone. Article 2 even coins the expression 'universal right to tourism' as corollary to the right to leisure of the Human Rights Declaration. It links the social rights of free use of leisure time and reconstitution of the workforce through rest.

The conflicting rights to the city between residents and tourists seem therefore rooted in the right to mobility tourists have been granted and the power tourists have acquired to exercise their rights. The examination of legal orders could be a step further in the political analysis of the right to the city exercised by temporary inhabitants.

Conclusion

The focus on mobile inhabitants coping with the city through competences, spatial capital and legal resources is aimed at a better understanding of the contemporary processes in metropolises. The analysis of some of the limits of existing frameworks tried to raise awareness of the complex relationship between urban and touristic dimensions of human societies. It is finally meant to disrupt the routinised practice of developing urban theory without tourism, and tourism theory without the urban dimensions. Both are pervasive elements of contemporary societies. If urban theory and tourism theory are to meet, a more general framework would take into account not only the territorial form of cities, but also urbanisation processes in general, i.e. the accumulation and complexification of urbanity. An articulation of urban theory and tourism through the reworking of three concepts, centrality, urbanity, urbanisation/de-urbanisation, could be put forward. With respect to tourism, this would lead, for example, to the concepts of 'touristic urbanity' as expressed in resorts, 'touristic centrality' of places, 'urban values of tourism', elements that could be detected in every kind of place, including cities.

Centrality as relational spatiality of social fields, especially in the context of globalisation allows for an understanding of 'global centralities' (Sassen 1991) and raises the question of 'touristic centralities' of cities, resorts, spots. If centrality is defined with reference to a specific 'social field', then there is an occasion to define relative centralities of places within a global tourism field. This would show the very importance of tourism as centralisation device in a global system of centralities. Moreover, the issue of symbolic centrality of cities (Monnet 2000) allows for the understanding of why tourism is a powerful tool for contemporary cities. Centrality is not only an economic problem *per se*. As spatial arrangements are recognised by actors, and transformed into knowledge, its symbolic dimension is key for the understanding of the emergence and reproduction of centralities. It would lead to an understanding of tourism as co-constitutive of cities' and resorts' positioning in a global economy. It also would open up an understanding for tourist resorts as urban places, even without all of the features of cities such as density and heterogeneity. Although urban theories now acknowledge that the city is no longer the sole territorial form of urbanity (Amin and Thrift 2002), there is still a lack of theoretical integration of the multiple forms urbanity can take; resorts develop a specific touristic urbanity, which is important to recognise for the sake of theoretical coherence and empirical relevance.

Moreover, the concept of urbanity Lefebvre puts in the centre of his urban theory can be defined as a specific quality of an urban place, based on public space, density, heterogeneity, centrality. Tourism modifies the urban qualities of places, especially in cities, but also in resorts. Tourists inhabit the city and therefore, through their practices, produce new urban qualities; in particular, public space is reconfigured through touristic practices. They contribute to the urbanity of the city by co-creating an inhabited space animated by mobile individuals (Sommer and Kip, Chapter 10 in this volume). This framework approaches the different qualities of space—city or centre—as 'inhabited space', which is constructed by a large array of actors, including day-to-day and tourist practices. As such, it provides the setting for situated actions. The increasing presence of mobile individuals, especially tourists, shapes contemporary urbanity. Tourism is co-constitutive of the contemporary metropolis; if it is lacking, a decrease in urbanity occurs.[24]

The question of urbanity also entails the classical sociological issue of the 'stranger' in the contemporary city because of new hospitality practices. Berliners go to Barcelona using Airbnb for a holiday, and Barcelonitos go to Berlin using Airbnb, which transforms the classical opposition between immobile residents and mobile tourists as an essentialist qualification. The contemporary tourist is no longer a stranger in the city: he/she is an urbanite who moves from one city to another, with spatial, social, economic and cultural capital, and equipped with digital technologies. This is precisely the transformation of people considered as strangers into people considered as consumers in the tourism industry or as alter egos in the so-called sharing economy. The imaginary of digital peer-to-peer platforms such as Couchsurfing or Airbnb (www.airbnb.com) transform the stranger into a friend. The Airbnb slogan reads now 'belong anywhere' after being 'feel like a local'. This imaginary of hospitality and home is key to understand the changing inhabitance of the contemporary city. Inhabiting the city touristically can be framed as a practice of the city where routinised urban competences are simply transferred, which tames the confrontation with otherness.

Finally, Lefebvre's idea of urbanisation as a process of accumulation and complexification of urbanity contains the idea of 'planetary urbanisation', recently discussed by Brenner and Schmid (2014). He thinks in terms of urban revolution, triggered by industry, which leads to an explosion of the city and the reconfiguration of the urban at other scales. How to link tourism to this urbanisation problem? The model of the 'double urban revolution of tourism' (Stock and Lucas 2012) proposes a two-fold process: first, the emergence of tourist resorts for the last 200 years can be interpreted as a form of planetary urbanisation through tourism via a 'transfer of urbanity' from the cities to the resorts. This has occurred at the seaside, in the countryside and in the mountain areas all over the world. Second, the ongoing touristification of cities within a global tourism field from the 1970s onwards can also be interpreted as an urbanisation of the city. It takes seriously the idea of centralisation as an urban process, and allows for an understanding of the city as a process in constant reworking, where urbanisation and de-urbanisation processes occur.

It implies defining urbanisation as an emergence and complexification of urbanity, which would apply to the understanding not only of the growth of cities, but also to the understanding of tourist resorts. In addition, we can conceive of ongoing urbanisation processes in tourist resorts since their inception. In Europe, many of the original resorts have developed into cities, Cannes, Garmisch-Partenkirchen, Montreux being cases in point. Finally, if urbanisation means accumulating urbanity, then we also have to reflect upon de-urbanisation processes. For instance, British tourist resorts, which were highly prominent in the British tourist culture until the 1950s, exited the tourist economy, with resorts in the Mediterranean and South-East Asia replacing them (Shaw and Williams 1997). Understanding the decline of resorts as de-urbanisation would point towards the process of replacement of tourist centralities by other kinds of centralities on the one hand, and the change of urbanity as replacement of touristic place-making by other forms of inhabitance on the other.

If we are to conceive of adequate frameworks for the urban in an urban, mobile, digital world, where tourism is a pervasive element of the late-modern human societies, there is an urgent need to articulate urban theory and tourism theory.

Notes

1 Exceptions are Mullins (1991) on 'tourism urbanisation', Soane (1993) on the urbanisation of resorts, Equipe MIT (2002, 2011) on the urbanity of resorts, Duhamel and Knafou (2007) on urban dimensions of tourism, Stock and Lucas (2012) on the 'double urban revolution of tourism', and Stock (2017) on 'touristic centrality' of resorts.

2 However, even Eurostat and UrbanAudit are unable to provide standardised and robust tourism statistics on cities. That makes Wöhler's attempt to provide

his TourMIS database (www.tourmis.info) even more valuable. See also Freytag (2007) for a statistical effort on European cities.

3 Glasgow in 1990, Lille in 2004, Liverpool in 2008, and Essen in 2010 as part of the Ruhr bid.

4 Please refer also to the recent discussion on the 'regimes of value in tourism' in the special issue of the *Journal of Tourism and Cultural Change*, 2014, 12 (3).

5 Airbnb (www.airbnb.com) as the now leading home-sharing platform has profoundly changed the city economy. It began as a traditional sharing platform in 2010, but has now attracted mainly business activities, which municipalities try to regulate (Dredge *et al.* 2016; see also Stors, Chapter 6 and Wildish and Spierings, Chapter 7 in this volume).

6 In the case of Berlin, the city estimates 4.7 million bed-nights in the so-called sharing economy and 33.2 million bed-nights with family and friends. However, no clue is offered to how it is estimated (Senat Berlin 2018, pp. 10–11).

7 See Lévy (1999) for an approach of 'gradients of urbanity' ranging from the 'hyper-urban' in the metropolis to the 'infra-urban' in the countryside and Schmid (2006) for patterns of urbanity in Switzerland.

8 The French original is: "Les urbains transportent l'urbain avec eux, même s'ils n'apportent pas l'urbanité" (Lefebvre 1968, p. 120).

9 See Shields' (1991) study on Brighton seen as placed at the social periphery of a cultural value system by Londoners.

10 I will use throughout the text the term 'urbanity' in order to designate the urban quality of place. Widely used since Lefebvre in French (*urbanité*) as a central element of urban theory, it is scarcely used in English. See however the work by Lévy (2014) as well as Brenner and Schmid (2014).

11 French sociologists Juan Salvador *et al.* (1997) report the meaning of holiday for a middle-aged woman who says in an interview: "I just exchange sinks", which means she just continues doing all the housework in the same way on holiday as she does at home.

12 See de Certeau (1980) and Lahire (1998) for a thorough critique of routinised practice theory and Elias (1995) for a critique of the notion of 'everyday life'.

13 The following formulations are used by Heidegger in order to define 'dwelling': "the way the mortals are on the Earth" (the German original is "die Weise, wie die Sterblichen auf der Erde sind" [Heidegger 2004a, p. 142]) and "relation of humans to places, and through places to spaces" (the German original is "Bezug des Menschen zu Orten und durch Orte zu Räumen" [Heidegger 2004a, p. 152]).

14 See most importantly, Seamon and Mugerauer (1985), Berque (1996) as well as Hoyaux (2002) for the pursuit of this endeavour. It has been an important research avenue in francophone geography for the last twenty years (Stock 2004, 2006, Lazzarotti 2006, Paquot et al. 2007) and the special issues of the journals *Travaux de l'Institut de Géographie de Reims* (2003) and *Annales de Géographie* (2015).

15 That is also the sense of the field of 'multilocality studies' where human beings inhabit several residences, but also a more or less complex system of places and mobilities (Rolshoven 2007, Stock 2009).

16 See Stock (2007a, 2007b) for a thorough critique of Heidegger's model of spatiality for lifeworlds informed by mobility and the development of a practice-based theory of dwelling.

17 This idea is based on the notion 'Lebensform' developed by Schütz (1973).

18 The French original is: "[E]nsemble des ressources, accumulées par un acteur, lui permettant de tirer avantage en fonction de sa stratégie, de l'usage de la dimension spatiale de la société" (Lévy 2003, p. 124).

19 See for example Ingold (2000) for whom "skill, in short, is a property not of the individual human body as a biophysical entity, a thing-in-itself, but of the total field of relations constituted by the presence of the organism-person, indissolubly body and mind, in a richly structured environment" (p. 291).

20 See the notion 'épreuve' (test) as part of the 'pragmatic regimes' (Thévenot 2000).

21 See Violier (2016), who shows how tourists cope with different metro systems in New York, Moscow and Shanghai.

22 However, the second-home market in metropolises has been an important vehicle and is accounted for 10 per cent of the housing stock in Paris.

23 I borrow from Lussault's (2009) French book title *De la lutte des classes à la lutte des places*, which can be translated as "from class struggle to place struggle".

24 Is it possible to imagine a city without tourists? The point made on New York by Lalia Rach (2003): "When the terrorism attacks occurred on September 11, 2001 the rhythm of travel was dramatically disrupted. Overnight, New York City experienced the unthinkable—hotels, stores, restaurants, attractions, museums, and convention centers echoed with silence. For an industry that thrives on movement, the sudden halt in travel created a zero-sum reality (no visitors = no spending = no revenues = no taxes). Suddenly the city was without tourists, and there was a noticeable loss of vitality, power and pace. When added to the loss of economic stimulation, the city fully realized the importance of travelers to its continued wellbeing."

References

Amin, A. and Thrift, N., 2002. *Cities: Reimagining the Urban*. London: Polity Press.

Antonescu, A. and Stock M., 2014. Reconstruction of the globalisation of tourism. *Annals of Tourism Research*, 45 (1), 77–88.

Ashworth, G., 1989. Urban tourism: an imbalance in attention. *Progress in tourism, Recreation and Hospitality Management*, 1 (1), 33–55.

Ashworth, G.J. and Tunbridge, J., 1990. *The Tourist-Historic City*. London: Belhaven Press.

Ashworth, G. and Page, S., 2011. Urban tourism research: recent progress and current paradoxes. *Tourism Management*, 32 (1), 1–15.

Berque, A., 1996. *Être humains sur la Terre*. Paris: Gallimard.

Bourdieu, P., 1994. *Raisons pratiques. Sur la théorie de l'action*. Paris: Seuil.

Bourdieu, P., 2000. *Esquisse d'une théorie de la pratique*. Paris: Seuil.

Brenner, N. and Schmid, C., 2014. The 'urban age' in question. *International Journal of Urban and Regional Research*, 38 (3), 731–755.

Butler, R., 1980. The concept of a tourist area cycle of evolution: implication for management of resources. *Canadian Geographer*, 23 (1), 5–12.

Butler, C., 2007. Sydney: aspiration, asylum and the denial of the right to the city. *In*: A. Philippopoulos-Mihalopoulos, ed., *Law and the City*. Abingdon: Routledge-Cavendish, 205–220.

Caillois, R., 1958. *Les Jeux et les hommes: le masque et le vertige*. Paris: Gallimard (transl. as *Man, Play, and Games*. Champaign, IL: University of Illinois Press, 2001).

Certeau, M. de, 1980. *L'invention du quotidien, I: Arts de faire*. Paris: Gallimard (transl. as *The Practice of Everyday Life*. Berkeley, CA: University of California Press, 1984).

Colomb, C. and Novy, J., eds, 2017. *Protest and Resistance in the Tourist City*. London: Routledge.

Crang, M., 2002. Grounded tourists, travelling theory. *In*: M. Crang and S. Coleman, eds, *Tourism: Between Place and Performance*. Oxford: Berghahn Books, 1–17.

Cresswell, T., 2006. *On the Move. Mobility in the Modern Western World*. London: Routledge.

Darbellay, F. and Stock, M., 2012. Tourism as complex interdisciplinary research object. *Annals of Tourism Research*, 39 (1), 441–458.

Dredge, D., Gyimóthy, S., Birkbak, A., Jensen, T.E. and Madsen, A.K., 2016. *The Impact of Regulatory Approaches Targeting Collaborative Economy in the Tourism Accommodation Sector: Barcelona, Berlin, Amsterdam and Paris*. Brussels: European Commission.

Duhamel, Ph. and Knafou, R., eds, 2007. *Les mondes urbains du tourisme*. Paris: Belin.

Edensor, T., 2000. Staging tourism. Tourists as performers. *Annals of Tourism Research*, 27 (2), 322–344.

Elias, N., 1986. Introduction. *In*: N. Elias and E. Dunning, eds, *Quest for Excitement. Sport and Leisure in the Civilising Process*. Oxford: Blackwell, 19–62.

Elias, N., 1995. Sur le concept de vie quotidienne. *Cahiers internationaux de Sociologie*, 99 (2), 237–246.

Enzensberger, H.-M., 1958. Vergebliche Brandung der Ferne. Eine Theorie des Tourismus. *Merkur*, 12, 701–720. (transl. as A theory of tourism. *New German Critique*, 68, 117–135 [1996]).

Equipe MIT, 2002. *Tourismes 1. Lieux communs*. Paris: Belin.

Equipe MIT, 2011. *Tourismes 3. La révolution durable*. Paris: Belin.

Eurostat 2016. *Urban Europe. Statistics on cities, towns and suburbs*. Luxemburg: Publications Office of the European Union (DOI: 10.2785/91120).

Franklin, A. and Crang, M., 2001. The trouble with tourism and travel theory. *Tourist Studies*, 1 (1), 5–22.

Freytag, T., 2007. Städtetourismus in europäischen Großstädten. Eine Hierarchie der Standorte und aktuelle Entwicklungen der Übernachtungszahlen. *DisP, The Planning Review*, 43 (169), 56–67.

Freytag, T., 2010. Déjà-vu: tourist practices of repeat visitors in the city of Paris. *Social Geography*, 5 (1), 49–58.

Füller, H. and Michel, B., 2014. 'Stop being a tourist!' New dynamics of urban tourism in Berlin-Kreuzberg. *International Journal of Urban and Regional Research*, 38 (4), 1304–1318.

Glick Schiller, N. and Salazar, N., 2013. Regimes of mobility across the globe. *Journal of Ethnic and Migration*, 39 (2), 183–200.

Graburn, N. 2002. The ethnographic tourist. *In*: G. Dann, ed., *The Tourist as a Metaphor of the Social World*. New York: CABI.

Gravari-Barbas, M. and Guinand, S., 2017. *Tourism and Gentrification in Contemporary Metropolises. International Perspectives*. London: Routledge.

Hannam, K., Sheller, M. and Urry, J., 2006. Editorial: mobilities, immobilities and moorings. *Mobilities*, 1 (1), 1–22.

Harvey, D., 1985. *Consciousness and the Urban Experience. Studies in the History and Theory of Capitalist Urbanization 1*. London: Blackwell.

Harvey, D., 2008. The right to the city. *New Left Review*, 53 (5), 23–40.

Harvey, D., 2001. *Spaces of Capital. Towards a Critical Geography*. London: Routledge.

Heidegger, M., 2004a. … dichterisch wohnet der Mensch… *In*: M. Heidegger, *Vorträge und Aufsätze*. Stuttgart: Klett-Cotta, 181–198 (transl. as …Poetically man dwells… *In*: *Poetry, Language, Thought*. New York: Harper & Row Publishers, 1971).

Heidegger, M., 2004b. Bauen, Wohnen, Denken. *In*: M. Heidegger, *Vorträge und Aufsätze*. Stuttgart: Klett-Cotta, 139–156 (transl. as Building, dwelling, thinking. *In*: *Basic Writings*. San Francisco, CA: Harper Collins Publishers, 1977).

Hennig, Ch., 1999. *Reiselust*. Frankfurt: Suhrkamp.

Hoffman, L., Fainstein, S. and Judd, D., eds, 2003. *Cities and Visitors: Regulating People, Markets, and City Space*. Oxford: Blackwell.

Hoyaux, A.-F., 2002. Entre construction territoriale et constitution ontologique de l'habitant. Introduction épistémologique aux apports de la phénoménologie au concept d'habiter. *Cybergeo – European Journal of Geography* [online], no. 102. Available from: http://cybergeo.revues.org/1824 [accessed 12 September 2018].

Hölderlin, F., 2008. In lieblicher Bläue. *In*: *Sämtliche Werke. Historisch-kritische Ausgabe*. 20 vol. Frankfurt: Stroemfeld.

Ince, A., 2016. Autonomy, territory, mobility: everyday (geo)politics in voluntary exchange networks. *Espace politique* [online], no. 28. Available from: https://espacepolitique.revues.org/3779 [accessed 12 September 2018].

Ingold, T., 2000. *The Perception of the Environment. Essays on Livelihood, Dwelling and Skill*. Abingdon: Routledge.

Jeuring, J. and Haartsen, T., 2016. The challenge of proximity: the (un)attractiveness of near-home tourism destinations. *Tourism Geographies*, 16 (1), 118–141.

Judd, D. and Fainstein, S., eds, 1999. *The Tourist City*. New Haven, CT: Yale University Press.

Kaufmann, V., Bergman, M. and Joye, D. 2004. Motility: mobility as capital. *International Journal of Urban and Regional Research*, 28 (4), 745–756.

Knafou, R., 2007. L'urbain et le tourisme: une construction laborieuse. *In*: Ph. Duhamel and R. Knafou, eds, *Mondes urbains du tourisme*. Paris: Belin, 9–21.

Krippendorf, J., 1977. *Die Landschaftsfresser*. Bern: Hallwag.

Lahire, B., 1998. *L'homme pluriel. Les ressorts de l'action*. Paris: Nathan.

Larsen, J., Urry, J. and Axhausen, K., 2007. Networks and tourism. Mobile social life. *Annals of Tourism Research*, 34 (1), 244–262.

Lazzarotti, O., 2006. *Habiter. La condition géographique*. Paris: Belin.

Lefebvre, H., 1968. *Le droit à la ville*. Paris: Anthropos.

Lefebvre, H., 1996. *Writings on Cities*. Oxford: Basil Blackwell (translated and edited by Eleonore Kofman and Elizabeth Lebas).

Lefebvre, H., 2000. *La révolution urbaine*. Paris: Anthropos (1st edition 1970).

Lévy, J., 1999. *Le tournant géographique*. Paris: Belin.

Lévy, J., 2003. Capital spatial. *In*: J. Lévy and M. Lussault, eds, *Dictionnaire de la géographie et de l'espace des sociétés*. Paris: Belin, 124–125.

Lévy, J., 2014. Science + space + society: urbanity and the risk of methodological communalism in social sciences of space. *Geographica Helvetica*, 69 (1), 99–114.

Löfgren, O., 1999. *On Holiday: A History of Vacationing*. Berkeley, CA: University of California Press.

Lucas, L., 2018. Le parcours des touristes à Los Angeles. Entre optimisation des déplacements et compétences spatiales. *Teoros*, 37 (1) [online], available from: https://journals.openedition.org/teoros/3246 [accessed 4 October 2018].

Lussault, M., 2009. *De la lutte des classes à la lutte des places*. Paris: Grasset.

Lussault, M., 2007. *L'Homme spatial*. Paris: Seuil.

Lussault, M. and Stock, M., 2010. "Doing with space". Towards a pragmatics of space. *Social Geography* [online], 5 (1), 1–8. Available from: www.soc-geogr.net/5/11/2010/sg-5-11-2010.pdf [accessed 12 September 2018].

MacCannell, D., 1976. *The Tourist: A New Theory of the Leisure Class*. Berkeley, CA: University of California Press.

Monnet, J., 2000. Les dimensions symboliques de la centralité. *Cahiers de géographie du Québec*, 123, 399–418.

Mullins, P., 1991. Tourism urbanization. *International Journal of Urban and Regional Research*, 15 (3), 326–342.

Novy, J. and Colomb, C., 2012. Struggling for the right to the (creative) city in Berlin and Hamburg: new urban social movement, new spaces of hope? *International Journal of Urban and Regional Research*, 34 (2), 1816–1838.

Obrador Pons, P., 2003. Being-on-holiday: tourist dwelling, bodies and place. *Tourist Studies*, 3 (1), 47–66.

Paquot, T., Lussault, M. and Younès, Ch., eds, 2007. *Habiter, le propre de l'humain*. Paris: La Découverte.

Pott, A., 2007. *Tourismusorte. Eine gesellschafts- und raumtheoretische Untersuchung am Beispiel des Städtetourismus*. Bielefeld: Transcript.

Pratt, A. and Hutton, T., 2013. Reconceptualising the relationship between the creative economy and the city. Learning from the financial crisis. *Cities*, 33 (1), 86–95.

Rach, L., 2003. Rebuilding tourism in an uncertain environment. A White Paper prepared for the Sister City Summit [online]. Available from: www.nyc.gov/html/ia/gp/downloads/pdf/rebuilding_tourism_paper.pdf [accessed 27 September 2018].

Reckwitz, A., 2002. Toward a theory of social practices: a development in culturalist theorizing. *European Journal of Social Theory*, 5 (2), 243–263.

Rolshoven J., 2007. Multilokalität als Lebensweise in der Spätmoderne. *Schweizerisches Archiv für Volkskunde*, 103, 157–179.

Salomon-Cavin, J. and Marchand, B., 2011. *Anti-urbain. Origines et conséquences de l'urbaphobie*. Lausanne: Presses Polytechniques et Universitaires Romandes.

Salvador, J., Largo-Poirier, A., Orain, H. and Poltorak, J.-F., 1997. *Les sentiers du quotidien. Rigidité, fluidité des espaces sociaux et trajets routiniers en ville*. Paris: L'Harmattan.

Sassen, S., 1991. *The Global City: New York, London, Tokyo*. Princeton, NJ: Princeton University Press.

Schatzki, T., Knorr-Cetina, K. and Savigny, E. von, eds, 2001. *The Practice Turn in Contemporary Theory*. London: Routledge.

Schmid, C., 2006. Theory. *In*: R. Diener, J. Herzog, M. Meili, P. de Meuron and C. Schmid, *Switzerland: An Urban Portrait*, Volume 1. Basel: Birkhäuser, 163–221.

Schütz, A., 1973. *Der sinnhafte Aufbau der sozialen Welt*. Frankfurt: Suhrkamp.

Scott, A., 2004. Cultural-products industries and urban economic development. Prospects for growth and market contestation in global context. *Urban Affairs Review*, 39 (4), 461–490.

Seamon, D. and Mugerauer, R., 1985. *Dwelling, Place and Environment. Towards a Phenomenology of Person and World*. Dordrecht: Martinus Nijhoff.

Shaw, G. and Williams, A., eds, 1997. *The Rise and Fall of British Coastal Resorts: Cultural and Economies Perspectives*. London: Cassell.

Sheller, M. and Urry, J., 2006. The new mobilities paradigm. *Environment and Planning A*, 38 (2), 207–226.

Shields, R., 1991. *Places on the Margin. Alternative Geographies of Modernity*. London: Routledge.

Soane, J., 1993. *Fashionable Resort Regions. Their Evolution and Transformation with Particular Reference to Bournemouth, Nice, Los Angeles and Wiesbaden*. Wallingford: CABI.

Spode, H., 2016. Mobilität, Reisen, Tourismus. Transformationen der Terminologie zwischen Fremdenverkehrslehre und Mobility Turn. *In*: H. Pechlahner and M. Volgger, eds, *Die Gesellschaft auf Reisen – Eine Reise in die Gesellschaft*. Wiesbaden: VS Verlag, 23–46.

Spode, H., 2009. Tourism research and theory in German-speaking countries. *In*: G. Dann and G. Liebman-Parrinello, eds, *The Sociology of Tourism*. Bingley: Emerald, 65–94.

Stephen, L., 1871. *The Playground of Europe*. London: Longmans, Green & Co.

Stock, M., 2004. L'habiter comme pratique des lieux géographiques. *Espacestemps.net* [online]. Available from: www.espacestemps.net/articles/habiter-comme-pratique-des-lieux-geographiques/ [accessed 17 July 2018].

Stock, M., 2006. L'hypothèse de l'habiter polytopique. *Espacestemps.net* [online]. Available from: www.espacestemps.net/articles/hypothese-habiter-polytopique/ [accessed 17 July 2018].

Stock, M., 2007a. Mobility as "arts of dwelling": conceptual investigations. Paper at the American Association of Geographers, San Francisco, CA. Available from: https://halshs.archives-ouvertes.fr/halshs-00366452/document [accessed 17 July 2018].

Stock, M., 2007b. Théorie de l'habiter. Questionnements. *In*: T. Paquot, M. Lussault and Ch. Younès, eds, *Habiter, le propre de l'humain*. Paris: La Découverte, 103–125.

Stock, M., 2007c. Towards a recreational turn of European cities? *Hagar. Studies in Culture, Polity and Identities*, 7 (1), 115–134.

Stock, M., 2009. Polytopisches Wohnen. Ein phänomenologisch-prozessorientierter Zugang. *Informationen zur Raumforschung*, 1–2, 107–116.

Stock, M. and Lucas, L., 2012. La double révolution urbaine du tourisme. *Espaces & Sociétés*, 151, 15–30.

Stock, M., 2014. "Touristisch wohnet der Mensch". Zu einer kulturwissenschaftlichen Theorie mobiler Lebensweisen. *Voyage*, 16, 54–68.

Stock, M., 2015. Habiter comme 'faire avec l'espace'. Réflexions à partir des théories de la pratique. *Annales de Géographie*, 704, 424–441.

Stock, M., 2017. Le concept de centralité à l'épreuve du tourisme. Réflexions critiques. In: N. Bernard, C. Blondy and P. Duhamel, eds, *Tourisme et périphéries : La centralité des lieux en question*. Rennes: Presses Universitaires de Rennes, 269–290.

Senat Berlin, 2018. Konzept für einen stadtverträglichen und nachhaltigen Berlin-Tourismus 2018+ [online]. Berlin: Senat Berlin. Available from: www.berlin.de/sen/web/presse/aktuelles-presseschau/tourismuskonzept_1senatsbefassung.pdf [accessed 17 July 2018].

Thévenot, L., 2000. Pragmatic regimes governing the engagement with the world. *In*: T. Schatzki, K. Knorr-Cetina and E. von Savigny, eds, *The Practice Turn in Contemporary Theory*. London: Routledge.

UNWTO, 2012. *Global Report on City Tourism – Cities 2012 Project*. Madrid: UNWTO.

UNWTO 2016. *Compendium of Tourism Statistics. Data 2010–2014*. Madrid: UNWTO.

Urbain, J.-D., 1991. *L'Idiot du voyage. Histoires de touristes*. Paris: Plon.

Violier, P., 2016. Mobilité des individus et familiarité construite: des arrangements qui offrent aux touristes des prises pour parcourir le monde. *Mondes du tourisme* [online], no. 12. Available from: http://journals.openedition.org/tourisme/1365 [accessed 17 July 2018].

Williams, A. and Shaw, G., 2004. *Tourism and Tourism Spaces*. London: SAGE.

4 Tourist valorisation and urban development

Fabian Frenzel

Introduction

Recent years have brought an increasing concern with the effects of urban tourism on gentrification; concerns shared by residents and expressed in anti-tourism social movements; concerns picked up in the media and in public policy; and concerns increasingly discussed by the tourism industry and tourism academics, too (Freytag and Bauder 2018). The linkages between tourism and gentrification have been widely explored (Gotham 2005, Lin, 2008, Colomb and Novy 2016). In his study of tourism gentrification in New Orleans, Gotham (2005) observed the transformation of the French quarter into a touristified district, involving increasing noise levels, and changes of local businesses from resident-facing to tourist-facing. He pointed to the role of policy deliberately developing tourist-oriented economies in cities. The case of Chinatown in Los Angeles is another example of such tourism-led gentrification (Lin 2008). Beyond the narrow confines of tourism studies and in debates of post-industrial urban development, cities in the UK were encouraged to develop 'night life economies', a form of leisure gentrification that led to changes in the urban fabric and certainly caused pain for permanent residents (Zukin 1987). This turn towards making 'culture' work for the economy did not primarily consider attracting (international) tourists, but shares the wider policy context of a political economy of tourism gentrification, namely the economisation and commoditisation of culture in the urban context (Florida 2004, 2014, Böhm and Land 2009, Catungal *et al.* 2009, Evans 2009). Touristified or otherwise economised local culture has affected residents in a number of ways. In recent years concern has specifically arisen with the gentrification of neighbourhoods as expressed and measured in the increasing exchange value of units of real estate which often leads to displacement of residents. Tourism has moved in the focus of concerns with this form of gentrification because of the emergence of new short-term rental brokerage systems made possible by sharing economy companies such as Airbnb (www.airbnb.com). The effects of this tourism gentrification are much more directly noticeable to residents (namely in higher value real estate), and also affect commercial rental properties. Anti-tourist social movements have emerged in various cities in recent years, not exclusively but often centrally concerned with tourism gentrification or 'overtourism' (Colomb and Novy 2016, Hughes 2018, Novy 2018).

There is a solid political economic analysis of this form of gentrification and the specific role of tourism in it, proposed by Harvey (2012). According to Harvey, urban real estate is valuable in relation to its place, which has monopoly power. A specific location, in its proximity to other places, is unique and can become a source of relative value. Owners of real estate can exploit the monopoly power of real estate that derives from its physical location. Place is not the only determinant of neighbourhood value, and Harvey recognises this. He points out how neighbourhoods become attractive because of the activities of people who live there and make their home. Residents are producing urban commons, shared goods which increase the collective wealth and well-being in an area. Harvey's interpretation of tourism gentrification relates to the ways in which neighbourhood value so produced can be made into capital gains via rent incomes. Tourism is one mechanism by which this commodification works. Tourists, according to Harvey (2012), exchange money for being in and part of a neighbourhood. They allow owners of real estate in locations with monopoly power to realise capital gains.

In this chapter, I contend that Harvey's proposal does not fully explain the processes that govern tourist gentrification. While offering a very useful starting point, his analysis does not give a valid account for how neighbourhoods become attractive in the first place. Thus, once we acknowledge that residents contribute to this process, how do we separate their activities from those of tourists? And how can we understand, theoretically, the processes in which neighbourhoods become attractive?

This chapter sets out to analyse this process and specifically aims to answer four questions.

(1) How do cities or neighbourhoods become attractive and what is the role of labour in the process?
(2) Is gentrification a necessary consequence of making neighbourhoods attractive?
(3) What is the relationship between diverse notions of attractiveness and value?
(4) What is the role of tourists, as opposed to everyday residents in this?

In this conceptual chapter, informed by data from my fieldwork in a number of global urban tourism destinations, and by secondary data, I will first discuss literature on gentrification, with a focus on contributions informed by political economic thought and namely Harvey. By elaborating of the production of neighbourhoods by residents' labour, I address some of the limitations of Harvey's view. In order to do so, I introduce ideas such as 'user-generated' cities and the logic of externalities as proposed by Hardt and Negri (2009) for the understanding of urban commons. In the following section, I discuss the role of tourists in the making of attractions, building on literature that considers the active role of tourists in tourism, using such concepts as 'co-creation' and 'pro-suming', but introducing an alternative view in which such activities are read as practices, akin but not equivalent to labour. I offer a theoretical take on modelling such activities, starting from the notion of 'commoning' and building on Virno's understanding of 'praxis'. In the last section, I discuss empirical examples drawing from different cases of field-work and highlighting in particular the question how tourist and every day 'praxis' may differ. I resolve that tourist 'praxis' is specific in its exceptionality in temporal and spatial terms, its relative ignorance and its autonomy. I conclude on the note that addressing the issue of tourism gentrification should be pursued not against, but with tourists, who may be allies of local residents in their struggles for attractive and affordable neighbourhoods.

Gentrification

The wide literature on gentrification generally converges around a focus on the tail end effect of gentrification, namely the rising value and cost of real estate. Rising costs mark gentrification processes across the world and are the cause of most concerns with gentrification, in particular displacement of residents who can no longer afford to live in a gentrified neighbourhood (Shin *et al.* 2016). The more complicated and contested question is what happens at the beginning: how are gentrification processes set off and who are their most important agents?[1] It is here that gentrification literature broadly diverges and varying approaches exist in parallel. There is no space in this chapter to discuss the wider literature at length (see for overview, Smith 2005, Porter and Shaw 2008, Maloutas 2012, Lees and Ferrerai 2016), so a focus will be placed on approaches from political economy which tend to take a more critical view on gentrification. Political economy perspectives on urban development have long proposed a view in which the process of creation of urban neighbourhoods is understood as closely related to wider labour processes. Harvey (2012) traces the 'housing question' to early debates on regeneration and displacement as an effect of deliberate urban planning by policy. He pointed to the forced erasure of Paris's working-class neighbourhoods and slums in Haussmann's urban regeneration program of the late 1800s. According to what Friedrich Engels called the 'Haussmann' method, this was a means to solving the housing question "in such a way that the solution perpetually renews the questions" (cited in Harvey 2012, p. 16). Engels understood that slum removal conducted in this way did not solve the housing needs of the working class who were displaced to the outskirts of the city. The inner-city areas thus 'regenerated', however, yielded higher rents for real estate developers than the working-class slums that were removed. This made a compelling case for 'urban regeneration' as an aspect of capitalist accumulation in the realm of rent. According to Harvey (2012), a key factor to the attractiveness of urban space derives from the 'monopoly power' of place, which is a proxy for convenience: there is only a limited amount housing available close to city centre, or close to a place of work, more generally. In a situation of private ownership of real estate, the relative scarcity of conveniently located housing creates increased profits or rents from real estate.

Beyond the centrality of policy and real estate owners in driving gentrification processes, a second factor needs to be considered from a political economy perspective, namely that there is a labour dynamic in the urbanisation process itself. This means that the creation of housing and associated aspects of social reproduction in the city are also autonomous valorisation processes initiated by those who dwell in the city. In such a reading, the initial creation of working-class urban spaces is a result not just of real estate owners exploiting 'monopoly power', but also of various rural to urban migrants creating their living spaces in the city (Hardt and Negri 2009). Historically speaking, such processes of 'user-generated' urbanity (Echanove and Srivastava 2014) are most vividly evident in the development of so-called slums: initial settlers establish a new urban neighbourhood in spaces that lie peripheral to the core city (outside the zones too expensive because of their relative centrality). In such new urban zones, housing and other services of social reproduction are produced more informally, without support by urban development agencies (Angélil and Hehl 2012). In these contexts, real estate interests and property regimes based on private ownership do exist and sometimes play really important roles, but the overall lack of formal recognition of property titles makes the exchange value of real estate highly precarious and speculative. Under conditions of informality the main value in real estate is its use value: day-to-day uses for commercial and social reproductive needs (Echanove and Srivastava 2014). As a city grows, such spaces may become increasingly centrally located, with pressure of formalisation rising and also affecting the exchange value of their real estate, at least theoretically. A paradigmatic case is the Dharavi neighbourhood in Mumbai, a place literarily built from mud and rubbish by subsequent generations of residents. Today this vast neighbourhood lies so central in the expanded city that it is the object of vivid regeneration desires. The potential value of the ground, initially created by the first inhabitants, has multiplied. Haussmann-type interventions, fiercely contested by some residents, have been proposed by Mumbai urban development elites since the mid-2000s (Campana 2013), but to date have not succeeded in fully integrating Dharavi into the formal property regimes of the city, arguably because of resident resistance.

The making of the city as a process of commoning

The example of Dharavi and other 'user-generated' neighbourhoods—or perhaps in a wider sense, localities, quarters and urban spaces—shows that neighbourhood attraction and its value is not set by their relative location to central points of production, or 'monopoly power' of space only, or any other physical or intrinsic values as such. Instead, attraction is produced, and residents of the city, its 'users', are its producers. Many political economists of the urban form acknowledge the importance of inhabitants in building neighbourhoods as their living spaces, for example in notions of urban commons, or commoning (Dellenbaugh *et al.* 2015, see also Sommer and Kip, Chapter 10 in this volume), in the already mentioned concept of 'user-generated urbanity' (Echanove and Srivastava 2014) or as value practices (De Angelis 2007).

Commons are often understood as resources that already exist. The example of urban commoning however shows its relevance as an activity. Urban commons are not only a shared resource, but they are also commonly produced, and this can include the urban fabric, whole neighbourhoods, as our previous example of Dharavi has shown. However, in a yet wider sense, urban commoning also describes the permanent re-production of neighbourhoods as spaces worth living in, as attractive places. Activities here concern the maintaining of infrastructures and social relations and their adaptation to new needs, e.g., activities such as the refurbishing of housing, the organisation of transport, the quality of air, security and safety, child-friendliness, the opening of coffee places and myriad other. Moreover, we need to consider here intangible commons, notions such as neighbourhood reputation and feel, which are also constantly re-produced.

For Hardt and Negri (2009), drawing critically from economics, such urban commons can be understood as 'externalities'. They play a crucial role in determining property value, but when we define ownership of a property and therefore the ownership of its economic value, these values are considered external. Arguably, the value of housing itself is to a large extent defined through things that have little to do with the relative quality of the house or apartment. Value is codetermined by externalities, which can be positive and negative towards the overall quality of housing. Just like the house or apartment itself, they need to be produced, but this production happens largely without the participation of the property's owners. It is very often not organised, paid for, or produced by the owners of the real estate, but still external to our understanding of ownership. Otherwise, every time a property is sold, some money should flow to the many people who produced the neighbourhood in which it lies, in common.

Often 'externalities' are produced in common or as public goods, for example by the DIY urbanism of squatters who render derelict buildings into usable housing, social centres or leisure facilities, or by the state that uses tax income to provide kindergartens. Immaterial commons such as neighbourhood reputation and feel are equally produced in common by any number of urban dwellers (Hardt and Negri 2009, Harvey 2012, Dellenbaugh *et al.* 2015). There is a wider literature considering these processes beyond the common's terminology (Hou 2010, Lydon and Garcia 2015, Fabian and Samson 2016). Seemingly inevitably, such practices of commoning increase the value of properties and owners can benefit and skim them off in rent income.

Conceptually, the process by which externalities are rendered 'external' to the value of individual properties resembles a classical labour process whereby the work of the many is appropriated to produce profit for the few, but with an important difference. Expropriation here does not happen as in the case of the factory owner, who controls her workers' labour time. Instead, the production of commons that increase property value is much more autonomous. People just do what they have to do to survive, what they like to do, but often under their own terms. They increase the living quality, the well-being of people, but such activities are not, from a political economy perspective, labour practices. In fact, mostly these are common everyday activities, such as neighbourhood meetings, or activities, volunteer work, engagement in artistic or sportive practices, political activities, even a chat with a neighbour. They are not subject to work regimes, but operate autonomously from it. People are not paid to do such activities; they use their free time to pursue them. Perhaps it makes sense to see the city as a "factory for the production of commons" (Hardt and Negri 2009, p. 260) with a number of agents involved in producing them. However, this factory has little external control, and few middle managers.

Gentrification as enclosure

Some urban scholars argue that autonomous production has become ever more important in post-Fordist, increasingly deindustrialised cities (Lazzarato 1996, Virno 2004, Gill and Pratt 2008). This is contested, but arguably more relevant for cities in the developed world. What remains evident throughout is the fact that urban commoning is a process of relative autonomous production of positive externalities contributing towards neighbourhood attraction, which are being harnessed for private gain because real estate is privately owned. In other words, in private ownership of real estate, urban commons are enclosed (Frenzel and Beverungen 2014). Harvie and Milburn (2010) have suggested a vocabulary that is useful to differentiate notions of attractiveness. They consider as 'wealth' all the assembled things human beings find valuable and 'values' (in plural) as the things we consider when we produce wealth. 'Value' (in the singular) is different from these two. It describes a unified measure of wealth and its sole purpose resides in aiding the appropriation of collectively produced wealth by the few in capital gains. Gentrification can then be defined as a process of enclosure of urban commoning, or with Harvie and Millburn (2010) as the translation of 'values' into 'value'. Diverse value practices can increase the worth (positive externalities) of a neighbourhood and produce attractiveness in common. As an area becomes more attractive, real estate is a way of realising, enclosing worth and attractiveness of urban commons in private rent income, which results in expropriation: owners of real estate profit, regardless of their contribution to the production.

People not owning property, conversely, are in danger of being displaced even if they participated in the commoning. Harvey (2012) calls this the 'tragedy of the urban commons': what used to be an attractive area becomes unaffordable because of rising property values and speculation, thus pushing many people out, potentially transforming the neighbourhood fabric— often relatively fewer producers of commons reside here. Paradoxically, the affected area has now a higher exchange value, but only small use values for those who live there. In current urban settings, such processes may lead to the full transformation of housing into a pure storage of value. Flats and houses are no longer used to live in, but as speculative investments. In the context of tourism, an equivalent development would be the transform- ation of what used to be a neighbourhood into an assemblage of short- term rentals in houses and apartments that no longer have permanent resident occupiers. In the extreme, a former neighbourhood would effect- ively become a resort.

To summarise, I separate two different processes: one is the process in which neighbourhoods become more attractive. This can happen in a number of ways, for example by a particular place 'moving' more into the centre of the city as a city expands. Yet, mostly it is the result of the activities or value practices by people who already live in a place. Their various activities con- spire to create neighbourhoods that are more attractive. Of course, this is not necessarily the case: there are obviously circumstances in which externalities are rather negative, in which neighbourhoods have terrible living conditions, which become consecutively worse in their re-production (Wacquant 2008). But even under conditions of 'advanced urban marginality' (Wacquant 2008), most people living in neighbourhoods will presumably try to improve their living quality and, in many cases, also succeed. The stigma itself is often harder to address then more material failings, evidenced in the cases I discuss later. Against the permanent re-production of neighbourhoods as liveable, and attractive places by residents, we can contrast a secondary process of gentrification. In these processes, increased attractiveness or 'wealth' becomes 'value' in purely economic terms, materialised in the rising prices of real estate. Those producing the 'wealth' of a place are 'externalised', initially as a way of appropriating their value practices in the enclosure of commons of private property, and secondly via displacement as the exchange value of a neigh- bourhood rises. When private property regimes exist, there is the almost per- manent danger of this secondary process colonising the first: the enclosure, in private ownership of urban space, of the commons produced by the many in the city. Both processes occur together but they are separated: one is doing, the other is appropriating what has been done (Holloway 2002). The link between the two is not natural or better: the latter often follows the former, but not necessarily. It is relatively difficult to imagine a situation where no private ownership of real estate exists. Closer to the status quo (in Western societies), several taxes (capital gains on property, or ground tax, for example) or enforced contributions of real estate owners to public transport projects, are arguably justified because we recognise the centrality of externalities that go into the value of property.

In order to move to the next argument, there is one more important point to add. We need to ask who contributes to the production of urban commons.

Until now, I have referred here mostly to residents, but they are not the only actors in the creation of wealth in neighbourhoods. I have already referred to the role played by the public sector in creating public goods such as educational facilities. Policy, real estate owners as well as businesses and other organisations all play roles and often contribute in one way or another to creating neighbourhood attractiveness; and importantly, so do tourists.

Tourism and gentrification

If we understand urbanites as active participants in making cities more or less attractive, then the next question to discuss is the role of tourism in this process. Harvey (2012, p. 74) argues: "The ambience and attractiveness of a city, for example, is a collective product of its citizens, but it is the tourist trade that commercially capitalizes upon that common to extract monopoly rents." According to Harvey, tourism is a way to valorise the vibrancy of the common, to translate a wonderful city life into monetary gain through tourist spending. In relation to the two processes of commoning and gentrification discussed above, Harvey sees tourists involved only in the latter. They help owners of property to appropriate positive externalities, produced in common, because tourists are willing to exchange money for the experience of these spaces. Tourists, not unlike new residents, are trying to buy themselves into the attractive neighbourhoods that residents have created. My argument is that this view of tourism is very limited because it does not consider their role in the first process.

In terms of theoretical implications of Harvey's (2012) approach, tourists are assumed to be consumers and all their activities are fully captured in processes of capitalist valorisation. Tourists have no agency, meaning here that the intensions and modalities of their actions have no bearings on the outcomes of their actions. Tourists are not considered to be able to participate in the commoning, to engage in value practices that increase neighbourhood value. In short, tourists are not expected to contribute anything meaningful to the places they visit beyond the money they spend: the money, however, only feeds into gentrification processes. In recent anti-tourist social movements, the application of such thinking is expressed as a rejection and even hostility against tourists (Hughes 2018). Tourists are understood as a temporary plague, offering benefits only to those engaged commercially in the tourist trade and undermining the social fabric of neighbourhoods.

Tourists as co-producers of attractions

In recent years, increasing attention has been paid to the ways in which consumption activities also have productive characteristics (Shaw *et al.* 2011, Blazquez-Resino *et al.* 2013). Within the narrow confines of a restaurant, this can be usefully exemplified. Thus, people visiting a restaurant, the customers, are evidently involved in producing the restaurant experience. The atmosphere of a restaurant is, among other things, dependent on how many people are visiting and how they act in the restaurant. In marketing literature, the analysis of such phenomena has led to the development of the so-called 'service dominant logic' (Shaw *et al.* 2011, Blazquez-Resino *et al.* 2013). The limitation of these approaches lies in their focus on the perspective of businesses who provide tourism products. In some way, one could say the interest is to better understand how tourists can be made to contribute to the value proposition of the company for free. There exists no moral problem for this type of research, because in their view tourists are involved in production processes out of their own self-interest, i.e., to maximise their cost–benefit.

In debates on the political economy of post-Fordist production, Virno (2004) offers perhaps the most useful theoretical framework to understand how tourists may contribute to the making of attractions beyond such cost–benefit logics. Virno is not concerned with tourism empirically, but considers the wider post-Fordist economy. The post-Fordist economy in its most basic sense describes an economy more tilted towards services, and one where manufacturing is of relatively less importance (Lash and Urry 1987, Lazzarato 1996). Virno marks this shift with reference to two different readings of human activities, drawing from Aristotle's differentiation between 'poiesis' and 'praxis'. 'Poiesis', connected to the making of things, is the dominant activity in the Fordist economy. As an activity, it is separated from its product and the product can be consumed or used independently from its production. 'Praxis', in difference, is more akin to a performance; thus production and product are inseparable. In Virno's reading, the product of 'praxis' is shared space of significance. Virno partly draws on Arendt's (1998) notion of the 'space of appearance' to make this argument more explicit: 'praxis' is a mode of human activity most closely associated with politics. Its product is the shared space in which action is performed and perceived. There is a very social and political character to this kind of production. According to Virno, it is increasingly used in the capitalist economy.

In the example of the restaurant experience, both guests and hosts have contributed to the making of the restaurant experience. However, it is the owner of the restaurant who takes away the profit: by being the owner of the space in which the common praxis occurs, the restaurant owner is able to enclose the production of commons that has taken place in the restaurant space. Importantly, the restaurant owner has very little power over the guests. They are free to leave, to chat or not, within the constraints of acceptable behaviour in a restaurant space. This participation is voluntary, and from a labour process perspective, not 'labour'. It means that the 'praxis' of visitors to the restaurant is not controlled, directed and owned by the restaurant owner. In contrast, the activities of the waiters and cooks are indeed controlled by the managerial impositions of the owner.[2]

To qualify the argument, it is important to say that restaurant waiters are not fully robotic. There is, in other words, an element of autonomy in all labour. Managerial control is never total, neither in the service industries, nor in other areas of production. This becomes obvious when cooperation between different workers is a crucial ingredient to the production of value. Labour process studies, dating back to Marx's analysis of the production process, show that capital often does avoid strict control, but seeks to exploit aspects of human collaboration that take place outside scripted job roles, in relative autonomy. Free cooperation is essential to many successful production processes. Autonomy is also central to the co-production, or 'praxis', of tourists, who are, like restaurants guests, involved in making the tourist experience.

Tourist valorisation in praxis

Bringing Virno into the study of tourism allows for a reconsideration of tourists' involvement in the production of attractions. In what follows I will describe some empirical examples of tourist value practices in which this involvement becomes evident. My main area of empirical study concerns relatively poor and disadvantaged neighbourhoods that turn into tourist attractions. One of the main contributions of tourism in this context is linked specifically to the desire of some tourists for difference. In urban sociology advanced marginality is described as the result of the compound effects of neglect and 'territorial stigma', most notably by Wacquant (2008). Thus, neglected neighbourhoods suffer from invisibility or the selected visibility of stigma, meaning that social problems (or negative externalities) are highlighted, while positive aspects are ignored.

Territorial stigma is biased and evidently not a truthful representation. Neighbourhoods subject to it can often be 'discovered' by tourists as radically different from their dominant representations. Tourists may thus produce visibility and also a specific positive visibility of neighbourhoods they visit. They do this, initially, by defying the injunctions of the stigmatic urban space organisation: they enter a stigmatised neighbourhood, branded as 'no-go area' in mainstream discourses, and against warnings that they should not go. They visit a place, although mainstream discourses and official tourism literature and destination marketing tell them that there is nothing to see.

Sometimes this rebellious neglect of the official guidance for tourists may become rather political. This is the case with activist groups, who use tourism as a way of telling their stories and attempting to create solidarities with tourists in the process. Thus, in Dharavi, some residents oppose the plans to transform the neighbourhood according to the Dharavi redevelopment plan because this will destroy much of the built structures while formalising the real estate regime; they told me about their hope that tourists may strengthen their case against the destruction of traditional, but informal, housing in the neighbourhood. In Rio de Janeiro, several community initiatives use tourism to advance their arguments with the city council over questions such as house removals or security. In one instance, tourists were characterised as potentially shielding residents against overtly violent police behaviour as potential witnesses (Frenzel 2016, 2017). The tourists themselves are involved in producing visibility.

It is useful in this regard to remember the example of the restaurant experience. Tourists are of course not 'discovering a place' off the beaten track, as tourism language seems to suggest. However, they do add new meanings and visibilities to a place that already exists. The action of viewing and visiting a neighbourhood can thus be understood as a 'praxis' in Virno's sense. All acts within this place contribute to the expansion of social action and possible experiences. In the language of Hardt and Negri (2009), this commoning can also be translated as 'joyful encounters'. In short, tourists are already contributing to the vibrancy of the place simply by being present and seeing the place.

Beyond seeing

Beyond the mere presence and the seeing, tourists also contribute in more material and immaterial practices, in particular in creating infrastructures and place representations themselves. Tourists often get more involved in the production of places than simply altering visibility. Tourism studies discuss numerous examples of tourism entrepreneurship where tourists start to set up tourism infrastructures, creating new destinations in the process (Ateljevic and Doorne 2000). Again, the place is not being 'discovered' but rather re-made, with new meaning added to whatever older meanings were already in place.

In an urban context such processes are also clearly visible, when neglected neighbourhoods become the place where tourist entrepreneurs start their own guesthouses. My research has shown that this is frequently the case in favelas in Rio de Janeiro (Frenzel 2016). Such production of infrastructures by tourists is pertinent for the consideration of how tourists take part in producing an attractive neighbourhood, although arguably the setting up of business is not strictly speaking a practice of commoning. What matters, however, are possibilities to enable 'joyful encounters' (Hardt and Negri 2009). There is evidence for such practices in the setting up of joint meeting spaces of institutional pressure groups that discuss common issues, sometimes triggered by tourists. This is the case, for example, in the favela Vidigal in Rio de Janeiro, where community activists, visitors and local universities organised public discussions about gentrification (Frenzel 2016). Such spaces do not only serve tourists but also have common functions in the community.

Valorisation 2.0

A particularly important aspect of practices of tourist valorisation is the role tourists play in telling stories about the places they visit. It may be of little surprise that one of the most significant brands of global travel books, the *Lonely Planet*, was started by two tourists re-telling their travel stories as a way of providing practical tips. Telling tales is a central element of tourism and travel. At the same time, it is also one of the most powerful practices in which tourists engage in creating attractions. In recent years, this age-old practice has been significantly enhanced with the advent of social media. The ability of tourists to share and rate experiences, to send images and give tales of locations, to provide feedback has significantly increased (see also Kramer *et al.*, Chapter 9 in this volume). The platforms on which tourists engage in valorisations are plentiful and range from well-known TripAdvisor (www.tripadvisor.com) to more specific comment sections on other social media.

In my empirical research I investigated the role of webpages like TripAdvisor to put disadvantaged neighbourhoods on the map (Frenzel 2014a). Thus, in Johannesburg some inner-city walking tours have become the most highly rated attractions for tourism in the city, ahead of all official sites of tourism promoted by the city tourism board. The places in which these tours were offered were widely considered to be no-go areas by most South Africans. Nevertheless, for tourists reflecting and rating on TripAdvisor, the tours became a top experience, putting the neighbourhoods in which they were conducted in a completely different light (Frenzel 2014b).

Tourism can be described as a social force that amplifies what tour organisers want to share, namely that these places are much better than their reputation. In practices of rating and re-posting, of telling tales of the stories experienced, tourists also actively participate in the re-making of these disadvantaged neighbourhoods. Johannesburg is an important example, partly because so much has changed in the general perception of the city, and particularly its inner-city sections. Over the last few years, Johannesburg's inner city has experienced a renaissance which has also led to an explosion of inner-city tours, often highly commercial in nature (Gregory 2016, Hoogendoorn and Giddy 2017). This return of the city has been some time in the making, and tourism plays an important part in it. However, it is also illustrative that many actors and intentions are involved. It is important to refrain from seeing tourism in isolation. Both urban policy and private real estate have been activist in their approach at urban regeneration, attempting to make the city more attractive. Whole sections of the inner city have been bought up by property developers, securitised and 'regenerated' in versions of a soft 'Haussmann'. In contrast to the place making from below done by small-scale tour operators, real estate operators ignore and displace the existing social fabric and replace it with imported models of urbanity, as in the case of the Maboneng development in Johannesburg (Gregory 2016).

Thus, we have to differentiate again between the more 'grassroots' practices described in the previous sections and attempts to make neighbourhoods attractive via large injections of cash. The latter is neither ineffective nor completely unwelcome by all residents. Nevertheless, it comes attached, from the beginning, with the following enclosure of all the practices people put into making places more attractive. In Maboneng, for example, there has been the displacement of those people who produced the existing urban fabric, rather than any earnest attempt at ensuring their involvement (Bahmann and Frenkel 2012, Gregory 2016).

Tourism and the everyday

Tourists and residents are thus both involved in practices of commoning that make places attractive. They may differ, but they also have a lot in common. Conceptually speaking, in both cases we see practices that can extend or diminish the living quality of neighbourhoods. On the positive, I described such value practices as ranging from simply viewing and utilising certain spaces to more active practices of place making, like activism, building of infrastructures and places of encounter. Both residents and tourists are also involved in the telling of tales, the processes in which information about certain places are shared more widely, practices of place branding from below, greatly enhanced by contemporary online technologies.

As already discussed, we can see those practices as 'praxis' in Virno's terms, borrowed from Aristotle: a production process that does not result in a final product, separated from the production, but one that leads to the creation and re-creation of shared spaces of experience. The process of such production is naturally open to all who enter a space, and all are taking part. The making of a neighbourhood is thus a truly integrative production process, with no restrictions related to the background or the status of residency—at least not theoretically. Practically speaking, many restrictions do structure such production processes and while some of these are external, and relate to questions of legal status, rights and access to resources (which I will not discuss here for reasons of space), there are also those that are connected to the different subjective positions that participants are in.

In this sense, I propose reconsidering the differentiation of residents and tourists,[3] or those engaging in the process of attraction making from an everyday and from an exceptional perspective. Tourist practices differ from those of everyday residents in a number of ways, of which I will discuss a few cases. In the examples presented earlier, the more material practices of tourists building infrastructures of encounter really only happen where tourists decide to become everyday residents of a place. Similar observations can be made for the creation of guided tours by visitors. Such practices seem to coincide with the transformation of a tourist to a resident, often via a hybrid state between those two categories. The transient temporary trans-migrant (or trans-tourist), who may spend years in a neighbourhood, but remains connected to other places and is never constructing their presence as one of origin, is an increasingly discussed figure of urban tourism considerations.

It is interesting to consider the theoretical implications of this coincidence between more material value practices and residential status: the more substantial contribution to the making of neighbourhoods often starts at the point where very temporary visitors become a bit more like everyday residents. This is of course, drawing on migration studies (Basch *et al.* 1994), the precise contribution of migrants in the city. They expand the meaning of places beyond those already in place, making the place their home in the process, and re-creating a neighbourhood in this way. If we look at the practices of more short-term visitors, then, we need to acknowledge that their contributions to the creation of infrastructures of encounter is often more ephemeral. As temporal visitors, they will use such spaces, write and tell about those spaces and in this way contribute to their viability, but there is perhaps a limit to how much they can do to set them up.

What is special about tourist attraction making?

Overall, it may be useful to understand the difference between tourist and everyday practices in the city by simply redefining tourist practices as exceptional for the tourist. Rather than pertaining to everyday experience, tourist practices are exceptional, because tourists are not pursuing such practices in this particular place every day. From the perspective of the place, these practices may not seem exceptional at all. Seeing tourists coming in day after day, residents may simply see a repetition and an everyday of certain practices; to the tourist though, the practices are exceptional. We have already noted that this brings constraints for long-term involvement and the value practices they rely on. However, exceptionality also provides specific openings. Exceptionally present, tourists are likely to view particular places differently and assert attractiveness differently from those permanently present. They may be more curious, for example, about the specific configuration of places, as a result of being largely ignorant towards existing meanings and understandings of place. Curiosity is of course a central motivation for travel and it is positively related to what tourists usually get derided for, namely their stupidity and ignorance (Grube, Chapter 11 in this volume). Urbain's work (2002) points to the idiotic character of tourism. By idiotic, he refers to the original meaning of the term in ancient Greek—namely of being an outsider and therefore unfamiliar with the rules and conditions of the place. This idiotic position may be causing anxiety (or *tourist angst* about being perceived as an idiot), but it is also, more positively, the precondition of tourist curiosity, their potential questioning of existing notions of place attractiveness.

In the empirical context of highly stigmatised neighbourhoods, for example, tourists may not be aware of existing negative externalities of places or they may find them exceptionally attractive. They are likely to not share everyday perceptions of specific situations as normal and non-noticeable. Exchanges on the rating platform TripAdvisor between tourists and Mumbai elite residents over the attractiveness of the Dharavi neighbourhood evidence the radically different approach tourists have. Elite Mumbai residents claim that Dharavi is not an attraction, at best just a normal neighbourhood and that there is nothing to see. Tourists highly rate Dharavi, thereby providing a different view to those present in Mumbai (Frenzel 2014a). The difference between everyday and exceptional views on attractions may be disruptive, and rebellious, too, questioning understandings of what is valuable and attractive or correcting territorial stigma.

A second aspect of tourist practices, apart from their exceptionality, is that they contribute to attraction making voluntarily, or autonomously. Much of our activities in normal, everyday life are in one way or another connected to work. Rojek (2010) has argued that much of our leisure time is also non-voluntary, and often connected to necessary elements of life. However, it is important to maintain a difference between activities that, in a polit-ical economy sense, can be described as labour, i.e., practices we conduct in exchange for a wage, and non-waged practices. Non-waged activities often form the precondition of labour, for example in activities linked to social reproduction, and they constitute important sources for the production of capitalist profit. However, the motivation they are pursued for is not linked to remuneration. Humans perform such activities for different reasons, often because they care, love or feel obliged in a number of other social senses. Frequently, such non-waged practices may be pursued for fun and desire, and because they provide fulfilment and give meaning. In tourism, many practices are conducted in such a context and they often come with a greater sense of playfulness or what Virno (2004) might call virtuosity. They concern interactions that are not scripted and open in their outcome, or encounters that are informal (Simoni 2015). As indicated earlier, such activities are far from being irrelevant to the production of profits. Indeed, conditions may arise in which such autonomous pursuit of practices feed into the making of profits. Gentrification is an example where many voluntarily activities feed into an increased value of real estate as already explained.

What matters, however, is that tourists are more likely to be engaged in such voluntary or autonomous practices than everyday residents, simply because tourists have a lot of free time at hand, derived from the exceptionality of the tourist experience. Many residents will juggle paid work with free time, which limits their ability to write about their experiences of the neighbour-hood. They have less time to reflect on its attractiveness, organise a protest or simply to sit in a café or join a musical event and in such a way contribute to the positive atmosphere of a neighbourhood.

As indicated earlier, the differences between tourism and everyday practices should not be overstated. In some ways, these are merely theoret-ical differences resulting from different conceptions of tourism and everyday life. Everyday residents may be seeing their neighbourhood in a new light, or 'like tourists'. Likewise, tourists may be drawn to not being very explorative or curious, following similar patterns of behaviour wherever they go and cre-ating their own everyday in tourism. It is illustrative, however, and important as well, to acknowledge that there are specific advantages to the tourist involvement in attraction making. Tourists contribute to the production of attractions and they do so in specific ways. Far from being merely realisers of capital gains, they contribute to neighbourhoods in exceptional, disruptive and rebellious ways.

Conclusion

This chapter analysed the process of attraction making and its links to gentrification. Specifically, it aimed to answer four questions, posited in the introduction, which are now set to be answered.

(1) How do cities or neighbourhoods become attractive and what is the role of labour in it?

The chapter discussed current analysis of the political economy of urban development, in which the attraction of a neighbourhood or a city is not simply understood as a consequence of intrinsic values, but as a result of production processes. Neighbourhood value is produced, often in processes that can be described as commoning. In contrast to regeneration as driven by the state or the private sector, residents produce neighbourhood attractiveness in various practices. Commoning can thus be understood as activity akin to work or labour, but not conducted in exchange for a wage, and thus in contrast more autonomous. This includes activities such as squatting, or attending and organising neighbourhood groups, helping neighbours moving in or writing about the neighbourhood in a blog. Together with other externalities, commons constitute a neighbourhood feel, its reputation and sense of place. This perspective on gentrification matters because it highlights the unjust appropriation of these activities in secondary processes of enclosure.

(2) Is gentrification a necessary consequence of making neighbourhoods attractive?

The chapter aimed to show that this is not the case. It argued that managerial and capitalist control is increasingly absent from contemporary production processes and this includes the production of neighbourhood attractiveness. Often regeneration is driven by state actors, or private sector capital, but a significant way in which neighbourhood attractiveness is translated from commons into profit is via the enclosure of the spaces in which relatively autonomous production of neighbourhood attractiveness takes place via value practices. In this light, gentrification can be understood as form of enclosure of autonomous production. This poses questions of justice, not dissimilar to other domains of capitalist production, as owners of real estate profit from production processes to which they have not contributed. Conversely, others who have contributed, but do not have the capacity or will to enclose spaces in which his production takes place, may seem themselves displaced by increasing property prices and rent costs. Importantly, gentrification is a secondary process, in which the commonly produced attractions are enclosed, predominantly via the private ownership of real estate. It is not a necessary consequence, but rather a specific result of the organisation of the political economy.

(3) What is the relationship between diverse notions of attractiveness and value?

Neighbourhood attractiveness cannot (directly) be translated into value and rent, or to be more precise, into capital gains. A key measure to translate 'values' into 'value' is the private ownership of land and housing. In enclosing the spaces in which collective production takes place, owners of private real estate also render what is a rather opaque and intangible 'worth' or 'feel' of an area into something that can be measured, quite neatly, by real estate prices. In today's world, investors buy with the tip of a finger on the keyboard, shares in property all over the world. In globalised property regimes, the collective production of attractiveness, the creativity, joy and energy that goes into living commonly, is being made to serve the growth of capital in ever more abstract ways. The crucial political question is how to prevent the transformation of neighbourhood attractiveness into neighbourhood value. The skimming of value in such processes is evidently unfair, but it is also detrimental to the production of further neighbourhood attractiveness. In gentrification, many of those who contribute are displaced as the process further develops. The tragedy of the urban commons means that fully gentrified neighbourhoods are no longer attractive beyond their exchange value.

(4) What is the role of tourists, as opposed to everyday residents in this?

Finally, this chapter discussed the specific character of tourist practices that contribute to the creation of neighbourhood attractiveness. The aim was to recognise the contribution of tourists to neighbourhood attractiveness, because they are still broadly considered to be passive consumers. The misperception of tourists as merely consuming is misleading and can propel and fuel anti-tourist social movement practices. Such practices, just like the theories underpinning them, are short-sighted and misleading in personalising the tourists as bearers of capital in the world. The issue is precisely not to personalise the functionalities of capital in identifying particular groups as their impersonation. Instead, it is important to understand the structural logics in which capital operates, its inherent contradictions in which production of value actually depends on relatively autonomous production processes. Harvey (2001, p. 411) expresses this clearly:

> It is here that the contradictions faced by the capitalists as they search for monopoly rent assume a certain structural significance. By seeking to

trade on values of authenticity, locality, history, culture, collective memories and tradition, they open a space for political thought and action within which alternatives can be both devised and pursued. That space deserves intense exploration and cultivation by oppositional movements. It is one of the key spaces of hope for the construction of an alternative kind of globalization. One in which the progressive forces of culture appropriate those of capital rather than the other way round.

Where Harvey goes wrong, is to disregard tourists as part of this 'mix of progressive forces'. They contribute to neighbourhood attractiveness in marked difference to the everyday resident. Categorically, tourist practices differ because of the exceptionality of their experience and the amount of free time in hand. Arguably, such a specific position of the leisured stranger is actually a key ingredient in the production of neighbourhood attractiveness.

Are tourists aware of the links between the production of neighbourhood attractiveness and gentrification to which they so specifically contribute? Can they help to prevent the neighbourhood attractiveness turning into neighbourhood value? I have witnessed attempts to bring tourists and residents together to create strategies that prevent the enclosure of commonly produced goods such as an increased neighbourhood reputation. A key strategy lies in tackling privately owned real estate. Tourists should be included in our calculation of struggles against the enclosures of commons. They may form an important part in the resistance against gentrification. They have a special place in the 'grammar of the multitude' (Virno 2004) because their practices are exceptional, rebellious and idiotic.

Notes

1 In Chapter 5 of this volume, Parish points out the special relationship between the emergence of urban wellness industries in a Toronto neighbourhood and its relation to gentrification.
2 Even though this classical restaurant setting with its clear distribution of roles becomes blurred in eating experiences mediated by online platforms, the owners, i.e., hosts, are still taking away the profit (Stoltenberg and Frisch, Chapter 8 in this volume).
3 Also refer to Chapter 7 by Wildish and Spierings in this volume.

References

Angélil, M. and Hehl, R., eds, 2012. *Informalize!: Essays on the Political Economy of Urban Form*. Berlin: Ruby Press.
Arendt, H., 1998. *The Human Condition*, 2nd ed. Chicago, IL: University of Chicago Press.
Ateljevic, I. and Doorne, S., 2000. 'Staying within the fence': lifestyle entrepreneurship in tourism. Journal of Sustainable Tourism, 8 (5), 378–392.

Bahmann, D. and Frenkel, J., 2012. Renegotiating Space – Arts on Main, 44 Stanley and Johannesburg. Report series produced by the South African Research Chair in Development Planning and Modelling, School of Architecture and Planning, University of the Witwatersrand, Johannesburg, p. 50.

Basch, L., Glick Schiller, N. and Szanton Blanc, C., 1994. *Nations Unbound: Transnational Projects, Postcolonial Predicaments, and Deterritorialized Nation-States.* New York: Gordon and Breach.

Blazquez-Resino, J.J., Molina, A. and Esteban-Talaya, A., 2013. Service-dominant logic in tourism: the way to loyalty. *Current Issues in Tourism.* Available from: www.tandfonline.com.ezproxy3.lib.le.ac.uk/doi/abs/10.1080/13683500.2013.863853 [accessed 13 June 2016].

Böhm, S. and Land, C., 2009. No measure for culture? Value in the new economy. *Capital & Class*, 33 (1), 75–98.

Campana, J., ed., 2013. *Dharavi: The City Within.* Noida: HarperCollins Publishers India.

Catungal, J.P., Leslie, D. and Hii, Y., 2009. Geographies of displacement in the creative city: the case of Liberty Village, Toronto. *Urban Studies*, 46 (5–6), 1095–1114.

Colomb, C. and Novy, J., eds, 2016. *Protest and Resistance in the Tourist City.* London and New York: Routledge. Available from: www.taylorandfrancis.com/books/details/9781138856714/ [accessed 9 February 2016].

De Angelis, M., 2007. *The Beginning of History: Value Struggles and Global Capital.* London: Pluto Press.

Dellenbaugh, M. *et al.*, eds, 2015. *Urban Commons: Moving Beyond State and Market.* Gütersloh and Basel: Birkhäuser.

Echanove, M. and Srivastava, R., 2014. *The Slum Outside Elusive Dharavi.* Moscow: Strelka Press.

Evans, G., 2009. Creative cities, creative spaces and urban policy. *Urban Studies*, 46 (5–6), 1003–1040.

Fabian, L. and Samson, K., 2016. Claiming participation: a comparative analysis of DIY urbanism in Denmark. *Journal of Urbanism: International Research on Placemaking and Urban Sustainability*, 9 (2), 166–184.

Florida, R., 2004. *The Rise of the Creative Class: And How It's Transforming Work, Leisure, Community and Everyday Life.* New York: Basic Books.

Florida, R., 2014. *The Rise of the Creative Class, Revisited.* New York: Basic Books.

Frenzel, F., 2014a. Should Dharavi be ashamed of itself? URBZ [online]. Available from: http://urbz.net/slum-tourism/ [accessed 1 July 2015].

Frenzel, F., 2014b. Slum tourism and urban regeneration: touring inner Johannesburg. *Urban Forum*, 25 (4), 431–447.

Frenzel, F., 2016. *Slumming It: The Tourist Valorization of Urban Poverty.* London: Zed Books.

Frenzel, F., 2017. Tourist agency as valorisation: making Dharavi into a tourist attraction. *Annals of Tourism Research*, 66, 159–169.

Frenzel, F. and Beverungen, A., 2014. Value struggles in the creative city: A People's Republic of Stokes Croft? *Urban Studies*, 52 (6), 1020–1036.

Freytag, T. and Bauder, M., 2018. Bottom-up touristification and urban transformations in Paris. *Tourism Geographies*, 20 (3), 443–460.

Gill, R. and Pratt, A., 2008. In the social factory? Immaterial labour, precariousness and cultural work. *Theory, Culture & Society*, 25 (7–8), 1–30.

Gotham, K.F., 2005. Tourism gentrification: the case of New Orleans' Vieux Carre (French Quarter). *Urban Studies*, 42 (7), 1099–1121.

Gregory, J.J., 2016. Creative industries and urban regeneration: the Maboneng precinct, Johannesburg. *Local Economy*, 31 (1–2), 158–171.

Hardt, M. and Negri, A., 2009. *Commonwealth*. Cambridge, MA: Belknap Press of Harvard University Press.

Harvey, D., 2001. *Spaces of Capital: Towards a Critical Geography*. New York: Routledge.

Harvey, D., 2012. *Rebel Cities: From the Right to the City to the Urban Revolution*. New York: Verso.

Harvie, D. and Milburn, K., 2010. How organizations value and how value organizes. *Organization*, 17 (5), 631–636.

Holloway, J., 2002. *Change the World Without Taking Power: The Meaning of Revolution Today*. London: Pluto.

Hoogendoorn, G. and Giddy, J.K., 2017. "Does it look like a slum?" Walking tours in the Johannesburg inner city. *Urban Forum*, 28 (3), 1–14.

Hou, J., 2010. *Insurgent Public Space: Guerrilla Urbanism and the Remaking of Contemporary Cities*. London: Routledge.

Hughes, N., 2018. "Tourists go home": anti-tourism industry protest in Barcelona. *Social Movement Studies*, 17 (4), 471–477.

Lash, S. and Urry, J., 1987. *The End of Organized Capitalism*. Madison, WI: University of Wisconsin Press.

Lazzarato, M., 1996. Immaterial labour. *In*: M. Hardt and P. Virno, eds, *Radical Thought in Italy: A Potential Politics*. Minneapolis, MN: University of Minnesota Press, 133–147.

Lees, L.C. and Ferrerai, M., 2016. Resisting gentrification on its final frontiers: learning from the Heygate Estate in London (1974–2013). *Cities*, 57, 14–24.

Lin, J., 2008. Los Angeles Chinatown: tourism, gentrification, and the rise of an ethnic growth machine. *Amerasia Journal*, 34 (3), 110–125.

Lydon, M. and Garcia, A., 2015. *Tactical Urbanism: Short-term Action for Long-term Change*. Washington, DC: Island Press.

Maloutas, T., 2012. Contextual diversity in gentrification research. *Critical Sociology*, 38 (1), 33–48.

Novy, J., 2018. "Destination" Berlin revisited. From (new) tourism towards a pentagon of mobility and place consumption. *Tourism Geographies*, 20 (3), 418–442.

Porter, L. and Shaw, K., 2008. *Whose Urban Renaissance? An International Comparison of Urban Regeneration Strategies*. London: Routledge (Routledge Studies in Human Geography, 27).

Rojek, C., 2010. *The Labour of Leisure: The Culture of Free Time*. London: SAGE.

Shaw, G., Bailey, A. and Williams, A., 2011. Aspects of service-dominant logic and its implications for tourism management: examples from the hotel industry. *Tourism Management*, 32 (2), 207–214.

Shin, H.B., Lees, L. and López-Morales, E., 2016. Introduction: locating gentrification in the Global East. *Urban Studies*, 53 (3), 455–470.

Simoni, V., 2015. *Tourism and Informal Encounters in Cuba*. New York: Berghahn Books.

Smith, N., 2005. *The New Urban Frontier: Gentrification and the Revanchist City*. London: Routledge.

Urbain, J.-D., 2002. *L'idiot du voyage: histoires de touristes*, 2nd ed. Paris: Petite Bibliotheque Payot.

Virno, P., 2004. *A Grammar of the Multitude: For an Analysis of Contemporary Forms of Life*, eds I. Bertoletti, J. Cascaito and A. Casson, trans. S. Lotringer. Los Angeles, CA; Cambridge, MA: Semiotext(e); distributed by MIT Press.

Wacquant, L., 2008. *Urban Outcasts: A Comparative Sociology of Advanced Marginality*. Cambridge: Polity.

Zukin, S., 1987. Gentrification: culture and capital in the urban core. *Annual Review of Sociology*, 13, 129–147. Available from: www.jstor.org/stable/2083243 [accessed 25 October 2011].

5 Escaping the global city?

Gentrification, urban wellness industries and the exotic-mundane

Jessica Parish

Introduction

This chapter draws on the tension between the local and the 'elsewhere' in contemporary urban tourism. As other contributions to this volume show, binaries between the resident and the tourist and between everyday life and extraordinary experience in the theory and practice of tourism exhibit 'increasing de-differentiation' (Urry 1995, Stors *et al.*, Chapter 1 in this volume). In this chapter, I draw on a case study of a gentrifying neighbourhood in West Toronto that has recently surfaced as both: an eminently desirable place for young professional families to acquire property, as well as an exemplary 'off the beaten track' (Füller and Michel 2014) tourist destination where visitors can blend in with young, hip "stroller pushing locals" (Kaminer 2011).

The surfacing of this neighbourhood as a place where visitors can participate in a rejuvenated vision of everyday life is an important context shaping the specific character of gentrification in the area (Parish 2017). However, this case study further emphasises a form of everyday escape to 'elsewhere' that is offered, ordinarily, to residents. As part of the broader gentrification process, the neighbourhood has recently seen a dramatic growth in what I call the 'new wellness industries'.[1] The appearance of costly and exclusive health and wellness consumption in the historically working-class neighbourhood of Parkdale is contemporaneous with the gentrification of the area. Through this process, the northern part of the neighbourhood has emerged as a distinct area (Valverde 2012) known variously as Roncy, Roncesvalles and Roncesvalles Village, and known by some as definitely "not [any longer] Parkdale" (MacKinnon 1999; see also Parish 2017).

Roncesvalles is now represented in mainstream media and everyday discourse as hip, white and middle class, while the more southern part is racialised as low-income and "multicultural" (Teelucksingh 2002, p. 132). Following the work of sociologist John Urry (1995), I pay particular attention to the reorganisation of space and time in the production and reproduction of 'consuming places' in these developments. On the one hand, the neighbourhood itself is presented as more laid-back and village-like than the rest of the city of which it is a part. On the other hand, the new wellness industries, which have proliferated in the context of intensified gentrification of the neighbourhood, promise the ability to get away from it all if only for an hour or two, to recover from the hectic pace of Toronto's urban everyday life through the consumption of exotifying wellness services.

New and re-emergent forms of health and self-care include yoga and Pilates services, naturopathic and holistic care clinics, day spas, nutritionists and healthy eating consultants, and so forth. Many of these modalities fall into the category of what are referred to as forms of complementary and alternative medicine (CAM). Indeed, observers in a range of fields have noted that a renaissance of alternative medicine is afoot (Achilles *et al.* 1999, Barcan 2011, Collyer 2004, Eisenberg *et al.* 1993, Esmail 2007, Ramsay 2009, Ross 2012). In Ontario, these modalities largely fall outside of the publically insured system, and must be paid for either out of pocket, or through employment-related insurance. As such, the growth and normalisation of the new wellness industries in the urban landscape is part of a broader privatisation of health care that raises new questions of access.

This research draws on a larger project that examines how the urban is problematised in relation to health in the twenty-first century. In order to document changes to the neighbourhood—defined in my study as broadly encompassing areas known as South Parkdale and Roncesvalles—the empirical dimension of my study relied on three main strategies: in-depth interviews with local health and wellness practitioners, targeted archival research, and discourse analysis of promotional materials such as websites as well as storefront signage, by using photography and observations in situ. The research focused on a roughly one-kilometre stretch of the three main commercial streets running through these areas: Roncesvalles Avenue, Queen Street and King Street. By visiting these areas, I documented the addresses of health and wellness organisations and used this information to cross-reference historical business directory listings, since the late 1980s. This allowed me to learn when current businesses were established as well as what preceded those businesses in the time period selected. Further, I conducted a scan of business names along the same streets and over the same period in order to reconstruct an image of the changing health and wellness landscape of these streets more broadly. This also allowed me to control for the possibility of, for example, a business moving locations, rather than newly starting up or closing down.

I further conducted a set of in-depth semi-structured interviews with health and wellness practitioners, to learn about their perceptions of the changing neighbourhood and the place of health and well-being within that. Finally, analysis of websites and other promotional materials allowed me to understand the density of offerings (i.e., how many practitioners at a given address?), as well as to analyse and make inferences about how and to whom these products and services are offered.

The analysis aims at understanding, first, what kinds of subjects of health are produced in these spatial practices, and second, in what ways contemporary wellness practices conform to or contest dominant problematisations of urban space and its relationship to health. I argue that even as the formerly working-class neighbourhood is re-emerging as a tourist destination (Condevaux *et al.* 2016), these new additions to the neighbourhood promise a temporary escape from the stresses and strains of everyday life in the capitalist metropolis. In brief, the new wellness industries in Toronto offer the opportunity to escape the hectic pace of everyday life in the global city, for a slice of time that can be slotted into the space between paid work and the labours of social reproduction (see, e.g., Katz 2017). In so doing, they draw on gendered and racialised assumptions about the exotic and the mundane in depictions of leisure, work, and the relationship between the two. We can see this, for example, in the gendered reimagining of the 'progress of man' meme that has recently been appropriated by various organisations to claim yoga as the latest and highest stage of 'evolution'. Figure 5.1, taken from a t-shirt produced by the US-based Spreadshirt company, shows an explicitly gendered version of this meme wherein a career woman is superseded by a woman in Natarajasana, or 'lord of the dance pose' (*Yoga Journal* 2017).[2]

Here, yoga is explicitly positioned as the highest stage of evolution, coming after the attainment of paid work and careers for white middle-class women. However, the (implicit) promise of wellness practices such as yoga is not the permanent emancipation from the capitalist exploitation of paid and unpaid labour. Rather, it is the creation of an extraordinary space to which to 'escape' and recuperate from the rigours of career life for the purposes of being able to "get up and do it over again tomorrow" (Berlant 2010).

The argument unfolds in three parts, followed by a conclusion. The first provides an overview of the literature and a discussion of the chapter's key theoretical commitments—namely heterotopias (Foucault 1984), and Orientalism (Said 1978) as they pertain to the new wellness industries. In the second section, I introduce the neighbourhood which is the subject of the case

Figure 5.1 Progress of "man".
Source: Spreadshirt 2016, copyright: Dale Keele 2008, reproduced with permission.

study, paying particular attention to recent changes pursuant to 'municipally managed gentrification' (Slater 2004) processes and the subsequent emergence of the neighbourhood as a laid-back urban tourist destination. In the third section, I focus on the discursive strategies of the new wellness industries in the neighbourhood to show how, even within this 'village-like' neighbourhood, escaping to an exotic elsewhere is presented as integral to everyday life and social reproduction.

Heterotopias, the exotic mundane and urban tourism in the twenty-first century

The newness of the *new urban tourism* arises, in part, from the long-standing preference of bourgeois and aristocratic classes for non-urban settings as ideally suited for rest, relaxation, sport and entertainment (Füller and Michael 2014, Lea 2008, Thorpe 2012, Wall 2009). In the industrial period of capitalist development, the city was regularly maligned as a necessary evil: a crucial node in circuits of production and consumption but also one marked by the spectre of the working urban masses and nineteenth-century theories of degeneracy and contagion associated therewith (Foucault 2000a, 2000b, Lupton 1995, Valverde 1991). The emergence of cities—and working-class areas in particular—as tourist destinations is thus part of a broader reproduction of the urban as a site of leisure and consumption, as its economic base has shifted from industry to service (Condevaux *et al.* 2016, Sassen 2005, Smith 1996, Urry 1995). A preference for 'ordinary' locations within the city thus challenges geographic assumptions about where tourism happens and what counts as a tourist experience.

However, the popularity of urban everyday life as a tourist experience co-exists with a long-standing romantic view of non-urban space as quieter, slower, more authentic and, therefore, healthier (Lea 2008, Little 2013, Matchar 2013). Indeed, this nostalgia for a simpler time is also implicated in the production of differentiated space within cities as well: consider, for example, the significance of farmers' markets and the fetish for all things 'local' and 'handmade' in contemporary processes of gentrification (Gray 2013, Kern 2015a, Sharzer 2012, Zukin 2008). These experiences, too, may be sought out as highly desirable urban tourist experiences. Forms of non-urban 'nature' tourism therefore exist alongside the *new urban tourism* and may even have much in common with it.

Scientific research into how and why 'reconnecting' with nature may produce specific health and well-being benefits is distinctively contemporary, drawing, for example, on developments in psychological and neurological research (Kler 2009, Smith 2017). However, the practice of 'retreating to nature' has a long history in Canada and elsewhere (Lea 2008, Thorpe 2012). For instance, in Canada, the practice of sending children to wilderness camps was an important part of the reproduction of class identities in the late nineteenth and early twentieth centuries (Valverde 1991, Wall 2009).

For the children of the wealthier classes, the physically remote summer wilderness camp was a place where leadership skills were inculcated and lifelong relationships with other members of the elite were nurtured (Wall 2009). For the children of poor households who had neither the time nor means for long-distance train travel, nineteenth- and early twentieth-century philanthropists raised money for 'fresh air camps' a short distance from the hustle and bustle of the city (Wall 2009). As environmental historian Jocelyn Thorpe (2012, p. 63) explains, promoters advertised the more distant Canadian north to wealthy travellers as:

> a place where tourists could escape the forward movement of time and access both traces of a past era and the nostalgia associated with its erasure. [...] As one [travel] writer put it, a wilderness vacation allowed 'the brain fagged, nerve-racked, denizens of our great cities' to recover from 'the hurry and worry of the ten months' grind in the treadmill of business life so that they might return to work with 'added zest and vim'.

Retreating to nature, then, is a practice that draws on the medical and sociological problematisations of urban everyday life. The therapeutic time-space is seen to be distinct from, and other to, the time-space of everyday life in the capitalist metropolis.

The recuperative and restorative capacities of 'retreating to nature' are well documented in the environmental psychology and therapeutic landscapes literatures. A number of studies have now shown that contact with 'nature', and especially 'forest environments', is "beneficial to human well-being and comfort" (Komppula *et al.* 2017, p. 120; see also Kler 2009, Leiper 2017, Louv 2009). Discourses which position contemporary urban life as characterised by a general lack of connection to nature and its potential health-giving benefits abound. They are perhaps best exemplified by the notion of "nature deficit disorder" (NDD) (Louv 2009). Rather than describing a specific medical disorder, NDD makes a broader claim about a general condition of alienation from nature and the 'human costs' thereof (Smith 2017). As Komppula *et al.* (2017, p. 120) write, wilderness tourism is frequently presented as a counterpart to "hectic urban life where visitors can enjoy peace and quiet and have space to breathe".

Similarly, the concept of therapeutic landscapes aims to describe and evaluate the extent to which spending time or undertaking activities in specific landscapes can produce tangible therapeutic outcomes. According to Lea (2008), therapeutic retreats "are characteristically located in 'aesthetically pleasing [and] environmentally lush' surroundings" which allow people to take a break away from everyday life and "re-connect with the quietness and stillness within ourselves, qualities that are often overshadowed by the demands of our busy everyday lives" (p. 95, citing interview participant). Likewise, in her research on rural spa retreats in the UK, geographer Jo Little (2013) finds that women, in particular, are increasingly "seeking 'time out' from busy lives in which they are frequently juggling responsibilities at home, at work and with friends, time in which to recover from the stress involved in managing the multiple demands placed upon them" (p. 43).

The literature on the new wellness industries has noted the persistence of Orientalism, but is divided on how to interpret the phenomenon. On the one hand, some see a form of 'medical pluralism' (Cant and Sharma 1999) in which different systems of belief and modes of being in the world are finally able to exist on more or less equal ground (Barcan 2011, Harrington 2008, Hoyez 2007, Klassen 2011). Others see the booming North American uptake of eastern well-being practices such as yoga, Ayurveda and Traditional Chinese Medicine as fundamentally connected to the availability of long-standing Orientalist tropes as an important part of the broader reproduction of race and class privilege in the twenty-first century (Lavrence and Lozanski 2014, Reddy 2004). With respect to yoga, there is even a whole journal, founded by graduate students at the University of California, Berkeley, devoted to the subjects of cultural appropriation and racialised exclusion from the North American incarnation of this practice (Race and Yoga 2018).

Orientalism describes a geographic imagination, based in expert discourses, that domesticates the people and places of the 'East' for European consumption. It is a mode of organising racialised and gendered knowledge-power, a concept that describes a European way of imagining, speaking and writing about the Orient in a way that presumes familiarity and therefore authority, power and worldliness. The Orientalist presumes to rescue the Orient "from the obscurity, alienation, and strangeness which he himself had properly distinguished" (Said 1978, p. 121). This 'obscurity' is simultaneously spatial and temporal in character. The Orient was understood as both geographically East and temporally 'backwards'. Outside of 'modernity', it inhabited what post-colonial scholar Anne McClintock (1995) has referred to as 'anachronistic space', or space which exists at an earlier moment in the linear progression of 'world history'. Thus, in travelling—and colonising—the globe, Europe can behold an image of itself at an earlier moment of development (McClintock 1995, Said 1978).

Historian of science Anne Harrington (2008) sees the contemporary popularity of Orientalist health services as emerging in response to what she calls the 'broken by modern life' narrative. Foundational to this narrative is the importation of the notion of 'stress' from metallurgy to physiology, circa 1970. This new notion of stress came to complement long-standing discourses and ideas pertaining to the deleterious effects of modernity and urban life on the body, mind and soul.[3] Harrington argues that another narrative, which she calls 'Eastward journeys', emerged as a neo-Orientalist 'balm' or antidote to the diagnosis offered in 'broken by modern life'. For Harrington, this neo-Orientalism entailed a 'moral inversion' relative to older forms of Orientalism, which historically played a key role in "advancing European colonialist and imperialist agendas" (2008, p. 208). As Harrington explains:

[s]till stylized, still exoticizing, this new, more romantic form of Orientalism used idealized images of the East to highlight Western moral and spiritual failings... By the second half of the twentieth century, as colonialism became a shameful legacy and Western cultures continued to grow more ambivalent about their modern values and lifestyles the romantic variant of Orientalism—an Orientalism dominated by visions of ancient teachers, texts filled with occult secrets, meditating monks on misty mountain tops and serene sanctuaries—gained a new lease on life, especially within alternative counter cultural circles.

(p. 208)

Likewise, communications scholar Sita Reddy (2004) shows how in the contemporary US, Indian Ayurveda is explicitly marketed as "a haven, an island of gentle breezes and calm sanity in this world of increasing violence, chaos and overmedication" (p. 219, citing *New Times*). Here, "educated liberal environmentalists [...] looking towards the East for an antidote to Western materialism and the stress created by capitalist life" (Reddy 2004, p. 217) constitute a core demographic.

Agents of the British Empire once set out to 'save' Eastern subjects through Christianisation. Today, "vague, homogenizing and orientalist concepts of Eastern spiritualties" (Lavrence and Lozanski 2014, p. 76) are increasingly positioned as holding the potential to 'save' the stressed-out subject of 'Western' capitalism. The CEO of Canadian billion-dollar yoga apparel brand *lululemon*, has even gone so far as to suggest that yoga can "elevate the world" (Christine Day 2012, cited in Lavrence and Lozanski 2014, p. 77). This is a paradigmatic example of the neo-liberalisation of health and the environment as they are moved "out of the collective public realm into the private, individualized arena of the market, where profits can be made by trading on consumers' desires and anxieties" (Power 2016, p. 56). It offers "the opportunity to consume with distinction", to purchase an epistemic and embodied distance from forms of mainstream consumption associated with "ill health, poverty and obesity" (Johnston 2008, cited in Power 2016, pp. 56–57).

French intellectual and historian of 'systems of thought' Michel Foucault used the term 'heterotopia' to name the spaces that are produced in order to be Other, or counter to, the dominant order of society. As he explained, heterotopias are different from utopias because "utopias are sites with no real place" (1984, p. 3). Utopias are "sites that have a general relation of direct or inverted analogy with the real space of society. They present society itself in a perfected form, or else society turned upside down, but in any case these utopias are fundamentally unreal spaces" (Foucault 1984, p. 3). At the same time, however, there are really existing sites that reflect society back onto itself:

There are also, probably in every culture, in every civilization, real places—places that do exist and that are formed in the very founding of society— which are something like counter-sites, a kind of effectively enacted utopia in which the real sites, all the other real sites that can be found within the culture, are simultaneously represented, contested, and inverted. Places of this kind are outside of all places, even though it may be possible to indicate their location in reality. Because these places are absolutely different from all the sites that they reflect and speak about, I shall call them, by way of contrast to utopias, heterotopias.

(Foucault 1984, pp. 3–4)

Foucault argued that historically there were two main types of heterotopia—heterotopias of crisis and heterotopias of deviance—but that in the twentieth century these two typologies were becoming less and less distinguishable from one another. By creating specialised spaces for recuperation embedded in the urban fabric, spaces such as the yoga studio and the spa simultaneously contest and make possible the economically productive work that sustains neoliberal capitalism. As MacDonald (2017) points out, in the 'creative city' one person's space of leisure and recuperation is often the location of another's low-paying, precarious job.

Expert knowledge—whether neurological, child developmental or anthropological—while powerful, is never neutral or objective. Rather, these forms of knowledge-power and modes of knowing and acting on the body are implicated in broader historical processes and political struggles (Foucault 1990, Lemke 2011, Osborne 1997, Rose 2001). From a feminist political economy perspective, what is being restored or reproduced is not simply a state of subjective well-being, however important this may be.[4] What is also being reproduced is the capacity for paid and unpaid work, and the raced, classed and geographically differentiated labour force upon which neoliberal capitalism depends (Katz 2017).

Destination Toronto: the 'city of neighbourhoods' as tourist desire

The emergence of Toronto and its residential neighbourhoods as tourist destinations is a product of broader processes, including a shift from manufacturing to services as the economic base of cities (Sassen 2005, Smith 1996), and a shifting spatial politics of race and class. Both of these are bound up with the near wholesale gentrification of the urban core in Canadian cities such as Toronto and Vancouver (Kern 2010, Ley 1996, Murray 2015, Parish 2017, Slater 2004). Under the influence of economic theories such as those of the 'creative class' (Florida 2002), and with the aid of federal immigration policies which heavily favour the mobility of the race and class privileged (Abu-Laban and Gabriel 2002), cities such as Toronto have sought to position themselves as 'magnets' (City of Toronto 2003) both for tourist dollars and for internationally mobile workers, including the so-called 'creative class' (Figueroa *et al.* 2017, Parish 2007) and the 'business class' produced through Canadian immigration policies (Abu-Laban and Gabriel 2002). In the twenty-first century the global competition for tourist dollars and distinction has been drilled down to the neighbourhood scale (Valverde 2012). With the encouragement of national and city governments, these local geographies of everyday life are increasingly engaged in forms of competitive place-branding (Blomley 2004, MacDonald 2017). However, implicit in the practices of 'ranking' neighbourhoods and other modes of normalising distinction is the logic of winners and losers (Parish 2017, Valverde 2012). Officially, the City of Toronto is divided into 140 contiguous neighbourhoods for planning and administrative purposes. But which of these neighbourhoods will surface as desirable urban tourist destinations, and why?[5]

The case of the West Toronto neighbourhood of Roncy is illustrative. In 2012 the neighbourhood, formerly understood as part of the historic-ally working-class neighbourhood of Parkdale (e.g., Dunkleman 1997, MacKinnon 1999), emerged as both a discrete neighbourhood and an ideal 'off the beaten track' tourism destination. Situated in the south-west of Toronto, the area is among the most income polarised in the central city. The area has a long history of working-class stigmatisation (Whitzman 2009, Slater 2004), following the de-institutionalisation of several thousand psychiatric patients in the 1970s 'social services ghetto' (Dear and Wolch 1987). The neighbourhood is also characterised by high levels of social solidarity and activism, having been the site of squatters' protests, and a recent rent strike by low income and racialised residents in protest of rent hikes in chronically under-maintained units (Sweetman 2011, Shum 2017). Like many gentrifying neighbourhoods, the area is also home to a wide and growing array of private health and well-being services and commodities (Kern 2012, Parish 2017).

While there is a large literature tracing the gentrification of Parkdale (e.g., Mazer and Rankin 2011, Slater 2004, Teelucksingh 2002, Whitzman 2009), no such literature exists for Roncesvalles. This is at least partly because wider, international cache of Roncesvalles as a distinct neighbourhood and tourist destination and uniquely 'authentic' (Zukin 2008, Zukin *et al.* 2009) place is a novel twenty-first-century creation. It follows a major three-year infrastruc-ture redevelopment project (2009–2011), to replace the streetcar tracks and water mains on the main street, Roncesvalles Avenue, and the concerted place promoting efforts of property developers and real estate agents in the 1990s and 2000s (Parish 2017, Whitzman 2009).

The infrastructure reconstruction is especially significant because it provided the local Business Improvement Association (BIA) with an oppor-tunity to advocate for a significant beautification project to be piggybacked onto the infrastructure redevelopment. As a result, the one-kilometre stretch that is the main street was endowed with twenty-one new flower gardens and some 100 new street trees. As reported in the *Toronto Star*, members of the local BIA, as well as the local city councillor, believed that a "pedestrian, cyclist and transit-user friendly street is the way to go" and could trans-form Roncesvalles "into a 'model village', a paradise for pedestrians, cyclists and shop owners alike" (Baute 2009). Further, it had the added advantage of fulfilling the imperative to be green: "And above all else, they say the street must be green" (Baute 2009). In addition to capturing these opportunities, Roncesvalles Renewed established a "'buy local' campaign to help our businesses survive this major reconstruction of Roncesvalles" (Veroncy 2014). The beautification project was made possible through a mix of city and national government funding, partnerships with locally based organisations, and forms of unpaid volunteer labour (Baute 2009, Parish 2017).

While public discourse centred on enhancing amenities for residents and enabling local businesses to survive a prolonged period of construction-related interruptions, Roncesvalles Village subsequently emerged as a local and global tourist destination the spring after the reconstruction of its main street was completed. Subsequently, the area surfaced as a 'leafy', 'tree-lined', 'low slung' place to while away a day shopping and sipping lattes. The area was featured, first in the *New York Times* travel section, where it was christened as "one of Toronto's most engaging strolls" (Kaminer 2011), and later in Toronto-based *Porter Airlines'* inflight magazine (Freed 2016). In both of these publications, the neighbourhood is depicted both as an ideal 'off the beaten track' tourist destination. Furthermore, in these and other forums the specific desirability of Roncesvalles emerges from its 'low slung small village in a big city feel': tucked away from the hustle and bustle of the city and just a little bit closer to nature.[6]

When British bourgeois lifestyle publication *Monocle* published its Toronto edition of their tourist guide series in 2016 (2016a), the city joined the growing ranks of urban destinations such as London, New York and Copenhagen as cities where quality of lifestyle connoisseurs can "make the most" of a visit by "feeling like a resident rather than a tourist" (*Monocle* 2016b). With an almost exclusively urban focus, the *Monocle* travel guide series is both a product and producer of *new urban tourism*. The company describes its travel guide series as one that "cuts through the hype and offers you real experiences" (2016c). Among the features the guides boast as being key to 'authentic' urban experiences are the "neighbourhood walks to get you away from the crowds" (*Monocle* 2016b). The Toronto guide features just five of the City's 140 neighbourhoods as especially worthy of and conducive to this brand of new urban/lifestyle tourism. Here again, Roncesvalles was singled out as noteworthy for its small-town feel. As the authors correctly note: "It's an odd quirk of Toronto that so many neighbourhoods bill themselves as villages, regardless of historical fact" (*Monocle* 2016a, p. 134). Nevertheless, they continue:

> Roncesvalles—Roncy for short—at least feels more so than most. [...] its main artery [Roncesvalles Avenue] has the air of a village high street; it's almost defiantly local and mostly free of big-name retailers. The area is also partly insulated from Toronto's bustle: south is Lake Ontario and to its west is the forest of High Park which at 161 hectares is the city's largest green space. [...] The community has been getting younger and more

diversified. Young families are drawn to the well-tended Victorian homes, amenities and quick commute downtown. Many of these newcomers have opened boutiques and restaurants that are bringing life to some of the areas more neglected corners. When people refer to Toronto's superior liveability, Roncy's the kind of area they're thinking about.

(*Monocle* 2016a, p. 134)[7]

Given Roncy's newfound acclaim as an ideally leafy, laid-back and liveable neighbourhood, it is curious that the proliferation of the new wellness industries and the distinctly natural aesthetic that accompanies them has gone largely unremarked on in these various publications. The neighbourhood is indeed becoming more boutique, as costs rise and the Polish bakeries and delis established by first-generation immigrants are closing down in response to falling profits and changing tastes of consumers (Mejia 2011).[8] As that happens, new storefront space becomes available, and increasingly, wellness organisations take their place as street-level, storefront shops and boutiques. This has the effect of visibly altering the streetscape, such that the presence of an array of therapeutic offerings has become an integral part of the shopping district and the shopping experience.

Escaping the global city: urban wellness industries in the twenty-first century

In addition to the changes associated with gentrification discussed above, the Roncesvalles area has, in recent years, seen the commercial landscape change in ways that privilege different forms of consumption than in the past. The growth of private 'holistic', 'natural' and 'alternative' health and wellness services has brought changes to the landscape that constitute an important and overlooked aspect of the specificity of the 'consuming place' (Urry 1995) that is twenty-first-century Roncesvalles. This is evident in both a quantitative shift in terms of the growing number of health commodities on offer, and the qualitative changes this brings to the streetscape. Concerning the latter, the use of naturalist and Orientalist discourses and images is noteworthy.

The late 1980s marked an important shift in the streetscape of services. In 1988 'Otani', a Shiatsu massage therapy organisation opened its doors in a small suburban drive-up plaza at the south end of Roncesvalles Avenue. The following year a medical doctor trained in Poland established 'Health From Nature' (Figure 5.2), a natural health products store, as a stand-alone storefront across the street from Otani. Otani and Health From Nature represented a new type of health service appearing in the midst of more mainstream health institutions at the south end of Roncesvalles, which include a retirement lodge, a medical arts building and a hospital. In the case of Health From Nature, the large flower mural covering its south-facing window also represents the emergence of a significant departure from the more clinical aesthetic of the surrounding establishments.

Figure 5.2 Boutiquing natural health.
Source: © photo by Jessica Parish, 2012, with permission from Health from Nature.

A detailed search of historical business directory listings held at the City of Toronto archives reveals that, as of the spring of 2016, of the eighteen new wellness organisations that existed in Roncesvalles, fourteen had been established since the year 2000. Moreover, the organisations established prior to 2000 tend to be located near the edges of Roncesvalles Avenue, in medical offices without storefronts and associated signage. The post-2000 emergence of these kinds of organisations in the more central part of the Roncesvalles strip constitutes a migration out of the medical arts-type building and into the street-level shopping area. Whereas in the 1980s an office tower/medical arts building would house numerous service providers at a single address, few if any of these would be 'alternative' health providers. Today, the converse is true. Storefronts in prime, street-level commercial space are home to alternative providers, and many such addresses boast numerous different practitioners and modalities. Most illustrative is the Village Healing Centre, which rents unused space from a large United Church. In addition to yoga and qui gong classes, the centre boasts some twenty healing practices including acupuncture, Ayurveda, naturopathy, reiki and massage therapy, as well as twenty-seven varieties of counselling services, including art therapy, life coaching, registered psychologist services and spiritual counselling.[9]

Further qualitative changes to the street and the place of the new wellness industries therein include a discernible shift away from working-class and ethnic-oriented, especially Polish/Eastern European services, and towards luxury and boutique-style offerings. Indeed, while the Polish community reached its demographic apex in the post-war period, the area's annual Polish Festival was established in 2005. Like other Toronto neighbourhoods, the 'ethnic' identity of a gentrifying neighbourhood is commodified precisely at the time when the demographic reality of ethnic concentration is in decline (Hackworth and Rekers 2005). The new, street-level presence of the wellness industries that has emerged in the meantime contributes to and plays upon a naturalist and at times Orientalist aesthetic sensibility (Said 1978). Ethnic-oriented and working-class shops and services such as used furniture shops and used clothing stores, the Polish Chamber of Commerce, a discount hair salon, a bulk food store and a dollar store have closed down or left. They have been replaced by businesses with quaint and exotic names like 'Ecotique', 'All One Holistic Clinic' and 'Qi Natural Foods'.

Even when wellness services and natural consumerism take the place of other health services, there is a shift in the substance of the offerings as well as in their discursive presentation. For example, around the year 2002 the Sanskrit-named 'Sukha Spa' (Figure 5.3) replaced a dental practice publicly listed as 'W. Matulak, DDS [Doctor of Dental Surgery]'. Sukha Spa offers a range of services, including massage therapy, acupuncture and facial treatments in a luxury day-spa environment. Similarly, the address of the pragmatically named 'Disability to Function Rehabilitation & Physiotherapy' has been, since 2013, the home of the exotically named 'Damask Studios'. Damask offers yoga, Pilates and fitness classes, as well as the services of a naturopathic doctor. Both of these newer establishments lay claim to 'the East' in naming and other discursive strategies. For example, Sukha Spa includes the Sanskrit rendering of its name on its signage, which, as the website explains, translates to "a state of happiness from within" (Sukha Spa 2015). Similarly, Damask invokes a reference to a type of weaving and a style of tapestry produced in, and traded through, Damascus on the Silk Road.

In South Parkdale, the typical signage announcing health products and services is qualitatively different. It is relatively unadorned and in plain text/font and names the health service(s) that are available are listed with few if any images or graphics. For example, a physiotherapy clinic in South Parkdale makes additional reference to the forms of insurance with which it is compatible: "Treatments covered by OHIP; WSIB; EHC/Private Insurance; MVA" (i.e., Ontario Health Insurance Plan; Workplace Safety & Insurance Board; Extended Health Care; Motor Vehicle Accident).[10] By contrast, in Roncesvalles Village, and especially along the main thoroughfare of

Roncesvalles Avenue, what is most notable are the references to nature, in images, words or both, as well as the biopolitical valued added claims that are made or implied. In addition to the word 'nature' and its derivatives, one of the more common references to nature are representations of lotus flowers. At times, these images are highly stylised and designed storefront business logos, suggesting a kind of meeting of ancient wisdoms and modern technology. Other times the image may take the form of a graffiti stencil or a stock photo imported into a more modestly designed poster stapled to a street post. Thus, aesthetically these small gestures of naming and claiming space align with broader practices that normalise the competitive neoliberal drive for neighbourhood distinction.

For example, Sukha Spa combines images of stonecrop and lotus flowers with the injunction to "live younger, longer". Figure 5.3 shows two exterior signs at Sukha Spa. The first (foreground) depicts a stonecrop plant. The second (background) bears a hand-drawn lotus flower near the bottom. The sign reads: "Éminence Products!!/Esthetics/Registered Massage Therapy/ Acupuncture". As the sign suggests, Sukha Spa offers alternative health services, as well as Éminence, a line of "natural, organic and biodynamic" skin care products from Budapest, a city where "East meets West" (Éminence Organic Skin Care 2012). Furthermore, "the key to living a happy and fulfilling life begins with good health. This means taking time for yourself.

Figure 5.3 "Live younger, longer".
Source: © photo by Jessica Parish, 2012, with permission from Sukha Spa.

Addressing your own needs now and then" (Sukha Spa 2012). Potential clients are invited to:

> [c]ome to our haven, and take a break from the outside world. Let us ease your aches and pains with massage therapy and Chinese medicine. Let us pamper your skin with decadent facials using the finest natural products. Revitalize your body and soul and we will take care of you. You deserve it.
>
> (Sukha Spa 2012)

Sukha Spa further emphasises its location in the 'heart' of Roncesvalles Village, perhaps suggesting a safe distance from its more working-class edges:

> Sukha Spa is a boutique spa located in the heart of Roncesvalles Village in Toronto, Canada. The spa operates in an Edwardian home built in the late 1800s. Our atmosphere is relaxed, warm and inviting. Sukha Spa prides itself on being a safe haven for our clients. We offer a unique, personal and caring experience to each of our guests. Enjoy your Sukha experience, we look forward to welcoming you. Live Younger, Longer.
>
> (Sukha Spa 2015)[11]

These references to "taking a break from the outside world" in a "safe haven" construct the space as a therapeutic retreat from the hectic pace of urban capitalist life (Little 2013). Meanwhile, the Orientalist tropes serve to underline the Otherness of the time-space of the spa relative to its broader environment. This Othering presents itself as unproblematic, and even 'good', in ways that are consistent with the moral inversion described by Harrington. However, evidence of the harsh realities of capitalism presumably includes the slow erasure (Kern 2015b) of the neighbourhood's former identity as a working-class Polish area with a local industrial employment base. The references to safety and care also serve to affirm that Sukha is the right kind of spa; one where 'therapeutic' benefits can be sought and obtained. Furthermore, in the pastiche of references to the 'East'—acupuncture, a Chinese therapeutic art; Sanskrit, a South Asian script; and Budapest, the capital of a former Soviet Bloc country—we see an exemplary instance of Orientalism as 'vague and homogenizing' (Lavrence and Lozanski 2014). Physical, cultural, religious and historical differences are erased. What matters is an exotified Otherness that *makes sense* as a space of luxury and escape for the race and class privileged subjects of health to whom the marketing speaks.

There is, however, nothing inevitable about the use of an Orientalist motif in the new wellness organisations, whether or not the proprietors happen to be migrants from the East. Established in the late 1980s, Japanese-owned Otani Shiatsu Clinic was one of the first 'alternative' health providers on Roncesvalles. Today this organisation is somewhat exceptional, both for the absence of an obvious emphasis on nature, trees and green consumption, and for the absence of the 'luxury theme' that is now prevalent within the new wellness organisations. The remarks of one Yelp reviewer are particularly instructive in highlighting how this establishment differs from the new mainstream in the neighbourhood. The reviewer writes: "No frills and the price is right. The owner is Japanese as are many of the masseurs. Think old school 70s Japan Ma & Pa shop... no Zen theme luxury decorator touches. A Roncesvalles staple for at least 15 years or more" (Meems 2012). In other words, this reviewer appears to be recommending the establishment based on the absence of Orientalist techniques—coded as "Zen theme luxury décor touches"—for producing a therapeutic experience. Further, the writer suggests that the creation of Orientalist experiences also leads to a higher price tag for services.[12]

What the spatio-temporal dynamics highlighted here amount to is a sustained effort to produce, in a material sense, a 'natural' world that extends from the interior arrangement of a wellness organisation to the exterior world of the streetscape. The production of this 'heterotopic Other space' (Foucault 1984) to capitalist urbanism relies in important ways on Orientalist tropes to produce a spatial and temporal experience that is different, and therefore an escape from the space and the temporality of capitalist urbanism. The effect, if not the intent, is the appropriation of an entire life world for urban capitalist production and social reproduction. While this is often presented as a technique of diversity, or at least as practices which conform to broader governmental consensus around the importance of diversity in a globally competitive economy (Abu-Laban and Gabriel 2002, Blomley 2004, Valverde 2012), these processes are part of a broader homogenisation of ways of living and being in the world, through gentrification.

We can see this in the ways that this process of exotification is integrally bound up with processes of gentrification. A naturopath and owner of wholesale herbal medicine business on Roncesvalles explained:

> It's as easy as saying pre- and post-construction. Because for almost two years [2009–2011] they tore the whole street up and it was incredibly unpleasant. Roncesvalles—the whole neighbourhood—it changed. So, that is a very clearly marked example. Before that, it was less gentrified and post-construction it's increasingly gentrified.
>
> (Anonymous interviewee #1 2015,
> personal communication, 28 March)

This informant noted that rents went up along the street, in some cases doubling. This had the effect of pushing some of the 'older' shops out. In order to cope with these pressures, businesses are self-consciously "boutiquing" themselves (Mazer and Rankin 2011, Zukin 2008). The same informant explained these concerns:

> As the neighbourhood got fancier, we had to—and I also kind of wanted to—have an increasingly nice space. The old junky, junk shop look just doesn't work in this neighbourhood anymore. [Now] we prefer to think of ourselves as a herbal boutique rather than an apothecary.
>
> (Anonymous interviewee #1 2015,
> personal communication, 28 March)

Paradoxically, this process of getting 'fancier' was also identified as a part of trends that actually undermined the therapeutic possibilities to 'take time out' or 'just stop'. One yoga studio owner made the difficult decision to close their business (anonymous interviewee #2 2015, personal communication, 22 April) due to an inability to compete with 'fancier' studios. For this person, yoga had in fact become deeply enmeshed in the fast, competitive pace of contemporary urban life. As the informant put it, people "think they're going to a yoga class, but they're just doing more, more, more in the yoga classes. To me that's not yoga, that's just an extension of the crazy pace of life that we're always trying to keep. Yoga should be a place where you can just stop" (anonymous interviewee #2 2015, personal communication, 22 April). Creating a place to 'just stop' on a daily basis was integral to this person's personal practice; and the inability to run an economically viable yoga studio without adding all of the 'more, more, more' was identified as a key challenge.

This informant noted the way in which both the Roncesvalles neighbourhood as well as the practice of yoga itself had changed:

> When I first started doing yoga a lot of classes were in churches, or in schools, and we'd practice on the wrestling mats. It didn't really matter much what the place was like. What mattered was what we were doing in the class and the surroundings were fairly basic. But now people are putting so much money into building yoga studios and they are creating an atmosphere that's more like a spa. They're adding saunas and change rooms and lockers, and the result is that these days, going to a yoga studio is like going to a high end, boutique gym.
>
> (Anonymous interviewee #2 2015,
> personal communication, 22 April)

Importantly, this informant associates 'spa-likeness' not only with an aesthetic, but also with the scale and variety of health and wellness services and options. They also associate the ability to attract a certain socio-economic demographic with its ability to "pay a bit more", "have a membership", "drive [to the location] and pay for parking" and enjoy "all the other add-ons that go with it" (anonymous interviewee #2 2015, personal communication, 22 April).

This is especially significant in light of Kern's (2015b) work on the temporality of gentrification. Roncesvalles in many ways conforms to the ideal of an 'eventful' and 'happening' neighbourhood identified by Kern. For example, it has a weekly farmers' market and annual street festivals such as 'Roncy

Rocks' and the 'Roncesvalles Polish Festival' (Roncesvalles Village BIA n.d.). However, this other dynamic, that of slowing down, 'pampering' and taking time out to 'recuperate' (Little 2013) is also important, and raises similar questions about who can participate. This aspect of time is also related in important ways to the naturalist (Lea 2008, Little 2013) and Orientalist (Said 1978) tendencies within the wellness industries (Harrington 2008, Lavrence and Lozanski 2014, Reddy 2004). More than being merely 'symptomatic' of broader neoliberal trends, these practices are integral to the social reproduction of urban neoliberalism at both bodily and neighbourhood scales.

Concluding remarks

Roncy has become a hip destination, in part for its relatively 'sheltered' feel. The area is nonetheless home to many neo-Orientalist wellness providers. These establishments draw on notions of an exotified Otherness to produce a time-space experience that is heterotopic to the time-space of twenty-first-century capitalist urbanism. Even though these places have a 'real' and relatively mundane urban location—around the corner from the grocery store, adjacent a residential neighbourhood and so forth, they nevertheless cultivate a spatial aesthetic that aspires to temporarily transport their clients to a place that is 'elsewhere' relative to everyday life. While much writing on nature tourism maintains the city–nature binary, this case study shows that this very binary is used as a technique for producing spaces of recuperation in the very midst of the city which is to be escaped. Furthermore, for those who have access and can otherwise afford them, these practices are increasingly normalised as essential to the daily reproduction of gendered, raced and classed bodies for the imperative of capitalistically productive work. They also tell a complex story about differentiation and de-differentiation of spaces. Even though Roncesvalles has, in some ways, emerged as a quintessential 'off the beaten track' destination it is also a place where long-standing tropes about the clear distinction between 'nature' and the 'city' are reproduced. And, as a gentrifying area of the creative city, it is also a space in and through which highly differentiated categories of workers and consumers are reproduced in relation to one another.

Notes

1 I use the new wellness industries to refer collectively to modalities that are both new and re-emergent. On the one hand, many of the therapeutic modalities of interest here have long histories. Yoga and acupuncture, for example, are disciplines that have been practised for thousands of years. Similarly, even the comparatively 'new' discipline of naturopathy has been practised in North America for over a hundred years. Thus, the term 're-emergent' seems appropriate. At the same time, however, there is a newness that is also important, in that the presence of these disciplines as mainstream services in the urban landscape are a testament to the uniqueness of their contemporary legal, social and cultural status.

2 For a sampling of other popular versions, see www.spreadshirt.com/center+
   evolution+yoga+t-shirts.
3 While Harrington speaks specifically of 'mind-body medicine', I use the formulation 'mind, body, soul' here as a gesture to the ubiquity of this formulation—
   vague and homogenising though it is—in North American yoga culture.
4 Bezanson and Luxton (2006) explicitly acknowledge neo-Foucaultian biopolitics
   perspectives as an under-utilised resource for feminist political ecology (FPE).
5 For an analysis of how tourists contribute to making a neighbourhood attractive,
   see Chapter 4 by Frenzel in this volume.
6 In Chapter 9 of this volume, Kramer, Winsky and Freytag also point to spatio-
   temporal sequences that allow escape and recovery from stressful urban life, such
   as parks or museums. However, they analyse these places of Muße, as they term
   them, concerning their significance for visitors.
7 As an ethnographic aside, when I saw the book for sale at a hip new bakery near
   Parkdale, I asked the woman behind the counter, "Who buys this book—locals,
   or people from out of town?" She replied that many people who purchased
   the book, at least from her, were in fact local neighbourhood residents. She
   explained that this was probably because Toronto is so big and "it's always
   great to discover new places". This remark captures the tension between the
   neighbourhood as a space of social reproduction and the emergence of some
   neighbourhoods as not only highly desirable places to live, but also as highly
   desirable tourist destinations.
8 "[W]e've noticed that desserts aren't as popular as they once were", says Elizabeth
   Klodas of her family's decision to close Granowska's Bakery after thirty-nine
   years in Roncesvalles (cited in Mejia 2011).
9 Information as listed on the website as of March 2016.
10 Physiotherapy and Chiropractic were delisted from the Ontario Health Insurance
   Plan (OHIP) in 2005. Publically insured services are now available only on phys-
   ician recommendation to those under 19 or over 65 years of age, at designated
   pubically funded clinics.
11 The type and character of housing available in Parkdale has been discussed by
   Whitzman (2009), in particular, who emphasises that the area was until recently
   one of the last places in inner Toronto where a Victorian or Edwardian home
   could be purchased by young families—hence Kaminer's (2011) reference to
   homes being "snapped up" by "young creative types". Of course, this aesthetic
   preference also carries raced and classed dimensions, not to mention the gendered
   discourse of "safety" (see Kern, 2010).
12 As of 6 March 2016, a one-hour treatment at Otani was CDN$65 plus taxes (Otani
   2010) compared with Sukha Spa, where a one-hour massage costs CDN$90 plus
   taxes (Sukha Spa 2015).

Acknowledgements

I would like to thank Karen Murray and Leslie Kern for helpful comments on
an earlier iteration of this work. I would also like to thank the editors of this
volume for their comments.

This research was supported by the Social Sciences and Humanities
Research Council of Canada [Grant Number 77522].

References

Abu-Laban, Y. and Gabriel, C. 2002. *Selling Diversity*. Peterborough, Ont.: Broadview Press.

Achilles, R. *et al.*, 1999. *Complementary and Alternative Health Care Practices and Therapies: A Canadian Overview*. Toronto: York University Centre for Health Studies.

Barcan, R., 2011. *Complementary and Alternative Medicine: Bodies, Therapies, Senses*. Oxford: Berg Publishers.

Baute, N., 2009. Roncesvalles gets a remake [online]. *Toronto Star*. Available from: www.thestar.com/news/gta/2009/08/21/roncesvalles_gets_a_remake.html [accessed 5 October 2018].

Berlant, L., 2010. Risky bigness: on obesity, eating and the ambiguity of "health". *In*: J. Metzl and A. Kirkland, eds, *Against Health: How Health Became the New Morality*. New York: New York University Press, 26–39.

Bezanson, K. and Luxton, M., 2006. *Social Reproduction: Feminist Political Economy Challenges Neo-liberalism*. Montreal: McGill-Queen's University Press.

Blomley, N., 2004. *Unsettling the City: Urban Land and the Politics of Property*. New York: Routledge.

Cant, S. and Sharma, U., 1999. *A New Medical Pluralism? Alternative Medicine, Doctors and the State*. New York: Routledge.

City of Toronto, 2003. Culture plan for the creative city, Toronto, City of Toronto [online]. Available from: www.torontocreativecity.ca/wp-content/uploads/2018/02/2003-Culture-Plan-for-the-Creative-City.pdf [accessed 29 November 2018].

Collyer, F. 2004. The corporatization and commercialization of CAM. *In*: P. Tovey, G. Easthope and J. Adams, eds, *The Mainstreaming of Complementary and Alternative Medicine: Studies in Social Context*. London: Routledge, 81–99.

Condevaux, A., Djament-Tran, G. and Gravari-Barbas, M., 2016. Before and after tourism(s). The trajectories of tourist destinations and the role of actors involved in "off-the-beaten-track" tourism: a literature review. *Via Tourism Review* [online], 9 (2016). Available from: https://journals.openedition.org/viatourism/413 [accessed 5 October 2018].

Dear, M. and Wolch, J., 1987. *Landscapes of Despair: From Deinstitutionalization to Homelessness*. Princeton, NJ: Princeton University Press.

Dunkleman, D., 1997. *Your Guide to Toronto's Neighbourhoods*, 1st ed. Toronto: Maple Tree Publishing.

Eisenberg, D.M. *et al.*, 1993. Unconventional medicine in the United States: prevalence, costs and patterns of use (special article). *New England Journal of Medicine*, 328, 246–252.

Éminence Organic Skin Care, 2012. The Facial Room [online]. Available from: www.thefacialroom.ca/page120.htm?gclid=CODpy8aaorQCFcU-%20Mgodd1sANA [accessed 8 December 2012].

Esmail, N., 2007. Complementary and alternative medicine in Canada: trends in use and public attitudes, 1997–2006 (Public Policy Sources No. 87) [online]. Vancouver, The Fraser Institute. Available from: www.fraserinstitute.org/sites/default/files/ComplementaryAlternativeMedicine.pdf [accessed 5 October 2018].

Figueroa, M., Gray, L.S. and Wieditz, T., 2017. Labour and the creative city. *In*: I.T. MacDonald, ed., *Unions and the City*. Ithaca, NY: Cornell University Press, 75–78.

Florida, R., 2002. *The Rise of the Creative Class*. New York: Basic Books.

Foucault, M., 1984. Of other spaces: utopias and heterotopias. *Architecture/ Mouvement/Continuité*, 5 (October), 1–9.

Foucault, M., 1990. *The Will to Knowledge: The History of Sexuality*. New York: Vintage Books.

Foucault, M., 2000a. The birth of social medicine. *In*: J. Faubion, ed., *Power: Essential Works of Michel Foucault 1954–1984*, vol. 3. New York: The New Press, 134–156.

Foucault, M., 2000b. The politics of health in the 18th century. *In*: J. Faubion, ed., *Power: Essential Works of Michel Foucault 1954–1984*, vol. 3. New York: The New Press, 90–105.

Freed, J., 2016. A Roncy good time. *re:Porter*, May/June, 7–11.

Füller, H. and Michel, B., 2014. 'Stop being a tourist!' New dynamics of urban tourism in Berlin-Kreuzberg. *International Journal of Urban and Regional Research*, 38 (4), 1308–1318.

Gray, M., 2013. *Labor and the Locavor: The Making of a Comprehensive Food Ethic*. Berkeley, CA: University of California Press.

Hackworth, J. and Rekers, J., 2005. Ethnic packaging and gentrification: the case of four neighbourhoods in Toronto. *Urban Affairs Review*, 41 (2), 211–236.

Harrington, A., 2008. *The Cure Within: A History of Mind Body Medicine*. New York: WW Norton and Company.

Hoyez, A.C., 2007. The 'world of yoga': the production and reproduction of therapeutic landscapes. *Social Science & Medicine*, 65, 112–124.

Kaminer, M., 2011. A low-slung piece of Toronto gains casual-hip cachet. *New York Times Travel*, 9 October [online]. Available from: https://archive.nytimes.com/query.nytimes.com/gst/fullpage-9804E2D81131F93AA35753C1A9679D8B63.html [accessed 5 October 2018].

Katz, C., 2017. Social reproduction. *In*: D. Richardson *et al.*, eds, *The International Encyclopaedia of Geography: People, the Earth, Environment and Technology*. Oxford: Wiley.

Kern, L., 2010. *Sex and the Revitalized City: Gender, Condominium Development and Urban Citizenship*. Vancouver: UBC Press.

Kern, L., 2012. Connecting embodiment, emotion and gentrification: an exploration through the practice of yoga in Toronto. *Emotion, Space and Society*, 5 (1), 27–35.

Kern, L., 2015a. From toxic wreck to crunchy chick: environmental gentrification through the body. *Environment and Planning D: Society and Space*, 33 (1), 67–83.

Kern, L., 2015b. Rhythms of gentrification: eventfulness and slow violence in a happening neighbourhood. *Cultural Geographies*, 23 (3), 441–457.

Klassen, P.E., 2011. *Spirits of Protestantism: Medicine, Healing and Liberal Christianity*. Berkeley, CA: University of California Press.

Kler, B.K., 2009. Tourism and restoration. *In*: J. Tribe, ed., *Philosophical Issues in Tourism*. Bristol: Channel View Publications, 117–134.

Komppula, R., Konu, H. and Vikman, N., 2017. Listening to the sounds of silence: forest-based wellbeing tourism in Finland. *In*: J. Chen and N. Prebenson, eds, *Nature Tourism*. Abingdon: Routledge, 120–130.

Lavrence, C. and Lozanski, K., 2014. 'This is not your practice life': lululemon and the neoliberal governance of the self. *Canadian Review of Sociology*, 51 (1), 76–94.

Lea, J., 2008. Retreating to nature: rethinking 'therapeutic landscapes'. *Area*, 40 (1), 90–98.

Leiper, C., 2017. 'Rewilding' the body in the Anthropocene and our ecological lives work. *Environment and Planning D: Society and Space*, forum on social reproduction [online]. Available from: http://societyandspace.org/2017/11/14/re-wilding-the-body-in-the-anthropocene-and-our-ecological-lives-work/ [accessed 5 October 2018].

Lemke, T., 2011. *Bio-politics: An Advanced Introduction*. New York: New York University Press.

Ley, D., 1996. *The New Middle Class and the Remaking of the Central City*. Oxford: Oxford University Press.

Little, J., 2013. Pampering, well-being and women's bodies in the therapeutic spaces of the spa. *Social and Cultural Geography*, 14 (1), 41–58.

Louv, R., 2009. No more 'nature-deficit disorder': the 'no child left inside' movement. *Psychology Today*, 28 January [online]. Available from: www.psychologytoday.com/ca/blog/people-in-nature/200901/no-more-nature-deficit-disorder [accessed 5 October 2018].

Lupton, D., 1995. *The Imperative of Health: Public Health and the Regulated Body*. London: SAGE.

MacDonald, I.T., ed., 2017. *Unions and the City*. Ithaca, NY: Cornell University Press.

MacKinnon, D., 1999. Toronto infill Victorian-style homes transform gritty site; Upscale project set for former industrial enclave in Parkdale. *The Toronto Star*, 16 October, p. 1.

Matchar, E., 2013. *Homeward Bound: Why Women Are Embracing the New Domesticity*. New York: Simon & Schuster.

Mazer, K. and Rankin, K., 2011. The social space of gentrification: the politics of neighbourhood accessibility in Toronto's downtown west. *Environment and Planning D: Society and Space*, 29 (5), 822–839.

McClintock, A., 1995. *Imperial Leather: Race, Gender and Sexuality in the Colonial Contest*. New York: Routledge.

Meems, C., 2012. Otani Shiatsu Clinic. *Yelp*, 28 November [online]. Available from: www.yelp.ca/biz/otani-shiatsu-clinic-toronto [accessed 5 October 2018].

Mejia, M.L., 2011. Roncesvalles staple Granowska's Bakery to serve its last paczki at the end of the month. *Toronto Life*, 13 December [online]. Available from: http://torontolife.com/food/restaurants/granowskas-to-close/ [accessed 5 October 2018].

Monocle, 2016a. *The Monocle Travel Guide Toronto*. Berlin: Gestalten.

Monocle, 2016b. Books/Travel Guides [online]. Available from: https://monocle.com/shop/books/?page=3 [accessed 5 October 2018].

Monocle, 2016c. Monocle Travel Guides: New York [online]. Available from: https://monocle.com/shop/books/travel-guides/the-monocle-travel-guide-new-york/ [accessed 5 October 2018].

Murray, K., 2015. Bio-gentrification: vulnerability bio-value chains in gentrifying neighbourhoods. *Urban Geography*, 36(2), 277–299.

Osborne, T., 1997. Of health and statecraft. *In*: R. Bunton and A.R. Petersen, eds, *Foucault, Health and Medicine*. London: Routledge, 173–188.

Otani, 2010. About-Rates [online]. Available from: www.otanishiatsuclinic.com/rates.html [accessed 6 July 2016].

Parish, J., 2007. Soup can sublime or why it matters to IR that Andy came to town. Master's thesis, York University.

Parish, J., 2017. The vital politics of gentrification: governing life in urban Canada into the 21st century. PhD thesis, York University.

Power, E., 2016. Fat children, failed (future) consumer citizens, and mothers' duties in neoliberal consumer society. *In*: J. Polzer and E. Power, eds, *Neoliberal Governance and Health: Duties, Risks and Vulnerabilities*. Montreal: McGill-Queens University Press, 43–65.

Race and Yoga, 2018. About [online]. Available from: https://escholarship.org/uc/crg_raceandyoga [accessed 6 October 2018].

Ramsay, C., 2009. Unnatural regulation: complementary and alternative medicine policy in Canada [online]. Fraser Institute, Vancouver. Available from: www.fraserinstitute.org/studies/unnatural-regulation-complementary-and-alternative-medicine-policy-canada [accessed 5 October 2018].

Reddy, S., 2004. The politics and poetics of 'Magazine Medicine': new age Ayurveda in the print media. *In*: R. Johnston, ed., *The Politics of Healing: Histories of Alternative Medicine in Twentieth-Century North America*. New York: Routledge, 207–230.

Roncesvalles Village BIA, n.d. Our Neighbourhood [online]. Available from: https://roncesvallesvillage.ca/about-roncesvalles-village/ [accessed 6 October 2018].

Rose, N., 2001. The politics of life itself. *Theory, Culture & Society*, 18 (6), 1–30.

Ross, A.I., 2012. *The Anthropology of Alternative Medicine*. London: Berg Publishers.

Said, E., 1978. *Orientalism*. New York: Random House.

Sassen, S., 2005. The global city: introducing a concept. *Brown Journal of World Affairs*, XI (2), 27–43.

Sharzer, G., 2012. *No Local – Why Small-Scale Alternatives Won't Change the World*. Alresford: Zero books.

Shum, D., 2017. Parkdale tenants organize rent strike to protest rent increases at MetCap buildings. *Global News*, 1 May [online]. Available from: https://globalnews.ca/news/3416279/parkdale-rent-strike-metcap-buildings/ [accessed 5 October 2018].

Slater, T., 2004. Municipally managed gentrification in South Parkdale, Toronto. *The Canadian Geographer*, 48 (3), 303–325.

Smith, M., 2017. Generation Y, nature and tourism. *In*: J. Chen and N. Prebenson, eds, *Nature Tourism*. Abingdon: Routledge, 46–56.

Smith, N., 1996. *The New Urban Frontier: Gentrification and the Revanchist City*. London: Routledge.

Sukha Spa, 2015. Our philosophy: your health is our pleasure [online]. Available from: http://sukhaspa.ca/philosophy/ [accessed 5 July 2016].

Sukha Spa, 2012. About Us—Our Philosophy [online]. Available from: www.sukhahealthspa.com/aboutus_philosophy.html [accessed 8 December 2012].

Sweetman, M., 2011. Occupying housing from the Pope Squat to Occupy Toronto. *rabble.ca*, 19 December [online]. Available from: http://rabble.ca/news/2011/12/occupying-housing-pope-squat-occupy-toronto [accessed 5 October 2018].

Teelucksingh, C., 2002. Spatiality and environmental justice in Parkdale (Toronto). *Ethnologies*, 24 (1), 119–141.

Thorpe, J., 2012. *Temagami's Tangled Wild: Race, Gender and the Making of Canadian Nature*. Vancouver: UBC Press.

Urry, J., 1995. *Consuming Places*. London: Routledge.

Valverde, M., 1991. *The Age of Light, Soap and Water: Moral Reform in English Canada 1885–1925*. Toronto: McClelland and Stewart.

Valverde, M., 2012. *Everyday Law on the Street: City Governance in an Age of Diversity*. Chicago, IL: University of Chicago Press.

Veroncy, 2014. Greening of Roncy part I. *RoncyWorks*, 12 September [online]. Available from: https://roncyworks.wordpress.com/2014/09/12/greening-of-roncy-part-1/ [accessed 5 October 2018].

Wall, S., 2009. *The Nurture of Nature: Childhood, Anti-modernism and Ontario Summer Camps, 1920–55*. Vancouver: UBC Press.

Whitzman, C., 2009. *Suburb, Slum, Urban Village: Transformations in Toronto's Parkdale Neighbourhood 1875–2002*. Vancouver: UBC Press.

Yoga Journal, 2017. Lord of the dance pose [online]. Available from: www.yogajournal.com/poses/lord-of-the-dance-pose [accessed 5 October 2018].

Zukin, S., 2008. Consuming authenticity. *Cultural Studies*, 22 (5), 724–748.

Zukin, S. *et al.*, 2009. New retail capital and neighbourhood change: boutiques and gentrification in New York City. *City and Community*, 8 (1), 47–64.

6 Living with guests
Understanding the reasons for hosting via Airbnb in a mobile society

Natalie Stors

Introduction

The capital of Germany, Berlin, has been experiencing a major tourism boom, both in terms of guest arrivals and Airbnb listings (www.airbnb.de). Visitors are no longer staying within the confines of tourist zones. They are venturing into residential neighbourhoods—a phenomenon discussed as 'off-the-beaten-track' tourism (Maitland and Newman 2009) or 'new urban tourism' (Füller and Michel 2014) in scholarly discourse. Airbnb, the online platform for peer-to-peer accommodation rental, has been fostering this development (Freytag and Bauder 2018). It enables all kind of temporary city users (Martinotti 1999)—such as cultural tourists, exchange students, temporary migrants or business travellers—to stay in (semi-) private apartments.

Airbnb is part of the 'sharing economy', an umbrella term for a large variety of business models that thrive on the sharing, lending, bartering, trading, renting, gifting and swapping of goods and services, instead of buying and owning them (Botsman and Rogers 2010, p. 13). Airbnb—one of the sharing economy's most famous and successful platforms—lists about five million accommodations in 191 countries worldwide (Airbnb 2018). Founded in 2008, the platform has experienced a rising number of hosts and guests ever since, and Berlin has turned into a popular destination among its users. The city is home to about 26,000 listings (Cox 2018a) accounting for about 710,000 guest arrivals in 2017 (Airbnb 2018a). The growth of the platform's portfolio has proceeded relatively unabated in spite of ongoing debate about the misappropriation of living space (Senatsverwaltung für Justiz und Verbraucherschutz Berlin 2014), and discourses on urban transformation, rent increases and gentrification (Holm 2016, Schäfer and Hirsch 2017, Stors and Kagermeier 2017) in Berlin.

While most research on *new urban tourism* and Airbnb in particular has focused on the tourist perspective—on visitors' motivations for venturing into off-the-beaten-track areas (Pappalepore *et al.* 2010, 2014) or for choosing Airbnb accommodations instead of hotel rooms (Tussyadiah and Pesonen 2016, Guttentag *et al.* 2017, Paulauskaite 2017)—and the effects that such a 'new' tourist behaviour has on urban everyday life and the city, the perspectives of hosts and their rationales for renting out private space have been less considered. The host has rarely been conceptualised in tourism research in general (Sherlock 2001, p. 274), and, as Kim *et al.* (2017) have recently highlighted, a great deal of work is still necessary to understand hosts' motivation to participate in online hospitality networks, such as Couchsurfing or Airbnb. The goal of this chapter is to tackle this research gap and to contribute to a still under-represented strand of literature that deals with local residents and how they engage in *new urban tourism* (Novy and Colomb 2017, Dirksmeier and Helbrecht 2015; Pinkster and Boterman 2017; Knaus 2018).

Research investigating tourism to residential neighbourhoods from a local resident perspective is frequently concerned with its negative implications. Scholars have criticised neighbourhood tourism for its contribution to a commodification of local culture (Novy and Huning 2009, Degen 2010) or have argued that residents' feeling of home is disrupted by visitors' 'inappropriate' usage of place (Pinkster and Boterman 2017). Besides simple annoyances that come along with the intense use of space, such as noise, dirt or crowded restaurants and public transport, scholars have also linked the rise of Airbnb to rent increases (Schäfer and Hirsch 2017), a lack of affordable living space (Mermet 2018), transformations in the social urban structure (Sans and Quaglieri 2016) and gentrification (Holm 2016, Gant 2016, Gravari-Barbas and Guinand 2017; Wachsmuth and Weisler 2018). Thus, local communities are mainly regarded as being negatively affected by tourism to residential neighbourhoods fostered through Airbnb, which is why some of them have begun to protest against off-the-beaten-track tourism (Novy and Colomb 2017) and the practice of renting out rooms and apartments in particular (Gant 2016, Opillard 2017).

Such a research perspective is founded on an underlying, clear-cut distinction between visitors and those being visited. From a resident's point of view, it seems that the 'other', the 'intruder'—i.e., the tourist—is causing, or at least contributing to, unwanted neighbourhood changes. As Dirksmeier and Helbrecht (2015, p. 277) pointed out, "there is only a fine line between residents' attitudes towards the intruders of their residential areas and prejudices". Regardless of who exactly is performing extraordinary practices, taking pictures, drinking beer on the streets or passing by with a trolley suitcase, "[t]he performances of new urban tourists, be they visitors from abroad or even residents themselves, function as a source of visible difference in terms of consuming practices and behaviour. Thus, the strange performing tourists may become the scapegoats for perceived evils" (ibid., p. 280; see also Grube, Chapter 11 in this volume). Crang (2014) criticised this binary thinking as well. Framing local urban communities as a "bounded, static, undivided, and happy culture prior to tourism" (ibid. p. 67) and understanding them as a "weaker receiving milieu" (Picard 1996, p. 110) that is affected by the global forces of tourism transforming their living environment is neither sufficient nor contemporary. For this reason, research on *new urban tourism* aims to disrupt such a binary thinking in distinct groups, and is concerned with how people co-construct and 'prosume' (Toffler 1980, cited in Pappalepore *et al.* 2014) space (Stors and Baltes 2018) as well as goods and services (see also Stors *et al.*, Chapter 1 in this volume).

Applying the lens of mobility, Meier and Frank (2016, p. 3) investigated spatialities formed and fashioned by mobility practices, and argued that there was no sense in understanding places like urban neighbourhoods as static and unaffected by global mobile forces. In mobile times, residing means "to dwell in a place that is open to an outer world and that is under influence by mobility practices of mobile persons, for example, who are not only crossing a place but are also leaving an impact" (Meier and Frank 2016, p. 3). The present chapter takes this line of argumentation, but illustrates that not only is the mobile tourist leaving such an impact. As Knaus (2018) has recently outlined, some local residents have adapted to an increase in mobility practices and "dwell with mobility". They (temporarily) transform their lifestyles, homes and roles in order to act as Airbnb hosts who live with the constant mobility of travellers passing through. As such, the Airbnb home, originally the most private space, the backstage area for family and intimacy, has turned into a place of encounter, a 'contact zone' for global flows of people, information, imaginaries and capital. As a result, the domestic space is not only reconfigured as a semi-public space (see Wildish and Spierings, Chapter 7 in this volume) but also turned it into a space for economic exchange relations (Stabrowski 2017, p. 340).

Against the backdrop of such a rise in mobility practices and their respective infrastructure—five million homes have turned into 'contact zones'—the present chapter investigates the complex entanglement between travel and dwelling, being home and not-home, how people settle and how they move (Hannam *et al.* 2006, p. 10). More specifically, it analyses how renting out private space on a regular basis turns into a central element of mundane, everyday life and an important source of revenue for Airbnb hosts. Unlike the work by Knaus (2018), this research is less concerned with how the home changes for those who stay put, but examines Airbnb hosts as mobile agents themselves and investigates how mobility practices produce the preconditions and at the same time the necessity to engage in the practice of subletting. It illustrates how unsteady, mobile lifestyles (Elliott and Urry 2010, Cohen *et al.* 2015) have increasingly blurred the notions of tourist and resident (see also Sherlock 2001) and how 'living with guests' also has contributed to stability and resilience in the lives of mobile Airbnb hosts.

In order to unravel the (im)mobilities that have recently become particularly apparent in the 'contact zone' of the Airbnb home, the chapter is structured as follows. The next section reviews existing literature on motivations for participating in the sharing economy in general and Airbnb in particular to reflect on the academic debate about why people engage in such services. After introducing the chosen research area and briefly discussing Berlin's housing market as one potential cause for the rising numbers of Airbnb rentals, the next section presents empirical findings based on twenty-five qualitative, semi-structured interviews with hosts. Private and semi-professional hosts' mobility patterns are examined as a central precondition for the emergence of unused or underused living space that is rented out via Airbnb. In addition, the text investigates hosts' rationales and the (non-)financial motivations they have, which are in turn linked to the medium- and long-term goals they have intended to accomplish by their subletting activities. The chapter concludes by outlining the thought that, in an increasingly mobile world, which includes flexible jobs, changing partners and temporary rental agreements, hosts transform their home into a place of encounter in order to keep it for themselves, their family members or significant others in the long term.

Airbnb and the sharing economy: considering reasons for participation

The term 'sharing economy' is far from being consistently defined. The genealogy of the concept, outlined by Gyimóthy and Dredge (2017), reinforces the idea that sharing is not a recent phenomenon (Belk 2010), but nevertheless one that gained momentum in the aftermath of the global financial crisis of 2008–2009. Fostered by the wide proliferation of mobile internet and fuelled by people's desires for more sustainable consumption (Heinrichs and Grunenberg 2012), peer-to-peer sharing of goods and services is believed to transform and disrupt capitalist structures in general and the traditional accommodation sector in particular (Guttentag 2015). As Dredge and Gyimóthy (2017, p. 2) explained, the 'collaborative economy', a term used synonymously with the 'sharing economy', "epitomises the disruptive rescaling of economic structures and practices of a postmodern, post-structuralist world". In order to understand Airbnb as an agent operating within the realm of this economy, this chapter utilises a conceptualisation of the term that follows a definition provided by the European Commission, which frames the collaborative or sharing economy as follows:

> [B]usiness models where activities are facilitated by collaborative platforms that create an open marketplace for the temporary usage of goods or services often provided by private individuals. The collaborative economy involves three categories of actors: (i) service providers who share assets, resources, time and/or skills—these can be private individuals offering services on an occasional basis ('peers') or service providers acting in their professional capacity ('professional services providers'); (ii) users of these; and (iii) intermediaries that connect—via an online platform—providers with users and that facilitate transactions between them ('collaborative platforms'). Collaborative economy transactions generally do not involve a change of ownership and can be carried out for profit or not-for-profit.
>
> (European Commission 2016, p. 3)

Such 'collaborative platforms' are classified along two dimensions (Codagnone and Martens 2016): the first dimension differentiates between for-profit and not-for-profit platforms; the second distinguishes business-to-consumer (B2C) versus peer-to-peer (P2P) offers. As a commercial platform, Airbnb operates within the realm of for-profit sharing (or letting) of accommodation, with the host either being a private person or a professional service provider.[1]

Motivations for participating in the sharing economy and Airbnb—a brief literature review

The motivations people have for participating in the sharing economy are diverse and depend on various aspects (Hamari *et al.* 2015). One decisive criterion is the type of service taken into account: they range from accommodation (e.g., Airbnb), transportation (e.g., Uber) and financial services (e.g., Startnext.com) to mini-jobs (e.g., TaskRabbit). In addition to the type of service, people's roles as producers or consumers also influence their decision to participate (or not). While many people consume goods and services provided via online platforms, the group of people acting as suppliers is much smaller (Andreotti *et al.* 2018, Böcker and Meelen 2017).

Academic research on users' motivations for participating in the sharing economy too often lacks distinct differentiation and tends to analyse motivations for (non-)participation on a very general level. These studies either fail to differentiate between the various types of platforms considered (see, e.g., Andreotti *et al.* 2018, Bellotti *et al.* 2015) or they do not differentiate between users' roles as receivers or providers of goods and services (Hamari *et al.* 2015). Accordingly, findings have remained on a very general level. For example, Hamari *et al.* (2015) found that perceived 'enjoyment' in sharing[2] is an important intrinsic motivation, while anticipated 'economic gains' is a relevant extrinsic one. Bellotti *et al.* (2015) likewise noted that both receivers and providers of sharing services agree on the importance of the 'social element' in sharing systems. Other studies pre-define possible motivations, such as social, economic and environmental reasons (Böcker and Meelen 2017), and limit themselves to positioning receivers and providers of various sharing services into such a trialectic.

Looking into Airbnb in particular, people's motivations for participation, either as hosts or guests, are more delimited. Environmental issues, for example, which were frequently expected to be a relevant driver for using sharing services in general (Bellotti *et al.* 2015, Böcker and Meelen 2017, Hamari *et al.* 2015, Heinrichs and Grunenberg 2012) have played a subordinate role for people's engagement in home sharing (Tussyadiah 2015 is an exception; she found sustainability issues to be relevant). Typically, motivational research on Airbnb focuses either on studying hosts or analysing guests—an approach that is plausible, given the different requirements each role involves. Nevertheless, Tussyadiah and Pesonen (2016) identified two central drivers for using Airbnb independent of the chosen role. They found out that both a 'social appeal', which mainly includes a desire for community, as well as an 'economic appeal', which translates into cost-saving, have a strong effect on the decision to use Airbnb either as a host or as a guest.

Since guests' expectations have an important impact on shaping hosts' services, it is logical to first examine the reasons for booking accommodation on Airbnb. The aforementioned two appeals identified by Tussyadiah and Pesonen (2016) were also prominent findings in several other studies focusing on guests' motives (Guttentag *et al.* 2017, Kagermeier *et al.* 2015, Quinby and Gasdia 2014). The 'social appeal', however, is not understood uniformly in the various studies under consideration, but is used with different emphases: while some researchers tie the feeling of authenticity to Airbnb's 'social appeal' (Guttentag 2015, Tussyadiah and Pesonen 2016, Kagermeier *et al.* 2015), others regard the host–guest interaction as its central element (see Guttentag *et al.* 2017). Only a few of the studies reviewed here went beyond relying on a narrow set of intrinsic or extrinsic motivational factors and acknowledged the broader context of guests' decision-making when choosing Airbnb. This is surprising, as Nowak *et al.* (2015), for instance, pointed out that an apartment's location is a key determinant for booking a listed accommodation. In addition, the availability of household amenities, the individuality of design and additional space compared to hotel rooms are significant factors influencing guests' decision-making (Kagermeier *et al.* 2015, Quinby and Gasdia 2014), but these factors cannot be linked to motivation in a narrow sense. These are rather structural or situational criteria determining visitors' choice of accommodation.

Turning to hosts' motivations for participating in short-term rentals, Ikkala and Lampinen (2015) and Lampinen and Cheshire (2016) have published two initial qualitative studies on this topic. Overall, both articles concluded that the platform's 'social appeal', understood as the host–guest interaction including the gratification for being 'a good host', are hosts' central intrinsic motivational factors. Insofar as renting space out on Airbnb also results in a financial benefit, the prospect of additional income was depicted as an important external motivation. Drawing on research in two different geographical settings, Finland and California in the USA, a comparison of the studies' results illustrate that earnings were of less relevance for Finnish hosts. The former did not regard the money made through Airbnb as an indispensable part of their total income—it was not needed to make ends meet. In contrast to the first study, earnings from hosting among Californians were regarded as supplementary income that helped to pay the rent or a mortgage. Other hosts invested the extra money in education or spent it to cover unexpected medical expenses (Lampinen and Cheshire 2016, p. 1675). Although these findings were derived from exploratory and qualitative studies, results may point to the relevance of spatial or social factors affecting hosts' decision to engage in short-term rental.

Approaching an in-depth analysis of hosts' rationales for renting out

The presented literature came to the conclusion that it was mainly two aspects—the social and the economic dimension—that drive users' engagement in Airbnb. Scholars, however, have so far mainly concentrated on individuals' motivations alone. More structural conditions, in terms of hosts' lifestyles, their living situation or employment status, as well as in terms of the geographical setting, the specific location of listings and the prevailing housing market, have not yet been considered when analysing the host perspective. However, such broader analytical categories appear to be useful tools to gain more in-depth knowledge about the various rationales for renting out that go beyond rather general economic or social motives and that can be linked to broader urban and societal processes, such as gentrification or an increasingly mobile lifestyle.

In this regard, psychological research on human behaviour can provide a useful contribution. Heckhausen and Heckhausen (2018, pp. 4–8) put forward the idea that human behaviour can be explained as interaction between people's traits, their character, their motives and their personality on the one hand, and the actual situation in which an activity takes place on the other hand (see also Bowers 1973, Endler and Magnusson 1976). With regard to Airbnb these findings indicate that it does not suffice to look into people's motivations alone to fully understand hosts' subletting activities. Structural or situational factors are likewise relevant since they produce the opportunity and induce significant stimuli to initiate the subletting.

Looking at structural factors first, they appear to play a key role because the availability of 'idling capacity' in terms of space to rent out, time to prepare the apartment and maintain its online representation is indispensable if a host is to engage in subletting activities. This 'idling capacity' concept, introduced by Botsman and Rogers (2010, pp. 105–109) is seen as creating the preconditions for participating in the sharing economy; it represents various kinds of unused or underused goods that can be redistributed via peer-to-peer sharing platforms. However, idling capacity "is related not just to physical products such as bikes, cars, and drills but to less tangible assets, such as time, skills, space, or commodities like electricity" (ibid., p. 109). The concept of idling capacity—which is intimately tied to hosts' mobility practices, as the following sections will demonstrate—is useful for investigating how empty space that is let via Airbnb emerges in the first place.

With respect to situational factors, Heckhausen and Heckhausen (2018; see also Endler and Magnusson 1976, p. 958) have shown that certain situations may cause stimuli that activate people to perform certain tasks, such as to start subletting. Such stimuli are mostly not directly related to the rental practice itself, but rather to the expected outcome, for example additional income or social contacts. These results, in turn, are related to the long-term goals that hosts intend to achieve. The following example will clarify the relations between stimulus, activity, immediate outcome and long-term goal. An unexpected rent increase may function as a stimulus triggering the intention to sublet. The power of this stimulus, however, is dependent on a person's individual situation. If a person has a secure, sufficient income, rising rents do not necessarily cause a change in behaviour. If monthly income is instead insecure or insufficient to cover additional housing costs, the stimulus becomes powerful and may cause a hosting activity. Here, the immediate benefit from subletting is earning money, a dimension that was frequently framed as the economic appeal of the platform and hosts' extrinsic motivation. However, even though hosts' long-term goals are related to the immediate consequence of an activity, they differ substantially from the situational impulse of renting out. In the example the anticipated consequence of renting out is earning money whereas the long-term goal might be to keep the apartment and avoid moving out despite rising living costs.

Against this background, it appears promising to look into the structural factors building the preconditions for hosts' engagement in short-term rental and hosts' situational conditions to identify stimuli triggering subletting activities. In addition, it is necessary to take into account the expected (long-term) goals that Airbnb hosts intend to accomplish through subletting.

Studying Airbnb hosts in Berlin: methodological considerations

The city of Berlin is experiencing a major tourism boom, both in terms of guest arrivals and Airbnb listings. In 2017, almost 13,000,000 people visited Berlin (guest arrivals) and completed about 31,150,000 overnight stays (Amt für Statistik Berlin-Brandenburg 2018). Compared to 2005, both guest arrivals and overnight stays have more than doubled. There is no such dynamic in tourism growth rates in any other European city (DWIF 2017, p. 10). Compared to the previous year, however, guest arrivals grew by only 1.8 per cent and overnight stays by 0.3 per cent (Amt für Statistik Berlin-Brandenburg 2018). Apparently, tourism in Berlin is stabilising at a high level.

Berlin has also gained a top position among European cities in terms of Airbnb listings. As of 9 June 2018, the website *Inside Airbnb* counted 26,295 listings (Cox 2018a). Only the cities of London (49,348 listings) and Paris (60,529 listings) offered more listings at that time (Cox 2018b, 2018c). Airbnb listings are distributed all over the city. The majority, however, are concentrated in the boroughs Friedrichshain-Kreuzberg (6,547 listings), Mitte (5,449 listings), Pankow (4,350 listings) and Neukölln (4,165 listings) (Cox 2018a)—areas that all have experienced large-scale gentrification processes (Holm 2013).

Several scholars have regarded Airbnb as another cause driving gentrification in residential neighbourhoods—an interrelation that has not only been identified in Berlin, but in several cities across Europe (Cócola Gant 2016, Sans and Quaglieri Domínguez 2016, Mermet 2017). While most researchers have been concerned with Airbnb's effects on the city's rental market, Holm (2016) briefly theorised upon people's rationales for partaking in the subletting of apartments. He differentiated between *professional hosts* who continuously rent out apartments with the primary aim of maximising turnover and *private hosts* who occasionally sublet in order to generate additional income or to compensate for rising rents. With regard to gentrification processes, he illustrated the fact that professional hosts take advantage of the rent gap that is derived from differing revenues in the long-term and short-term rental market (see also Mermet 2017; Wachsmuth and Weisler 2018). The conversion of relatively cheap apartments into holiday rentals—being most promising from an economic perspective—is particularly problematic since such transformations result in the displacement of the apartment's inhabitants. While he noted that professional hosts contribute to gentrification processes, he likewise illustrated the fact that non-professional, private hosts use Airbnb as an opportunity to generate supplemental income that they need to compensate for rising rents. In this regard, non-professional hosts' subletting activities have turned into a strategy to fight displacement. Holm's argumentation points towards the complex entanglement between dwelling and mobility in the context of Airbnb. While professional hosts seem to foster tenants' mobility in terms of displacement, non-professional hosts co-finance rising rents in order to be able to remain in the apartment themselves.

In order to gain more in-depth insights into hosts' rationales for renting out, a qualitative research design was carried out. Twenty-five semi-structured interviews were conducted with Airbnb hosts all over Berlin. At the time of data collection, during August and September 2014, no exact figures on the total number of listings in the city of Berlin and its boroughs or other solid demographic information about the Airbnb hosts were available. Therefore, the interviewees were selected based on the location of their listings. While more attention was paid to districts with larger numbers of listings, fewer interviews were conducted in areas with only a few Airbnb listings. This information was accessible at that time, since Airbnb indicated on its website if districts provided more than 1,000 listings. All in all, more than 100 Airbnb hosts were contacted via the platform's website, and twenty-five interviews were ultimately carried out. As Table 6.1 illustrates, most interviews took place in the districts of Prenzlauer Berg, Friedrichshain, Kreuzberg, Moabit and Neukölln. The length of each interview ranged from 25 minutes to more than 1.5 hours.

In order to examine the collected data, all interviews were recorded and later transcribed and coded using the CAQDAS software MAXQDA (see also Saldaña 2012, p. 28). Particularly with regard to people's rationales for engaging in short-term subletting activities, the research design was exploratory, with no underlying theory tied to it before data collection. For this reason, Charmaz's (2014) constructivist approach of grounded theory coding was applied in order to develop larger concepts and theoretical directions explaining people's engagement in short-term rental. Following her argument (2014, p. 113), "[c]oding is the pivotal link between collecting data and developing an emergent theory to explain these data". In addition, Charmaz's (2014) constructivist approach acknowledges the researcher's as well as the interviewees' involvement in the research design and process, which allows theory building that also takes into account the perspective of the local people involved. More specifically, data analysis was divided into several coding

Table 6.1 List of interviewed hosts (source: compiled by the author)

ID	Location of listing	Type of Airbnb offer	No. of listings	Owned or rented space	Sex	Job
*[1]	Charlottenburg	room	5	rented commercial space	M	Project developer (Airbnb mini hotel)
[2]	Friedrichshain	room	1	rented	M	Theatre director
[3]	Friedrichshain	room	1	rented	M	Computer scientist
[4]	Heiligensee	room/apartment	2	owned	M	Product designer
[5]	Kreuzberg	room	1	rented	M	Consultant
[6]	Kreuzberg	room/apartment	2	rented	F	Chauffeur
[7]	Kreuzberg	shared room/room	2	owned	F	Student
[8]	Mitte	room	2	rented	F	Pensioner
[9]	Moabit	apartment	1	rented	F	Actress
[10]	Moabit	shared room	1	rented	F	-
*[11]	Moabit	apartment	15	rented	F	Marketing employee
[12]	Moabit	room/apartment	2	rented	F	Architect, Language teacher
[13]	Moabit	room	1	rented	M	Engineer
[14]	Neukölln	apartment	1	rented	M	-
*[15]	Neukölln	apartment	11	owned	F	Bar owner
[16]	Neukölln	apartment	2	owned	M	Architect
*[17]	Neukölln	room	5	rented	M	Sociologist
[18]	Prenzlauer Berg	room	1	owned	M	-
[19]	Prenzlauer Berg	apartment	1	owned	F	Architect, bar owner
[20]	Prenzlauer Berg	apartment	1	rented	M + F	Artist + art manager
[21]	Rummelsburg	apartment	1	rented	F	Parental leave
[22]	Schöneberg	room	1	rented	M	Photographer
[23]	Wedding	apartment	1	rented	F	Housewife
[24]	Weißensee	room	2	rented	M	Nurse
[25]	Wilmersdorf	room	1	rented	F	Student

* Empirical results derived from interviews marked with an asterisk are not presented in this chapter. The following analysis focuses on private hosts only providing one or two Airbnb listings.

cycles: (1) *initial coding* was applied in order to stick closely to the data and to take on the interviewees' perspective, (2) *focused coding* was deployed to identify, group and categorise repeating themes (see also Saldaña's [2012, p. 207] second coding cycle) and (3) broader, *theoretical concepts* were developed based on the most salient categories. This process of qualitative data analysis, which includes identifying categories and developing concepts, is also reflected in Figures 6.1 and 6.2, presented in the following section.

Understanding the host perspective: empirical results

This section presents and discusses the findings derived from the twenty-five qualitative interviews with Airbnb hosts in Berlin. First, the emergence of idling capacity in terms of empty living space is outlined as a precondition for engaging in subletting activities, and the empirical results are tied to the concept of mobility. Figure 6.1 provides an overview of the type of accommodation rented out and people's rationales for not using the space themselves. Figure 6.2 then pays close attention to the medium- and long-term goals that hosts intend to accomplish through their subletting activities. It illustrates the fact that economic gains can barely be seen as the sole driver of this activity, but instead hosts' desire to earn supplemental income must be set in a broader context of increasingly unstable relationships in terms of housing, work, capital and social relations.

The origin of idling capacity

The Airbnb listings in the sample all had different purposes before they were turned into accommodation for strangers—they served as homes of parents, children, partners, etc. Increasingly mobile lifestyles, however, made these places sit temporarily idle. Based on the interview material, three key factors that cause idling capacity emerged: First, the temporary mobility of significant others including flatmates, second, hosts' desire to accumulate additional living space for future use and third, the temporary mobility of the hosts themselves are factors which result in empty living space. For two of these factors, the maintenance or facilitation of a mobile lifestyle proves to be a strong rationale for keeping these rooms or apartments despite their current lack of inhabitants. The concept 'production and accumulation of space' is also tied to mobility, yet in the sense that hosts intend to avoid mobility (moving out) in case their familial relations change.

The temporary mobility of significant others

As empirical data revealed, idle living space mainly emerges due to the private or professional mobility of people. In the majority of cases analysed, certain phases in the course of their lives or lifestyle changes required individuals to move out and leave their previously inhabited space empty. The mobility

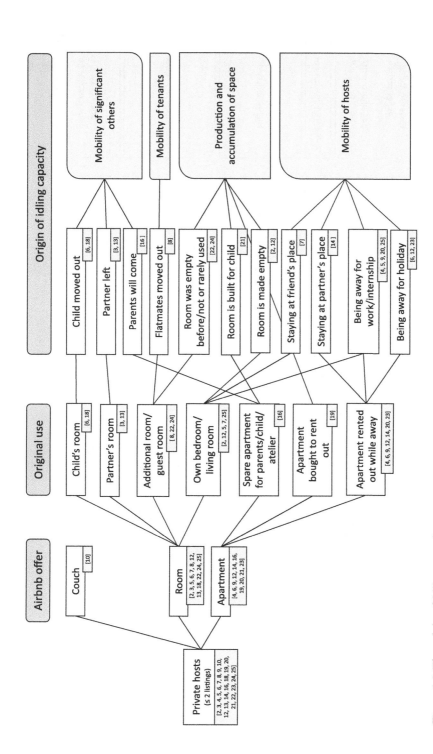

Figure 6.1 The origin of idling capacity.
Source: own depiction.

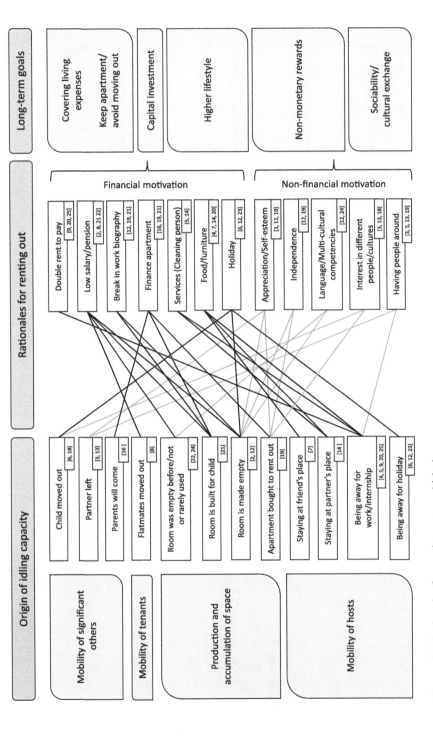

Figure 6.2 Rationales for renting out on Airbnb.
Source: own depiction.

of significant others is one observation that is derived from the data. Many Airbnb hosts explained that the rooms they are renting out on Airbnb were originally dedicated to their family members [3, 6, 13, 16, 18].[3] They offer places in which their children used to live [6, 18] or which their partners used to inhabit [3, 18]. The increasing mobility of children, for educational, professional or social reasons, thus produces unused space, as one interviewee explained:

> Actually, we intended for our son to live in these rooms. However, he is now travelling the world as well, so we are using his place for Airbnb [18].

The man interviewed combined two small apartments years ago in order to provide sufficient living space, particularly for the adolescent child. Securing space for potential future use appears to be common practice among Airbnb hosts, as the following cases will exemplify. Hosts [3] and [13] acted similarly but did not provide spare space for their respective children, but for their partners. Both hosts are single men with secure incomes; they both moved into large apartments while in a relationship. When their relationships ultimately ended, each man decided to keep his apartment. Host [3] explained his rationale as follows:

> In the end, it didn't work out with my girlfriend, that's why I am living here alone. At the beginning, I looked for a flatmate [...]. That didn't work out either [...]. That's when I started with Airbnb. The platform provides so much flexibility: [...] people stay for only a very limited amount of time. Or I can say I need that space for myself or my girlfriend. I can very easily stop renting out. In a shared apartment, it is much more difficult. You make friends with your flatmate and at the end you have to throw out a friend. That's not good, you don't do that.[4]

Instead of moving into a smaller apartment, both hosts secured living space for future partners. Moreover, due to their sufficient incomes they do not rely on the money made through Airbnb, but appreciate the social contact with their guests. Offering a room on a long-term basis, however, is not an option for either of them; they do not intend to take responsibility for long-term flatmates. Instead, they prefer to use the additional spatial capacities for their individual purposes whenever it pleases them.

Production and accumulation of space

The previous section already pointed to another category that continuously emerged in the data and that gains particular relevance when considering the increasingly tight housing market in Berlin. Besides the mobility of significant others, people's desire to accumulate additional space for family members appears to be linked to subletting activities on Airbnb, as the example of Host [21] illustrates:

We have a three-room apartment, me, my husband, and my husband's son; he is twelve years old. He lives one week with us and one week with his mother. So, we have two rooms and the third room, the child's room, is one week used and one week empty. At first, we had the idea to rent out his room when he stays at his mother's place. But then, another possibility emerged: the tenant next door moved out.

We [...] thought, we have to get this apartment. Because we [...] have a baby and we are lacking one room [...]. We desperately need an additional room but we don't want to move out. We are so rooted in this house, we have our friends around and we get along with the landlord. We don't want to move out, and that's why we rented this apartment. We are planning to combine both apartments and thus enlarge our apartment [...]. We are planning to do this in two years when our baby needs his own room. Until then, we want to rent out the apartment on Airbnb in order to finance the studio in the meantime [21].

The quote highlights the fact that the older child's mobility initiated the idea of renting out temporarily empty space. However, instead of subletting the older child's room, the couple ended up renting out a whole studio next door in order to secure sufficient living space for their growing family. Host [21]'s rather unconventional approach is related to the housing situation in Berlin. Finding affordable apartments, particularly for larger families, is becoming increasingly difficult, so much so that Host [21] feared losing her social relations in case they had to move further away. Then, renting out on Airbnb turns into a coping strategy: supplemental income made through subletting finances the enlarged living space and thus postpones the family's displacement from their neighbourhood. Accumulating additional living space or, at least, keeping the space currently inhabited are central rationales for many Airbnb hosts. Hosts [2], [8], [12] and [22] live in larger apartments that they can barely afford. They rent out guest rooms (see [22]), rooms of previous flatmates (see [8]) or their own bedrooms or living rooms (see [2] and [12]) to avoid moving out. These hosts artificially created their idling spatial capacity by purposefully changing the original use of the rooms they sublet. Reasons for their precarious situation and their need to monetise living space will be discussed later on.

The temporary mobility of the hosts themselves

Besides the temporary mobility of family members, the mobility of the hosts themselves is another frequently occurring source of idling spatial capacity. Hosts' mobility can be differentiated into work, leisure and social mobility in terms of maintaining social relations.

Hosts [6], [12] and [23] noted that they rent out their apartment while away on holiday. They rely on the supplemental income to co-finance their trips. For these hosts, renting out while away was the starting point for engaging in short-term subletting activities. Over the course of her subletting, Host [12] began renting out her own bedroom even when she was not on vacation. She would then stay at her partner's place or sleep in the living room. Financial reasons drove her to adapt and expand her subletting activities. Like other hosts in this group [6, 23], earning supplemental income is a key motivation for renting out via Airbnb.

Besides leisure mobility, a large group of hosts sublet their places while on a journey for educational or professional reasons. Being away on business trips has become part of a regular work schedule. Many companies require their employees to travel to customers, training seminars, or 'workation' events (see [5]). Self-employed or freelance people, such as artists, journalists, photographers and designers (see [4], [9] and [20]) travel to meet potential clients, to pitch the concept of a new product, or to participate in an exhibition. Even students travel to complete an internship abroad or to participate in an international exchange programme (see [25]). Thus, educational or professional travel becomes part of people's everyday life. The travel expenses, however, are not always fully covered by the sending institutions. Students and self-employed people, in particular, often pay for most of their travel costs themselves. As empirical data revealed, such people make use of Airbnb to cover travel expenses while on business trips. The following quote vividly illustrates the motivations of a couple of freelance actors:

> We are both freelancers and we are both a lot on the move; we are both actors. Therefore, we frequently work away from home and our apartment sits idle [...]. First of all, we still have to pay the rent. And nobody is paying for your rent at home while you are living at a different place where you have to pay the rent as well [...]. However, we cannot afford to pay a €600 to €700 monthly rent while staying somewhere else. Now, I am shooting a series for four to five months and I have to pay another €400, €500, €600 monthly rent. Who can afford that? How is that supposed to work? And that was actually the main reason why we started to try out Airbnb [9].

Living at multiple localities for private or professional reasons is becoming more and more common in late-modern societies (Hilti 2016). Flexibilisation of the work environment that is manifested in project-based jobs, unsteady work contracts and varying working hours often requires people to move from one locality to another, commute long distances, or find a second home at the place of employment (see Brenner 2002, Szydlik 2008). As the quote of Host [9] indicates, despite companies providing financial benefits, many employees and self-employed workers, in particular, have to cover a large amount of their travel expenses themselves. The empirical data revealed that such flexible working environments produce underused living space, which is then rented out on Airbnb. For many hosts who work in such mobile environments, covering their travel expenses or higher living costs is a central rationale for using Airbnb (see [9], [20] and [25]).

A last type of mobility detected in the empirical data is socially oriented mobility practices to maintain relationships with partners or family members that produce idle living space. Host [14] and his girlfriend live in two separate apartments in Berlin. Despite being in a relationship, they both want to keep their own flats in order to remain independent and flexible. Scholars refer to such multi-local lifestyles as "living apart together" (Petzold 2013, p. 32). Although both intend to keep their apartments, they frequently visit each other or spend a weekend together. In such situations, they become Airbnb hosts and rent out their own apartment while staying at their partner's place. Since both can afford to live in a comfortable flat, supplemental income is not their sole rationale for renting out. It is rather the flexibility of monetising the apartment whenever they like that both hosts appreciate. Moreover, their rationales point towards the housing market again—hosts don't dare to give up once acquired living space only for moving in together. They would rather keep their apartments and monetise the unused living space from time to time instead of giving it up irretrievably.

Rationales for renting out and long-term goals

Rationales for renting out are highly diverse, as Figure 6.2 depicts. Hosts' motivations can be both financially and non-financially driven—a finding in line with Ikkala and Lampinen's (2015) and Lampinen and Cheshire's (2016) previous studies. The long-term goals that hosts intend to achieve, however, are much more complex, ranging from avoiding displacement or affording higher lifestyles to non-monetary rewards, such as education, self-esteem and sociability. The following pages discuss the empirical findings regarding hosts' long-term goals along financial and non-financial rationales.

The financial motivation: covering living expenses, capital investment and higher lifestyle

Earning money is a prominent motivation for hosting on Airbnb and often the pivotal reason for initiating subletting activities. In order to understand this phenomenon more broadly, however, it does not suffice to look into people's motivations alone. As Heckhausen and Heckhausen (2018) have depicted, intentional and motivated behaviour depends on people's internal needs and desires as well as on their external conditions—the situation in which their action is embedded. Since the previous section already dealt with hosts' living conditions and the origin of their idling capacity, the following sections examine the intended long-term outcomes of hosts' subletting activities.

More than one-third of hosts in the data sample use supplemental income to cover their respective living expenses. This finding comes close to the data Airbnb published itself in 2016: the company claims that 38 per cent of its hosts use Airbnb income to make ends meet (Airbnb 2017, p. 10). During the interviews, hosts described their rationales for renting out as a strategy to cover financial shortfalls, resulting from low wages (see [2] and [22]), a small pension (see [8]) or because they had two rents to pay due to project-based work at different locations (see [9], [20] and [25]). Others had to interrupt their careers because of pregnancy, child care or illness (see [12], [19] and [21]).

Hosts [2] and [22] both work in creative professions, one as a theatre director, and the other as a photographer. Host [2] is only temporarily employed and relies on the additional income to cover bouts of unemployment. Host [22] works as a freelance photographer; he uses the supplemental income to bridge periods with fewer projects. Both sublet rooms in their own rented apartments: Host [22] rents out underused space, whereas Host [2] even transformed his living room into a guest room to make additional income. These examples demonstrate that unsteady income is one stimulus that triggers hosts' needs to earn additional money, which they have accomplished through subletting. Besides insufficient income, a double cost burden for mobile professionals, in particular, is another reason to sublet. Host [9] works as an actress and Host [20] as an art manager; both sublet their apartments while away for work. For both, the primary rationale for renting out is to cover their fixed costs for the apartment while on business trips. The argumentation of Host [25] is similar; as a student, she sublets her room in a shared apartment when she is away doing an internship.

The empirical data showed that people employed in creative and mobile professions have made use of Airbnb in order to close their income gaps or to compensate for double rent burdens. Unemployed hosts or those with breaks in their careers argued similarly; their reliance on Airbnb earnings, however, is even higher. For Hosts [8], [12], [19] and [21], money made through Airbnb is an indispensable part of their income. All the hosts in this group were women who have not returned to their jobs after periods of pregnancy, child care or illness; Host [8] is retired. Their subletting activities transformed into semi-professional businesses that replaced or supplemented their previous professions. While some still intend to get back into their jobs—mainly as self-employed professionals (see [9], [12], [19], [20] and [22])—Host [8] relies solely on Airbnb income, since her pension does not suffice to keep her apartment. She states:

My daughter got the apartment when she came back to Berlin, 13–14 years ago […]. At that time, the apartment was not renovated […]. I took [it] over […]. The apartment is pretty big, four rooms, and at the beginning, I rented it out as a shared apartment. I cannot live there all by myself, I don't have enough money […]. But now, I rent it out to tourists […] and that's fantastic. It works much better than the shared apartment. In the shared apartment, I always had some problems. It was just the total rent, the rent was so high, if I had divided it fairly it would have been too expensive for the students [8].

Hosts in this category rely on supplemental income made through Airbnb to cover their living expenses, in particular, to be able to pay the monthly rent. This aspect becomes even more important in light of the fast-rising rental prices in Berlin (IBB 2017). As Holm (2016) discussed theoretically, empirical data has shown that several hosts sublet their private living space in order to keep pace with the rental market and thus fight—or at least postpone— displacement. Yet, developments on Berlin's housing market are not hosts' sole rationale for renting out. Precarious working conditions in terms of temporary work contracts or self-employment and breaks in hosts' careers are likewise important drivers for subletting.

Another concept identified that may drive Airbnb's boom in Berlin, is the opportunity it provides for non-institutional investors to achieve a comparably high return on investments in real estate. Hosts (see [16] and [19]) who purchased small apartments for the purpose of subletting may have expected a two-fold economic gain. Host [16] regards his short-term subletting as much more lucrative than long-term rental since monthly revenue is significantly higher (see also Holm 2016, Mermet 2017). Host [19] even explains that she cannot rent out on a long-term basis, for example to students or other residents with lower income, since the economic return would be too low to pay back her bank loans for the apartment. These two cases exemplify that apartments bought for subletting have lost their use value for owners. They are, instead, transformed into assets, forms of capital investment, intended to produce profits due to their specific location or the overall development of the real estate market (see also Frenzel, Chapter 4 in this volume). As Heeg (2013) outlined, real estate has gone from a commodity to a financial product.

Besides this form of capital investment, Host [16] depicts another reason for subletting related to Heeg's (2013) concept of 'responsibilisation'. He not only bought a second apartment in order to break the spiral of rising rent, but also to secure additional property for his wife's parents, who plan to move to Berlin when they are older. He thus invested in real estate not only to provide for his own pension but also to take care of his parents-in-law's future housing situation. As already discussed in the previous section, some hosts intended to accumulate living space—owned or rented—because they expect further price increases and fear their inability to afford living space in the future. These hosts bought (see [16] and [18]) or even rented (see [21]) additional property as provision for their own retirement or to secure living space for their relatives. Their subletting activities thus turn into a temporary solution to liquefy investments bound in concrete.

A last reason for renting out that can be linked to financial motivations is hosts' desire for a higher lifestyle. Several hosts explained that they sublet while away as a means to co-finance their holiday [6], [12], [23]. Others use the supplemental income to pay for household services, such as a cleaner [5], [14], or to renovate, respectively maintain, the apartment [7], buy beautiful furniture [14], technological devices [3] or better food [7]. Hosts in this group do not rely on the supplemental income; they only rent out if it pleases them and if they have sufficient idling temporal and spatial capacities.

The non-financial motivation: non-monetary rewards and sociability

While supplemental income is the central driver for those who rely on Airbnb money to cover their living expenses, non-monetary rewards are often of primary relevance for those who have secure, full-time jobs, sufficient space at home or who do not assign great importance to financial security. In addition, many people in this group search for and enjoy social interactions, and they find the interpersonal relationships rewarding.

Non-monetary rewards are intangible benefits that hosts receive for their engagement apart from monetary compensation. 'Independence' and 'self-esteem' were central outcomes for two female hosts (see [12] and [19]) who initiated hosting after a break in their careers. Host [19] explains her considerations and motivation:

> I started it [renting out via Airbnb] after I got pregnant—but I really wanted to work during that time […]. I am an architect and there is still this real estate boom in Berlin. […] We found this small apartment when I got pregnant and we bought it. Then, I equipped the apartment with furniture and opened up a business […]. If these revenues declined, that would be bad for my livelihood and for my ego in general […]. I am an architect, but I have never worked as one, because I studied for a long time and afterwards I got pregnant. For me—for my ego—I built up something else [19].

As Host [19] vividly depicts, she developed self-esteem from her subletting activities; hosting became important for her ego since she managed to initiate a small business all by herself. Host [12] tells a similar story; she worked as an architect but got sick and left her job. She is investing her Airbnb money in covering her expenses while she completes a period of professional reorientation and retraining to become a language teacher. Renting out via Airbnb enabled her to become temporarily independent from her fixed monthly salary. Moreover, Host [12] claimed to appreciate the diverse multicultural experiences she now has, and she is using her international guests to improve her language skills. Getting to know different cultures and practising language skills is also the primary reasons for Host [24] to rent out via Airbnb. He regards such multicultural experiences as an important element of his children's education.

The last overarching concept derived from the empirical data includes the concept of sociability and cultural exchange. Very few hosts mentioned non-monetary rewards as their central motivation for renting out—Host [13] was one of them: he considers the social experience to be crucial to his subletting activities. He works as an engineer, with a busy work schedule and a high monthly salary. However, he does not meet many people, which is why he decided to rent out his ex-girlfriend's room to visitors:

> I started it [renting out via Airbnb] […] after I broke up with my girlfriend. There was so much space that nobody used anymore […]. I thought maybe someone would come over every now and then. And you get the opportunity to meet someone from anywhere on earth—someone who is from the USA or from Asia. Since then, I have had visitors from all inhabited continents—that's so cool [13].

Being interested in different cultures and having people around was mentioned by several hosts. However, the majority of them used this argument to counterbalance their economic motivation. While renting out via Airbnb has often been used as a coping strategy to bridge financial shortfalls, only hosts with secure, full-time jobs and sufficient income focused on the social appeal of this practice. Only Host [13] seemed to be truly motivated by the "sheer pleasure of the company of others" (Ikkala and Lampinen 2015, p. 1034)—a motivation inseparably linked to the task of hosting, and thus the only intrinsic motivation (Ryan and Deci 2000) identified that explains people's subletting activities.

Conclusion

This chapter identified people's rationales for sharing their own private space with strangers. This meant applying Botsman and Roger's (2010) concept of 'idling capacity' as a lens to investigate how short-term rental is tied to hosts' mobility practices. In addition, this chapter shines a light on the structural and situational conditions of Airbnb hosts, thereby identifying various stimuli that trigger hosts' subletting activities and fostering an understanding of the long-term goals that hosts hope to achieve by subletting.

Framing Airbnb hosts as mobile agents helps scholars to better understand the intimate entanglement between hosts' dwelling and mobility practices. The evidence presented here demonstrates that their diverse mobility patterns are a frequent cause for idling spatial capacity rented out via Airbnb. Hosts travelling for social, professional or leisure reasons produce un(der)used space that is sublet via Airbnb, and the money earned is in turn used to cover travel costs. In this regard, renting out while on the move exemplifies the ambiguity and mutability of the categories of 'host' and 'guest'—a binary conceptualisation that has lost much of its explanatory power at a time when travelling has become a mundane part of people's lifestyles (Cohen *et al.* 2015, p, 154). As Crang (2014) noted, hosts can no longer be framed as the sedentary community visited by the mobile tourist. On the contrary, Airbnb hosts are similarly mobile; they can simultaneously act as a host at one place while being a guest at another.

Despite mobility practices structuring much of hosts' lives, including the mobility of significant others, having a solid home was crucial for every one interviewed in this sample. Although hosts' private living spaces have often turned into a contact zone for various people, the home has never lost its function as a place of retreat. On the contrary, having a home that is affordable and large enough for themselves and their family members was an issue commonly raised by Airbnb hosts. Renting out temporarily underused spatial capacity was thus transformed into a strategy to secure living space. This issue of keeping, securing or expanding one's own private space was a recurring narrative in interviews with Berlin Airbnb hosts. As Meier and Frank (2016, p. 5) very aptly stated, "[t]he transformations that have led to more mobility are accompanied by transformations in the arrangements and forms of dwellings as well". Despite many Airbnb hosts having highly mobile lifestyles, they intend to keep their rooms or apartments—their homes—under all circumstances. They rent it out and share it with strangers in order to cover the costs for (additional) space, while aiming to inhabit the space themselves together with their family members in the long run.

While hosts' mobility practices were found to be a central cause for the origin of idling spatial capacity, the rationales of these hosts for renting out that space are tied to increasingly flexible conditions in the realm of work, social life and even capital investment. Parent concepts derived from the empirical data illustrated the fact that subletting activities are frequently triggered by precarious living conditions and the need to earn supplemental income. Airbnb provides a business opportunity for hosts with breaks in their careers, but also for those with unsteady employment or a low income. These hosts engage in subletting activities on an everyday basis; some have substituted their jobs for Airbnb, others rent out during phases of unemployment. As such, the home "has emerged as an increasingly important site of entrepreneurship" (Stabrowski 2017, p. 340). Some hosts have turned their living space into a means of production, and turned the act of hosting into work. The accumulating of property as an asset turned out to be an important driver for those hosts with larger economic opportunities—their hosting activities do not resemble work, but financial speculation. They transform their homes or the homes of others into assets and engage in subletting as a form of capital investment. Finally, the platform's social appeal is of primary relevance for those with only a few or relatively unsteady social relations. These hosts may engage in cultural exchange, practise language skills or feel more integrated in a community. However, many hosts also used the social argument to counterbalance their financial rationales. Only one host in the sample mentioned sociability as the primary rationale for subletting via Airbnb.

In light of the above presented findings, Airbnb turns out to be as much tied to mobility practices as it is to dwelling. While hosts are highly mobile, they often engage in subletting activities to secure the stability of their home—a finding that should be further investigated with particular attention to developments on the Berlin housing market. Moreover, short-term rental is frequently applied as a coping strategy to deal with increasingly unstable and flexible relationships in the private and professional realm, i.e., with regard to working conditions and social relations. Against this background, the monetisation of the home—more voluntarily for some than for others—seems to be the price to pay for living in mobile and flexible times.

Notes

1 See Stoltenberg and Frisch (Chapter 8 in this volume) for an analysis of another online service named Eatwith (www.eatwith.com) which connects users for joint meals at a resident's home.
2 Despite the broad variety of platforms and the various interpretations of sharing, they have not explained what types of sharing platforms they have included in their research.
3 When citing an interview, the number of the respective interview is stated in square brackets.
4 See also the quote by Host [13] in the Sociability section.

References

Airbnb. 2017. The Airbnb Community in Berlin 2016 [online]. Available from: https://community.withairbnb.com/t5/Berlin/ct-p/berlin [accessed 1 August 2018].
Airbnb. 2018. Airbnb in Berlin [online]. Available from: www.airbnbcitizen.com/data/#/en/berlin [accessed 1 August 2018].
Amt für Statistik Berlin-Brandenburg. 2018. Tourismus. Lange Reihen [online]. Available from: www.statistik-berlin-brandenburg.de/statistiken/langereihen.asp?Ptyp=450&Sageb=45005&creg=BBB&anzwer=7 [accessed 1 August 2018].
Andreotti, A. *et al.*, 2018. Participation in the Sharing Economy. Report from the EU H2020 Research Project Ps2Share: Participation, Privacy, and Power in the Sharing Economy [online]. Available from: www.bi.edu/globalassets/forskning/h2020/participation-working-paper.pdf [accessed 1 August 2018].
Belk, R., 2010. Sharing. *Journal of Consumer Research*, 36, 715–734.
Bellotti, V. *et al.*, 2015. A muddle of models of motivation for using peer-to-peer economy systems. *Proceedings of the 33rd Annual ACM Conference on Human Factors in Computing Systems*, 1085–1094.
Botsman, R. and Rogers, R., 2010. *What's Mine is Yours: The Rise of Collaborative Consumption*. New York: HarperBusiness.
Bowers, K.S., 1973. Situationism in psychology. An analysis and a critique. *Psychological Review*, 80 (5), 307–336.
Brenner, C., 2002. *Work in the New Economy. Flexible Labor Markets in the Silicon Valley*. Malden, MA: Blackwell.
Böcker, L. and Meelen, T., 2017. Sharing for people, planet or profit? Analysing motivations for intended sharing economy participation. *Environmental Innovation and Societal Transformations*, 23, 28–39.
Charmaz, K., 2014. *Constructing Grounded Theory*. London: SAGE.
Cócola Gant, A.C., 2016. Holiday rentals: the new gentrification battlefront. *Sociological Research Online*, 21 (3), 1–9.
Codagnone, C. and Martens, B., 2016. Scoping the Sharing Economy: Origins, Definitions, Impact and Regulatory Issues. JRC Technical Reports, Institute for Prospective Technological Studies Digital Economy Working Paper 2016/01

[online]. Available from: https://ec.europa.eu/jrc/sites/jrcsh/files/JRC100369.pdf [accessed 1 August 2018].

Cohen, S.A., Duncan, T. and Thulemark, M., 2015. Lifestyle mobilities: the crossroads of travel, leisure and migration. *Mobilities*, 10 (1), 155–172.

Colomb, C. and Novy, J., eds, 2017. *Protest and Resistance in the Tourist City*. Abingdon: Routledge.

Cox, M., 2018a. Inside Airbnb. Adding data to the debate. Get the data. Berlin [online]. Available from: http://insideairbnb.com/berlin/ [accessed 1 August 2018].

Cox, M., 2018b. Inside Airbnb. Adding data to the debate. Get the data. London [online]. Available from: http://insideairbnb.com/london/ [accessed 1 August 2018].

Cox, M., 2018c. Inside Airbnb. Adding data to the debate. Get the data. Paris [online]. Available from: http://insideairbnb.com/paris/ [accessed 1 August 2018].

Crang, M., 2014. Cultural geographies of tourism. *In*: A.A. Lew, C.M. Hall and A.M. Williams, eds, *The Wiley Blackwell Companion to Tourism*. Chichester: Wiley, 66–77.

Degen, M., 2010. Consuming urban rhythms: let's Ravalejar. *In*: T. Edensor, ed. *Geographies of Rhythm*. Aldershot: Ashgate, 21–32.

Dirksmeier, P. and Helbrecht, I., 2015. Resident perceptions of new urban tourism: a neglected geography of prejudice. *Geography Compass*, 9 (5), 276–285.

Dredge, D. and Gyimóthy, S., 2017. Collaborative economy and tourism. *In*: D. Dredge and S. Gyimóthy, eds, *Collaborative Economy and Tourism. Perspectives, Politics, Policies and Prospects*. Cham: Springer, 1–12.

DWIF, 2017. 12 mal Berlin er Leben. Konzept für einen stadtverträglichen und nachhaltigen Berlin-Tourismus 2018+ [online]. Available from: https://about. visitberlin.de/materialien/toolkit/tourismuskonzept [accessed 1 August 2018].

Elliott, A. and Urry, J., 2010. *Mobile Lives*. Abingdon: Routledge.

Endler, N. and Magnusson, D., 1976. Toward an interactional psychology of personality. *Psychological Bulleting*, 83 (5), 956–974.

European Commission, 2016. A European agenda for the collaborative economy [online]. Available from: http://ec.europa.eu/DocsRoom/documents/16881/attachments/2/translations [accessed 1 August 2018].

Freytag, T. and Bauder, M., 2018. Bottom-up touristification and urban transformations in Paris. *Tourism Geographies*, 20 (3), 443–460.

Füller, H. and Michel, B., 2014. 'Stop being a tourist!' New dynamics of urban tourism in Berlin-Kreuzberg. *International Journal of Urban and Regional Research*, 38 (4), 1304–1318.

Gravari-Barbas, M. and Guinand, S., eds, 2017. *Tourism and Gentrification in Contemporary Metropolises. International Perspectives*. Abingdon: Routledge.

Guttentag, D., 2015. Airbnb: disruptive innovation and the rise of an informal tourism accommodation sector. *Current Issues in Tourism*, 18 (12), 1192–1217.

Guttentag, D. *et al.*, 2017. Why tourists choose Airbnb: a motivation-based segmentation study. *Journal of Travel Research*, 57 (3), 342–359.

Gyimóthy, S. and Dredge, D., 2017. Definitions and mapping the landscape in the collaborative economy. *In*: D. Dredge and S. Gyimóthy, eds, *Collaborative Economy and Tourism. Perspectives, Politics, Policies and Prospects*. Cham: Springer, 15–30.

Hamari, J., Sjöklint, M. and Ukkonen, A., 2015. The sharing economy: why people participate in collaborative consumption. *Journal of the Association for Information Science and Technology*, 67 (9), 2047–2059.

Hannam, K., Sheller, M. and Urry, J., 2006. Editorial: mobilities, immobilities and moorings. *Mobilities*, 1 (1), 1–22.

Heckhausen, J. and Heckhausen, H., 2018. Motivation und Handeln: Einführung und Überblick. *In:* J. Heckhausen and H. Heckhausen, eds, *Motivation und Handeln*. Berlin: Springer, 1–11.

Heeg, S., 2013. Wohnungen als Finanzanlage. Auswirkungen von Responsibilisierung und Finanzialisierung im Bereich des Wohnens. *Sub\urban. Zeitschrift für kritische Stadtforschung*, 1, 75–99.

Heinrichs, H. and Grunenberg, H., 2012. Sharing Economy: Auf dem Weg in eine neue Konsumkultur? [online]. Available from: https://www.ssoar.info/ssoar/bitstream/handle/document/42748/ssoar-2012-heinrichs_et_al-Sharing_Economy__Auf_dem.pdf?sequence=1 [accessed 1 August 2018].

Hilti, N., 2016. Multi-local lifeworlds: between movement and mooring. *Cultural Studies*, 30 (3), 467–482.

Holm, A., 2013. Berlin's gentrification mainstream. *In*: A. Holm, B. Grell and M. Bernt, eds, *Berlin Reader. A Compendium on Urban Change and Activism*. Bielefeld: Transcript, 173–189.

Holm, A., 2016. Wie verändert Airbnb den Wohnungsmarkt? Eine Politische Ökonomie der Ferienwohnungen am Beispiel Berlin [online]. Available from: https://gentrificationblog.wordpress.com/2016/07/05/berliin-wie-veraendert-airbnb-den-wohnungsmarkt-eine-politische-oekonomie-der-ferienwohnungen/#more-4577 [accessed 1 August 2018].

Ikkala, T. and Lampinen, A., 2015. Monetizing network hospitality: hospitality and sociability in the context of Airbnb. *CSCW '15 Proceedings of the 18th ACM Conference on Computer Supported Cooperative Work & Social Computing*, 1033–1044.

Investitionsbank Berlin IBB, 2017. IBB Wohnungsmarktbericht 2016 [online]. Available from: www.ibb.de/media/dokumente/publikationen/berliner-wohnungsmarkt/wohnungsmarktbericht/ibb_wohnungsmarktbericht_2016.pdf [accessed 1 August 2018].

Kagermeier, A., Köller, J. and Stors, N., 2015. Share Economy im Tourismus. Zwischen pragmatischen Motiven und der Suche nach authentischen Erlebnissen. *Zeitschrift für Tourismuswissenschaft*, 7 (2), 117–146.

Kim, S. *et al.*, 2017. Examining the influencing factors of intention to share accommodations in online hospitality exchange networks. *Journal of Travel & Tourism Marketing*, 35 (7), 938–957.

Knaus, K., 2018. At home with guests: discussing hosting on Airbnb through the lens of labour. *Applied Mobilities*, 1–18.

Lampinen, A. and Cheshire, C., 2016. Hosting via Airbnb: motivations and financial assurances in monetized network hospitality. *CHI '16 Proceedings of the 2016 CHI Conference on Human Factors in Computing Systems*, 1669–1680.

Maitland, R. and Newman, P., eds, 2009. *World Tourism Cities. Developing Tourism Off the Beaten Track*. London: Routledge.

Martinotti, G., 1999. A city for whom? Transients and public life in the second-generation metropolis. *In*: R. Beauregard and S. Body-Gendrot, eds, *The Urban Moment*. Thousand Oaks, CA: SAGE, 155–184.

Meier, L. and Frank, S., 2016. Dwelling in mobile times: places, practices and contestations. *Cultural Studies*, 30 (3), 362–375.

Mermet, A.-C., 2017. Airbnb and tourism gentrification: critical insights from the exploratory analysis of the 'Airbnb syndrome' in Reykjavik. *In*: M. Gravari-Barbas and S. Guinand, eds, *Tourism and Gentrification in Contemporary Metropolises. International Perspectives.* Abingdon: Routledge, 52–74.

Novy, J. and Huning, S., 2009. New tourism (areas) in the 'New Berlin'. *In*: R. Maitland and P. Newman, eds, *World Tourism Cities. Developing Tourism Off the Beaten Track.* London: Routledge, 87–108.

Nowak, B. *et al.*, 2015. Internet, lodging, leisure and hotels. Global insights: who will Airbnb hurt more – hotels or OTAs? [online]. Available from: www.morganstanley. com/ideas/hotels-vs-online-travel-agencies [accessed 1 August 2018].

Opillard, F., 2017. From San Francisco's 'Tech Boom 2.0' to Valparaíso's UNESCO World Heritage Site: resistance to tourism gentrification from a comparative political perspective. *In*: C. Colomb and J. Novy, eds, *Protest and Resistance in the Tourist City.* Abingdon: Routledge, 129–151.

Pappalepore, I., Maitland, R. and Smith, A., 2010. Exploring urban creativity: visitor experiences of Spitalfields, London. *Tourism, Culture and Communication*, 10, 217–230.

Pappalepore, I., Maitland, R. and Smith, A., 2014. Prosuming creative urban areas. Evidence from east London. *Annals of Tourism Research*, 44, 227–240.

Paulauskaite, D. *et al.*, 2017. Living like a local: authentic tourism experiences and the sharing economy. *International Journal of Tourism Research*, 19 (6), 619–628.

Petzold, K., 2013. *Multilokalität als Handlungssituation. Lokale Identifikation, Kosmopolitismus und ortsbezogenes Handeln unter Mobilitätsbedingungen.* Wiesbaden: Springer.

Picard, M., 1996. *Bali: Cultural Tourism and Touristic Culture.* Singapore: Archipelago Press.

Pinkster, F.M. and Boterman, W.R., 2017. When the spell is broken: gentrification, urban tourism and privileged discontent in the Amsterdam canal district. *Cultural Geographies*, 24 (3), 457–472.

Quinby, D. and Gasdia, M., 2014. Share this! Private accommodation & the rise of the new gen renter. *Phocuswright* [online]. Available from: www.phocuswright.com/ Travel-Research/Consumer-Trends/Share-This-Private-Accommodation-the-Rise-of-the-New-Gen-Renter [accessed 1 August 2018].

Ryan, R.M. and Deci, E.L., 2000. Intrinsic and Extrinsic Motivations: Classic Definitions and New Directions. *Contemporary Educational Psychology*, 25, 54–67.

Saldaña, J., 2012. *The Coding Manual for Qualitative Researchers.* London: SAGE.

Sans, A.A. and Quaglieri Domínguez, A., 2016. Unravelling Airbnb: urban perspectives from Barcelona. *In*: A.P. Russo and G. Richards, eds, *Reinventing the Local in Tourism.* Bristol: Channel View Publications, 15–31.

Schäfer, P. and Hirsch, J., 2017. Do urban tourism hotspots affect housing rents? *International Journal of Housing Markets and Analysis*, 10 (2), 231–255.

Senatsverwaltung für Justiz und Verbraucherschutz Berlin, 2014. Verordnung über das Verbot der Zweckentfremdung von Wohnraum (Zweckentfremdungsverbot-Verordnung – WwVbVO) vom 4. März 2014 [online]. Available from: http:// gesetze.berlin.de/jportal/portal/t/hhn/page/bsbeprod.psml/action/portlets. jw.MainAction?p1=7&eventSubmit_doNavigate=searchInSubtreeTOC&sh owdoccase=1&doc.hl=0&doc.id=jlr-WoZwEntfrVBEpP6&doc.part=S&toc. poskey=#focuspoint [accessed 1 August 2018].

Sherlock, K., 2001. Revisiting the concept of hosts and guests. *Tourist Studies*, 1 (3), 271–295.

Stabrowski, F., 2017. 'People as businesses': Airbnb and urban micro-entrepreneurship in New York City. *Cambridge Journal of Regions, Economy and Society*, 10, 327–347.

Stors, N. and Baltes, S., 2018. Constructing Urban Tourism Space Digitally: A Study of Airbnb Listings in Two Berlin Neighborhoods. *Proceedings of the ACM on Human-Computer Interaction*, 2, 166, 1–29.

Stors, N. and Kagermeier, A., 2017. The sharing economy and its role in metropolitan tourism. *In*: M. Gravari-Barbas and S. Guinand, eds, *Tourism and Gentrification in Contemporary Metropolises. International Perspectives.* Abingdon: Routledge, 181–206.

Szydlik, M., 2008. Flexibilisierung und die Folgen. *In*: M. Szydlik, ed., *Flexibilisierung. Folgen für Arbeit und Familie.* Wiesbaden: VS Verlag, 17–22.

Tussyadiah, I.P., 2015. An exploratory study on drivers and deterrents of collaborative consumption in travel. *In*: I.P. Tussyadiah and A. Inversini, eds, *Information and Communication Technologies in Tourism 2015.* Cham: Springer, 817–830.

Tussyadiah, I.P. and Pesonen, J., 2016. Drivers and barriers of peer-to-peer accommodation stay: an exploratory study with American and Finnish travellers. *Current Issues in Tourism*, 19, 1–18.

Wachsmuth, D. and Weisler, A., 2018. Airbnb and the rent gap: gentrification through the sharing economy. *Environment and Planning A: Economy and Space*, 50 (6), 1147–1170.

7 Living like a local

Amsterdam Airbnb users and the blurring of boundaries between 'tourists' and 'residents' in residential neighbourhoods

Bianca Wildish and Bas Spierings

Amsterdam Airbnb and neighbourhood familiarisation

When investigating the urban tourism context, tourists and residents are often focused on as clearly defined and distinct groups, yet the boundaries between tourist/resident and insider/outsider are increasingly dissolving. Peer-to-peer accommodation platforms, like Airbnb (www.airbnb.com), contribute to increasing tourist–resident encounters in residential neighbourhoods and the blurring of boundaries between 'tourists' and 'residents' (Bock 2015). Tourists and residents are city users who visit the same places, engage in similar practices, share experiences, variably feel at home and interchangeably identify and are perceived as insiders and outsiders. Frequenting regular but diverse others' lively neighbourhoods is also as much, if not higher, on the tourist agenda as officially designated tourist attractions (Dirksmeier and Helbrecht 2015). Tourists increasingly seek authentic and home-like experiences (Füller and Michel 2014). In this context, Airbnb—whose marketing promotes feeling at home—facilitates millions of overnight stays in everyday environments and is a valued means of 'living like a local' for new urban tourists.

For Amsterdam, the most populous Dutch city and a key European tourist destination with a proliferation of Airbnb sites, keeping the balance between a liveable city while maintaining the tourist industry is a pertinent issue (Gemeente Amsterdam 2013). A largely negative narrative about tourists and Airbnb from the residents' perspective dominates literature and media about popular tourist cities, while research on tourist–resident encounters lacks qualitative approaches and tends to exclude the tourist perspective (Sharpley 2014). The dissolving of boundaries between tourists and residents has been recognised in *new urban tourism* studies (Stors *et al.*, Chapter 1 in this volume), however in light of the proliferation and spatial geography of Airbnb, how this process actually plays out through everyday neighbourhood encounters from the perspective of tourists requires examination. Focusing on Airbnb users in Amsterdam, this chapter therefore explores how Airbnb users practise and experience boundary blurring between 'tourists' and 'residents' in residential neighbourhoods.

To develop an understanding of this blurring of boundaries, we apply a novel lens to *new urban tourism* by focusing on multidimensional familiarisation processes in residential neighbourhoods.[1] Founded on the discussion of 'living like a local', two key aspects of boundary blurring are explored: first, the blurring between tourists and residents in the sense of participation in 'local life' through the performance of practices and visiting particular neighbourhood spaces; and second, between insiders and outsiders through experiences of belonging and feeling at home in the neighbourhood. From semi-structured in-depth interviews and mental mapping exercises, we selected three Airbnb user stories to present a diverse and detailed picture of the specific 'tourist–resident' contact zones. These stories identify a number of residential neighbourhood spaces such as Airbnb accommodation, shops, restaurants, bars and the street as contact zones with important implications for feelings of inside(r)/outside(r)ness. Examining neighbourhood encounters through the lens of familiarisation processes has proven useful, foregrounding diverse aspects of dynamic and relational boundary blurring. This chapter discusses these results which have specificity for private, semi-public and public contact zones in residential neighbourhoods.

New urban tourism and the blurring of boundaries between 'tourists' and 'residents'

It has become progressively more apparent that urban tourism and its associated impacts on urban fabric are not bound to clearly defined tourist precincts within cities nor certain tourist cities. Such "changing patterns of urban tourism" (Novy and Huning 2009, p. 88) have recently been highlighted and labelled '*new urban tourism*' by Füller and Michel (2014). New urban tourists strive to 'live like a local' where they visit—involving diverse aspects of boundary blurring between 'tourist' and 'resident' as well as the highly related binary categorisation of 'outsider' versus 'insider'.

Living like a local: who is the tourist, who is the resident?

The *new urban tourism* debate recognises a shift from 'sightseeing' to 'lifeseeing' (Bosschart and Frick 2006), a shift away from inner cities being the standard destination area, to gentrified, previously working-class neighbourhoods short of any iconic tourist attractions other than everyday life. This type of tourism is premised on the preference and motivations to experience cities outside official tourist attractions, wander 'off the beaten track' through 'ordinary' but diverse and lively neighbourhoods (Maitland 2010, Maitland and Newman 2014), explore 'alternative' urban spaces (Pappalepore *et al.* 2010), feel part of 'everyday' activities, and consume locally sourced and 'authentic' produce and services (Füller and Michel 2014). The aim is not to escape from everyday life by visiting extraordinary places—as traditional, mass tourists are expected to do (Larsen 2008)—but to participate in everyday life and find the extraordinary in these daily practices (Spierings 2006). The shift towards *new urban tourism* and the rise of private short-term rentals such as Airbnb are closely intertwined because such accommodation options provide access to local 'authentic' city life, not only geographically, by staying in the neighbourhood, but also through access to recommendations of local hosts regarding what to see and do in the area.[2] New urban tourists seem to share the aim to 'live like a local', and even become like a resident temporarily, through the experience of and/or participation in local neighbourhood life (Pappalepore *et al.* 2010, Airbnb 2013). As such, the motivations of tourists to visit a neighbourhood and the activities they undertake there converge with motivations and activities of residents—complicating any binary distinction being made between who the 'tourist' is, and who the 'resident' is in the neighbourhood or city.

This convergence applies both ways—according to Novy (2011), local residents can also be considered (new urban) tourists. Drawing on Urry (1995), Novy (2011) argues that everyone is a tourist, being a tourist and engaging in tourist activities is ever more a part of mundane daily life; it is an element of contemporary culture and forms how we perceive and experience our surroundings. This is especially the case when residents seek to experience the unfamiliar, unexplored and extraordinary in their own neighbourhood, city and country (Spierings 2006).

Living like a local: who is the outsider, who is the insider?

Living like a local is not only related with boundary blurring between tourists and residents in terms of motivations for visiting the neighbourhood and activities performed there. The use of the word 'live' also implies some level of involvement and deeper engagement with the neighbourhood—alluding to Relph's (1976) concept of 'insideness'. When analysing tourists' and residents' experiences of involvement and engagement with the neighbourhood, it is important to consider "not just the identity *of* a place […] but also the identity that a person or group has *with* that place, in particular whether they are experiencing it as an insider or as an outsider" (ibid., p. 45). According to Relph (1976), the distinction between an insider and outsider can be grasped by realising the various levels of intensity through which insideness and outsideness are experienced. These levels are not discrete yet are appreciated as relatively distinctive ways of experiencing places. One extreme entails 'belonging' to a place and a "deep and complete identity with a place" (ibid., p. 55), which can be aligned with the notion of feeling 'at home'. This is juxtaposed by the other extreme of 'not belonging', 'alienation' and 'homelessness' (Relph 1976, p. 51).

New urban tourists strive to 'live like a local', experiencing their destination through an insider perspective by becoming somewhat involved and engaged in the local neighbourhood—complicating any clear-cut characterisation of the tourist as an 'outsider' in an unfamiliar place. This is supported by Germann Molz's argument that tourists are capable of feeling at home anywhere through "embodied, embedded and localized acts of habitability" (2008, p. 326). New urban tourists are able to experience home-like feelings through the development of 'personal familiarity', 'private comfort' and 'public belonging' with and in the neighbourhood (Wildish 2017). For example, they can become personally familiar with neighbours, local entrepreneurs, the Airbnb accommodation and non-professional hosts.[3] Private comfort is related to having a place of retreat and relaxation, the Airbnb accommodation, for instance, where one can feel safe and secure. Public belonging implies feeling at home in the neighbourhood streets, parks, shops and other (semi-) public spaces, involving a feeling of attachment to and inclusion in the local community.

Going beyond resident–tourist or insider–outsider binaries, Massey (2010) argues that place is not fixed and isolated but rather fluid, dynamic and 'extrovert'—characterised by heterogeneous identities and produced through a multiplicity of translocal connections to the rest of the world. Tourist spaces, or residential neighbourhoods in this case, should therefore be understood as 'hybrid and unbounded', co-produced by a large variety of city users with many variations of mobilities, networks, memories and activities (Sommer 2018). This not only troubles any distinction between resident and tourist as well as between insider and outsider but, consequently, also questions notions of place which pit residents as insiders, or 'us', against tourists as outsiders, or 'them'. In a similar fashion, Allon and Anderson (2010) argue that 'tourists' stir "insider/outsider sensibilities of entitlement and belonging. Modes of encounter with and among such visitors expose and, above all, confuse the lines between 'itinerant' and 'host'" (p. 20). In doing so, they stress the importance of encounters in co-producing who is being considered an 'insider', 'outsider', 'resident' or 'tourist', and it is to these multifaceted encounters that we now turn.

Tourist–resident encounters in residential neighbourhoods

The nature of *new urban tourism*, including dwelling in residential neighbourhoods, and the supportive geography of Airbnb accommodation, entails increasing encounters between 'residents' and 'tourists' in neighbourhood settings. According to Matejskova and Leitner (2011, p. 722), encounters "hold open the possibility of either reinforcing or disorienting us from firmly held habits, stereotypes, and prejudices" and "they may both (re)inscribe and help transcend existing boundaries and differences between individuals and groups" (ibid.). Thus, the encounter is more than just the coming together of difference, the encounter itself is the circumstance in which differences and related boundaries are produced (Ahmed 2000). The element of difference in the tourist-resident encounter entails not just personal characteristics; different bodily attributes, temporalities, motivations and activities in neighbourhood spaces become salient. Ideas around who does and does not belong in a particular neighbourhood—potentially pinpointing tourists as outsiders—play a significant role in shaping social space and the extent to which visitors feel welcomed into the community and at home in the local area.

Drawing on Valentine (2008), Lawson and Elwood (2014) stress the spatial context of encounters by talking about 'zones and sites of encounter' as spaces where differences are (re)negotiated in the context of history, power relations and material conditions.[4] As such, encounters can involve both human and non-human elements, as defined by Crouch (1999, p. 1), "encounter occurs between several things. It occurs between people, between people and space, amongst people as socialised and embodied subject, and in contexts in which leisure/tourism is available. The encounter is also between expectations and experience, desire, and so on".

When analysing encounters in diverse urban contact zones, two main types are often distinguished. The key difference is that one is a shallower, fleeting, often non-verbal, daily encounter typically taking place in urban public space (Lofland 1989), while the other lasts longer, involving continuous interaction arising from a shared activity or repetitive encounters (Matejskova and Leitner 2011). Valentine (2008) emphasises that the key difference is that the latter entails more 'meaningful' contact. These types have been labelled by Goffman (1963) who differentiates between unfocused and focused encounters; respectively entailing people simply sharing the same space without direct contact, such as observing others while walking by in the street, versus individuals being in direct contact and engaging in activities together such as conversations in a bar. The latter may also involve secondary or 'segmental' contact when people only bring limited segments of their personality—based on an occupational role, for instance—to the encounter. In the context of this research, an example is when tourists get food recommendations from local bartenders. When hosts and guests connect in the Airbnb accommodation, however, these encounters involve primary contact, which is when biographical and emotional aspects of the self are being shared (Lofland 1989). These types of tourist–resident encounters are highly influential for the neighbourhood familiarisation of 'tourists' and 'outsiders', as will be explained next.

Becoming like a 'resident' and 'insider' through neighbourhood familiarisation

Developing familiarity with people and places involves dynamic and relational familiarisation processes, unfolding through an interplay between 'informational', 'experiential' and 'proximate' dimensions (Szytniewski and Spierings 2014). Informational familiarity develops when gaining 'knowledge' of people and places, with access to and quality of information as key properties. Knowledge about cultural norms and values, physical highlights and 'authentic' functional facilities, can be obtained through both indirect information sources—e.g., via family, friends and media—and direct information sources—through experiences during previous encounters with the neighbourhood (Baloglu 2001). According to Lofland (1971), encounters may be restricted to visual and brief verbal interactions only, resulting in a 'simple' knowing or categorisation of others based on often stereotypical information about their roles and statuses—including 'tourist' and 'resident'. More 'complex' or 'personal knowing' may develop through both visual and verbal encounters when 'categoric knowing' is supplemented by adding depth and detail-based biographical information. As such, 'tourists' and 'residents' may realise that they actually have more in common than expected when not only focusing on their categorical differences.

Experiential familiarity develops when tourists gain direct experiences in and with the city and its neighbourhoods during the current and previous visits (Baloglu 2001). Experiences are gained through fleeting, unfocused encounters in co-presence of others in a variety of public and semi-public spaces, including streets and bars. More meaningful, focused interactions can be experienced with local hosts in the private space of the Airbnb accommodation, for instance. Memories of previous encounters and visits mediate present moments of experience with neighbourhoods and those who reside there. Current experiences may be influenced by current and/or past experiences in that city and its neighbourhoods but also with other, potentially but not necessarily similar, places (Degen and Rose 2012). Neighbourhood experiences also involve and are influenced by social differentiation taking place between 'tourists' and 'residents', or rather the boundary blurring between both categories. In this context, Valentine and Sadgrove (2012) argue that daily life experiences of social differentiation should not be understood by theorising social identity—including 'tourist' versus 'resident'—based on static signifiers—including 'place of residence'—or simple 'categoric knowing' as Lofland (1971) would put it. A deep understanding of "constant processes of differentiation evident in sociospatial relationships" (2012, p. 2058) is required to capture the dynamism of personal positioning and related daily life experiences.

Even with a great deal and variety of knowledge about people and places obtained and experiences gained, tourists may still feel socially distant during encounters in and with the residential neighbourhood—reflected in a degree of proximate unfamiliarity. According to O'Donoghue (2013, p. 406), "proximity [or distance] is not about being fixed, neither is it solely about movement [...] it is about recognizing the positioning of ideas, concepts, and selves as they come into being through interaction with or alongside other beings". This coming into being during encounters with people and places involves 'affective', 'normative' and 'interactive' understandings of proximity and distance (Szytniewski *et al.* 2017). Affective proximity implies that people who are socially and culturally close also feel close (Karakayali 2009). Moreover, Valentine and Sadgrove (2012) add that felt closeness or intimacy may develop through encounters and these feelings also help overcoming obvious differences and related categorisations, including 'tourist' and 'resident'— pointing at dynamics and negotiations of social distance. Normative social distance implies that people may feel proximate or distant when recognising and sharing norms and values, also generating a degree of differentiation between 'us' as 'insiders' and 'them' as 'outsiders' (Karakayali 2009). As such, cultural identity and group membership are being defined and 'strangers' are identified as not belonging and out of place (Ahmed 2000). Interactive social distance implies that the less tourists have to modify their behaviour in unfamiliar settings—in the sense of required 'cross-cultural code-switching' for accommodating different norms and values (Molinsky 2007)—the more socially proximate they may feel with residents, and the more they will also feel familiar with and at home in the neighbourhood. Tourists may get accustomed to and develop skills to behave in accordance with norms and values during everyday repetition but they also occasionally challenge, change and improvise during encounters with and in the local environment (Edensor 2007).

Mental mapping and interviewing in Amsterdam

Amsterdam was selected as the case study because tourism is a contentious topic in this city. Tourists are on the rise, as is the amount of Airbnb accommodation and consequently the implications for residents. Amsterdam has a population of nearly 835,000 and just over half (51.7%) are non-Dutch residents (Gemeente Amsterdam 2017). Residents can legally rent their property to tourists provided regulations are respected. In total, Amsterdam has approximately 19,000 Airbnb listings (Inside Airbnb 2018).

Airbnb accommodation prevails in neighbourhoods within Amsterdam's nineteenth-century Ring (bound by Highway 10); no neighbourhood outside has a percentage of Airbnb accommodation greater than 1 per cent, while inside, percentages reach up to 7.6 per cent (Hogeweij 2016). Amsterdam's core is historically a very touristic area with a high density of attractions, hotels and now Airbnb accommodation—it is unsurprising to find many tourists there. This chapter discusses encounters between tourists and residents in traditionally non-touristic residential neighbourhoods and therefore focuses on tourists staying in Airbnb accommodation outside the city centre—defined as outside the canal district.

This chapter is based on research done for a larger research project on urban tourism and Airbnb in Amsterdam with specific attention to encounters between tourists and residents and their feeling at home in residential neighbourhoods. This entailed in-depth interviews and mental mapping exercises with thirteen residents and sixteen tourists. Semi-structured in-depth interviews were employed as they simultaneously enable comparability between interviews and provide rich, descriptive data, capturing the diversity of participants' responses and allow for an exploration of links between feelings and experiences. The interview guide consisted of four key topics: spatial practices; neighbouring, hosting or staying in Airbnb accommodation; tourist–resident encounters; and feeling at home in the neighbourhood.

Participants were asked to draw a mental map of their neighbourhood, including their accommodation and places they visited. While mental mapping is challenging, depicting three-dimensional space in two dimensions, relying on participants memory, drawing and creative abilities, it is a useful tool to represent what is known and felt about places (Bell 2009). It uncovers participants' spatial knowledge of, and familiarity with, a place. The maps were used as "conversation points for further discussion" (Gieseking 2013, p. 716) during the interviews, helping participants to think spatially, provide detailed stories and, most importantly, tell their stories instead of providing a more general picture of the neighbourhood.

For this chapter, three narratives are discussed, that of James, a repeat visitor, a small group—Priya, Jay, Leah and Nikita—and a first-time visitor George. They have been selected to present a diverse and detailed picture of tourist–resident encounters in Amsterdam from the perspective of the Airbnb users. These visitors were recruited through a gatekeeper. The peer-to-business-to-peer company Airbnbutler, which assists hosts with running their Airbnbs, provided the connections with Airbnb users in Amsterdam who were approached via email to participate.

James: a story about friendship, sense of community, anonymity and observation mode

James is 43, from South Africa, and works in theatre. He has previously been to Amsterdam for work and is a repeat visitor to the Airbnb accommodation in Oosterpark (marked 'X' beside the street name Vrolik in Figure 7.1). At the point of the interview James had already stayed five days and would stay an additional two weeks. When describing what kind of visitor he was, James expressed that he wants to "feel like part of the city" rather than "just flashing through". He likes "experiencing a city and kind of riffing off it you know, what is the energy, what can the energy of the city do".

Private space: Airbnb accommodation

James is a repeat visitor to his Airbnb accommodation which is owned by Sanne. She lives upstairs and rents the bottom floor to Airbnb guests. After James's first stay in Amsterdam for a work project, he clicked with Sanne, they formed a friendship and kept in touch. James felt at home in his Airbnb accommodation, an identity with a place which is closely bound up with feeling like an insider (Relph 1976). James was familiar with his host and his accommodation, but even more than this, he felt connected to both. Feeling at home for James was defined by a combination of privacy, which was as simple as having his own room where he could "close the door and be like okay, now it's just me" and sentimentality. James points at a large beautiful vase and explains:

> Like look over there, you get the artworks that are sentimental, then you see there are similarities in taste, she has a great music collection, upstairs and sort of dotted around and lots of instruments, so we can connect on

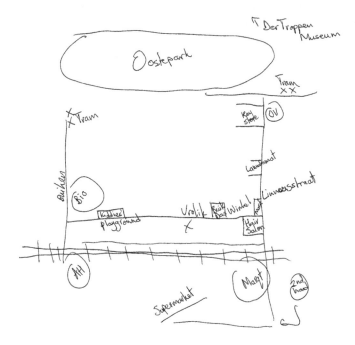

Figure 7.1 Mental map drawn by James.
Source: compiled by the authors.

that and if I am playing something late at night, she will pop down and sit and have a listen and vice versa, so there's this great feeling of flow.

For James, the type of encounters with Sanne were focused; engaging in activities together such as making music, having dinner and "talking *kak* [shit] and catching up". These types of interactions and the fact they share interests, exemplifies 'affective' proximity, in that James experienced 'closeness' (Karakayali 2009) to Sanne. Sharing and recognising emotional aspects of the self intensifies feelings of closeness. James felt humbled to be so welcomed into Sanne's accommodation, "it's her home, it's very open, and what's remarkable is how trusting she is of people who stay here". The accommodation is full of her precious things which resonate with him, and the fact she shares her time, space and belongings contributes to his sense of 'flow'.

Contrasting his Airbnb experience at Sanne's place which has "a lot of soul and love in it" to that of hotels which he regards as 'soulless', enabled James to further articulate why he felt at home:

It's like this ridiculous saying, home from home, which gets overused but it's really so true… There is no pressure on one to get up at a certain time, or what have you, it's just like respect the rules and help yourself.

So that's great, you don't get that kind of hustle from a hotel or something like that, you can actually wander in and out as you please and just this morning… it was raining and I was like ah, I actually don't feel like hurrying out anywhere and kind of lay on the bed for a few hours reading which is wonderful. Very often in hotels it is so impersonal that you're just like oh fuck this and go into the street and do something.

Because the accommodation is physically comfortable and he feels the freedom to do as he pleases meant that James felt happy to relax there, as if it were his own home. James's informational familiarity on behavioural codes is based on 'personal knowing' through his past experience at this Airbnb. He contrasts this to the more impersonal 'categorical knowing' of hotel staff based on roles and rigid regulations. His Airbnb experience is characterised by a sense of insideness compared to a sense of outsideness through his experience of feeling out of place in hotels. Thus, the personal knowing, informational familiarity, residential location and unique decor of the Airbnb makes it feel "more real than a hotel". It is important to James to feel at home when in a foreign city, and these elements plus the social closeness felt with Sanne are the "little things that help one anchor".

Semi-public space: local shops

Through his visits to local shops, James picked up on the sense of local ownership, regular patronage and locals' deep-rooted sense of belonging. Because he could recognise this, James felt like he could relate and partake in this connection. James was impressed by:

the sense of local ownership, that's very, very diverse, there are some very small businesses, like the cheese maker, the fish guy, the bread guy, the what have you, but they have been doing this for a very long time, it's in the family… you can feel that the people inside are regulars and they go there to get it and gossip.

Although his encounters with and in these local shops are unfocused and characterised by observation, James is attentive to small details—contributing to detailed informational familiarity. James senses many locals' strong sense of community and projects this onto his general experience and understanding of the local inhabitants. The way James talks about the neighbourhood goods, services and ownership hints that it is more authentic than the commercialised city centre and therefore more special, charming and local.

James gave an anecdote of being in the organic supermarket where "there was an old lady that obviously everyone knows and she was there with her bottle of wine, but she was a little bit frail and she started to fall and out of nowhere someone came rushing in with a chair and slid it underneath her at the till. And that's lovely". From his perspective, the residents are 'intensely loyal', everyone knows everyone and there is a friendly and supportive togetherness—potentially reflecting a romanticised stereotype of how local people live their lives. Be that as it may, for James, picking up on others' strong sense of belonging was infectious and made him feel like an insider because he both recognised and adjusted to the local rhythms. Furthermore, because James did not need to adapt so much culturally, particularly in terms of language, he felt socially proximate to the general population. As he explained about service encounters, he would "stumble through" his "pigeon Dutch, and they will just switch to English, and be super nice about all of that". Shopkeepers switching to English signified to James this inclusive camaraderie, evoking a sense of insideness. Yet in general not knowing the language also evoked a sense of outsideness for James as when asked whether he felt a sense of belonging to the neighbourhood he responded: "In a weird way, yeah, like you know, one feels quite loyal to it, I mean I am an outsider in that I am visiting and I don't speak the language fluently, but yeah."

Public space: neighbourhood streets

The street featured prominently in James's narrative and this contact zone exemplifies processes of his experience of blurring boundaries. That is, in some instances James identifies and feels identified as a new urban tourist, whilst in other moments a local city user. James explained that his encounters in public space were fleeting and unfocused: "[W]hen I walk around the park, and in the streets, on the tram and just generally missioning through, yeah just part of the hustle and bustle of daily life. It is not like I will sit somewhere and interact, it's more that I will just wander at this point." This wandering itself however is very important to James's experience of feeling like a local, he expressed that he is "a lot more alone in Cape Town" because it is so autocentric. In Oosterparkbuurt, James was motivated to explore the area and went for daily morning walks to be among the "hustle and bustle" of local neighbourhood life. James felt more involved by gaining context-specific spatial and sensory knowledge, getting accustomed to the sounds, smells and physical layout of the neighbourhood as well as the local rhythms:

> [I]t's a whole particular rhythm of people you know getting ready for school, and the biking culture, so there's always sounds going around on the streets, the kids or the rubbish truck… one has to get used to the noises obviously, each place has its own particular noise, but then yeah, smells, people cooking different things or you walk around the corner and there is a different restaurant or what have you, it's got a little bit more space to breathe than the city centre, where it is just coming at you the whole time.

Being cognisant of these happenings increased James's familiarity of place and also helped him feel in place. Staying in a residential neighbourhood, an appeal to new urban tourists who want a local experience, means one can more manageably get a sense of the rhythms and subtleties, as James mentions, compared to the city centre which is a sensual overload.

James differentiates himself from mass tourists because he is more attuned to everyday life of the city, but also goes as far as feeling like a local. James felt like an insider when walking through the neighbourhood because the diversity of Amsterdam's population meant he was able to blend in, specifically in terms of skin colour and general appearance. This relates to the individual level of the 'experiential' component of familiarity, where James is typically used to being regarded as 'different' for his appearance. He explained that "in South Africa or other places I would sort of stand out more because of oh the hair, or oh the black clothes you know... [here] it doesn't seem to ruffle anyone's feathers". When discussing whether he felt if he was identifiable as an outsider, James felt others were not necessarily even aware of him, that he was "quite invisible". He enjoyed this anonymity, it reinforced his feeling of fitting in and belonging such that he could go about his business as a city user without being conscious of being foreign or different. In his words, "it's a tacit acceptance from people and just the ease and comfort and leaving me the fuck alone in a way, it's quite nice".

To highlight James's experience of blurring boundaries, despite feeling like an insider because of knowing where to walk and passing from an onlooker's point of view as an insider, James also expressed that he felt like an outsider, "but not an ostracized one". He felt like an outsider because of the lack of interaction with locals, as he was not "in the business of making friends" and rather than participating in local life, he was more in "observation mode". Considering also temporality, walking the streets at night brought James's outsideness to the fore of his experience because he was able to notice that the atmosphere "relaxed that sort of heightened South African awareness". James was aware of how different The Netherlands made him feel regarding safety in public space at night. This was influenced by the streets being well lit, the fact that "people are quite open, and their curtains are open" and witnessing the confidence asserted by women. Although a positive experience, it is still a contrast from the social norms and values he is used to, evoking some degree of normative distance; not walking streets at night, bars across locked windows, and assuming strangers are potentially dangerous. For James is more familiar with "an instilled fear of violence, of being attacked, so what is wonderful here is the confidence that people have, particularly the women, they can just be wandering the streets at half past eleven at night and no problem you know". Thus, in public space, namely walking the streets of his neighbourhood, James exemplifies how fleeting, unfocused encounters with people and space which involve observation afford anonymity and related experiential familiarity that in turn evoke a sense of insideness. However, key experiential differences become salient through unfocused encounters, which combined with the lack of meaningful (focused) encounters with locals, also results in moments of feeling like an outsider.

James feels comfortable in mobility, feeling at home is not confined to his Airbnb accommodation, nor the neighbourhood itself, rather in exploring the area, the act of walking, the act of physically travelling makes him feel at home: "Definitely [feel at home] here [in the Airbnb] or on the move, so it is either static, like being here, or just passing through and wandering. There isn't like a place I'll go to, to kind of feel settled or what have you." Akin to the findings of Germann Molz (2008, p. 333) who asserts that travellers practise a sort of mobile attachment through the continuity and familiarity of travel itself, the world becomes a 'global abode'—a place of belonging established by a privileged access to both mobility and stability. Travellers translate their ability to feel at home in mobility into a sense of being at home in the world, which can be recognised in James with his cosmopolitan sensibility and engagement in everyday practices while travelling.

Priya, Jay, Leah and Nikita: a story about in-group dynamics, local recommendations, minding one's own business and transport rhythms

Priya, 30, who works in digital communications and her husband Jay, 31, a chartered accountant, travelled to Amsterdam for a long weekend with Leah, 30, a finance banker and Nikita, 31, a technology consultant. These four British Indian friends rented an entire apartment in Oud-West for three nights (marked '*' on Kinkerstraat in Figure 7.2). This was a "friendship renewal trip". When travelling they like walking, finding nice food and as Leah explained are "not that bothered about actual sightseeing", they "just like to see".

Private space: Airbnb accommodation

Priya, Jay, Leah and Nikita stayed in a two-bedroom apartment in Oud-West. They expressed *new urban tourism* sentiments when selecting the location of their accommodation, desiring to stay in a local neighbourhood away from overly touristy areas:

PRIYA: We knew we wanted to do Airbnb from the beginning, so it was finding one in an area that was close enough to central so you could go in, but also far enough out that we could again see the local neighbourhood as well, I think that was key…

JAY: We wouldn't have chosen one near Dam or the central station, because we knew it would've been hyper touristy, we wanted to be away from that…

LEAH: …the description indicated that it was a lively and local neighbourhood.

The group emphasised the importance of being immersed in a local neighbourhood and the Airbnb description highlighted this opportunity. Feeling like an insider can mean having access to local life. This is understood to play

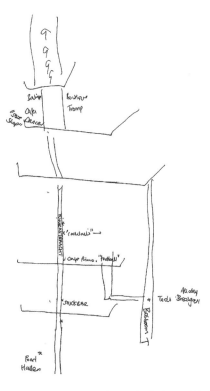

Figure 7.2 Mental map drawn by Priya, with input from Leah, Jay and Nikita.
Source: compiled by the authors.

out in residential neighbourhoods rather than the city centre which is marked
as commercialised, touristified and inauthentic (Maitland 2010).

Priya explained that they chose Airbnb because they wanted their "own
space [...] to be together". Like James, Priya contrasted Airbnb with hotel
accommodation, expressing that "if you're in a hotel room you've got two
separate rooms and there's nowhere to sort of relax and chill out". Hence,
building on James's perspective, a physically comfortable, private space which
affords the freedom to engage in familiar activities which make one feel at
home was important for this group to feel like insiders. When explaining what
feeling at home in the accommodation meant to them, they expressed:

PRIYA: Being in my pyjamas.
NAKITA: Feeling the freedom to just have a walk around, make a cup of
    tea, sit on the sofa with your legs up, watch TV, have music on in the
    background.
JAY: Yeah it was cosy it was warm, with music, when us lot go away there's
    always music on in the background so that was nice.

This highlights how familiarity is not necessarily context specific, engaging in familiar routines can make people feel a sense of insideness. While being familiar with a place and its people are typically context specific, familiar activities and objects are transportable across contexts. Here they mention pyjamas, drinking tea, watching TV and listening to music. Familiar possessions and objects can serve as "signifiers of familiarity and continuity through which homely feelings are evoked" (Germann Molz 2008, p. 334). Thus, feeling like an insider in a foreign context can be triggered by familiar practices and in novel settings. Although engagement with the novel setting is shallow, the strength of feeling at home comes from the shared affective familiarity.

Semi-public space: local restaurants and bars

Despite staying in a residential neighbourhood, access to local recommendations was lacking for this group. Their host did not provide them with "any context, any ideas, it was just how to lock the front door" (Priya), which they felt was a shame because they "always like to find out where locals like to go" (Nikita). This lack of insider knowledge made them feel more like outsiders when it came to choosing what to see and do, and particularly where to eat in the local neighbourhood. In the case of *new urban tourism*, accessibility and quality of information are substantially determined by locals. Without direct or indirect interaction with locals who hold such tacit knowledge, the indirect information from social media and tour guides lost some validity. However, the group combined online research about their neighbourhood with direct experience of looking where 'locals' go, to develop their informational familiarity. Priya felt the shops and restaurants she saw were "going to be good" because they seem "to be frequented by locals, which means something".

The group did not specifically seek to encounter locals in bars, rather they left it up to chance. They were conscious that they were observing, curious and open to encounter, but their intention was to socialise within their group which therefore meant they limited their willingness to encounter locals. They described themselves as a "self-contained unit" who knew what they wanted to do and valued "spending time together" (Leah). Familiarity is about close relations with other people and in this case, this group of friends are extremely familiar with one another and focused on this connection. Inevitably they felt like insiders in their group, despite—but also due to—their unfamiliar surroundings.

One particular semi-public contact zone we can zoom in on is the pub 'Primo' Jay visited to watch football. This experience clearly marked processes of boundary blurring as he entered the pub without any desire to converse, feeling a bit lost and unfamiliar and his initial conversation with the bar staff and other patrons was centred on his foreign accent—evoking some degree of outside(r)ness. Jay explained: "they were talking to me about English football, because they could tell straight away that I was a tourist". Yet after some time he became "quite chilled", he was participating in the same practices as the other locals in the bar and despite being on his own, he felt at home in the "cosy neighbourhoodly pub".

Public space: neighbourhood streets

Local residents helped this group feel like locals in some instances, while in others made them aware of their outsideness. Feeling local was instilled by the manner in which Dutch people interacted, they were polite, however not too polite.

PRIYA: …in some countries they're like over-friendly, that makes you feel quite different from home.

NIKITA: It's like London in some ways, people are just walking around getting on with their lives and we're getting on with ours.

JAY: If we sought out help, we knew we'd get it.

NIKITA: It's not been an extreme on either way so it's been quite nice because we just feel like we're blending and just doing what we do at home.

Not being treated like tourists enabled the group to feel like they fitted in more, gave them both a sense of confidence and a level of anonymity. This narrative also highlights the similarities in terms of interactive social distance experienced between London and Amsterdam. They did not need to stretch themselves to behave very differently from London, there was little 'cross-cultural code-switching' (Molinsky 2007). Minding their own business or the "getting on with life" code of conduct—for 'tourists' and 'residents' alike—translated across contexts, the effort required to adapt was not strenuous as they were just doing what they do at home. This social interaction element of familiarity was appreciated and enabled an experience of "blending" (Nikita).

An array of experiences of walking on Kinkerstraat exemplify boundary blurring. The group identified cycling and specifically observing and being among Dutch cyclists on the street as a key experience that marked their outsideness—reflecting a normative distance related with traffic habits and behaviours.[5] As Nikita exclaimed "trying to cross a road is really scary". Cycling was seen as an activity to try in the park, not a mode of transport, and navigating the foreign transport rules was challenging and disconcerting. The speed and volume of cyclists was intimidating. Recognising the confidence of local cyclists while feeling nervous and unsure about how to behave in relation to cyclists on the street, emphasised their outsideness and lack of familiarity with the local transport rhythm. However, in different moments walking down this same street, Jay expressed how they came to feel like residents and be perceived as so through walking "around with confidence, like we know where we're going" and not having "heads in a map" or "a massive camera". This was during their second and third days, but again when adorned with such tourist markers, the group were conscious of their visible identity as outsiders, particularly when carting around their wheelie bags upon arrival to and departure from their accommodation. Nevertheless, Jay exclaimed "we will always remember Kinkerstraat, it's our place".

The feeling of walking down Kinkerstraat was compared to streets in the city centre. The city centre was "*so* busy, *so* many people. You can tell obviously it's like where tourists will automatically flock... Here [Kinkerstraat], you can tell it is just full of local people that live here. It's not as busy, it's not as rowdy". Walking on Kinkerstraat meant this group encountered a different rhythm of daily public life from the city centre. Leah felt "smug about it", staying in a residential neighbourhood and walking streets such as this one made her feel like she had "won a bit more", had her own novel personal experience (Bock 2015). This feeling of having access to authentic local areas, and therefore goods and services, meant that Leah felt "less pressure that I am going to get ripped off". As Jay summarised it, they have "been on enough holidays that we know we don't need to be staying smack bang in the centre of the city to have a good time [...] [W]e're not I suppose fearful about being off the beaten track a little bit and we're happy to walk". Walking is an important practice which as highlighted here, depending on individual gait, accessories and focus, can be experienced as a tourist and/or resident practice.

George: a story about sense of security, knowing the way, genuine bluntness and cycling cultures

George is a 24-year-old British lighting designer who came to Amsterdam with his Australian girlfriend and two Australian friends for four days. They rented a whole Airbnb apartment for themselves (marked 'house' in Figure 7.3). It was his first time in The Netherlands and although he was "quite impartial" about visiting Amsterdam, because when he travels he likes to "go places for a reason", he was "keen to see new bits of Europe". The interview took place after his visit via Skype.

Private space: Airbnb accommodation

Like the other interviewees, George felt at home in his Airbnb accommodation due to the private comfort it gave him, but his experience of comfort was not just physical, but also mental. He felt a "sense of security more generally not just from a threat point of view but from a general wellbeing point of view". Not only was it "nicely furnished", "warm and cosy" with good lighting, but he felt "safe and secure" in the location, describing words suggestive of feeling at home (Wildish *et al.* 2016). This meant not being "worried about what might be going on near the property" and feeling "like you can be yourself, you can watch TV without worrying about bothering other people". Even knowing that he had this private place to retreat to, a familiar and safe haven, meant he felt a sense of security while out during the day. George explained:

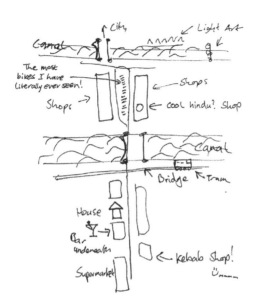

Figure 7.3 Mental map drawn by George.
Source: compiled by the authors.

> I quite like to have a solid base to come back to because at the end of the
> day you are in a foreign country, you don't know the area necessarily and
> you don't know what kind of mysteries or trouble you might end up in so
> I think it is quite nice… knowing you have somewhere to come back to
> and kind of relax, kick back and chill out… I am a creature of comfort,
> I like having a base.

Staying in an Airbnb in a residential area outside the city centre afforded
George a more local experience than staying in a hotel—referred to as
a "bubble of no culture". He appreciated that their neighbourhood had a
"slower pace" and provided "a buffer from the hustle and bustle" of the centre.
    Opposite to James but similar to Priya's group, George had minimal con-
tact with his Airbnb host, to the point that the accommodation provider
became insignificant. This segmental contact, where George engaged as a
guest with the host minimally about practicalities, was not about exchan-
ging biographical or emotional information. Due to having only segmental
encounters combined with experiential familiarity in the accommodation,
George felt like it was his own place:

> To be perfectly honest I quite quickly forgot I was with Airbnb, for
> example my friend has quite red hair, she dies it, so it was on one of the
> towels, so there were a few moments where we had to make contact…

but personally I didn't think about Airbnb much at all. It just felt like we owned a little flat in Amsterdam for a few days, it was quite nice.

The diminished focus and awareness of being an Airbnb user, meant George's experience was in some instances framed through feeling like a resident, that he owned the place. Living with or like locals can include imagining what locals' lives are like (Maitland 2010). Because of the "homey environment" and "residential area", George explained that "you do kind of almost picture yourself living there".

Ley-Cervantes and Duyvendak (2017) contend that fostering feelings of home depend on personalising space; demarcating material or symbolic boundaries through displaying identity(ies). Additional to appreciating how the space was decorated, George personalised his Airbnb with some of his own familiar objects and touches closely tied to his identity: "So yeah, we changed a few little things, and being lighting designers, we immediately got on some chairs and started readjusting all the lights that were pointing at the wall and not quite at the photograph so we immediately started fiddling around with everything." He also decorated the Airbnb with gifts he received from a "Secret Santa event" at work. These acts helped entrench his feeling at home through surrounding himself with familiar objects, tweaking the environment to reflect his taste and comfort, adding that personal touch.

Semi-public space: local supermarket

Despite his brief stay, George quickly got familiar with his location and frequented certain places like the local supermarket. George explained how personal familiarity of place as well as routine produced the feeling of being at home for him: "I think it came with the familiarity of being there, and going to the shop every morning, you do start to feel like you're a local and you've got that kind of sense of feeling comfortable somewhere, you know the way down to the shop." Duyvendak (2011) asserts that familiarity takes time, yet the surface level of recognising landmarks and regular walking routes is sufficient for some city users to feel at home. Routines stimulate feeling at home for city users who can rapidly and enthusiastically attach to places and in doing so establish homely routines in short time frames; even experiencing being a 'regular' after a couple of visits (Germann Molz 2008).

The main shop George mentioned was the supermarket. His experience and behaviour exemplify an instance of feeling like a tourist and a resident in the same space. George expressed his delight at the local cheese and "Dutch things" on offer at the supermarket: he felt like an outsider/tourist as he "spent quite a long time just wandering around the shop looking at all the different local bits and pieces". Yet when he arrived at the cashier to pay and was told in a "very matter of fact" way that they do not accept Mastercard, he was very surprised. In this exchange he expected the store clerk to be friendly and offer an alternative, instead of being short and direct. Although this circumstance highlighted George's informational unfamiliarity about the local payment method, which might mark one as an outsider, the way it was dealt with the blunt reaction, made him feel accepted and like an insider because they were not treating him like a tourist, "they weren't patronising [...]. I found it quite nice that they just accepted me and you know that was it, I was someone trying to buy their stuff [...], there wasn't any special treatment, it was just raw Amsterdam". This exemplifies a moment where George was simultaneously feeling like an insider and an outsider. Just like Jay, Priya, Nikita and Leah appreciated the direct nature of Dutch people, this also made George feel like he had a local experience: "I think the people, they didn't put on a show for us or anything, they were the people they are every day, going about their daily lives as if we are just daily people. I think the interactions we did have were very genuine."

Public space: neighbourhood streets

Unlike the other interviewees, George felt like he stood out as a tourist. He explained: "I think we stood out a little bit because we were so obviously, we were touristy tourists, wandering around with our cameras and stuff but I think if I was there for a bit longer and doing less of that camera stuff, I think I would have felt quite comfortable to blend in and get on with things." Again because of physical appearance, namely 'tourist' markers and "slight fashion differences", George was conscious of his outside(r)ness and believed others to be also. While the other interviewees granted being treated as local as a sign that they blended in, George felt that he got this treatment regardless, explaining that "people weren't going out of their way to be helpful to tourists, they were just treating us as locals". But again, being treated as a local still had the impact of making him feel more like an insider. As he also mentioned: "I think enjoying the localness and just taking all that in and being open to them, I think that made me feel they would perhaps be open back, to give me that sense of belonging." Experiencing and being open to local culture, enabled George to feel in place and connected to his neighbourhood.

Upon arrival, the cycling culture struck George as very surprising, particularly compared to the UK where "cyclists are the people underneath the cars!" In Amsterdam however, cyclists "are the king of the road" with "the right of way, their own traffic signals and lanes". The most shocking aspect was seeing people not wearing helmets. This different cycling culture was so unfamiliar to George that it made him feel strange and uncomfortable, until he tried it for himself in a biking tour—which made him realise that he could switch cultural codes quite easily referring to interactive familiarity with the cycling culture. He argued that this gave him a different perspective and a "sense of being a local and what it was like to cycle through [the city]". Engaging in the activity, albeit guided, enabled George to be exposed to the cycling rhythms, feel more comfortable and feel more like an insider. Through this experience,

George was more positive about the cycling culture and experience than the other interviewees.

Overall, George felt between an insider and an outsider. This mainly boiled down to his informational and experiential familiarity of place whereas his ability to navigate the area was still limited: "I don't want to say outsider, because I could go to the shops and I could get on my way and do things, but I don't feel like I have that kind of confidence where I could be like oh yeah we can just duck down this street and pop out here or do this or do that." Again, like the other interviewees, George got around on foot, he "ended up walking everywhere" and "quickly forgot about buses and trams". Walking was a means to really engage with the city and familiarise himself with the area. Like he expressed, "if you just jump on a bus then you get used to just counting stops or whatever, you don't really get a sense of where you are". After a short period of time, George started to get his bearings, at first it was a little confusing, but then he said "it really helped us familiarise ourselves with different streets and avenues and things. You're like oh I recognise this avenue, with these buildings and these decorations. I think it was a nice way to get familiar".

Conclusion: walking the line between 'tourist' and 'resident'

The three stories of Amsterdam Airbnb users reveal diverse and complex boundary blurring between 'tourists' and 'residents' as well as 'outsiders' and 'insiders', unfolding in and across a variety of contact zones in residential neighbourhoods. To develop an understanding of this boundary blurring in the context of *new urban tourism*, we adopted a novel lens by focusing on multi-dimensional familiarisation processes. In so doing, we looked at the development of informational, experiential and proximate familiarity (Szytniewski and Spierings 2014) in the private space of the Airbnb accommodation, the semi-public space of local shops, supermarkets, bars and restaurants and the public space of streets.

In the private space of the Airbnb accommodation, familiarisation *of* and *with* the physical and social setting of the accommodation turns out to be important for tourists to feel like a resident and insider in the neighbourhood. Familiarisation of these settings often occurs through personalisation, including decorating with familiar objects, and performing homely activities and routines, including watching TV. Familiarisation with both accommodation settings seems related to feeling welcome and comfortable in the accommodation because of its personal atmosphere, creating a space where one can be themselves, relax and participate in in-group dynamics when sharing the accommodation with friends. In addition, familiarisation with the social setting of the accommodation may further develop based on social connections with the local host, when receiving local recommendations but also, and especially, when friendship develops. However, even when interactions with the host are superficial and minimal, tourists may still feel like an insider due to diminished awareness of being an Airbnb user in someone else's house. Furthermore, just having access to local life through the location of the accommodation in a residential neighbourhood with a relatively calm pace already makes tourists experience inside(r)ness.

In the semi-public space of local shops, supermarkets, bars and restaurants, neighbourhood familiarisation occurs through a variety of service-related encounters, contributing to feeling like a resident and insider. This includes the observation of local activities and cultures in order to find out where locals eat, drink and shop, and grasping the composition and connectedness of the local community. Picking up on a strong sense of local community and being able to relate to it seems highly supportive of a sense of inside(r)ness. Furthermore, frequenting local businesses and partaking in local life within these spaces makes people feel that they are locally embedded and have access to local culture. However, not speaking the language and having an accent made tourists feel like they stood out as outsiders—although when locals switch to English this evokes a sense of inside(r)ness again. Not experiencing over-friendly interactions or receiving any special treatment during service encounters was considered as participating in local life, being treated as an insider instead of an outsider, and having genuine interactions. However, searching for and asking about local specialities did evoke a sense of outsiderness again.

In the public space of neighbourhood streets, familiarisation and feeling like a resident and insider seems to develop largely through the ability to blend in and be anonymous. Blending into multicultural diversity, accessing a sense of anonymity, allowed our interviewees the freedom to just get on with their life and mind their own business. In this respect, not receiving special treatment when asking for help in the street was found to be constitutive for an experience of inside(r)ness. However, being in observation mode with a lack of interaction with locals when walking around in the neighbourhood also made people feel to some degree like outsiders. When walking around, the ability to navigate the neighbourhood and develop walking routines already evokes a sense of inside(r)ness and adds more detail to the mental map—which, when still basic and underdeveloped, contributes to a feeling of outsiderness. Walking around also helps in getting accustomed to local habits, sounds and rhythms—related with understanding cycling traffic in particular. However, feeling uncomfortable or intimidated by the number and speed of cyclists and not feeling secure and confident enough to participate in cycling activities makes visitors feel like outsiders. Walking around with wheelie bags and cameras and wearing different fashion styles also contribute to a sense of outside(r)ness. Such outside(r)ness can also be experienced when noticing norms and values in stark contrast to 'normal' daily life—for example, when witnessing people's confidence to walk around at night as opposed to a night-time situation of fear 'at home'.

Altogether, encounters with and in the residential neighbourhood—mediated through memories of previous encounters—have shown to be

relationally constitutive of Airbnb users' experiences of outside(r)/inside(r)
ness, practised and experienced differently, to varying degrees in private,
semi-public and public spaces. As such, a sense of inside(r)ness and outside(r)
ness cannot be directly related to, and is also not prerogative to, 'resident' or
'tourist' in the context of *new urban tourism*. This implies that tourist–resident
and insider–outsider binaries fail for developing an understanding of contemporary urbanism, including its complications and challenges in relation
with tourism in particular. When trying to keep the balance between a liveable city while maintaining the tourist industry—a policy in Amsterdam as
in many other popular tourist cities—going beyond these traditional binaries
is pertinent and pivotal. Following Costa and Martinotti (2003), we argue
for shifting attention towards practices and experiences of a large variety of
'city users', but also beyond different types of visitors. Future research in the
field of *new urban tourism* could further analyse, through the lens of familiarisation processes, encounters between different types of city users where the
line between 'tourist' and 'resident' as well as 'outsider' and 'insider' is fluid
and blurring. Such 'hybrid' types of city users include Airbnb users but also
expats, international students, commuters, people with a holiday home, and
migrants and other 'new arrivals' in the city and its neighbourhoods.

The blurring of boundaries between tourists and residents has proven to
be dynamic through familiarisation processes, unfolding in diverse neighbourhood contact zones and complementary in the sense that they together
produce and enrich knowledge and understanding of the neighbourhood and
its local community. The act of walking, as performed in public space, turned
out to be of utmost importance for boundary blurring between 'tourists' and
'residents', or 'insiders' and 'outsiders'. Walking is crucial for getting to know
where best to go and how to get there, finding landmarks and developing
everyday routines—all feeding into a mental map of the neighbourhood and a
sense of inside(r)ness. Future research in the field of *new urban tourism* should
pay more attention to the mobilities of neighbourhood walking—through
applying 'walk-alongs' as research methods, for instance—their implications
for being and belonging in a place, and effects on 'living like a local' in residential neighbourhoods.

Notes

1 Stock (Chapter 3 in this volume) conceptualises how tourists can be understood
  as temporary inhabitants of a city equipped with spatial capital and competences
  which allow similar familiarisation processes.
2 Stoltenberg and Frisch (Chapter 8 in this volume) explore this connection of new
  urban tourism and the search for 'local life' via another online service named Eatwith
  (www.eatwith.com) which connects users for joint meals at a resident's home.
3 For a detailed distinction between professional and non-professional hosts in terms of
  their motivations for renting out their space, refer to Stors, Chapter 6 in this volume.

4 For an example of a specific place of encounter, see Sommer and Kip, Chapter 10 in this volume.
5 Larsen (Chapter 2 in this volume) also highlights how cycling is seen as a 'local' practice in Copenhagen, Denmark.

Acknowledgements

We would like to express our gratitude to the respondents for their participation in the fieldwork and for the permission to use their mental maps as illustrations in this chapter.

References

Ahmed, S., 2000. *Strange Encounters: Embodied Others in Post-coloniality*. New York: Routledge.

Airbnb Inc., 2013. New study: Airbnb community makes Amsterdam economy stronger [online]. Available from: www.airbnb.com/press/news/new-study-airbnb-community-makes-amsterdam-economy-stronger [accessed 7 September 2017].

Allon, F. and Anderson, K., 2010. Intimate encounters: the embodied transnationalism of backpackers and independent travellers. *Population, Space and Place*, 16 (1), 11–22.

Baloglu, S., 2001. Image variations of Turkey by familiarity index: informational and experiential dimensions. *Tourism Management*, 22 (2), 127–33.

Bell, S., 2009. Mental maps. *In*: N. Thrift and R. Kitchin, eds, *The International Encyclopaedia of Human Geography*. Philadelphia, PA: Elsevier Science, 70–75.

Bock, K., 2015. The changing nature of city tourism and its possible implications for the future of cities. *European Journal of Futures Research*, 3 (1), 1–8.

Bosschart, D. and Frick, K., 2006. *The Future of Leisure Travel: Trend Study*. Zurich: Gottlieb Duttweiler Institut.

Costa, N. and Martinotti, G., 2003. Sociological theories of tourism and regulation theory. *In*: L.M. Hoffman, S.S. Fainstein and D.R. Judd, eds, *Cities and Visitors: Regulating People, Markets, and City Space*. Oxford: Blackwell, 53–71.

Crouch, D., 1999. *Leisure/Tourism Geographies: Practices and Geographical Knowledge*. London: Routledge.

Degen, M.M. and Rose, G., 2012. The sensory experience of urban design: the role of walking and perceptual memory. *Urban Studies*, 49 (15), 3271–3287.

Dirksmeier, P. and Helbrecht, I., 2015. Resident perceptions of new urban tourism: a neglected geography of prejudice. *Geography Compass*, 9 (5), 276–285.

Duyvendak, J.W., 2011. *The Politics of Home: Belonging and Nostalgia in Europe and the United States*. Basingstoke: Palgrave Macmillan.

Edensor, T., 2007. Mundane mobilities, performances and spaces of tourism. *Social & Cultural Geography*, 8 (2), 199–215.

Füller, H. and Michel, B., 2014. 'Stop being a tourist!' New dynamics of urban tourism in Berlin-Kreuzberg. *International Journal of Urban and Regional Research*, 38 (4), 1304–1318.

Gemeente Amsterdam, 2013. *Structuurvisie Amsterdam 2040 – economisch sterk en duurzaam*. Amsterdam: Gemeente Amsterdam.

Gemeente Amsterdam, 2017. 2017_stadsdelen_1_06.xlsx. Excel file, population by migration background [online]. Available from: www.ois.amsterdam.nl/feiten-en-cijfers/wijken/ [accessed 8 February 2017].

Germann Molz, J., 2008. Global abode: home and mobility in narratives of round-the-world travel. *Space and Culture*, 11 (4), 325–342.

Gieseking, J.J., 2013. Where we go from here: the mental sketch mapping method and its analytic components. *Qualitative Inquiry*, 19 (9), 712–724.

Goffman, E., 1963. *Behavior in Public Places: Notes on the Social Organization of Gatherings*. New York: The Free Press.

Hogeweij, M., 2016. Gedeelde winst of vergrote ongelijkheid? Airbnb en gentrification in Amsterdam. Unpublished thesis, University of Amsterdam.

Inside Airbnb, 2018. Amsterdam [online]. Available from: http://insideairbnb.com/amsterdam/ [accessed 22 August 2018].

Karakayali, N., 2009. Social distance and affective orientations. *Sociological Forum*, 24 (3), 538–562.

Larsen, J., 2008. De-exoticizing tourist travel: everyday life and sociality on the move. *Leisure Studies*, 27 (1), 21–34.

Lawson, V. and Elwood, S., 2014. Encountering poverty: space, class, and poverty politics. *Antipode*, 46 (1), 209–228.

Ley-Cervantes, M. and Duyvendak J.W., 2017. At home in generic places: personalizing strategies of the mobile rich. *Journal of Housing and the Built Environment*, 32 (1), 63–76.

Lofland, L.H., 1971. A world of strangers. Order and action in urban public space. PhD thesis, University of California.

Lofland, L.H., 1989. Social life in the public realm: a review. *Journal of Contemporary Ethnography*, 17 (4), 453–482.

Maitland, R., 2010. Everyday life as a creative experience in cities. *International Journal of Culture, Tourism and Hospitality Research*, 4 (3), 176–185.

Maitland, R. and Newman, P., eds, 2014. *World Tourism Cities: Developing Tourism Off the Beaten Track*. Abingdon: Routledge.

Massey, D., 2010. A global sense of place [online]. Available from: aughty.org/pdf/global_sense_place.pdf [accessed 15 October 2017].

Matejskova, T. and Leitner, H., 2011. Urban encounters with difference: the contact hypothesis and immigrant integration projects in eastern Berlin. *Social and Cultural Geography*, 12 (7), 717–740.

Molinsky, A., 2007. Cross-cultural code-switching: the psychological challenges of adapting behaviour in foreign cultural interactions. *Academy of Management Review*, 32 (2), 622–640.

Novy, J., 2011. Marketing marginalized neighborhoods. Tourism and leisure in the 21st century inner city. PhD thesis, Columbia University.

Novy, J. and Huning, S., 2009. New tourism (areas) in the 'New Berlin'. *In*: R. Maitland and P. Newman, eds, *World Tourism Cities: Developing Tourism Off the Beaten Track*. Abingdon: Routledge, 87–108.

O'Donoghue, D., 2013. 'The otherness that implicates the self': towards an understanding of gendering from a theory of proximity. *International Journal of Qualitative Studies in Education*, 26 (4), 400–413.

Pappalepore, I., Maitland, R. and Smith, A., 2010. Exploring urban creativity: visitor experiences of Spitalfields, London. *Tourism Culture and Communication*, 10 (3), 217–230.

Relph, E., 1976. *Place and Placelessness*. London: Pion.

Sharpley, R., 2014. Host perceptions of tourism: a review of the research. *Tourism Management*, 42, 37–49.

Sommer, C., 2018. What begins at the end of urban tourism, as we know it? *Europe Now* [online], 17, Available from: www.europenowjournal.org/2018/04/30/what-begins-at-the-end-of-urban-tourism-as-we-know-it/ [accessed 10 May 2018].

Spierings, B., 2006. Cities, consumption and competition: the image of consumerism and the making of city centres. PhD thesis, Radboud University Nijmegen.

Szytniewski, B. and Spierings, B., 2014. Encounters with otherness: implications of (un)familiarity for daily life in borderlands. *Journal of Borderlands Studies*, 29 (3), 339–351.

Szytniewski, B.B., Spierings, B. and Van der Velde, M., 2017. Socio-cultural proximity, daily life and shopping tourism in the Dutch–German border region. *Tourism Geographies*, 19 (1), 63–77.

Urry, J., 1995. *Consuming Places*. London: Routledge.

Valentine, G., 2008. Living with difference: reflections on geographies of encounter. *Progress in Human Geography*, 32 (3), 323–337.

Valentine, G. and Sadgrove, J., 2012. Lived difference: a narrative account of spatio-temporal processes of social differentiation. *Environment and Planning A*, 44 (9), 2049–2063.

Wildish, B., 2017. Urban tourism and Airbnb: tourist-resident encounters and feeling at home in Amsterdam residential neighbourhoods. Unpublished thesis, Utrecht University.

Wildish, B., Kearns, R. and Collins, D., 2016. At home away from home: visitor accommodation and place attachment. *Annals of Leisure Research*, 19 (1), 117–133.

8 Commensality and 'local' food

Exploring a city with the help of digital meal-sharing platforms

Luise Stoltenberg and Thomas Frisch

Introduction

A promising slogan welcomes Eatwith (www.eatwith.com) website visitors: "Taste the World with Locals". In the background, a 40-second-long sequence of quickly changing short video snippets in a repeating loop supports this virtual culinary tour around the world. It shows close-ups of different foods, people cooking or sharing a meal at what seems like a private home and places emblematic for certain cities like the Eiffel Tower (Eatwith 2018a). Online meal-sharing platforms such as Eatwith, BonAppetour (www.bonappetour.com) and Traveling Spoon (www.travelingspoon.com) represent a new group of actors in the sharing economy. As such, they need to be addressed in the context of disrupting media technologies that not only transform traditional business models, but also enable new ways of touring a city. With the help of specific digital infrastructures, they connect hosts and guests online in order to arrange face-to-face group eating experiences, which typically take place at the host's home. Meal-sharing platforms offer an innovative way to explore a city for all city users (Martinotti 1996), including but not restricted to tourists. As such, they are—like short-term rental providers—a driving force in the dedifferentiation processes that define *new urban tourism* (see Stors *et al.*, Chapter 1 in this volume), but remain largely under-researched (Ketter 2017).

This chapter aims to shed some light on the nexus of meal-sharing platforms and city tourism by analysing Eatwith, the largest and most popular platform of this kind. Given the rudimentary research status of meal-sharing platforms in general, our major aims are to identify relevant theoretical concepts to approach shared meals from a sociological point of view and to put some initial empirical findings up for discussion. The text is structured around four major sections. First, a brief overview of meal-sharing platforms, particularly focusing on Eatwith, provides insights into the business model of such services. Based on this short description, we argue that commensality—the act of sharing a meal with others—is an adequate starting point for further theoretical exploration, as it lies at the very heart of Eatwith's commercial concept. The third section is an examination of the status of food in tourism, paying special attention to branding strategies of food as a cultural signifier and its perception among travellers. The findings of these two literature reviews are then used to study the role of commensality as well as the framing of food as 'local' that Eatwith itself and its users employ. For this purpose, this chapter analyses the platform's websites as well as users' profiles and reviews to detect prominent narratives. Rather than providing a comprehensive in-depth study, we attempt to test the previously developed theoretical arguments with the help of selected empirical examples. Drawing on this combination of theoretical findings and empirical data, we conclude with three essential characteristics of meal-sharing platforms: they frame everyday activities as exceptional sensations; they open up private homes for their users and frame these places as 'local'; and they connect people who temporarily share the same geographical location. Finally, we claim that these characteristics not only apply to Eatwith and other meal-sharing platforms, but they are also distinctive qualities of many phenomena that have been discussed as *new urban tourism*.

Digital meal-sharing platforms

Conventionally, eating and drinking while on vacation have been tied to rather institutionalised semi-public places, such as bars, markets, restaurants and street-food stands (e.g., Germann Molz 2007, Boniface 2003, Cohen and Avieli 2004, Sims 2009, Simopoulos and Bhat 2000). Due to technological innovations, digital meal-sharing platforms such as BonAppetour, Eatwith and Traveling Spoon have introduced new places for experiencing food to their worldwide communities: amateur or even professional chefs invite guests to their homes in order to cook for them. Despite some differences in fee-based or free services, the emergence of meal-sharing platforms is intrinsically related to the rise of media-based business models frequently referred to as the sharing economy. This umbrella term has been used for a variety of activities, including traditional sharing, bartering, lending, trading, renting, gifting and swapping (Botsman and Rogers 2010). As a result, heterogeneous definitions exist to describe sharing economy companies (e.g., Ketter 2017, Belk 2014). However, what all these different approaches have in common is that they describe an economic shift that prioritises temporary access of services or goods over permanent ownership (Richardson 2015, Stoltenberg 2017).[1] This shift is largely attributed to the technological innovations made possible by the internet, specifically the advent of Web 2.0 applications. Online meal-sharing platforms organise their sharing and networking services through digital infrastructures, and embed the power of food to create and maintain social relations (Poulain 2017, Grignon 2001) in digital networks, thus inscribing their algorithmic culture and logics into organised encounters between their users (Striphas 2015, Beer 2017). This affects interactions between users and the respective platforms, and can be observed in processes such as signing up as a host or guest, creating a user profile, searching for food experiences, or booking and reviewing eating events.

By targeting travellers and locals alike, meal-sharing platforms not only celebrate food as an outstanding, commensal event, but also praise its ability to function as a mediator for cultural and authentic experiences for all city users. As a consequence, visitors can satisfy their desire to 'live like a local', whereas residents can take advantage of the cultural diversity of contemporary urban metropolises for a culinary journey in their own city. As mentioned previously, one special characteristic of these services is that the encounters take place in the host's home. As a result, the digitalisation of commensality opens up private homes for city users, thus imposing restaurant-like settings on users' kitchens and dining rooms. Furthermore, several studies have pointed out that such online networks need a dense urban environment in order to successfully establish themselves in the market, because these are the only types of areas that can gain a critical mass of users (Ketter 2017, Davidson and Infranca 2016). It is therefore not surprising that the most popular meal-sharing platform, and our case study, Eatwith, features Barcelona, Tokyo and Tel Aviv as some of their top locations (Eatwith 2018a).

Eatwith was founded in 2012 by Guy Michlin and Shemer Schwartz in Tel Aviv, but soon relocated their headquarters to San Francisco in 2014. Recently, one of its strongest competitors, the French website VizEat, acquired the California-based company. As a result, VizEat has adopted Eatwith's name and is now the biggest provider for fee-based social dining experiences. According to its own description, "Eatwith is the world's largest community for authentic food experiences with locals, in over 130 countries" (Eatwith 2018b). Besides San Francisco, the company has offices in Paris, Barcelona, Tel Aviv and New York. Eatwith allows registered users to offer meal-sharing events—which the company calls 'social eating experiences'—for other users. When setting up a profile, Eatwith users can sign up in the roles of 'hosts' or 'guests'. According to the company's website, 20,000 hosts and 150,000 guests have done this as of May 2018 (ibid.). As a host, they promote their cooking skills via personal profiles depicting their menu and pictures of their home. Every potential cook has to apply via the company's website and undergoes a selection process in order to ensure high-quality services (Eatwith 2018c). As a result, the number of culinary experiences available is 5,000, lower than the actual number of hosts (Eatwith 2018b). After passing the company's inspection, hosts are able to advertise their home-cooked order of courses.[2] As a guest, users do not have to meet certain standards. As soon as they register, they can browse through menu suggestions by entering a specific city in the search bar. After eating together, users can review their hosts, and vice versa. The implementation of such a reciprocal review system is regarded as a fundamental safety tool, and is therefore a common feature in online-based peer-to-peer services (Frisch 2018, Frisch and Stoltenberg 2018).

Against this background, we argue that Eatwith is an excellent research object for studying the technological infrastructures that open up places, scenes and representations of urban local life, a defining feature of *new urban tourism*. Through its digital architecture and interface design, Eatwith creates the desire for particular types of commensal experiences and, at the same time, shapes behavioural norms. Thus, we will focus on the meal-sharing platform as an important actor for branding certain kinds of commensality and food as key qualities of its service. Without a respective body of literature on meal-sharing platforms, this chapter approaches the issue first and foremost theoretically, by exploring two key aspects of such services: the social power of a shared meal and the branding of food as 'local' in tourism.

Commensality: sharing a meal together

Recent sociological analyses have interpreted eating as a universal, yet also a particular and complex practice (Poulain 2017, Warde 2016) which is performed in different ways, sometimes alone, but most of the time together with others. Commensality, the practice of eating together, is a particularly noteworthy field of study for our purposes (Grignon 2001, Fischler 2011). The French sociologist Claude Grignon (2001, p. 24) has defined commensality as a "gathering aimed to accomplish in a collective way some material tasks and symbolic obligations linked to the satisfaction of a biological individual need". He continues by emphasising the importance of not confusing commensality with conviviality, which he regards as a possible, euphoric outcome of the former. In contrast, commensality is in most cases the result and manifestation of an already existing social group, and fulfils the function of strengthening its inner coherence and boundaries. Grignon distinguishes six types of commensality, which he presents as three pairs of contrasting categories for the analysis of eating situations: domestic vs institutional; everyday vs exceptional; and segregative vs transgressive commensality (Grignon 2001). Before these rather static typologies are explained in more detail and given a critical reflection regarding their relevance for the study of meal-sharing platforms, it is necessary to recapitulate some important findings based on a review of social science literature.[3]

Commensality is very strongly connected with the concept of the meal, which has been addressed by various social theorists, most notably by Georg Simmel and Mary Douglas. Whereas commensality is the more general term and focuses on the practice of eating in socio-material settings, the shared meal needs to be understood as a way of realising commensality in a particular and institutionalised form. Simmel regards eating and drinking as the most egoistic human trait, but also as its least common denominator. In contrast to Grignon, Simmel ([1910] 1997, p. 130) emphasised its particular sociological value precisely because people "who in no way share any special interest can gather together at the common meal". Within the event of the meal, people's most primitive physiological need is socially structured, e.g., through temporal regularity, the aesthetics of food arrangement or eating techniques. Douglas, inspired by Lévi-Strauss's classic *The Raw and the Cooked* ([1964] 1997), was particularly interested in identifying the structures and components of meals and their meaning for social relations.

In 'Deciphering a meal' (1972), she put the sharing of food (solid) over the sharing of drinks (liquid) in the sense that the former reflects greater intimacy among its participants. Furthermore, she also pays attention to the sequence of meals and rules for social interaction. Others have used the concept for studying the 'decline of the family meal' (Murcott 1997) or as a powerful symbol for social distinction (Bourdieu 2003).

Although commensality in the form of meals might be regarded a universal social practice, it is also very much culturally and historically specific. As omnivores, humans have the ability to eat many different foodstuffs, and can thus adapt easily to changing environments (Fischler 1988). However, each society has its rules of what is acceptable for consumption as well as certain food taboos (Douglas 1972, Harris 1998). Commensality realised by a meal has both a temporal and spatial dimension. Mary Douglas (1972) was among the first who emphasised the importance of time-structured patterns and the interconnectedness of meals. She referred to sequences of the day (breakfast, lunch, dinner), the week (weekday lunch and Sunday dinner) and the year (festive events such as birthdays, weddings, Christmas) and showed how more important events are characterised by more elaborate formats and more prestigious food categories (Douglas 1972). Grignon also clearly distinguished between everyday and exceptional commensality, and understood them as two oppositional ideal types. Everyday commensality is low, unstressed and defined by regularity and repetition, whereas exceptional commensality is high, stressed, rare but memorable (Grignon 2001). However, a single dish or even the same food category can also be attached with meaning and become a signifier for exceptional commensality: "[T]he changeover from ordinary bread to *pain de mie* involves a difference in what is signified: the former signifies day-to-day life, the latter a party" (Barthes [1961] 1997, p. 22, italics in original).

In spatial matters, it has been very common to distinguish between eating at home and eating out, i.e., away from home. Grignon (2001) is again a starting point, as he separated domestic (linked to private life and the family) from institutionalised commensality (hierarchical and dominated by the respective institution's rules). Interestingly, eating out for leisure contains an element of both; in his terms "[e]xtra-domestic commensality of 'free' people... leading a private life outside any institution, takes place between the domestic and institutional types" (Grignon 2001, p. 26). Jack Goody (1982) already pointed out that the nineteenth-century idea of cuisine as high culture was very much related to eating food prepared by male chefs in public ceremonies and documented by writing, whereas everyday food was prepared by female cooks at home and off the record. In short, "Women are cooks whereas men are chefs" (Mennell *et al.* 1992, p. 96). Both eating in (home) and eating out (in restaurants) have been popular subjects for sociological studies since the 1980s, criticising the aforementioned structural inequality (Murcott 1982, Greene and Cramer 2011, Guptill *et al.* 2016). At the same time, they predominantly keep up the separation between the nexus everyday-home and exceptional-away. The common spatial expression of 'away' is the restaurant, which is "essentially a commercial innovation of the twentieth century" (Warde and Martens 2000, p. 23).

Semioticians have highlighted the significance of food as "a system of communication, a body of images, a protocol of usages, situations, and behaviour" (Barthes [1961] 1997, p. 21). Due to the circumstance that we tend to attach meaning to the food we eat, it also becomes "central to our sense of identity" (Fischler 1988, p. 275; more generally, see also Greene and Cramer 2011, Guptill *et al.* 2016). Grignon's final pair of commensality types works well in this regard: segregative commensality is a means by which a group becomes visible and reflective of itself in order to confirm hierarchies and solidarity or identify potential conflicts (Grignon 2001). Transgressive commensality, on the other hand, is less strict and essentially characterised by ambivalence. Through inviting strangers, the group redefines its borders but also measures the newcomer's value, based on the offering of food and drink (Grignon 2001). Food has received great attention as a signifier for gender (Murcott 1982, 1997), class (Bourdieu 2003, Ferguson 2011) and ethnic or national identity (Lockwood and Lockwood 2000, Appadurai 1988). Although some theorists have been critical of reading food as symbols of identity on display for others, insofar as "most consumption is ordinary and inconspicuous" (Warde 2016, p. 4), we can conclude that commensality is of course not the only, but one of the significant techniques by which identity can be defined and maintained (Grignon 2001).

Meal-sharing platforms nevertheless need to be analysed according to what they actually offer. Their product is commensality, predominantly realised in the event of the meal. Drawing on the mentioned theoretical considerations from selected social science literature, they challenge conventional ways of analysing eating situations, such as the typology put forward by Grignon. On the one hand, digital technologies bring about social arrangements that have not been there before by connecting previously unknown and unrelated individuals, and thus break a fundamental principle of Grignon's typology. On the other hand, the meals mediated by these platforms are in no way mere 'encounter commensalities' (Grignon 2001), i.e., spontaneous acts of eating together like sitting at the same table in a restaurant. They are thoroughly planned and have a relative certainty of expectations: the date and time are scheduled, the courses and ingredients are predominantly specified, and the host's profile as well as reviews from former guests provide detailed information about what to expect from the event. Furthermore, commensality realised through using meal-sharing platforms requires questioning strict spatial distinctions such as domestic/institutional or home/away, as well as looking at the dynamics that frame eating as an exceptional and cultural experience. It is especially this notion of eating, its ability to function as a cultural signifier, that is also a prominent issue in tourism studies.

Food and tourism: tasting a travel destination

When considering the rich sociological meaning of eating and drinking, it is not surprising that the consumption of food and beverages can hold great significance for tourism as well. While on vacation, eating and drinking may facilitate the creation of pleasant memories. First, this power is obviously rooted in food and beverages themselves, as they can offer unique taste experiences. While trying unknown dishes and tasting new ingredients may enrich a holiday trip in and of themselves, the setting in which food is consumed can be equally crucial. This includes not only the locality, e.g., a fancy restaurant or a street market, but also everyone and everything involved in contributing to its characteristic atmosphere. Therefore, depending on how, where, when, with what purpose, and by and with whom food is eaten, it can add meaningful moments and encounters to a trip. It may be the food itself, the memorable atmosphere it is consumed in or a well-balanced combination of both—eating and drinking create profound travel experiences, thus linking travel memories to a visited destination. The various facets of this strong relationship between food and place attachment in tourism constitute a wide-ranging research field in tourism studies. This section explores some of these facets along food's great importance for promoting a travel destination, its widespread interpretation of being a signifier for local culture, its status in times of increasing globalisation as well as its link to authenticity and the experience of place.

Several studies have found that food can act as a positive impetus on travel satisfaction, thus emphasising its value for promoting a destination (Björk and Kauppinen-Räisänen 2014, Henderson 2009). Obviously, this does not apply to food in general, but to national or regional specialities in particular. In this regard, common examples are trying exclusive red wine when visiting France, attending a traditional tea ceremony in Japan or eating pancakes with maple syrup in Canada. The branding of foods and drinks as 'local' or 'national' as well as the specific ways of consuming them both enable the establishment of intense connections between travellers and a visited destination (Hedegaard 2018, Sims 2009).

For this reason, the development of successful branding strategies for food has proven to be a prominent objective in tourism management and marketing studies (e.g., Mkono 2013, Henderson 2009, du Rand *et al.* 2003). One effective way to turn food into an attraction itself is to stress its rich cultural dimension. In fact, many travellers actually consider tasting unknown dishes as a way to experience local cultures (Fields 2002, Sims 2009). They associate food with excitement, use it as an escape from eating habits, regard it as a way to learn about other countries, and value it as a chance to experience authenticity (Kim and Eves 2012, Chang *et al.* 2010). 'Tasting the Other' while travelling can thus turn into an essential vacation mission (Germann Molz 2007). Folklorist Lucy M. Long (2012) has even stated that some tourists turn their trip into a 'food pilgrimage', as they value local foods and drinks as a means to elicit a deeper understanding of another culture. She has also introduced the broad term 'culinary tourism' in order to describe vacations aiming specifically at exploring dishes and flavours (Long 2004). Since 'culinary tourism' encompasses a wide range of intentions and interests that can motivate travellers to focus particularly on food experiences, subcategories of culinary tourism have been established to account for this variety. 'Gourmet tourism' or 'gastronomic tourism', for instance, applies to tourists who attach high importance to sophisticated cuisine, exclusive ingredients or selected wineries (Hall and Sharples 2008, Hall and Mitchell 2005).

However, approaching another culture by what is regarded as its 'typical food and eating styles' can turn out to be challenging, due to various impediments such as hygiene standards, health concerns and unpleasant bodily reactions (Gyimóthy and Mykletun 2009, Cohen and Avieli 2004). Yet even such impediments bolster the perception of food as an extraordinary sensation, because they let differences between food and eating habits become more apparent and therefore turn food into an attraction itself.

While branding food as an ambassador for a country's cuisine by tourism marketing seems to be an efficacious practice as travellers actually perceive certain dishes as cultural signifiers, such strategies rely on a rather narrow understanding of culture. Maintaining such a limited understanding proves especially difficult amidst the ongoing processes of globalisation. Mobility studies have made an important contribution in emphasising that not only people but also information, objects and material things travel around the world, and thus certain ingredients, dishes and cuisines do as well (Hannam *et al.* 2006, Urry 2000, Gibson 2007). Initially, it was predicted that global networks of food consumption and preparation would lead to a process called 'McDonaldization' (Ritzer 1998), which describes the rationalisation of food preparation and consumption, for example by the worldwide spread of international fast-food chains. Apart from global food chains, fusion cuisine is another effect of globalisation that adds a new facet to the presumed relationship between food and a country. It has been presented as a driving force for establishing a 'new global cuisine' (Scarpato and Daniele 2003).

Despite such developments, which point to a homogenisation of dishes and eating experiences (albeit not losing a minimal 'local touch'), progressive globalisation reportedly supports an even stronger desire by tourists to try novel specialities. Therefore, the spread of global food chains as well as fusion cuisine give rise to a further differentiation of food and beverages, triggering an impulse to empower the branding of food as 'local' and to strengthen its cultural attachment (Gössling and Hall 2013, Boniface 2003). In other words, "tourists' desire to seek 'symbolic' meanings of food may provide further impetus for destination marketers and culinary suppliers to reinvent or reconstruct the local food culture and identities" (Mak *et al.* 2012, p. 189). As pointed out earlier, such a reconstruction relies on a somewhat restricted understanding of culture—which nevertheless proves to be powerful among tourists. In order to frame food and beverages as cultural signifiers despite globalisation processes, their place attachment has to be perceived as 'real'. For this reason, emphasising food's local embeddedness in tourism means succeeding in portraying it as authentic (Hughes 1995).

However, the debate about the (im)possibility to experience authenticity has probably been the single most controversial debate in tourism studies ever since social scientist Dean MacCannell published his famous work *The Tourist: A New Theory of the Leisure Class* in 1976. Here, MacCannell argued that tourists sought out authentic experiences, but were often stuck in settings where a manufactured, 'staged' authenticity is produced exclusively for them. This view opened a fundamental academic debate discussing various concepts of authenticity and questioning whether it is an objectively measurable quantity at all. Based on extensive research on literature on the nexus of authenticity and tourism, Wang (1999) distinguished among three key concepts of authenticity: objective authenticity, constructive authenticity and existential authenticity. Whereas objective authenticity declares authenticity to be a fixed attribute of an item, constructive authenticity is projected onto an object by the travellers themselves (Wang 1999, Lau 2010). Objective authenticity results in the problem of authentication, i.e., who determines what is authentic and what is not (Reisinger and Steiner 2006). By contrast, constructive authenticity employs a more dynamic concept, by including the subjective perception of travellers into the process of interpreting an object as authentic (Reisinger and Steiner 2006, Beer 2008). The third conceptualisation of authenticity, existential authenticity, represents the most common and convincing approach today (e.g., Brown 2013, Kim and Jamal 2007, Steiner and Reisinger 2006). Wang (1999, pp. 365–366) described it as postmodern; it applies to travel experiences where tourists seek "their own authentic selves and intersubjective authenticity, and the issue of whether the toured objects are authentic is irrelevant or less relevant".

In light of the vital dimension of eating and drinking and its role as a cultural intermediary in tourism settings, existential authenticity has been used to analyse visits to ethnic restaurants while on vacation (Mkono 2013). Mkono found that the total experience determined whether tourists perceived their meal time as (existentially) authentic, and thus the article recommended that restaurant businesses kept in mind "the importance of thinking beyond the food on the plate" (Mkono 2013, p. 359). The development of authentication strategies aiming for a credible presentation of the restaurant itself is one potential way to facilitate moments of existential authenticity among travellers. This includes labelling the served food as 'authentic' or 'exotic'— a practice which has been heavily criticised as 'food colonisation' (Heldke 2003)—by creating a matching atmosphere (e.g., via the interior selected, skilled personnel, the choice of music). In addition, eating together while on holiday may strengthen social ties (Ignatov and Smith 2006, Lashley *et al.* 2004),[4] and thus other guests may similarly contribute to feelings of existential authenticity.

Here, tourism marketing benefits from food's rich sensuous appeal. Tasting unknown dishes, trying a new ingredient and eating in an ethnic restaurant go beyond nutritional values and nutritive characteristics. They present a sensation in their own right and link tourists' food experiences to 'sensuous tourism'—a type of tourism which relies on the embodied, multisensory experience of travelling, thus putting emphasis on the experience economy in tourism (Crouch and Desforges 2003, Pritchard and Morgan 2011). With its focus on travellers' own subjective perceptions, enabling novel sensuous adventures supports experiences of existential authenticity. For tourists, consuming food and beverages has the potential to trigger a strong place attachment with a visited destination. Due to diligent branding strategies by tourism agencies, it may even provoke feelings of gaining a deeper understanding of local cultures, and facilitate the experience of existential authentic moments.

With their international communities, meal-sharing platforms mark an interesting research area concerning the relationship of food and tourism. Based on the findings of these two literature reviews, we now continue on, to explore how commensality and branding strategies of food as 'authentic' can be used to study those services.

Deciphering Eatwith's social eating experiences

When researching the dominant logics and structures that infuse meal-sharing experiences, deciding on a perspective is a pivotal requirement. We pay special attention to the online platform itself, as its ways of presenting and framing food have a profound impact on its users. In addition, its digital architecture shapes users' online profiles, the depiction of the menus offered, and their interactions. It plays a fundamental role in prefiguring how face-to-face encounters and food are perceived among its users and thus substantially influences their expectations and imaginaries.

In order to reflect the previously mentioned theoretical considerations, we selectively analyse Eatwith. This procedure serves to evaluate whether the theoretical results actually promise categories to study these services. We draw on results gained by a website analysis to reveal the power of the digital architecture that enables user participation. Relying on a thick description of a platform's homepage and the structure of its user profiles, as well as other important pages such as 'About us' or 'FAQ', we study how the specific design and the implementation of tools and features support the arousal of certain imaginaries and desires among the user community. The online representation of food and eating together—be it with pictures or with the help of texts—is therefore an important force that shapes users' expectations and behaviour.

We combine this method with a netnographic approach. While a website analysis is particularly valuable for deciphering the power of digital infrastructures, netnography pays special attention to the ways users interact with each other through a website. It "adapts common participant-observation ethnographic procedures... to the contingencies of online community manifesting [themselves] through computer-mediated communications" (Kozinets 2010, p. 18). When researching meal-sharing websites, this means taking into account how users fill out their online profiles, how menus are described and presented, and which topics are commonly addressed in reviews. During the research process, active engagement is recommended for researchers, as this ensures a comprehensive understanding of the online community or interaction under investigation (Kozinets 2006). Following this advice, we both signed up as guests on Eatwith and documented each step of this process with notes and screenshots. By taking this procedure, we sought to unfold how the digital architecture modulates user behaviour right at the beginning of their membership.

Whereas virtual ethnography can be challenging due to the massive amounts of data available (Rokka 2010), we avoid this problem by applying a narrow focus, which strictly concentrates on studying commensality and the branding of food as 'local'. Reflecting the theoretical considerations earlier on, we use a broad definition of commensality as the practice and event of eating together, which, however, not only happens solely for the sake of eating. In contrast to Grignon, who was interested in the function of commensality for existing social groups, we pay attention to the mediation and emergence of encounters through sharing a meal. On the other hand, we focus on Eatwith's attempts to label food as 'local', and explore how users perceive their 'total experience'. Following the findings of the two theoretical explorations, our empirical investigation is structured along three steps.[5] First, we examine how commensality and food itself are used to promote joint meals as extraordinary experiences. Second, we study their dependency on distinctive spatial settings, as the private home of the host is often the venue for the social eating experience. Finally, we look closer at the people involved and how they shape such encounters in order to detect who actively participates in such global digital networks.

Framing eating as extraordinary

First, we address the question of how eating together is framed as an extraordinary, festive experience on Eatwith, and how the company turns the rather ordinary practices of eating and drinking into singular and memorable events. A key mechanism in this process is stressing the exceptional and convivial potential inherent in commensality (Grignon 2001, Simmel 1997). In order to illustrate how Eatwith and its users address this potential, we consider how the company brands its services as 'authentic' and 'local', how hosts translate a multi-sensuous experience into visual representation by text and images, and how guests evaluate their meal-sharing experiences in their reviews. These issues need to be answered alongside the particular logics and structures of interaction enabled and suppressed by the medium of the digital infrastructures.

The homepage is the starting point for most website users and as such it is central for defining and branding the company's image. Eatwith welcomes its visitors with the slogan "Taste the world with locals", a sequence of quickly changing videos—showing food, people eating and references to different cultural settings—and a search bar to find eating experiences. This is followed by a short explanation of Eatwith's services structured around three verbs in capital letters: "DISCOVER – BOOK – ENJOY" (Eatwith 2018a). The ultimate goal of using the platform (ENJOY) is described as to "[i]mmerse yourself in local food and culture, meet other travelers at your table, and experience the magic of social dining" (ibid.). The remaining sections of the homepage include ten top destinations, illustrated by large pictures, six hand-selected hosts and their experiences, three enthusiastic guest reviews and references to well-known press and media that have already featured the company's services.

The content available on the homepage is saturated with the nexus locality, authenticity and extraordinariness based on the sharing of a meal. This connection is presented very straightforwardly and depicted by beautifully arranged dishes, happy people around a table and reports of intercultural learning. Although food and eating is very much the purpose and reason for gathering hosts and guests together, it also becomes clear that this is only the foundation of a much deeper social event, enabled by the 'magic of social dining'. Looking up the question "How do I know that the host is a good chef?" in Eatwith's FAQ section provides additional evidence. After advising users to scrutinise the chefs' profiles and reviews, Julie, a representative of the platform, concludes her help article as follows: "Our community of food fans gets to share so much more than a meal—it's an unforgettable Eatwith experience!" (Eatwith 2018d). Through all these mechanisms, Eatwith makes use of food's potential as an intermediary in order to brand its social eating events as singular and exceptional.

However, Eatwith users also place themselves within the discourse on commensality, locality and authenticity put forward by the platform. A popular San Francisco host presents a vivid and savoury description of what guests can expect from a dinner at his home:

> The evening starts with tropical sounds, a sultry cocktail, followed by a menu seasoned by the 'Spice Trail' cuisines of The Caribbean with a modern twist. African, Spanish, Taíno, and Middle Eastern (Jewish & Arabic) flavors come together to make up traditional, Dominican, dishes-paired with a glass of a 'silky-white' wine from California. It ends with a creamy rum-dessert and stories, through 'The Host's Questionnaire'.
>
> (Host, San Francisco)[6]

The quote exemplifies well how hosts try to translate a multi-sensuous experience into text and images, in this case by addressing non-visual senses with expressive adjectives (sultry, silky, creamy) and an interesting fusion of ethnic cuisines. Hosts' attempts to promote their skills and meals on their user profiles are dependent on the particular structures and logics of the technical infrastructure. Whereas most of this limited set of tools is restricted to choosing a predefined category and is primarily intended to facilitate the selection of suitable experiences for searching guests,[7] hosts have some freedom in deciding on a title, uploading pictures, or adding a description. A closer look at the 'menu' profile section reveals two interesting aspects when thinking about the dynamics of promoting commensality as an exceptional (travel) experience. First, hosts put a great deal of effort into creating elaborate and prestigious dishes and describing them accordingly, resonating with Mary Douglas's findings on the typical patterns of extraordinary meals. Second, the way in which these dishes are presented and arranged on the profile pages strongly resembles the specific form of restaurant menus and thereby echoes more traditional places of dining out.

Compared to hosts, guests even have fewer possibilities to participate in the platform's content production. Nevertheless, by posting reviews they add another crucial and powerful layer to framing social eating experiences as extraordinary and memorable events. Although we have not analysed Eatwith user reviews systematically, they mostly seem to be very positive, and thus share a characteristic feature of similar platforms in the tourism sector like Airbnb (Bridges and Vásquez 2016, Frisch 2018, Frisch and Stoltenberg 2018). An Eatwith guest evaluates a dinner event in Tokyo with great excitement:

> We had an amazing time with [host] and her friend. The food was fresh and delicious and quite different from what we can find in any restaurants in Tokyo. We talked a lot about our different cultures. [Host] also gave us some great tips about the city and thanks to her we got to see the fireworks. This meal with [host] was a real local experience that I would recommand [*sic*] to everyone.
>
> (Guest, Tokyo)

In this enthusiastic report, the author is very much in line with the discourse presented by the platform. From the user's perspective, the promise of an outstanding and memorable event is fulfilled, the review a good example of linking locality to commensality. By differentiating between the food served at the social dining experience and restaurant meals, the guest emphasises the exclusivity of the event. Eating in a Tokyo home and getting recommendations on what to do during a Japan vacation is portrayed as an enhancement of the overall trip. Whereas the review does not mention authenticity *per se*, it describes the dinner as a 'real local experience'.[8] Thus, it confirms and further legitimises Eatwith's narrative of social eating events as a means of getting in touch with locals.

Private homes

In order to frame meal-sharing experiences as extraordinary events, Eatwith capitalises on distinctive spatial settings as well. Therefore, we examine which spaces and places are central for Eatwith's notion of commensality and 'local' food. By looking at the availability of experiences, it becomes apparent that eating with Eatwith is an almost exclusively urban phenomenon. Although the company employs a worldwide network, its services are tied to metropolises. Furthermore, Eatwith emphasises the private spaces of their chefs as signifiers for local attachment, and presents such settings as inherently authentic. The company's self-description on its homepage and various subsites all thoroughly evoke this interesting chain of associations. For example, under the section 'About us', Eatwith summarises its services as follows:

> Eatwith is the world's largest community for authentic food experiences with locals, in over 130 countries. From a dinner party in an elegant Paris home, to an Italian feast with a Roman family, to a cooking class in Tokyo, we connect hand-selected local hosts with travelers seeking unique, immersive experiences. Whether they're home-cooks, food-lovers, MasterChefs, or Michelin-starred chefs, our hosts all share one special ingredient: a passion for bringing people together through food.
>
> (Eatwith 2018b)

This statement connects the outstanding potential of eating together to famous capitals around the world and private spaces in particular. Eatwith's commensality takes place at a chef's home, and the platform declares this place as local and thereby authentic—a strategy which aims to shape users' perceptions that meal-sharing experiences offer the chance to explore a city 'off the beaten track'. What is noteworthy here is that, even though the platform operates a global network that supports the emergence of cosmopolitanism, the private home is still branded as a signifier for locality and a way to gain insight into urban everyday life.

Users pick up this notion of home as an authentic space, either as hosts in their personal profiles and menu descriptions or as guests in their reviews. For example, a French host promotes her dinner by explicitly pointing out unique features of her home. She writes:

> Join me and my husband for a luxury candlelit dinner in a Parisian style apartment of the XIX century, with an amazing view over the royal chapel of Louis XVI. We will offer you a complete menu with dishes of both modern French cuisine (Escoffier style), preferred by worldwide known French Chefs, and Traditional French cuisine. This way, the guests that come from abroad will have the possibility to understand better the history and the soul of the French cooking.
>
> (Host A, Paris)

This chef particularly emphasises the local embeddedness of her meal-sharing experiences. First, she uses her home interior, then the specific location of her apartment—which offers a view on a unique historical French building—and finally her style of cooking to brand her dinner as truly Parisian. Her invitation promises the fulfilment of the desire to 'Taste the Other' and thereby learn about a destination's culture.

The chef's private home plays not only a key role for introducing guests to the 'local lifestyle' of a visited city, it also helps to create a welcoming atmosphere for the commensality which is about to take place. Although private space is often described as 'intimate' or 'true' in the reviews of guests (and particularly valued for these qualities), Eatwith experiences impose restaurant-like settings onto chef's homes. After all, guests are paying in order to sit at their hosts' dinner table. For them, commensality turns into a balancing act between facilitating closeness and delivering a high-quality meal. If this is mastered well, guests praise their hosts and their performance as the following review for a dinner in Rio de Janeiro illustrates:

> We then proceeded to his apartment just half a block away and he imme-diately made us feel at home. His apartment is tastefully decorated with art pieces from various places around the world—the lighting created the perfect atmosphere! Food plating and presentation were outstanding and each course was out-of-this-world delicious! Overeall [*sic*], the location, food, and experience were absolutely incredible. 5+ stars!!!
>
> (Guest, Rio de Janeiro)

Despite noting that she felt at home, the guest highlights features that are reminiscent of restaurants: an appealing plating of each dish, an attractive preparation of the food, and being served different courses. This allusion to restaurants is already apparent in Eatwith's online presentation of the promoted meals, which shows remarkable similarities to menu cards. If chefs also choose pictures to advertise their menus, they often include photographs of past events, which depict at least four people gathered around a carefully decorated dining table in their homes. This illustrates quite well that meal-sharing experiences depend not only on eating together, but also on a hospit-able host and a pleasant, homely atmosphere. Such a setting contributes to creating the 'total experience', which then may facilitate moments of exist-ential authenticity, of immersive dinner experiences. The third step requires addressing the question of who is eating together with whom. After all, the people taking part in Eatwith experiences play an important role in shaping food and the host's place as 'local'.

Travellers, residents and locals

With the help of their digital infrastructures, meal-sharing platforms bring together different types of users. Connecting people and gathering them at private dinner tables in cities all over the world is a practice that deeply influences urban tourism. The third step of our analysis investigates this interpersonal dimension of social eating experiences. Who are the guests that meal-sharing platforms are aiming for? Who is sitting down at their host's dinner table?

In one part of Eatwith's FAQ section, Julie briefly explains the company's service. She concludes with the following appeal. "Around the world, or just around the corner, re-discover the surroundings in a delicious and authentic atmosphere" (Eatwith 2018e). In her post, she highlights this promise in bold characters. It reveals the types of users Eatwith is seeking to attract. While originally targeting travellers who are looking to get a taste of 'local culture' through food, Eatwith guests are often locals themselves who want to meet new people and explore their own place of residence (Ketter 2017). The platform no longer exclusively targets travellers; other city users are likewise invited. This includes temporary visitors, long-term residents, recent settlers, tourists and everyone who defines himself or herself as a local. Here, Eatwith frames commensality as a coming together of these different types of users, thus supporting the celebration of food as an extraordinary sensuous event.

One chef's profile reflects this notion as well. She lists three types of guests who typically book a place at her table:

> My guests are usually foreigners living in Paris, people who share a general interest in food, and tourists who are looking for an authentic culinary experience 'at home'. You are welcome in my apartment and in my kitchen!
>
> (Host B, Paris)

This differentiation is in line with the company's description. She invites all these heterogeneous users into her private home. Therefore, Eatwith's experiences rest on a get-together of diverse types of city users who are willing to share food and personal stories. Given this potential, eating with Eatwith is presented as a means for social interaction and interpersonal exchange. Commensality becomes a catalyst for local encounters, which are framed as being authentic in themselves and enabling feelings of existential authenticity. Guests also utilise this vivid mixture of meeting others, localness and tourism 'off the beaten track'. In his review of an Eatwith dinner taking place in Mexico, one user describes how a meal connected him with others and how attending his host's birthday turned his experience into a memorable one:

> This was one of the coolest travel experiences I have done! [The hosts] were amazing hosts and they even invited a few of their friends to the dinner. From the decoration of the house to the presentation of the dishes, and unique flavours this is a must do! During the dinner [one of the hosts] revealed it was almost his birthday and we stayed talking and drinking until midnight for a birthday toast. Such a unique way to experience Mexico City!
>
> (Guest, Mexico City)

This statement not only mentions the exceptional character of the event, it also refers to the interior of the home and the preparation of the plates which contribute to turning this commensal meal into a 'unique way to experience Mexico City'. In addition to these two aspects already examined in the previous sections, the guest highlights the company of his host's friends, and evaluates his Eatwith dinner as a great way to get in touch with locals. Using meal-sharing platforms enables different people staying in a city to meet and eat together, and thus allows for a third way of framing commensality and locality as deeply intertwined concepts. Before sorting algorithms, online profiles and user reviews started to bring people together, such encounters were matters of chance, or at least complex tasks for individuals. Especially for short-term visitors who were looking for possibilities to satisfy their wish to immerse in urban everyday life, this proved to be a tough challenge. Their options were limited, and so their goal was to find "that 'hidden' little restaurant patronized only by 'locals'" (Fields 2002, p. 42). Nowadays, travellers can easily gain access to local homes where they will enjoy food and beverages together with other city users.

Conclusion

The online networks of companies in the sharing economy connect users worldwide and facilitate new encounters that have a profound impact on travelling in general and urban tourism in particular. By focusing on the meal-sharing platform Eatwith, this chapter highlights how digital technology mediates and structures social interaction while bringing together users for joint meals. Since 'social eating experiences' represent a relatively new phenomenon, an established body of research is not yet available. Therefore, we used two literature reviews in order to identify possible theoretical starting points for addressing meal-sharing platforms: one focusing on the social power of food, and the other concentrating on food's significance for tourism. The framing of commensality and food as promising local and thereby desirable experiences was then examined through selected empirical material taken from Eatwith's website.

This chapter argues that meal-sharing experiences profoundly rely on three characteristics: they (a) present eating—a rather everyday activity—as an outstanding event; (b) open up private homes for their users and frame these places as 'local'; and (c) connect various types of people in a city. Even though the users gathered together to share a meal do not represent a previously existing social group, they engage in what Grignon labelled 'exceptional commensality': eating, an everyday practice, turns into a rare, memorable event. Here, commensality becomes branded as an opportunity to feel a local connection (as a visitor) or to experience the cultural diversity of a contemporary metropolis (as a resident).

Eatwith presents social eating as an extraordinary event deeply infused by a city's atmosphere. This notion is reinforced by users' reviews, which stress the commensal meal as an outstanding, multi-sensuous experience. With the chef's home as the typical venue, private dwelling spaces are interpreted as signifiers for locality supporting the 'local touch' that Eatwith attaches to commensality. By targeting travellers and residents alike, this meal-sharing platform connects various types of city users. Altogether, these three aspects characterise Eatwith's services. Further research is needed to study users' feelings and perceptions of Eatwith's face-to-face encounters. Onsite ethnography and qualitative interviews with hosts and guests would be able to uncover how commensality is actually lived out, and could reveal which particular moments are tipping points for arousing feelings of existential authenticity. These two methods would also present efficient ways to study whether the purchasability of a meal-sharing experience affects the emergence of existential authenticity. While virtual ethnography is a great way to explore prominent narratives online, critical perspectives are absent in Eatwith's profiles and reviews. A wider approach could include critical points of view from disappointed guests or frustrated chefs. Moreover, with the sharing economy becoming an established business model, researching associated companies and their networks would offer scholars the chance to shed light on the complex entanglement of online and offline spheres in their regard to social life.

The three characteristics—framing everyday activities as exceptional sensations, opening up private homes, and connecting people who temporarily share the same geographical location—are largely facilitated and enabled by technological innovations. However, they cannot be restricted to analysis of online meal-sharing platforms or short-term rental providers. Instead, we argue that they are distinctive qualities of *new urban tourism* phenomena. With the help of digital mobile technology, these phenomena soften well-established theoretical categories, for example by blending the differentiating boundaries of who is 'a traveller' and who is 'a local'. A new urban tourist is anyone who is discovering a city using apps, online platforms and social networks in order to reveal its everyday life. As such, he or she does not rely solely on sightseeing tours and does not engage in stereotypical touristic practices.[9] Rather, *new urban tourism* is about striving to immerse oneself into a city's everyday life and to feel (at least temporarily) a sense of local belonging. In the case of meal-sharing platforms, this immersion is hoped to be achieved by commensality.

Notes

1 See also the chapters in this volume by Stors (Chapter 6) and Wildish and Spierings (Chapter 7), which focus on Airbnb, a popular short-term rental platform.

2 Eatwith charges 20 per cent commission for every booked service.

3 We are aware that food consumption is a huge field and we only touch on a very specific topic within it. Due to the focus of our analysis, we cannot address important issues such as food production, food insecurity, hunger or food-related health or illnesses. For good general overviews, see Mintz and Du Bois (2002), Pilcher (2012) and Murcott (2017).

4 This function becomes particularly apparent in studies on drinking and tourism. Alcotourism, party tourism or stag tourism occurs when the joint consumption of alcoholic beverages is used to create and promote social bonding experiences (Thurnell-Read 2012, Bell 2008).

5 Eatwith's social eating experiences are classified into three categories: meals, cooking classes or wine/food tastings, and food tours. Due to our theoretical interest, the analysis will only look at experiences categorised as 'meals'. Eatwith considers the categories of lunch, brunch, dinner, aperitif, picnic and teatime as 'meals'.

6 Whereas we do not see the need to anonymise quotes taken from Eatwith's own self-descriptions because these are the company's official statements, we decided to hide the names of users out of courtesy. However, all material we cited is publicly accessible online—even without logging in.

7 Among them are the type of experience, cuisine, additional drinks, special diets, the minimum and maximum number of guests, the price and some characteristics of the place, such as parking and WiFi.

8 The powerful influence of online recommendations is thoroughly analysed by Kramer et al. (Chapter 9 in this volume).

9 For the stereotypical and conflictive figure of the tourist, see also Grube, Chapter 11 in this volume.

Acknowledgements

This research was conducted within the project 'Tourism 2.0—Network-Based Forms of Participation and Digital Detox', a sub-project of the interdisciplinary research group 'Media and Participation'. We would like to thank Deutsche Forschungsgemeinschaft (DFG) for generously allocating the funding for our research activities. In addition, we thank our student assistant Gertruda Kaczmarek for her competent support throughout the project's duration.

References

Appadurai A., 1988. How to make a national cuisine: cookbooks in contemporary India. *Comparative Studies in Society and History*, 30 (1), 3–24.

Barthes, R., 1997. Toward a psychosociology of contemporary food consumption. *In*: C. Counihan and P. Van Esterik, eds, *Food and Culture: A Reader*. New York: Routledge, 20–27.

Beer, D., 2017. The social power of algorithms. *Information, Communication & Society*, 20 (1), 1–13.

Beer, S., 2008. Authenticity and food experience: commercial and academic perspectives. *Journal of Foodservice*, 19, 153–163.

Belk, R., 2014. Sharing versus pseudo-sharing in Web 2.0. *Anthropologist*, 18 (1), 7–23.

Bell, D., 2008. Destination drinking: toward a research agenda on alcotourism. *Drugs: Education, Prevention and Policy*, 15 (3), 291–304.

Björk, P. and Kauppinen-Räisänen, H., 2014. Culinary-gastronomic tourism: a search for local food experiences. *Nutrition & Food Science*, 44 (4), 294–309.

Boniface, P., 2003. *Tasting Tourism: Travelling for Food and Drink*. London: Routledge.

Botsman, R. and Rogers, R., 2010. *What's Mine is Yours: The Rise of Collaborative Consumption.* New York: HarperBusiness.

Bourdieu, P., 2003. *Distinction: A Social Critique of the Judgement of Taste.* London: Routledge.

Bridges, J. and Vásquez, C., 2016. If nearly all Airbnb reviews are positive, does this make them meaningless? *Current Issues in Tourism*, 1–19.

Brown, L., 2013. Tourism: a catalyst for existential authenticity. *Annals of Tourism Research*, 40, 176–190.

Chang, R.C.Y., Kivela, J. and Mak, A.H.N., 2010. Food preferences of Chinese tourists. *Annals of Tourism Research*, 37 (4), 989–1011.

Cohen, E. and Avieli, N., 2004. Food in tourism: attraction and impediment. *Annals of Tourism Research*, 31 (4), 755–778.

Crouch, D. and Desforges, L., 2003. The sensuous in the tourist encounter. *Tourist Studies*, 3 (1), 5–22.

Davidson, N.M. and Infranca, J.J., 2016. The sharing economy as an urban phenomenon. *Yale Law & Policy Review*, 2, 215–279.

Douglas, M., 1972. Deciphering a meal. *Daedalus*, 101 (1), 61–81.

du Rand, G.E., Heath, E. and Alberts, N., 2003. The role of local and regional food in destination marketing. *Journal of Travel & Tourism Marketing*, 14 (3–4), 97–112.

Eatwith, 2018a. Eatwith Homepage [online]. Available from: www.eatwith.com/?c=EUR [accessed 3 May 2018].

Eatwith, 2018b. Food experiences in 130+ countries [online]. Available from: www.eatwith.com/pages/about-us?c=EUR [accessed 3 May 2018].

Eatwith, 2018c. Host your own food experience [online]. Available from: www.eatwith.com/landings/become-a-host?c=EUR [accessed 3 May 2018].

Eatwith, 2018d. How do I know that the host is a good chef? [online]. Available from: https://intercom.help/eatwith/faq-english/getting-started/how-do-i-know-that-the-host-is-a-good-chef [accessed 3 May 2018].

Eatwith, 2018e. What is Eatwith? [online]. Available from: https://intercom.help/eatwith/faq-english/about-us/what-is-eatwith [accessed 3 May 2018].

Ferguson, P.P., 2011. The sense of taste. *The American Historical Review*, 116 (2), 371–384.

Fields, K. 2002. Demand for the gastronomy tourism product: motivational factors. *In*: A.-M. Hjalager and G. Richards, eds, *Tourism and Gastronomy*. London: Routledge, 36–50.

Fischler, C., 1988. Food, self and identity. *Social Science Information*, 27 (2), 275–292.

Fischler, C., 2011. Commensality, society and culture. *Social Science Information*, 50 (3–4), 528–548.

Frisch, T., 2018. Digitale Bewertungskultur im Tourismus 2.0 Grenzüberschreitung und Normalisierungsdruck. *In*: J. Kropf and S. Laser, eds, *Digitale Bewertungspraktiken: Labore der Grenzziehung in vernetzten Welten*. Wiesbaden: Springer VS, 39–68.

Frisch, T. and Stoltenberg, L., 2018. Affirmative Superlative und die Macht negativer Bewertungen. Online-Reputation in der Datengesellschaft. *In*: D. Houben and B. Prietl, eds, *Datengesellschaft: Einsichten in die Datafizierung des Sozialen*. Bielefeld: transcript, 85–106.

Germann Molz, J., 2007. Eating difference: the cosmopolitan mobilities of culinary tourism. *Space and Culture*, 10 (1), 77–93.

Gibson, S., 2007. Food mobilities. Traveling, dwelling, and eating cultures. *Space and Culture*, 10 (1), 4–21.

Goody, J., 1982. *Cooking, Cuisine and Class: A Study in Comparative Sociology*. Cambridge: Cambridge University Press.

Gössling, S. and Hall, C.M., 2013. Sustainable culinary systems: an introduction. *In*: C.M. Hall and S. Gössling, eds, *Sustainable Culinary Systems: Local Foods, Innovation, and Tourism & Hospitality*. London: Routledge, 3–44.

Greene, C.P. and Cramer, J.M., 2011. Beyond mere sustenance: food as communication/communication as food. *In*: J.M. Cramer, C.P. Greene and L.M. Walters, eds, *Food as Communication/Communication as Food*. New York: Peter Lang, ix–xix.

Grignon, C. 2001. Commensality and social morphology: an essay of typology. *In*: P. Scholliers, ed., *Food, Drink and Identity: Cooking, Eating and Drinking in Europe since the Middle Ages*. Oxford and New York: Berg, 23–33.

Guptill, A.E., Copelton, D.A. and Lucal, B., 2016. *Food and Society. Principles and Paradoxes*. Cambridge: Polity Press.

Gyimóthy, S. and Mykletun, R.J., 2009. Scary food: commodifying culinary heritage as meal adventures in tourism. *Journal of Vacation Marketing*, 15 (3), 259–273.

Hall, C.M. and Mitchell, R., 2005. Gastronomic tourism. Comparing food and wine tourism experiences. *In*: M. Novelli, ed., *Niche Tourism*. London: Routledge, 73–88.

Hall, C.M. and Sharples, L., 2008. Food events, festivals and farmers' markets: an introduction. *In*: C.M. Hall and L. Sharples, eds, *Food and Wine Festivals and Events Around the World: Development, Management and Markets*. Amsterdam: Elsevier/Butterworth-Heinemann, 3–22.

Hannam, K., Sheller, M. and Urry, J., 2006. Editorial: mobilities, immobilities and moorings. *Mobilities*, 1 (1), 1–22.

Harris, M., 1998. *Good to Eat: Riddles of Food and Culture*. Long Grove, CA: Waveland Press.

Hedegaard, L., 2018. (Re)tasting places. *Gastronomica: The Journal of Critical Food Studies*, 18 (1), 66–75.

Heldke, L., 2003. *Exotic Appetites: Ruminations of a Food Adventurer*. London: Routledge.

Henderson, J.C., 2009. Food tourism reviewed. *British Food Journal*, 111 (4), 317–326.

Hughes, G., 1995. Authenticity in tourism. *Annals of Tourism Research*, 22 (4), 781–803.

Ignatov, E. and Smith, S., 2006. Segmenting Canadian culinary tourists. *Current Issues in Tourism*, 9 (3), 235–255.

Ketter, E., 2017. Eating with Eatwith: analysing tourism-sharing economy consumers. *Current Issues in Tourism*, 1–14.

Kim, H. and Jamal, T., 2007. Touristic quest for existential authenticity. *Annals of Tourism Research*, 34 (1), 181–201.

Kim, Y.G. and Eves, A., 2012. Construction and validation of a scale to measure tourist motivation to consume local food. *Tourism Management*, 33 (6), 1458–1467.

Kozinets, R.V., 2006. Click to connect: netnography and tribal advertising. *Journal of Advertising Research*, 46 (3), 279–288.

Kozinets, R.V., 2010. *Netnography: Doing Ethnographic Research Online*. London: SAGE.

Lau, R.W.K., 2010. Revisiting authenticity: a social realist approach. *Annals of Tourism Research*, 37 (2), 478–498.

Lashley, C., Morrison, A. and Randall, S., 2004. My most memorable meal ever! Hospitality as an emotional experience. *In*: D. Sloan, ed., *Culinary Taste – Consumer Behavior in the International Restaurant Sector*. London: Routledge, 165–184.

Lévi-Strauss, C., 1997. The culinary triangle. *In*: C. Counihan and P. Van Esterik, eds, *Food and Culture: A Reader*. New York: Routledge, 28–35.

Lockwood, W.G. and Lockwood, Y.R., 2000. Continuity and adaptation in Arab American foodways. *In*: N. Abraham and A. Shryock, eds, *Arab Detroit: From Margin to Mainstream*. Detroit, MI: Wayne State University Press, 515–559.

Long, L.M., 2004. Culinary tourism. A folkloristic perspective on eating and otherness. *In*: L.M. Long, ed., *Culinary Tourism*. Lexington, KY: University Press of Kentucky, 20–50.

Long, L.M., 2012. Culinary tourism. *In*: J.M. Pilcher, ed., *The Oxford Handbook of Food History*. Oxford: Oxford University Press, 389–407.

MacCannell, D., 1976. *The Tourist: A New Theory of the Leisure Class*. New York: Schocken Books.

Mak, A.H.N., Lumbers, M. and Eves, A., 2012. Globalisation and food consumption in tourism. *Annals of Tourism Research*, 39 (1), 171–196.

Martinotti, G., 1996. Four populations: human settlements and social morphology in the contemporary metropolis. *European Review*, 4 (1), 3–23.

Mennell, S., Murcott, A. and van Otterloo, A.H., 1992. *The Sociology of Food: Eating, Diet, and Culture*. London: SAGE.

Mintz, S.W. and Du Bois, C.M., 2002. The anthropology of food and eating. *Annual Review of Anthropology*, 31, 99–119.

Mkono, M., 2013. Existential authenticity in cultural restaurant experiences in Victoria Falls, Zimbabwe: a netnographic analysis. *International Journal of Culture, Tourism and Hospitality Research*, 7 (4), 353–363.

Murcott, A., 1982. On the social significance of the 'cooked dinner' in South Wales. *Social Science Information*, 21 (4–5), 677–696.

Murcott, A., 1997. Family meals: a thing of the past? *In*: P. Caplan, ed., *Food, Health, and Identity*. London: Routledge, 32–49.

Murcott, A., 2017. The sociology of food. *In*: K.O. Korgen, ed., *The Cambridge Handbook of Sociology: Specialty and Interdisciplinary Studies*. Cambridge: Cambridge University Press, 199–206.

Pilcher, J.M., ed., 2012. *The Oxford Handbook of Food History*. Oxford: Oxford University Press.

Poulain, J.-P., 2017. *The Sociology of Food: Eating and the Place of Food in Society*. London: Bloomsbury.

Pritchard, A. and Morgan, N., 2011. Tourist bodies, transformation and sensuality. *In*: P. Bramham and S. Wagg, eds, *The New Politics of Leisure and Pleasure*. London: Palgrave Macmillan, 153–168.

Reisinger, Y. and Steiner, C.J., 2006. Reconceptualizing object authenticity. *Annals of Tourism Research*, 33 (1), 65–86.

Richardson, L. 2015. Performing the sharing economy. *Geoforum*, 67, 121–129.

Ritzer, G., 1998. *The McDonaldization Thesis: Explorations and Extensions*. London: SAGE.

Rokka, J., 2010. Netnographic inquiry and new translocal sites of the social. *International Journal of Consumer Studies*, 34 (4), 381–387.

Scarpato, R. and Daniele, R., 2003. New global cuisine: tourism, authenticity and sense of place in postmodern gastronomy. *In*: C.M. Hall *et al.*, eds, *Food Tourism Around the World*. Oxford: Butterworth-Heinemann, 296–313.

Simmel, G., 1997. Sociology of the meal [1910]. *In*: D. Frisby and M. Featherstone, eds, *Simmel on Culture: Selected Writings*. London: SAGE, 130–135.

Simopoulos, A.P. and Bhat, R.V., eds, 2000. *Street Foods*. Basel: Karger.

Sims, R., 2009. Food, place and authenticity: local food and the sustainable tourism experience. *Journal of Sustainable Tourism*, 17 (3), 321–336.

Steiner, C.J. and Reisinger, Y., 2006. Understanding existential authenticity. *Annals of Tourism Research*, 33 (2), 299–318.

Stoltenberg, L., 2017. Zur urbanen Ökonomie des Teilens: Airbnbs Einfluss auf den städtischen Raum. *INDES*, 3, 59–65.

Striphas, T., 2015. Algorithmic culture. *European Journal of Cultural Studies*, 18 (4–5), 395–412.

Thurnell-Read, T., 2012. Tourism place and space: British stag tourism in Poland. *Annals of Tourism Research*, 39 (2), 801–819.

Urry, J., 2000. *Sociology Beyond Societies. Mobilities for the Twenty-First Century*. London: Routledge.

Wang, N., 1999. Rethinking authenticity in tourism experience. *Annals of Tourism Research*, 26 (2), 349–370.

Warde, A. and Martens, L., 2000. *Eating Out: Social Differentiation, Consumption and Pleasure*. Cambridge: Cambridge University Press.

Warde, A., 2016. *The Practice of Eating*. Cambridge: Polity Press.

9 Places of *Muße* as part of new urban tourism in Paris

Clara Sofie Kramer, Nora Winsky and Tim Freytag

Introduction

Over the past few decades urban tourism has been shaped by the emergence and diversification of visitor practices with a focus on urban everyday life. Being widely referred to as *new urban tourism*, this trend has affected and transformed urban neighbourhoods and has stretched out well beyond the established tourist attractions in the city (Maitland 2008). The sprawl of *new urban tourism* and the increasing importance of digital technologies tend to blur or even wipe out traditional boundaries between tourists and local residents in the tourist destination (Stors *et al.*, Chapter 1 in this volume). In other words, it becomes easier for tourists to relate to the everyday life and activities of locals. At the same time, digital technologies enable visitors to follow or even interact with relatives, friends and colleagues while being away from home.

The main aim of this chapter is to explore a set of practices that allow urban tourists to slow down, open up and experience a moment of quality time during their stay. In particular, we study representations of places that can help visitors to temporarily have a rest or escape from other tourist activities.[1] We call such places 'places of *Muße*', drawing on the German concept of *Muße* (Latin: *otium*) to better understand when and how visitors get away from a rather stressful urban environment, recover from their various tourist activities and occasionally enjoy feelings of comfort and inspiration. Potential urban tourist places of *Muße* include, but are not limited to, parks and gardens, cemeteries, churches, museums, exhibition halls and other buildings, galleries and department stores, bars and restaurants, but also avenues, squares and pedestrian areas in the city. We assume that *Muße* is a niche phenomenon with growing importance, which so far has been widely neglected in *new urban tourism* research. Up to now, our research has been limited to the exploration of travel guides and travel blogs, which form the empirical basis of our work. In the future, we plan to extend our research activities to a series of field observations and interviews. The research questions to be addressed in this chapter are:

(1) Which places of *Muße* can be identified in urban tourism based on travel guides?

(2) How can the identified places of *Muße* be described and categorised in a typology to be set up based on our study of travel guides?

(3) According to selected travel blogs, how does a particular place of *Muße* operate when being visited by tourists?

By focusing on Paris, we have chosen a leading destination in European city tourism to study places and practices of *Muße* within the broader field of *new urban tourism*. Paris is a suitable object of study as the city attracts extremely high numbers of visitors, provides a wide range of potential places of *Muße* and they are well represented in travel guides and travel blogs. Moreover, the key role of tourism and touristification in shaping and transforming the French capital has been addressed in a large number of studies (e.g., Pearce 1998, Fagnoni and Aymard 2002, Duhamel and Knafou 2007, Chapuis *et al.* 2013, Gravari-Barbas and Fagnoni 2013, Gravari-Barbas and Guinand 2017). However, we have been unable to identify any empirical study of *Muße* that is related to urban tourist practices in Paris.

This chapter is organised in four main sections. In the first section we discuss the concept of *Muße* in urban tourism studies and reflect on the role of *Muße* in *new urban tourism* and related practices. In the following section, we sketch out the sources and methods of our empirical work. The third section is based on a qualitative content analysis of three German-language travel guides. Here, we identify a set of linguistically constructed *Muße* places that are visualised and summarised in a map. On the basis of our travel guide analysis, we suggest a typology and illustrate particular characteristics and qualities of our four identified types of *Muße* places: cultural places, extensive places, green places and culinary places. In the fourth section, we draw upon two selected travel blogs to take a closer look at a few places of *Muße* identified in the travel guides. Here, our aim is to get a better understanding of how *Muße* places operate when being shared by travellers and residents in the city. In doing so, we take into account the notion of authenticity, which is often ascribed to places of *Muße*, and we discuss the fragility of places of *Muße* that may result from growing tourism, and potential tensions among tourists or between tourists and locals.

Theoretical background and conceptual framing

To start with the theoretical contextualisation, we will introduce the term *Muße*. Then we will take a closer look at encounters between tourists and locals that can be understood as involving both potential conflicts and the experience of *Muße*. Finally, we reflect upon tourist practices as a basis for the analysis.

Conceptualising Muße *in urban tourism studies*

Muße is a German term with a long history. It is equivalent to the Latin word 'otium' which encompasses a whole set of different meanings. In

German-speaking countries, the term went through a long process of conceptualisation. Hence, the term *Muße* refers to a complex phenomenon that in turn embraces a huge semantic field. *Muße* is not the same as leisure, as it exceeds the meaning of leisure. For instance, a person can experience *Muße* while working, which is not leisure by definition. The same applies to other translations—they do not adequately depict the concept of *Muße*, as we understand it in the interdisciplinary Collaborative Research Centre 1015 Otium (CRC 1015).[2]

A current social need for *Muße* stems from the prevalent impression that the capacity to feel moments of *Muße* is endangered and may get lost due to an achievement orientation and efficiency enhancement in postmodern society (Goldammer 2014, Leder 2007). For this reason, the need for, and the awareness of, mindfulness, placidity and self-determination have moved into the centre of the societal discourse and therefore also the scientific discourse (Leder 2007). Consequently, an emerging question for tourism geography is whether and how this trend will have an impact on the production and transformation of tourist spaces.

In the tourism context, *Muße* can be considered as a motive for travel (Leder 2007). However, in the context of urban tourism, a particular geographical environment comes into play. Urban spaces are usually not associated with the general characteristics of *Muße* but rather with the opposite: noise, smelliness, hustle and bustle (Claßen and Kistemann 2017, Fontaine 2017). Nevertheless, it can be assumed that tourists tend to look for experiences and places of *Muße* during their stay in urban environments, which opens up a new field of research to be explored in tourism studies (Leder 2007).

As Leder (2007) points out, the understanding of *Muße* lacks a general definition and its various meanings are framed according to the particular ideas of varying epochs, societies and discourses. Consequently, the attempt to define *Muße* will inevitably reduce its diversity, exclude alternative meanings and necessarily prioritise a particular form of understanding. In the CRC 1015, given the complexity of the term and the related difficulty of finding an adequate definition, a variety of academic disciplines have been confronted with the demanding and captivating task of conceptualising and studying aspects of *Muße*. However, from an urban tourism studies perspective the phenomenon of *Muße* appears to be widely unexplored in existing theoretical and empirical studies.

Based on CRC contributions, Kramer (2018) has elaborated four key features which characterise experiences of *Muße* in urban tourism and build the starting point for this analysis. *Muße* in urban tourism is considered as experienced moments of placidity, freedom, indulgence and recreation (Gimmel and Keiling 2016, Kramer 2018). The major consequences and effects of experiencing *Muße* include independence, energy and creativity, as well as self-determination and a new sense of the self. *Muße* gives peace of mind and a feeling of balance and satisfaction (Leder 2007).

Muße is embedded in a spatial context. Architects and urban planners, for example, try to take the need for *Muße* into account. Typical places of *Muße* include tea rooms, gardens, cloisters and libraries (Blum *et al.* 2016, Figal 2015). However, there is no guarantee that *Muße* will be experienced in such places: this depends on a wide range of external circumstances, together with the momentarily prevailing subjective mental state of the persons concerned. For personal reasons, other locations may be considered as preferred places of *Muße* (Figal 2015). Thus, the production and perception of places of *Muße* depends to some extent on individual norms and values. *Muße* means something different for each individual (Leder 2007). Despite this inherent subjectivity, potential places of *Muße* have parameters that may facilitate experiencing *Muße*. These can be identified in both the physical and the symbolic dimensions, the latter in the sense of the movements and practices of individuals in space which constitute potential places of *Muße*.

Beside its spatial embeddedness, *Muße* also has to be considered as a temporal phenomenon. *Muße* occurs detached from predominant temporal structures: in moments of *Muße*, time and potential time constraints do not play an important role anymore (Lengert 1957, Figal 2015, Schäfer 2015a). Furthermore, together with various external circumstances that may negatively affect experiences of *Muße*, the temporal component of *Muße* has to be taken into account. Visiting the same place may be experienced differently depending on the time of day and the time of the year. Moreover, for different people the conditions of access to a place may vary over time and consequently affect the experience of *Muße*. Thus, an identified place of *Muße* may be transformed temporarily into a place that is hostile to the experience of *Muße*.

Considering Muße *in* new urban tourism

New urban tourism is widely characterised by a contested relationship between tourists and locals. The attracted tourists play an ambivalent role because they have both positive and negative impacts on the city and its inhabitants. On the one hand, urban tourism can substantially contribute to the local economy because of earnings in the sectors of accommodation, gastronomy, retail, culture, entertainment and leisure. Tourism can be considered as an increasingly important factor in urban economies.[3] Moreover, cities usually benefit from the promotion of their image. This can lead to growing investments in the cultural sector, support of the inner-city public transport system, and initiatives for maintaining green areas and efficient infrastructures in the city. In this sense, urban tourism has the potential to improve quality of life for both locals and tourists (Andereck *et al.* 2005, Archer *et al.* 2005). On the other hand, the growth of urban tourism may result in overcrowded inner-city areas and let cities and their inhabitants suffer from a general overload of their infrastructure (Popp 2012, Stors and Kagermeier 2013). This often comes along with damage to buildings and monuments, and rising costs for maintenance and repair (Steinecke 2011). Tourists penetrate more and more into residents' neighbourhoods or home environments, in order to experience the authentic flair of the city, to explore secret places and to slip into the residents' world beyond the hustle and bustle of mass tourism (Kreisel 2007, Maitland and Newman 2008). This has negative impacts on the residents' spaces of retreat and their well-being (Freytag 2010, Bauder and Freytag 2018). To regulate flows of tourists, highly frequented cities have developed visitor management tools, such as increased entrance fees for certain tourist attractions, driving bans or specific rules of conduct in densely touristified inner-city areas (Steinecke 2011).

The problems associated with intense touristification result from the above-mentioned negative impacts of urban tourism: crowding, noise, litter, inappropriate behaviour, increased prices, and sometimes even displacement of residents. These radical transformations have provoked dramatic conflicts with residents in several major cities (Füller and Michel 2014, Colomb and Novy 2017, Gravari-Barbas and Jacquot 2017, Sommer and Kip, Chapter 10 in this volume). In this chapter, we refer to the current debates on *new urban tourism* reflecting the experience of *Muße*. In doing so, we follow the hypothesis that increasing numbers of visitors may endanger the experience of *Muße* for tourists (Kramer 2018). We argue that potential encounters between tourists and locals can play a crucial role in experiencing *Muße* and in searching for authenticity.

On the one hand, the search for authenticity corresponds with the wish to experience the original and genuine, which tends to disappear in postmodern ordinary life (Kreisel 2007, Urry and Larsen 2011). To achieve this aim, tourists look for ordinary places; they are keen on insider tips and perform practices of integration. They want to live like the locals. On the other hand, tourists tend to consider authenticity as the extraordinary, as the absence of what constitutes their own day-to-day life. Thus, ordinary life in the city becomes the extraordinary in the context of urban tourism.

Practices of integration neutralise the distance between tourists and the visited destination, as the tourists take part in and become part of the destination (Wöhler 2011).[4] Such practices enable tourists to experience authenticity, to perceive ordinariness as extraordinariness—they observe a city's everyday life from an extraordinary perspective (MacCannell 2013). This trend of integration may also operate the other way round. Tourist practices can spread into the day-to-day life of the locals, so that they can feel as if they are at least temporarily on holiday in their own city (Walla 2010). In other words, the boundary between tourists and locals becomes blurred in the context of *new urban tourism*.

Based on these theoretical reflections, we discuss the question of whether tourists experience *Muße* through the feeling of proximity to, and encounters with, residents. We suggest the hypothesis that a contact with locals can foster both an experience of authenticity and an experience of *Muße*. Considering authenticity as a general tourist aim, we assume that having authentic experiences promotes placidity, freedom, indulgence and recreation, the key features of *Muße*. Thus, we empirically explore to what extent residents can be considered as a constitutive element of experiencing *Muße* in urban tourism, and how authenticity perceived by tourists can be understood as a component of *Muße*. However, tourists find themselves in a dilemma: they destroy what they are looking for the moment they find it (Enzensberger 1958). Ordinary places are trapped in a cycle: as authentic havens within the waves and flows of growing urban tourism, they necessarily attract more and more visitors because they are regarded as insider tips. Over time, they become transformed into touristified places and—if we connect authenticity and *Muße*—lose their potential as places of *Muße*. Hence, there is a constant need to find new and secret authentic places, and so the cycle is complete. Taking up two examples from travel blogs, we discuss this fragility of places of *Muße*.

Tourist practices

In this section, we focus conceptually on tourist practices to address the question of what tourists do in places of *Muße*. Tourist practices are marked by repetition and regularity. They are routine forms of doing and collective habits that are socially bounded (Baerenholdt *et al.* 2004, Crouch 2004). With regard to such practices, we can expect particular routine forms of doing (Dalichau 2016, Walla 2010; see also Larsen, Chapter 2 in this volume). Tourist practices are socially and medially constructed, for example by travel guides, travel literature and the travel accounts of friends or relatives (Weber 2012). They express and transmit knowledge and awareness of how tourists (are expected to) act, move and behave in specific settings and contexts. By this collective internalisation of action patterns, roles and stereotypes are constantly produced and reproduced. Tourist practices can give orientation in unfamiliar environments and help when exploring travel destinations (Dalichau 2016, Weber 2012). They also comprise the visual tourist perception: under social and medial influences, the 'tourist gaze' is shaped and articulated (Urry and Larsen 2011, Walla 2010).

From a social constructivist perspective, tourist practices can be seen as modes of construction. When doing tourism, visitors do not just consume tourist spaces but also produce, change and load them with meaning. Accordingly, tourist practices and tourism are part of a constant process of reproduction (Dalichau 2016, Lefebvre 1991). The following tourist practices are very common in urban tourism: shopping, eating, gazing, sightseeing, strolling, consuming art and culture, going out and experiencing nightlife, as well as sleeping (Urry and Larsen 2011, Weber 2012). But by imitating the practices of residents, tourists may try to overcome the boundaries between themselves and the (unfamiliar) tourist destination.

Methodology

In order to identify and characterise places of *Muße* in Paris, we conducted a qualitative content analysis of prominent travel guides. We decided to focus on classical guidebooks and online travel blogs. Qualitative content analysis is a standard method for systematic text analysis and is suitable for an investigation of materialised communication. It is an empirical method for the systematic and intersubjective documented description of content-related and formal characteristics of communication (Kohlbacher 2006). A key advantage of content analysis is that it can be applied very efficiently to a high quantity of text material because it allows reducing of extensive and complex data sets (Bowen 2009, Mayring 2010). The system of categories forms the method's core and serves to reduce, structure and interpret the text corpus (Bowen 2009, Mayring 2010). Relevant passages from the text material—in this case descriptions of tourist sites—are assigned to the corresponding categories in order to subsequently analyse and evaluate them.

Following Kramer (2018), we set up categories based on the following key features related to *Muße* in urban tourism: indulgence, freedom, placidity and recreation. These categories serve to identify and characterise the linguistically constructed places of *Muße* and to investigate the activities that constitute practices of *Muße* in urban tourism. Using the system of categories is a valuable aid to sketching out a set of main characteristics of *Muße*-facilitating spatial structures in the context of urban tourism. The difficulty is that the word *Muße* is not used in the travel guides, so that the places we have identified as places of *Muße* are not labelled as such and we need all four categories to identify them.

In a first step, we use travel guides to explore the linguistic construction of potential places of *Muße*. Reflecting a tourist perspective, we take the travel guides to identify and characterise places of *Muße* and to study related practices. To analyse the text material, the linguistically constructed places of *Muße* are identified, then characterised and subsequently categorised as four types of places of *Muße*. In the next step, our suggested four types of places are illustrated, and finally, we address the practices described in relation to the particular types of places. Overall, our text corpus contains 232 entries from the travel guides, which describe tourist sites: 124 entries from the *ADAC* travel guide (Schenk 2016), fifty-nine entries from the *Baedeker* travel guide (Reincke and Maunder 2016) and forty-nine entries from the *Reise Know-How* travel guide (Kalmbach 2015). With these three travel guides, we cover a wide range of different forms of linguistic constructions of places of *Muße*. While *ADAC* represents a travel guide suitable for beginners, *Baedeker* can be seen as a travel guide for generalists and *Reise Know-How* is primarily meant for individual travellers (Scherle 2001). Thus, the three travel guides have different target groups with specific needs and expectations.

In a second step, we take a closer look at a few places that are presented and discussed in two travel blogs. In doing so, we focus on blog entries referring to places of *Muße* that were identified in our analysis of the travel guides. The aim of studying the blogs is to complement the findings from the travel guides. Travel blogs are becoming increasingly popular and are important for preparing individual trips and tourist activities. This trend is part of the fundamental transformation of tourism and the tourist economy in the digital age since the mid-1990s (Sari *et al.* 2006). Instead of consulting the information from booking engines, many travellers prefer to rely on user-generated content provided, for example, in travel newsgroups, online review websites and travel blogs. Travellers or local experts create the content of travel blogs for other travellers, thus enhancing the exchange of information among tourists via new media (O'Connor 2008). Akehurst (2008) states that travel blogs are often perceived as "more credible and trustworthy than traditional marketing communication" (p. 51). The variety of existing travel blogs covers many regions of the world, various types of destinations and different forms of travel (Klemm 2016). Moreover, the complexity of travel blogs is reflected by the different user groups, whether backpackers, best agers, luxury class travellers or families with children.

While the travel guides reflect a tourist perspective, the travel blogs were selected to represent the perspective of bloggers who act as mediators between tourists and locals. Covering the period from 1 January 2015 to 7 March 2018, the travel blogs considered in this chapter are *Paris mal anders* (www.parismalanders.com) by Roman Kugge and *HelpTourists* (www.help-tourists-in-paris.com) by Denise Urbach. Both authors are Germans living in Paris who write their blogs in German. They see themselves as experts in respect of the city and its cultural dimensions (Kugge 2015–2018, Urbach 2015–2018). Both travel blogs have a professional design because they are highly commercialised. All recommendations function as word-of-mouth communication and have the ambition to reach beyond the well-known tourist hot spots and to unveil authentic and hidden places of Parisian day-to-day life (Akehurst 2008). These places correspond to the emerging trend of *new urban tourism*. Many of them are located outside the city centre, are not equipped with classical sightseeing tourist attractions, and so far have not been planned and used for tourism activities (Novy and Huning 2009).

Four types of places of *Muße* identified in the travel guide analysis

The map in Figure 9.1 is one result of the qualitative content analysis. It visualises the localisation of the identified places of *Muße* in Paris. Overall, sixty-three sites are identified as places of *Muße*. The cartographic symbols distinguish between the places of *Muße* mentioned in one, two or three of the analysed travel guides. Moreover, a distinction is made between four different types of places of *Muße* that are derived from the data material of the travel guides.

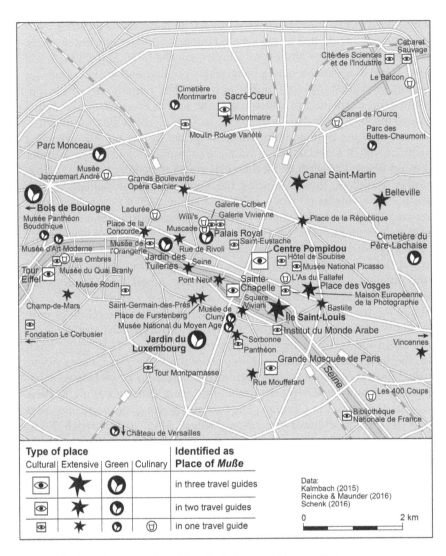

Type of place				Identified as	
Cultural	Extensive	Green	Culinary	Place of *Muße*	
◉	★	◐		in three travel guides	Data: Kalmbach (2015) Reincke & Maunder (2016) Schenk (2016)
◉	★	◐		in two travel guides	
◉	★	◐	ⓤ	in one travel guide	0 2 km

Figure 9.1 Overview map of the identified places of *Muße* in Paris.
Source: own depiction.

The places of *Muße* pictured on the map (Figure 9.1) represent the
following four different types of places: (1) cultural places, like churches and
museums, (2) extensive places, such as squares and streets, (3) green places,
for instance parks and cemeteries, and (4) culinary places, like restaurants and
cafés. They are listed and classified according to the relevant references in the
travel guides. The overview in Table 9.1 indicates the prevailing type for all
sixty-three identified places of *Muße*.

Table 9.1 The four types of the identified places of *Muße* in Paris

⊙ Cultural Places	★ Extensive Places	◑ Green Places	🍴 Culinary Places
Bibliothèque Nationale de France	Bastille	Bois de Boulogne	Bar Canal de l'Ourcq
Cabaret Sauvage	Belleville	Château de Versailles: Parc	Bistro les 400 Coups
Centre Pompidou	Canal Saint-Martin	Cimetière du Père-Lachaise	Ladurée tea room
Cité des Sciences et de l'lIndustrie	Champ-de-Mars	Cimetière Montmartre	Muscade tea room
Fondation Le Corbusier: Gallery	Grands Boulevards/ Opéra	Jardin des Tuileries	Musée Jacquemart André: Café
Galerie Colbert	Garnier	Jardin du Luxembourg	Restaurant L'As du Fallafel
Galerie Vivienne	Île Saint-Louis	Musée d'Art Moderne de la Ville	Restaurant Le Balcon
Grande Mosquée de Paris	Montmartre	de Paris: Garden	Restaurant Les Ombres
Hôtel de Soubise: Salon Ovale	Place de la Concorde	Musée de Cluny: Garden	Wine bar Willi's
Institut du Monde Arabe	Place de la République	Musée du Panthéon	
Maison Européenne de la	Place des Vosges	Bouddhique: Patio and garden	
Photographie: Library	Place de Furstenberg	Musée National du Moyen	
Moulin Rouge Variété	Rue de Rivoli	Age: Jardin Médiéval	
Musée de l'Orangerie	Rue Mouffetard	Palais Royal: Garden	
Musée du Quai Branly	Saint-Germain-des-Prés	Parc des Buttes-Chaumont	
Musée National Picasso	Seine	Parc Monceau	
Musée Rodin	Sorbonne		
Panthéon	Square Viviani		
Pont Neuf	Vincennes		
Sacré-Coeur			
Sainte-Chapelle			
Saint-Eustache			
Tour Eiffel: Viewing platform			
Tour Montparnasse			

Source: own depiction.

In the next step, we characterise the four types of places of *Muße* on the basis of the data given in the travel guides. This characterisation goes beyond the categories of indulgence, freedom, placidity and recreation.

(1) The first type—cultural places—is described in the travel guides as architecturally exciting, exotic and charming, and can be described as soft, for instance with curved components. Furthermore, this type of place is characterised as light, airy, quiet and spiritual. Cultural places in the travel guides feature elements of water and greening, and they are usually considered as being authentic. In addition, cultural places include an educational dimension and they often contain art, culture or music, which allows the tourists to contemplate, to learn and to listen. Moreover, these places, or at least some of their elements, are often elevated and offer a nice view. The building of Fondation Le Corbusier, and in particular its gallery, can serve as an example of a cultural place, as suggested by an entry in the *ADAC* travel guide:

> The picture gallery—with Le Corbusier's first swinging front supported by free-standing columns—forms a unit with the cubist central building. This comes out very clearly in the communication of the interior rooms. An elevated entrance hall, which is open to all three storeys, is surrounded by a complex circulation system: stairs, a smoothly rising ramp and a connecting pathway allow various combinations and invite the visitor to continuously explore new perspectives and perceptions of space. Huge panorama windows and horizontal bands of windows let the interior blend into the exterior.
>
> (Translated from the German original, Schenk 2016, p. 143)

(2) The second type—extensive places—is described as authentic and truly French. As suggested by the name of this type, such places are rambling, free and open. Like cultural places, but even more so, extensive places tend to feature green and blue components: plants and water. Extensive places contain charming and amusing elements, and they can be characterised as diversified, compelling and inviting. Moreover, they include nostalgic components, which enable tourists to slip into former times and to give room to wider thoughts. Extensive places are linguistically constructed as safe havens and oases in the urban hustle and bustle. Place de la République can be taken as an example of an extensive place. The *Baedeker* states that locals and tourists "[can] enjoy this location since 2014 as an open-air oasis with an urban park of 12,000 square metres and an open area of 8,000 square metres around the Marianne" (translated from the German original, Reincke and Maunder 2016, p. 296). Another example of an extensive place is listed in the *ADAC* guidebook, the Belleville neighbourhood:

> This as well is Paris, and is worth being discovered. However, its harsh character is not expressed in tourist attractions, but it has to be explored step by step in the steeply ascending alleyways, dark backyards and

narrow passages that the inhabitants consider as their gardens. [...] Old crooked houses [...]. Up here, one has a splendid view over the city [...]. There are markets in several streets on many days of the week.

(Translated from the German original,
Schenk 2016, pp. 134–135)

(3) Green places—the third type—contain primarily green and blue components and are rambling. Just like cultural and extensive places, they are often characterised as authentic, hence truly French. They are described as being restful, calm, airy, invigorating, pleasant, charming and inviting. Additionally, green places include nostalgic and romantic aspects. They are timeless: here, tourists feel liberated from the time structure that is prevalent in other places. Green places form a contrast to the rest of the urban landscape and they are linguistically constructed as oases and islands. Like extensive places, they are seen as an opportunity to escape from a stressful urban environment. Père Lachaise cemetery can serve as an example to illustrate the characteristics of a green place. *Reise Know-How* describes it as follows:

The tranquillity of the hill is worth a visit even without hunting for celebrities. The Parisian cemeteries are virtually cities of the dead. [...] One can leave it to chance, the park-like cemetery stretches extensively over some 43 hectares and 15 kilometres of pathways—a temptation to take a long walk to the great mausoleums and the bizarre or pretentious tomb figures.

(Translated from the German original,
Kalmbach 2015, p. 97)

According to the *ADAC* travel guide, another example of a green place can be found in the Tuileries Garden:

André Le Nôtre's harmonious arrangement—a prime example of French landscape gardening—is beautiful and appears in new splendour. [...] the Tuileries Garden [is] a restful island within the metropolis that is very popular with both tourists and Parisians. Its generously designed alleys and carefully arranged statues and water basins still transmit a feeling of the splendour of the Grand Siècle when it was created.

(Translated from the German original,
Schenk 2016, p. 69)

(4) Finally, the fourth type—culinary places—is marked by aimlessness, openness, comfort and cosiness, as well as restfulness and authenticity. To provide such a setting can be seen as a key characteristic of the localities dedicated to eating and drinking. Just like green places, culinary places tend to disrupt the prevalent time structure and invite the tourists to forget the schedule that otherwise dominates their stay. Many culinary places are

elevated—such as panorama rooftops and terraces on high floors—and offer a pleasant view to visitors. The Muscade tea room can serve as an example of the timelessness of a culinary place. *Reise Know-How* states: "In the Muscade tea room one can easily spend a whole afternoon chatting [...]" (translated from the German original, Kalmbach 2015, p. 74).

Since potential places of *Muße* must have structures that facilitate experiencing *Muße*, we outline the commonalities of the four types to give an idea of what these structures can be. The four types of places of *Muße* are often characterised as authentic and truly French, and they are perceived as calm and restful. Their main characteristics include their particular charm—something that needs to be explored more specifically in future research—and plants and water as their green and blue components. Only two types of places are described as airy and rambling. Particularly important is the opportunity they offer to break with the time structure that tends to determine tourist activities. In addition, places of *Muße* often provide a nice view and they serve as a safe haven, oasis or island within a stressful urban environment.

A closer look at the travel guides allows us to better understand the main activities carried out by tourists in such places. For the first type of places of *Muße* (cultural places), the travel guides point out the following practices as suitable: enjoying the view, eating and drinking, looking at art, learning about different cultures, discovering new things and strolling around. The educational dimension comes out very clearly. According to the travel guides, in extensive places tourists enjoy the view, consume art and music, discover new things, go shopping, eat, drink and stroll around. It seems that this second type involves many urban tourist practices of *Muße* which are also found in the following types of places. In green places (the third type of places of *Muße*) tourists primarily relax, sit and stroll around. Other activities in these places are playing, practising sports, eating and drinking. The clear dominance of practices related to play and relaxation underlines the function of green places as an island or safe haven. As indicated by the name, the main tourist practices in culinary places, the fourth type of places of *Muße*, are eating and drinking, and in many cases enjoying the view.

This leads to the following conclusion: the practice of eating and drinking is the only one that applies to all four types of places of *Muße*. Strolling around and enjoying the view apply to three types of places (strolling around: cultural, extended and green places; enjoying the view: cultural, extensive and culinary places). These are the three most dominant tourist practices of *Muße* in our analysis of the travel guides. Regarding the four categories of indulgence, freedom, placidity and recreation, it is clear that all four contain at least two of the three main practices:

- Indulgence: eating and drinking, enjoying the view
- Freedom: walking and strolling around, enjoying the view
- Placidity: all three main practices
- Recreation: eating and drinking, enjoying the view

Enjoying the view fits into all four categories. However, at this point, the subjectivity of *Muße* becomes obvious, because the assigning of practices to the different categories depends on our individual experiences and subjective preferences.

Authenticity and fragility of places of *Muße* shown by the travel blog analysis

In the following sections, we present our analysis of the two selected travel blogs reflecting *new urban tourism* in Paris. The list of places of *Muße* identified in the travel guides served as a basis for the subsequent content analysis. In the blog posts we found Canal Saint-Martin, Île Saint-Louis and Rue Mouffetard as places of *Muße* that are frequented by both locals and tourists. We regard these places as part of the *new urban tourism* in Paris because they are frequented by Parisians in their day-to-day life. The three places are described by the two bloggers as highly authentic. Our hypothesis is that ascribed authenticity is supported by a higher visibility of locals compared with tourists, remembering that the distinction between locals and tourists is neither objective nor stable. In the following sections we also discuss the fragility of places of *Muße* within *new urban tourism*.

Looking for authenticity

Bloggers are expected to use their own 'personal voice' and to express their own thoughts and knowledge of specific topics (Tan and Chen 2012). Talking about personal encounters and experiences, presenting the written text as if spoken, including pictures of oneself at tourist sites, and responding to comments and questions—all this suggests proximity between the bloggers and their readers and facilitates credibility among readers. Tan and Chen (2012) have pointed out that readers of a travel blog get "first-hand accounts of visitor's experience, advice on which destination to visit, and use online recommendations to make trip decision" (p. 453). One of the places that the bloggers of *Paris mal anders* and *HelpTourists* describe as authentic and worth a visit is the Canal Saint-Martin. It is one of the Parisian places of *Muße* that we classified as an extensive place in the previous section of this chapter. Roman reports in a blog post:

> The Canal Saint-Martin with its locks and iron bridges is a popular meeting place on summer evenings. Get a tasty baguette, a bottle of red wine and some cheese and enjoy the Parisian evening by the canal. Canal Saint-Martin picnics are somehow part of a tradition—here one is mainly in the company of Parisians. If you want to experience the 'real' Paris, this is the right place. People gather at 'Quai de Valmy' near the street 'Rue de Marseille'.
>
> (Translated from the German original, K1)

By classifying this place as the 'real' Paris, Roman claims to be an expert in the matter. The Canal Saint-Martin is portrayed as a place where ordinary Parisians go in the evening to spend time eating and drinking together. 'Baguette', 'red wine' and 'cheese' are cited as typically French food and thus framed as authentic. The blogger associates authentic places with places rarely frequented by tourists. The image constructed in the blog post has an impact on the potential practices and behaviour of incoming tourists (Wang 2012). This takes us to the phenomenon of *new urban tourism*. It is not the extraordinary, but rather the ordinary that qualifies the Canal Saint-Martin as an authentic place. The prevalent practices (eating, drinking, spending time together) have a double function: first, they are activities that clearly refer to the categories of indulgence and placidity, which contain a high potential for *Muße*. Second, the *Muße*-related practices have the function of integrating tourists by offering opportunities to come closer and get in touch with local residents. This is an essential goal for new urban tourists, as Freytag (2010) explains: "Establishing a privileged relationship with the local population is regarded as the most valuable form of spending time in the city" (p. 55). If and how locals and tourists have contact with each other—for example, having a conversation or sharing meals or drinks—is not part of Roman's blog posts on the canal.

In both analysed blogs, the Île Saint-Louis is described as another authentic place with potential for *Muße* experiences. Denise from *HelpTourists* writes:

> Île Saint-Louis is one of the two city islands in Paris, and it is definitely the calmer one, because most of the time there is more of a rush on Île de la Cité. The small Île Saint-Louis is primarily a residential area for affluent Parisians and with its small and calm streets it offers the potential for a romantic walk.
>
> (Translated from the German original, U1)

This example shows that many individual tourists, who form the main target group of the blogs, are not interested in tourism hot spots (here, Île de la Cité with Notre-Dame cathedral) as much as in areas shaped by the characteristics of *new urban tourism* (here, Île Saint-Louis). Contrasting with Île de la Cité in this blog post, the 'calm' island is valued because of its lack of tourists and its residential character.

In his blog post "Île Saint-Louis in Paris—a hidden jewel?" (title translated from the German original), Roman distinguishes between purely tourist places and urban areas. According to him, 'hidden jewels' are urban areas located off the beaten track. The word 'hidden' refers to the relatively low number of (international) tourists visiting this area:

> Actually, Île Saint-Louis is extremely picturesque and after (or before) visiting Notre-Dame cathedral, one can take a lovely walk in this area,

away from the tourist hype, exploring one of the many deli stores, browsing through little shops, eating ice cream or enjoying the sunny terraces.

(Translated from the German original, K2)

This passage addresses several issues. First, the practices are everyday practices. They are not related to a particular tourist attraction. There are several potential ways of using this urban space, such as shopping or eating ice cream. Second, the passage underlines the vast extent of the area. The openness of the place and the variety of possible practices give visitors to the island a greater freedom of choice compared to crowded sightseeing places like Notre-Dame cathedral, for example. Île Saint-Louis is made attractive to visitors by being presented as a place for ordinary everyday activities. Authenticity is suggested as being part of the experience of *Muße* in urban tourism. In order to experience *Muße*, it is important to distance oneself from one's own everyday life. This is the aim of tourists who spend time in a context they do not know well and that is not part of their day-to-day life.

Rue Mouffetard is located in the Quartier Latin, which is an extensive place as well. According to both blogs, this street is a venue for experiencing Parisian everyday life. Roman presents Rue Mouffetard to his readers as a suitable place for going out in the evening because it is "actually very much recommendable and not so touristy and noisy as the other restaurant and nightlife districts" (translated from the German original, K3). Moreover, he frames the district as more appealing because of the lack of tourists. Further on, he labels this street as authentic by stating: "In the evening, numerous fondue and raclette restaurants open their doors in this beautiful and authentic street in the Quartier Latin" (translated from the German original, K3). Once more, the blogger mobilises stereotypes that refer to gastronomy. Schäfer (2015b) mentions that the typical is presented as a signifier of authenticity and originality. For example, trying French cuisine qualifies as a 'real' experience in Paris.[5] We suggest that reproducing stereotypes creates a feeling of authenticity in tourists' minds, such as eating baguette with Camembert and drinking red wine in Paris.

Denise from *HelpTourists* chooses another strategy to promote Rue Mouffetard. While Roman recommends the whole area, she points out particular cafés. She proves her insider know-how by her knowledge of "10 addresses for good coffee in Paris" (title translated from the German original). She even seems to be familiar with the menu, as in the case of the café "DOSE" in Rue Mouffetard: "the brownies and muffins together with a spicy Chai latte are highly recommendable" (translated from the German original, U2).

In her blog post about "The best crêperies in Paris: 10 addresses for a delicious crêpe in Paris", she once more confirms her authority as a connoisseur of Paris and warmly recommends to her readers the crêperie "La petite Bretonne" located in the "popular and lively Rue Mouffetard" (translated from the German original, U3). Denise gives a colourful description of the café and indicates that gluten-free cakes are available (U3). By offering such detailed information, she increases the credibility and the quality of her blog posts. Readers get the impression of having access to exclusive first-hand information from a Parisian. If they visit Paris, they can adopt the Parisian practices presented in the blog and in doing so they will fulfil their desire to experience authenticity.

The cited blog posts characterise Rue Mouffetard in the first place as an ordinary street which is then presented as a unique attraction for new urban tourists. The street's cafés and bars are portrayed as places where residents and tourists come together to engage in similar practices (going out, eating, drinking, etc.). Such spaces are labelled as authentic.

By designating particular urban areas as 'real' and 'typical', Denise and Roman contribute to the production of geographical imaginations that shape readers' expectations. According to both bloggers, authenticity is directly linked to the presence of Parisians. Together with travel guides and other media aimed at tourists, they ascribe such a quality to a place. But the experience of authenticity is shaped by the situation and practices observed *in situ* (Weber 2012). Therefore, these specific urban tourist practices that are said to allow immersion in the everyday life of Parisians are not more than recommendations given by the two bloggers. The practices mentioned here are clearly *Muße*-related as they mainly belong to the category of indulgence.

Fragility of places of Muße

According to the analysed travel blogs, urban tourism in Paris takes place between two major poles. On the one hand, the travel blogs focus on tourism hot spots that are very popular and attract many visitors. On the other hand, they address areas of *new urban tourism* that represent the opposite of these hot spots. As the examples show, the latter are often described as *Muße*-related places. They are considered as non-tourist and therefore authentic places. However, places that fit in between these two categories can build a bridge between the two poles, and they show the alterability of places depending on the number of visitors and their tourist practices. If a *Muße*-related place becomes more popular—and paradoxically this might be the consequence of recommending such a place in a blog—the number of visiting tourists might increase. The two bloggers evaluate overcrowded places as being not authentic. From their point of view, places lose their appeal if they are visited by too many people.

Below, we explore two tourist sites that illustrate the life cycle and the fragility of a place of *Muße*. Taking two examples of the places of *Muße* identified in the travel guides, we show that Tour Montparnasse and Père Lachaise cemetery, which are considered there as insider tips, may transform into highly touristified places.

A linguistic strategy used by the two bloggers consists in comparing two places with similar characteristics to valorise the place that is less popular among tourists. This contrasting approach can be found in both blogs. *HelpTourists* asks in one blog post: "Where does one have the best view of Paris? This is a question that I am often asked. Apart from the Eiffel Tower and several Parisian rooftops, I would not hesitate to mention Tour Montparnasse" (translated from the German original, U4). Both bloggers praise the "amazing view in all directions" (translated from the German original, U4) and the "panorama" (translated from the German original, K4). The blog posts underline two advantages of Tour Montparnasse compared with the Eiffel Tower, namely the considerably shorter waiting time and the fact that Tour Montparnasse offers a splendid view of the Eiffel Tower, the city's landmark. The Eiffel Tower, Denise and Roman agree, still attracts many tourists, but "more and more visitors decide against the Eiffel Tower and opt for Tour Montparnasse" (translated from the German original, K5). This example shows that visitor flows are gaining more and more importance in both tourism hot spots and non-tourist places. As waiting queues and visitor crowds are detrimental to *Muße*, places with fewer tourists around become increasingly attractive to visitors. The Tour Montparnasse and the Eiffel Tower represent cultural places. Unlike the extensive places of *Muße* addressed above, both towers are single places of tourism in Paris. It seems likely that in the future increasing numbers of tourists will be attracted by these two locations.

With regard to the practices of residents and tourists, Père Lachaise cemetery is an example of a place connected with different stages of the life cycle. "This last resting-place is indeed not at all an insider tip, but everybody, no matter whether tourists or locals, lets themselves be captivated again and again by the atmosphere, which is almost magical" (translated from the German original, K6), writes Roman in *Paris mal anders*. The coexistence of tourists and locals and the alterability of a place as a result of the numbers of visitors form the key message of the cited blog entry. Nevertheless, it is suggested in the blog that the increasing number of visitors has not yet had a negative impact on the attractiveness of the place. The cemetery still allows "its visitors to forget the noisy metropolis for a while once they have passed the entrance gates" (translated from the German original, K6).

Tour Montparnasse and Père Lachaise cemetery are two examples of the alterability and fragility of places of *Muße*. Having not been very popular among tourists in the first place, these two sites illustrate how classical and modern travel media can linguistically and visually contribute to the diffusion of specific geographical imaginations. This can lead to an increase of incoming tourists, which may result in phenomena such as crowding, queues, noise and so on, that hinder or impede the experience of *Muße*. We can assume that similar transformations will increasingly affect the everyday spaces of residents in the future, because the interests of individual tourists will be oriented more and more towards the areas of *new urban tourism*.

Conclusion and outlook

By exploring the leading tourist destination of Paris using travel guides and travel blogs, we have identified a wide range of *Muße* places that are frequented and experienced by visitors in the broader context of *new urban tourism*. Experiencing places of *Muße* and the related practices can be conceptualised as spatio-temporal sequences that allow visitors to temporarily have a rest or escape from other tourist activities. We would stress that the experience of *Muße* is not just embedded in space and time, but it is also influenced by both context-related and individual conditions. In the case of Paris, we suggest a typology of *Muße* places: cultural places, extensive places, green places and culinary places. These four types of *Muße* places and their related practices can be identified and described on the basis of their particular characteristics. However, the typology is not meant to strictly separate these places from each other. Here, our aim is rather to point out a set of characteristics that may overlap and converge in our empirical observations, such as the combination of extensive and green places or cultural places combined with culinary places. Consequently, the analytical distinction between the four identified types of *Muße* places can be complemented by a more comprehensive or holistic perspective that would focus on the shared characteristics of *Muße* places.

The Parisian *Muße* places identified in the travel guides are also described in travel blogs. Studying travel blogs allowed us to take a closer look at these places. We selected two blogs in which the bloggers take on the role of experts and mediators who are primarily addressing individual tourists. In our analysis, it becomes very clear that the attribute of 'true' or 'authentic' is ascribed to places that are recommended to be visited because they are not touristified, but are perceived as being frequented mainly by Parisians. Therefore, the experience of *Muße* in urban tourism appears to be related to a notion of authenticity that is defined by the presence of locals in opposition to tourists, who represent the non-authentic. Hence, bloggers and tourists adopt an ambiguous position here: by recommending and visiting 'authentic' non-tourist places, they contribute to the fragility and potential destruction of these places which may imply their gradual transformation into tourist places.

Finally, our study remains within the limits of our empirical sources. Travel guides and travel blogs are suitable sources for exploring representations of places and practices of *Muße*, but they cannot substitute for in-depth observations and research *in situ*. For example, the selected travel guides and travel blogs do not take into account possible conflicts between tourists and locals in places of *Muße*. Here, substantial field research can help us to gain a better understanding of the interplay and potential conflicts between tourists and locals, and possibly also among tourists. Another question that still has to be explored in more detail is the role of perceived authenticity and the presence of local residents as a condition for experiencing *Muße* in urban tourism.

Notes

1 For an analysis of new wellness industries as places of temporary escape from the urban for residents, see Parish, Chapter 5 in this volume.
2 For more information, please visit: www.sfb1015.uni-freiburg.de/en.

3 See also Frenzel, Chapter 4 in this volume.
4 Stock in this volume (Chapter 3) even suggests to understand (new urban) tourists as temporary inhabitants of a city equipped with spatial capital and competences.
5 In their analysis of the promotion of social meal-sharing experiences, Stoltenberg and Frisch (Chapter 8 in this volume) focus on the link between branding food as 'local' or 'national' and its perception as 'authentic' by travellers.

Acknowledgements

Our research was conducted as part of the project 'Experiencing places and moments of otium in contemporary European city tourism' in the Collaborative Research Centre 'Otium. Boundaries, Chronotypes, Practices SFB 1015, Projektnummer 197396619'. We would like to thank the Deutsche Forschungsgemeinschaft (DFG) for generously allocating the funding for our research activities.

References

Akehurst, G., 2008. User generated content: the use of blogs for tourism organisations and tourism consumers. *Service Business*, 3 (1), 51–61.
Andereck, K.L. *et al.*, 2005. Residents' perceptions of community tourism impacts. *Annals of Tourism Research*, 32 (4), 1056–1076.
Archer, B., Cooper, C. and Ruhanen, L., 2005. The positive and negative impacts of tourism. *In*: W.F. Theobald, ed., *Global Tourism*. Burlington, VT: Elsevier, 79–102.
Baerenholdt, J.O. *et al.*, 2004. *Performing Tourist Places. New Directions in Tourism Analysis*. London: Ashgate.
Bauder, M. and Freytag, T., 2018. Bottom-up touristification and urban transformations in Paris. *Tourism Geographies*, 20 (3), 443–460.
Blum, B. *et al.*, 2016. Muße-Orte. *Muße. Ein Magazin*, 2 (1), 54–58.
Bowen, G.A., 2009. Document analysis as a qualitative research method. *Qualitative Research Journal*, 9 (2), 27–40.
Chapuis, A. *et al.*, 2013. Dynamiques urbaines et mobilités de loisir à Paris: pratiques, cohabitations et stratégies de production de l'espace urbain dans le quartier du Marais. *In*: E. Berthold, ed., *Les quartiers historiques: pressions, enjeux, actions*. Québec: Presses Universitaires de Laval, 43–65.
Claßen, T. and Kistemann, T., 2017. Urbane Grünräume und Gewässer. Ressourcen einer integrierten, gesundheitsfördernden Stadtentwicklung der Zukunft? *Geographische Rundschau*, 69 (5), 38–43.
Colomb, C. and Novy, J., eds, 2017. *Protest and Resistance in the Tourist City*. New York: Routledge.
Crouch, D., 2004. Tourist practices and performances. *In*: A.A. Lew, C.M. Hall and A.M. Williams, eds, *A Companion to Tourism*. Oxford: Blackwell, 85–95.
Dalichau, D., 2016. *Rationalisierung im Konsum*. Wiesbaden: Springer VS.
Duhamel, P. and Knafou, R., 2007. Le tourisme dans la centralité parisienne. *In*: T. Julien and R. Le Goix, eds, *La métropole parisienne: Centralités, inégalités, proximités*. Paris: Belin, 37–64.
Enzensberger, H.-M., 1958. Eine Theorie des Tourismus. *Merkur*, 126 (12), 701–720.

Fagnoni, E. and Aymard, C., 2002. Entre inertie et dynamique touristique: le cas parisien. *Téoros*, 21 (1), 4–11.

Figal, G., 2015. Muße als Forschungsgegenstand. *Muße. Ein Magazin*, 1 (1), 15–23.

Fontaine, D., 2017. Raum und Landschaft: Konzeptionen und Wahrnehmungsmuster. *In*: D. Fontaine, ed., *Simulierte Landschaften in der Postmoderne. Reflexionen und Befunde zu Disneyland, Wolfersheim und GTA V*. Wiesbaden: Springer, 49–84.

Freytag, T., 2010. Déjà-vu: tourist practices of repeat visitors in the city of Paris. *Social Geography*, 5, 49–58.

Füller, H. and Michel, B., 2014. 'Stop being a tourist!' New dynamics of urban tourism in Berlin-Kreuzberg. *International Journal of Urban and Regional Research*, 38 (4), 1304–1318.

Gimmel, J. and Keiling, T., 2016. *Konzepte der Muße*. Tübingen: Mohr Siebeck.

Goldammer, D., 2014. *After Work Balance: Die Zeit danach. Die Perspektiven der Älteren*. Wiesbaden: Springer VS.

Gravari-Barbas, M. and Fagnoni, E., eds, 2013. *Tourisme et métropolisation: Comment le tourisme redessine Paris*. Paris: Belin.

Gravari-Barbas, M. and Guinand, S., eds, 2017. *Tourism and Gentrification in Contemporary Metropolises: International Perspectives*. New York: Routledge.

Gravari-Barbas, M. and Jacquot, S., 2017. No conflict? Discourses and management of tourism-related tensions in Paris. *In*: C. Colomb and J. Novy, eds, *Protest and Resistance in the Tourist City*. New York: Routledge, 31–51.

Kalmbach, G., 2015. *Reise Know-How CityTrip Paris*. Bielefeld: Reise Know-How Verlag.

Klemm, M., 2016. Ich reise, also blogge ich. Wie Reiseberichte im Social Web zur multimodalen Echtzeit-Selbstdokumentation werden. *In*: K. Hahn and A. Schmidl, eds, *Websites & Sightseeing. Tourismus in Medienkulturen*. Wiesbaden: Springer, 31–62.

Kohlbacher, F., 2006. The use of qualitative content analysis in case study research. *Forum: Qualitative Social Research*, 7 (1), 1–30.

Kramer, C.S., 2018. Die sprachliche Konstruktion von Mußeräumen im Städtetourismus am Beispiel von Florenz, Italien. *Zeitschrift für Tourismuswissenschaft*, 10 (1), 29–47.

Kreisel, W., 2007. Trends in der Entwicklung von Freizeit und Tourismus. *In*: C. Becker, H. Hopfinger and A. Steinecke, eds, *Geographie der Freizeit und des Tourismus. Bilanz und Ausblick*. München: Oldenbourg, 74–85.

Kugge, R., 1 January 2015–7 March 2018. *Paris mal anders. Geheimtipps für das ungewöhnliche Paris!* [online]. Available from: www.parismalanders.com [accessed 14 July 2018].

Leder, S., 2007. Neue Muße im Tourismus. Eine Untersuchung von Angeboten mit den Schwerpunkten Selbstfindung und Entschleunigung. PhD thesis, Universität Paderborn.

Lefebvre, H., 1991. *The Production of Space*. Cambridge: Blackwell.

Lengert, R., 1957. Die anthropologische Bedeutung der Muße. *Bildung und Erziehung*, 10, 705–714.

MacCannell, D., [1976] 2013. *The Tourist. A New Theory of the Leisure Class*. Berkeley, CA: University of California Press.

Maitland, R., 2008. Conviviality and everyday life: the appeal of new areas of London for visitors. *International Journal of Tourist Research*, 10 (1), 15–25.

Maitland, R. and Newman, P., 2008. Visitor–host relationships: conviviality between visitors and host communities. *In*: B. Hayllar, T. Griffin and D. Edwards, eds, *City Spaces – Tourist Places: Urban Tourism Precints*. New York: Elsevier, 223–242.

Mayring, P., 2010. Qualitative Inhaltsanalyse. *In*: G. Mey and K. Mruck, eds, *Handbuch qualitative Forschung in der Psychologie*. Wiesbaden: VS Verlag für Sozialwissenschaften, 601–613.

Novy, J. and Huning, S., 2009. New tourism (areas) in the "New Berlin". *In*: R. Maitland and P. Newman, eds, *World Tourism Cities: Developing Tourism Off the Beaten Track*. London: Routledge, 87–108.

O'Connor, P., 2008. User-generated content and travel: a case study on Tripadvisor.com. *In*: P. O'Connor, W. Höpken and U. Gretzel, eds, *Information and Communication Technologies in Tourism 2008*. Wien and New York: Springer, 47–58.

Pearce, D.G., 1998. Tourist districts in Paris: structure and functions. *Tourism Management*, 19 (1), 49–65.

Popp, M., 2012. Positive and negative urban tourist crowding: Florence, Italy. *Tourism Geographies*, 14 (4), 50–72.

Reincke, M. and Maunder, H., 2016. *Baedeker Paris*. Ostfildern: Mairdumont.

Sari, Y., Kozak, M. and Duman, T., 2006. A historical development of "IT" in tourism marketing. *In*: M. Kozak and L. Andreu, eds, *Progress in Tourism Marketing*. Oxford: Elsevier, 33–44.

Schäfer, R., 2015a. Die gegensätzlichen Gegensätze touristischer Traumbilder. *Sozialer Sinn*, 16 (1), 49–70.

Schäfer, R., 2015b. *Tourismus und Authentizität. Zur gesellschaftlichen Organisation von Außeralltäglichkeit*. Bielefeld: transcript.

Schenk, G., 2016. *ADAC Reiseführer Paris*. München: Travel House Media.

Scherle, N., 2001. Touristische Medien aus interkultureller Perspektive. Gedruckte Urlaubswelten aufgezeigt am Beispiel von Reiseführern. *Tourismus Journal*, (3), 333–351.

Steinecke, A., 2011. *Tourismus*. Braunschweig: Westermann.

Stors, N. and Kagermeier, A., 2013. Crossing the border of the tourist bubble: touristification in Copenhagen. *In*: T. Thimm, ed., *Tourismus und Grenzen*. Mannheim: MetaGis, 115–131.

Tan, W.-K. and Chen, T.-H., 2012. The usage of online tourist information sources in tourist information search: an exploratory study. *The Service Industries Journal*, 32 (3), 451–476.

Urbach, D., 1 January 2015–7 March 2018. *HelpTourists: Informationen für Touristen, Reisetipps & Insidertipps für Paris* [online]. Available from: https://help-tourists-in-paris.com [accessed 14 July 2018].

Urry, J. and Larsen, J., 2011. *The Tourist Gaze 3.0*, 3rd ed. London: SAGE.

Walla, J., 2010. Performing tourism – doing IKEA. Gedanken zu touristischen Praktiken in "Nicht-Orten" des Konsums. *In*: K. Wöhler, A. Pott and V. Denzer, eds, *Tourismusräume. Zur soziokulturellen Konstruktion eines globalen Phänomens*. Bielefeld: transcript, 125–140.

Wang, H.-Y., 2012. Investigating the determinants of travel blogs influencing readers' intention to travel. *The Service Industries Journal*, 32 (2), 231–255.

Weber, H.-J.L., 2012. Die Paradoxie des Städtetourismus: zwischen Massentourismus und Individualität. Eine Studie zu touristischen Praktiken und Mobilität unter Verwendung von GPS- und Fragebogendaten sowie Reiseführerliteratur am Beispiel der Stadt Berlin. PhD thesis, Albert-Ludwigs-Universität Freiburg.

Wöhler, K., 2011. *Touristifizierung von Räumen. Kulturwissenschaftliche und soziologische Studien zur Konstruktion von Räumen.* Wiesbaden: VS.

Blog references

K1: Kugge, R., 19 June 2017. Available from: www.parismalanders.com/sommer-in-paris/ [accessed 14 July 2018].

K2: Kugge, R., 1 September 2016. Available from: www.parismalanders.com/ile-saint-louis-in-paris/ [accessed 14 July 2018].

K3: Kugge, R., 23 November 2015. Available from: www.parismalanders.com/stadtviertel/quartier-latin/ [accessed 14 July 2018].

K4: Kugge, R., 6 March 2017. Available from: www.parismalanders.com/tour-montparnasse-in-paris/ [accessed 14 July 2018].

K5: Kugge, R., 7 March 2017. Available from: www.parismalanders.com/aussichtspunkte-paris-bester-ausblick-und-blick-ueber-paris/ [accessed 14 July 2018].

K6: Kugge, R., n.d. Available from: www.parismalanders.com/friedhoefe-in-paris/ [accessed 14 July 2018].

U1: Urbach, D., 23 May 2016. Available from: http://help-tourists-in-paris.com/2016/05/23/top-10-romantische-orte-in-paris/ [accessed 14 July 2018].

U2: Urbach, D., 5 November 2017. Available from: http://help-tourists-in-paris.com/2017/11/05/paris-kaffee-kaffeeroesterei-kaffeehaeuser/ [accessed 14 July 2018].

U3: Urbach, D., 15 December 2017. Available from: http://help-tourists-in-paris.com/paris-die-besten-creperien-10-empfehlungen-crepes/ [accessed 14 July 2018].

U4: Urbach, D., 6 June 2015. Available from: http://help-tourists-in-paris.com/paris-sehenswuerdigkeiten-im-ueberblick/turm-montparnasse-besichtigen/ [accessed 14 July 2018].

10 Commoning in new tourism areas

Co-performing evening socials at the Admiralbrücke in Berlin-Kreuzberg

Christoph Sommer and Markus Kip[1]

Introducing urban hang-out commons and socio-material gatherings

What emerges when tourists and residents rub shoulders? Tourism is not a discrete activity, taking place in bounded localities, but is a key aspect of current social life (Cohen and Cohen 2017). Places of *new urban tourism* are characterised by the way in which practices of leisure and tourism have become indistinguishable (Maitland 2010). Recent debates on the negative impacts of overtourism indicate that tourism also matters beyond profit. This chapter draws on a study of the summertime evening gatherings at a location called the Admiralbrücke, a small bridge in Berlin-Kreuzberg, Germany. Our research started from the observation of conflicts between neighbourhood residents and party crowds that are widely portrayed as young tourists in the local media. Several residents have protested that hang-out parties on the Admiralbrücke disturb their night-time peace and make the area dirty. However, as we claim in this contribution, visitors and residents also produce synergies (Maitland 2010; see also Frenzel, Chapter 2 in this volume) in this space of encounter. Our explorative inquiry outlines this tourism-related co-production of urban life and we propose to understand it as commons—a socio-material assemblage operating beyond economic considerations and political administration.

Our interest in researching the event-like summertime gatherings at the Admiralbrücke (Figure 10.1) was sparked by Kaschuba's (2014) article, which discussed the controversy about the evening 'bottle parties' as an instance of an urban conflict requiring specific forms of negotiation. Our reading of the phenomenon connected with our interests on *new urban tourism* (C. Sommer) and the commons (M. Kip). Both of us had been acquainted with the gatherings as we had occasionally passed through them. We became curious as to how these summertime hang-out events have sustained themselves over more than a decade in the face of a changing set of visitors with constantly new ones pouring in every night and in the face of the controversies in the neighbourhood. How come these significant gatherings have continued in such fashion for more than ten years, with such a changing cast of people? How can these temporary fleeting encounters be understood and

Figure 10.1 Evening social at the Admiralbrücke, September 2016.
Source: C. Sommer.

analysed? We found no systematic attempt to explain this particular form of social organisation. Indeed, these questions become even more relevant when looking at other cities in Europe that have similar popular hang-outs. Prominent examples include the Canal Saint-Martin (Paris),[2] the Colonne di San Lorenzo (Milan), Gärtnerplatz (Munich), the Piazza Dell'immacolata (Rome), the Plaza Del Dos de Mayo (Madrid) and the Wohlwillstraße/Beim Grünen Jäger crossing (Hamburg). Conflicts about the use of space as new tourism areas erupt in all of these locations and it therefore appears important to better understand these phenomena.[3] As a change of perspective, our first goal here is to frame the tourism-related co-production of such public gatherings as hang-out commons and a way of producing urban space. For this purpose, we elaborate on the non-commercial and spontaneous character of such gatherings that evolve in a certain seasonal and daytime rhythm. The second aim was to discuss our explorative case study in relation to the existing literature on *new urban tourism*. We suggest that the 'new mobilities paradigm' (Mavrič and Urry 2009, Sheller and Urry 2006) is particularly useful in explaining how the hang-out commons at the Admiralbrücke emerge through encounters of highly mobile people, objects, imaginings and immoveable material components. Working with the idea of a performative co-production of the urban at the bridge, we also show how this co-production co-exists with controversies about the legitimate use of such places.

We decided to take an abductive approach (Peirce 1903, Paavola 2004), i.e., we start by making observations and then develop a hypothesis to explain the phenomenon based on available theoretical models. This hypothesis is then tested in the case at hand, leading to new observations. Such circular loops between observation, interpretation and testing are also characteristic of research informed by Grounded Theory (see Glaser and Strauss 1967, Flick 2014, p. 87 ff.). For the sake of presentation, we do not reproduce each circular loop, but describe the approach in a straightforward way. For this reason, we first describe the observation that intrigued us, then develop the hypothesis of hang-out commons as rhythmic enactments of socio-material gatherings, and finally explore the plausibility of the hypothesis through inductive reasoning. It should be noted upfront that more empirical research will be important to further test the hypothesis.

In the subsequent part, we contextualise the situation at the Admiralbrücke based on the empirical insights of literature on *new urban tourism*. In the third section, we describe our ethnographic approach and depict the empirical material in a condensed way. We then propose considering the evening socials as urban hang-out commons, a notion that helps to understand its productive dimension. To address the spatial and temporal dynamics of this production, we then suggest extending the analysis with the help of the 'new mobilities paradigm' and theoretical perspectives informed by the 'performance turn' within tourism studies. In the concluding part, we point to areas for more empirical research and specify a number of important conceptual needs.

The Admiralbrücke as a new tourism area

The concept of *new urban tourism* (Stors *et al.*, Chapter 1 in this volume) could be used to make sense of some significant phenomena related to urban tourism. Generally speaking, research on *new urban tourism* primarily focuses on distinct *motivations* of distinct *types of people* to visit distinct *new tourism areas* off the beaten track (Maitland 2008, 2010, Maitland and Newman 2004, 2009, Pappalepore *et al.* 2010). Empirically, case studies conducted by Maitland and his collaborators build a key reference for *new urban tourism* research.[4] We refer to this literature for two distinct reasons. First, we aim to show the similarity of the Admiralbrücke and its surroundings with other new tourism areas. Such areas are urban places with "overlapping activities of tourism and leisure" (Maitland 2010, p. 176). Second, the observation that tourism(-like) activities *somehow* co-produce urban life and that there are "potential synergies between some visitors and some residents" (ibid.) begs the question of how such co-production takes place. In addition, it is necessary to study how the phenomenon sustains itself in spite of the changing cast of participants.

Tourism in Berlin-Kreuzberg is not a new phenomenon, as it became part of Kreuzberg's daily life as early as the 1970s and 1980s with visitors from other parts of Berlin and Germany as well as—to a lesser extent—from abroad

(Novy 2011). Equally, genuine tourist interest in the everyday life of others is certainly not new (MacCannell 1973). Rather it has been the intensity and focus on certain aspects of urban everyday life that have increased awareness of *new urban tourism* as a phenomenon in its own right (Dirksmeier and Helbrecht 2015). Nevertheless, having a reputation as a hub of Berlin's alternative, bohemian and creative scene (Novy and Huning 2009), Berlin-Kreuzberg offers visitors an "integral element in the appeal of the [new tourism] area[s]", namely the "opportunity to observe and mingle with residents, workers, and with co-tourists" (Pappalepore *et al.* 2010, p. 220). Therefore, foreign urbanites play a role as "people as attractions" (Pappalepore *et al.* 2014, p. 234) or as protagonists being gazed upon in a manner of "life seeing" (Wöhler 2011, p. 129). However, gazing on the other is only part of the experience because new urban tourists "want to fit in, rather than stand to one side" (Maitland and Newman 2009, p. 135).

Graefekiez, the neighbourhood surrounding the Admiralbrücke, appeals to visitors who are seeking mundane city life off the beaten track. In terms of *new urban tourism*, the everyday activities of city residents and public street life in Graefekiez seem to be a promising way to experience the 'real' Berlin. It is an important characteristic of *new urban tourism* that only particular features of everydayness in residential urban areas seem to attract visitors. Smith and Pappalepore (2015, p. 97) pointedly describe this as "distinct ordinariness", which differs, for example, from features of everydayness in large housing estates or single-family housing areas. 'Distinct ordinariness' could, for example, be found in creative, edgy and unpolished urban neighbourhoods lacking standardised commerce, such as Deptford in London (Smith and Pappalepore 2015). Alternatively, London's Islington exemplifies the idea that areas well equipped with the infrastructure of everyday consumption, such as pubs, cafes, clubs or shops, appeal to new urban tourists (Maitland 2008). In Berlin-Kreuzberg, it is especially the multicultural 'flair' that accounts for the 'distinct ordinariness' attracting visitors (Novy 2011).

The Admiralbrücke is located in the northern part of Graefekiez, an ethnically diverse neighbourhood in Kreuzberg. The bridge spans the Landwehr water canal and is only a few minutes by foot from Kottbusser Tor, a busy traffic junction. This junction not only offers diverse dining and shopping possibilities, it is also a notorious meeting point for the local drug scene as well as a place for nightlife. A lawn area is adjacent to the southern part of the bridge, and several visitors take the opportunity to sit down and rest there. Within a distance of 50 metres from the bridge, there are two Italian restaurants, three cafes (one of which sells ice cream) and a late-night kiosk.

The bridge with its wrought-iron railings was built between 1880 and 1882 and is now listed as a landmark. When its foundations were found to be deteriorating in the 1990s, car traffic on the bridge and the surrounding streets was reduced. Therefore, it is only possible to drive across at pedestrian speed. The middle section was separated from car traffic by concrete bollards. Since around the first decade of the millennium, the bridge became known as a site where tourists gather in summer evenings (Figure 10.2).

Figure 10.2 "Oooh Berlin"[5] poster displaying an evening social at the Admiralbrücke. Source: Nils Grube, 2016, produced with permission.

The (extra)ordinary qualities of the Admiralbrücke result from its ordinary infrastructural function as a bridge for slow car, cycle and pedestrian traffic while also offering space for people to linger in the area. Overall, the Admiralbrücke features characteristics of new tourism areas (Novy 2017). It is located off the beaten track; and it is a suitable place to observe and mingle with locals and to experience (extra)ordinary street life. Nevertheless, it remains unclear what the potential synergies between visitors and residents postulated by Maitland (2010) specifically look like in places of *new urban tourism* such as the Admiralbrücke. In the next section, we aim to tackle this empirical question in an explorative way. Conceptually, we are guided by the basic idea of tourism studies informed by the notion of performance, namely that venues of (new urban) tourism are "unfixed for places are not reified and fixed stages but are made and refashioned, contested, and transformed through the performances of tourists" (Edensor 2009, p. 556) and other urbanites. Approaching the case of the Admiralbrücke, we know that the constitutive potency of *new urban tourism* on the bridge is an ambivalent one. The bridge's popularity has created conflicts. On the one hand, there is sympathy for the largely peaceful and lively gatherings involving mostly young people with different national backgrounds; on the other hand, local residents' complaints about night noise disturbance or pollution from garbage and urine have raised public attention.

Empirical research

To investigate the co-production of places by tourists and residents, we have engaged in an exploratory case study. With an approach geared towards 'understanding' rather than explaining, we started to look for theoretical models that would help us make sense of our initial insights. The investigation involved two main paths: first, internet research to identify popular narratives about the evening gatherings; second, ethnographic site visits. The advantage of internet research is that it gives us a better impression of what attracts potential and actual visitors to the bridge. We assume that many visitors assess potential sites to visit by searching the internet, and that they rely on information from both official tour guides and web forums. Our exploratory research suggests that there are significant postings about tourist sites, including the Admiralbrücke. Ethnographic visits help us verify and triangulate these representations on the internet. For the purpose of this study, ethnography means that we immersed ourselves in the gatherings on various occasions to gain our own subjective accounts of what it feels like to be at the site and what it is that we find attractive. Working as a research team, the two of us were able to double-check our observations and interpretations with each other. Participant observations were complemented with random conversation samples with people who were hanging out on the bridge. In such conversations, we were able to concretise our impressions and hypotheses, and receive feedback on them.

The Admiralbrücke on internet platforms

Due to our explorative approach, which aimed to develop an overview of the phenomenon, we structured our internet research along two criteria. First, we wanted to learn more about the things people like or dislike about the gatherings at the Admiralbrücke. Second, we decided to look for direct quotes from urbanites (e.g., neighbours, other Berliners, visitors) on issues related to the bridge. We did not seek to provide a systematic analysis of the discourse about the Admiralbrücke, but rather looked for focused reflections about the place. Following these criteria, we drew on the online recommendation platform Yelp (www.yelp.com) and a mediation report by Streit Entknoten, a Berlin-based association that was commissioned to help settle the dispute in 2010.

The selected accounts on the internet illustrate different perspectives of the participants on the evening hang-outs. At first glance, such accounts could be distinguished as to whether the gatherings were perceived as annoyances or as a fun attraction, even though there is also some balancing of arguments in such accounts. The online recommendation platform Yelp provides some statements and reflections about participants' experience of particular sites. We cite three of them at full length; each one highlights distinct aspects of the gatherings at the Admiralbrücke. The first statement was written by 'Yukie S.', a person who had obviously just moved to Berlin when she visited the Admiralbrücke:

> This place had quite an impact on me since it was my first impression of Berlin. And it was this place that made me fall in love with Berlin. People in suits, musicians, parents with children, punks, homeless people, everyone is sitting together with a beer in their hands on the bridge and enjoying the last sunrays. The view of the water is very beautiful and represents Kreuzberg from its most beautiful side. It is worth going there![6]

In her recommendation, the author notes that the place embodies positive aspects of Berlin-Kreuzberg, in particular, the diversity (in terms of lifestyles or age) of the people gathering there. This experience of diversity can be regarded as a precondition for urban self-experiences that new urban tourists and other urbanites seek in the lively density of authentically sensed neighbourhoods (Holm 2015, Kleinen and Kühn 2016). The anonymous author of the second statement also stresses this diversity. Indeed, this Berlin-based user is undecided on how to evaluate the scenery:

> I move between affection and aversion. On the one side, it is fascinating that such a small bridge turned into such a lively gathering place for all kinds of people, who sit together, drink and make music. On the other side, it is almost dangerous to drive a car or ride a bike across, and there is just too much swigging and accosting going on. And still, somehow the bridge has charm. I think of the bottle caps driven and trampled into the cobblestones.[7]

On the one hand, this contributor criticises the excessive drinking and traffic obstruction. On the other hand, the author stresses the distinct charm of the bridge, which she sees exemplified in the game to press bottle caps in the tar joints between the cobblestones. This specific action—and the Yelp post about it—is a good example of the *way* new tourism visitors seek to inscribe themselves in the scene rather than merely observing it.

Last but not least, the third Yelp recommendation we cite refers directly to the way travel guidebooks frame the gatherings at the Admiralbrücke; it seizes on its qualities to party outdoors:

> The Admiralbrücke is called an 'insider tip' in many travel guidebooks. In Lonely Planet, the warm evening with beer, wine, and guitar thrashing

is called a 'bottle party' which is something special for tourists if only for the fact that drinking alcohol in public is prohibited in most countries. I was there at one of the first warm nights of the year and I liked it a lot. Around 30 friends and acquaintances of mine made their contribution and we celebrated the birthday of a buddy from Ireland. The police didn't come until around 1 am that night, even though someone turned up the sound system of his car. I also don't feel sorry for the neighbours, because many of them enjoy their after-work beer on the Admiralbrücke. Funny how the old folks collected the beer bottles (for the deposit) in an almost organised manner. The notion of 'deposit vultures' [*Pfandgeier*] fits really well for them, since they literally draw circles around you, until the bottle is finally emptied ;o).[8]

This post is not so much written as a recommendation but more likely as retrospection of an evening out to celebrate a birthday on the bridge; some side notes hint at the potential noise conflicts with neighbours and the 'fun fact' that people collect empty bottles for the deposit. In this case, touring the bridge seems to be primarily motivated by the aim to celebrate and drink together with significant others.[9]

In sum, the descriptions of the scenery from the Admiralbrücke taken from Yelp indicate what the authors find attractive: people from different backgrounds and lifestyles come together, drink beer, enjoy the sunset, make or listen to music, push bottle caps into tar gaps, etc. Some of them also indicate sympathy for the neighbours who are concerned about the noise and unruly behaviour on the bridge.

The perspective of local residents who have expressed their concerns can be found in a condensed form in a mediation report written in February 2011. This report was the result of a concerted mediation effort between neighbourhood residents and visitors of the Admiralbrücke from May to December 2010. The deputy mayor of the Friedrichshain-Kreuzberg district commissioned such mediation as an attempt to address complaints. Residents of the area started to organise themselves and sought resolution from public authorities at the district level. The report states,

Since more than 300 people may be on the bridge at peak times, the acoustic noise meant significant noise disturbances for resident neighbours, even if all individuals speak quietly. The visitors began to stay on the bridge especially at night, and mostly young people partied on this part of the bridge, and sometimes live music was played during night hours. In the late hours, alcohol consumption increased among visitors such that they were often no longer responsive when residents approached them and asked them to be quiet. This led to frequent disturbances at night—occurring every night on warm days. On top of this, there were significant annoyances due to the quantity of garbage and the glass shards lying on the bridge in the morning and the bottle caps that were pushed in the gaps of the

cobblestones... Since there is no public toilet close to the bridge, people used building entrances and backyards to relieve themselves. There was vandalism and, as some residents stated, also drug consumption and sales.
(Streit Entknoten 2011, p. 4; our translation)

One consequence of the mediation process were more frequent patrols by the municipal regulatory authority and police to ensure that crowds would disperse by 10 pm, the legal hour for night-time peace, which lasts until 6 am in Germany. However, eight years after the mediation, these evening gatherings are still taking place regularly. In recent years, the conflict has aroused less public controversy, but it is still ongoing.

Due to the continued public relevance of the issue and our emerging interest in trying to grasp the sustainability of this collective gathering, in summer 2016 we decided to embark on a systematic investigation of the site with regular visits. Up until October 2017, at least one of us observed the scene once a month during summer and early autumn. The following is an account that we produced as a result of two fieldwork visits we undertook together in order to establish a common understanding of the setting.

Hanging out at the Admiralbrücke – ethnographic field observations

In August and September 2016, we spent two late evenings together on the site for about four hours between 7:30 and 11:30 pm. We wanted to see what would happen at 10 pm when the municipal regulatory authority or the police were expected to start telling people to move away. We walked around at different moments to count the number of people congregating on the bridge and to map the locations at which they would meet and how large the different groups were.

'Where is the best position to understand what's happening here?' we asked ourselves, as we approached the bridge the first time. The wall of the bridge to the South looked like a useful starting point. Walls frame the iron railing on both sides of the banks. Some visitors have taken a seat on it. We occupy a spot on the wall. We see many people, mostly sitting on the street or sidewalk, rarely standing, talking, drinking, smoking, laughing in small groups of two or three.

It is 8 pm on Wednesday, 7 September 2016. The sun is already setting and the evening temperature is mild. It is about 23 degrees Celsius. A T-shirt is sufficient to keep warm. The number of visitors on the bridge remains fairly constant over the next two hours. At 9 pm, we count 141 people on the bridge. Most of them are sitting on the paths on each side or in the middle section. The concrete bollards and bridge railings are used by many as backrests. We change position and sit down on the cobbled street in the middle of the bridge.

The ground is still pleasantly warm from the heat of the day. Indeed, there are many bottle caps pushed into the tar gaps between the cobblestones. The two-armed iron lamppost in the middle of the bridge on each side has been turned on. The orange-coloured lighting of the streetlights creates an evening atmosphere that is reminiscent of the Mediterranean. People appear to be relaxed, the background noise consists of conversations, mostly in English, German, French, Turkish and Spanish. The age range covers the spectrum from teenagers to seniors; however, we estimate that the predominant majority is somewhere between 20 and 40 years old. Most are drinking beer from bottles, most likely bought from one of the nearby late-night kiosks. There is always some movement in the crowd. New people arrive, others leave. After about one hour, we estimate that the composition of the crowd has changed by about two-thirds. On and off, cars cross the bridge, carefully, since many people sitting on the sidewalk corner still have their legs stretched out onto the street. At one point, an angry driver honks twice. Pedestrians and cyclists also pass by. We saw a handful of collectors of empty beverage containers throughout the evening, on the move to earn cash from the deposit. A photographer offers to take a Polaroid picture of us for three euros (Figure 10.3). Speaking in English, he says he recently came from Afghanistan.

Figure 10.3 Polaroid souvenir from the Admiralbrücke, September 2016.
Source: C. Sommer.

Sitting in a group of seven friends, a male takes out his guitar and starts jamming. He plays famous rock covers and others in the group start singing along at moderate noise level. Today, there is no performance on the bridge as at other times with the explicit intention to entertain the crowd.

At around 9:30 pm, an apparently unlicensed vendor with a cargo bike with colourful lighting parks on the middle section to sell cold drinks. We ask a group of two sitting on the wall for a cigarette. A conversation is struck up about what we are doing here. One of them is a resident. She says that she had also asked herself several times what kind of people gather here.

No police officers or regulatory officials show up at 10 pm, the official night-time curfew, or even later. The noise level this evening may not be a great nuisance for local residents, as long as they keep any windows facing the street closed. During warm nights, however, this may be a real inconvenience. Slowly, over the next hour and a half, the crowd disperses and by midnight, when we left, there were just over a dozen people still hanging out on the bridge absorbed by their conversations.

This short account illustrates some of the social dynamics of the bridge and the material specifics that we both experienced as pleasant and interesting. It is fun to sit at the site during a warm evening. What was most interesting to us as researchers was the observation that while the cast of people appeared to be constantly changing, we rarely identified people we had seen before at the site, such as musicians or vendors. In spite of this, significant dynamics and gatherings on the bridge were rather stable over the period of our observation. About eighty or more people were consistently present when temperatures exceeded 23 degrees in the evening. We saw them arranged in groups of two to eight people, drinking and having conversations in different languages. Other regular events included cars slowly driving by; musicians busking; people collecting cans and bottles, etc. Clearly, there were no explicit agreements or coordinated efforts among participants to bring these gatherings into being, there was no apparent profit-driven venture that would explain most people's motivation to go the bridge. We argue that the notion of the commons helps us understand the social organisation of this phenomenon.

The hang-out party as a commons

Following Massimo de Angelis's (2010) definition, commons are a non-commodified means to fulfil people's needs, sustained by a group of 'commoners' through constant reproduction, distribution and consumption. A commons amounts to an assemblage entailing shared resources, a group of commoners taking care of and benefiting from the resource, and practices and institutions that constitute the relationship among commoners with respect to the resource as well (Kip *et al.* 2015). This process of satisfying needs thus stands in significant contrast to selling and buying in a capitalist market or making legal claims vis-à-vis the politico-administrative apparatus.

So, what makes these evening hang-outs a commons?

If we follow a definition of the commons based on three dimensions—the resource, the community and the institutions (Kip *et al.* 2015)—we can find all three at play in these evening gatherings. The *common-pool resource* is the atmosphere of conviviality, its sensual qualities and the opportunities to watch and relax in a crowd and to come into contact with strangers. Even though it is immaterial, it is a produced good that is collectively consumed for its sensual pleasures of seeing, hearing and smelling a crowd of (mostly) joyful and diverse people. The setting and experience of a social collectivity simultaneously allows for both relative anonymity and the prospect of unforeseen and exciting personal contacts. In significant distinction to traditional commons, such as meadowlands or fisheries, the use of this commons does not subtract utility from other potential users (Hess and Ostrom 2007). On the contrary, its use can even add to the commons. Kornberger and Borch (2015, pp. 7–8) suggest that this non-subtractive character of the resource is characteristic for urban commons: "consuming the city is nothing but the most subtle form of its production". The community of *commoners* is made up of everyone who partakes in the gathering. It is an open and fluid community. Everyone can enter and leave as he or she wishes, provided their behaviour is civilised. The *institutional rules* may not be explicit, but some of them can be discerned easily: it is okay to sit close to strangers, but it also requires respect of each individual's and each group's space and privacy. Another rule seems to be that the space is used for friendly and casual conversations, not primarily for business negotiations or personal disputes. Voices are kept relatively low, at regular conversation volume, etc.

As a collective good, the evening gatherings are not organised by administrative or profit-seeking organisations. They are self-organised by the people who simultaneously consume the atmosphere and the different attractions and offers. The self-organisation we are speaking of does not occur in a reflexive fashion. There is no explicit and agreed-upon plan among participants, and the set-up does not require an explicit position or defined process for monitoring or regulation. The gatherings occur as an aggregation of individual interests to participate in a collective endeavour that is driven by neither economic nor regulatory interests.[10] Nevertheless, there are elements of these gatherings (such as various small groups conversing while sitting on the ground) that are related in a particular fashion (conviviality and relative anonymity) that justifies speaking of a social organisation that is sustained over time.

What we found most fascinating is the fact that these evening gatherings have been happening in a fairly consistent manner over the years. This is remarkable for two reasons. First, the gatherings amount to an 'urban commons' (Kip *et al.* 2015) involving divergent if not conflicting interpretations and usage of the same material resource: the bridge as a picturesque space of night-time quiet versus the bridge as a joyful party. Using the terminology 'commons' is thus by no means intended as a normative assessment of the events (as if all types of commons were to be viewed as positive *per se*), but for analytical purposes. It is noticeable how, in spite of the conflicts and the involvement of municipal authorities for greater regulation, these gatherings continue to be held. Second, most 'hang-out commoners' consist of a changing cast of people. Still, the structure of different roles that people co-perform on the bridge remains relatively stable. We might even consider this a division of labour in the production of the hang-out atmosphere. Roles include 'normal' participants, musicians and other entertainers, bottle collectors and beverage vendors, and other small entrepreneurs selling their goods and services. The interplay of these roles produces the hang-out atmosphere, even though the cast of actors changes constantly over time. While some musicians appear with a certain regularity, there are also new people putting on shows, and others leaving. Although short-term visitors to Berlin make up a significant portion of 'normal' participants, there is always a flow of new visitors, which keeps the attendance of these events fairly even over the years. The line-up is never the same on any given day, over the course of the summertime season, over the years. In other words, in spite of the fluidity of the actors, the performance has exhibited significant consistency over time in view of the roles assumed on the bridge. And it occurs without any collective decision-making processes.

The phenomenon thus defies the rather static ideas of commoners as a clearly defined group of people, as proposed by neo-institutionalist commons theorists. This relates in particular to the first of Elinor Ostrom's (1990, p. 90) famous design principles for common-pool resources: "clearly defined boundaries" of the group of commoners. As this principle appeared to be consistently violated in our case, we focused on the social mechanisms that ensured the rhythmic stability of the evening hang-outs. The 'new mobilities paradigm' proves especially valuable for theoretically analysing this phenomenon.

Intersecting mobilities and co-performing commoners

The 'new mobilities paradigm' (NMP) offers a focused perspective to look at social phenomena through the lens of movement (Sheller and Urry 2006, Salazar 2017). Social phenomena such as tourism can be considered "as comprised and created by various intersecting mobilities (and immobilities) or as networks stretching from local to global" (Mavrič and Urry 2009, p. 650). This premise seems to be helpful when approaching urban places "in which overlapping activities of tourism and leisure now form part of its [the city's] fabric and life" (Maitland 2010, p. 176). The 'network' metaphor helps in thinking of urban (tourist) places not as fixed containers, but as unbounded (Sommer 2018). The idea of 'intersecting mobilities' (Baerenholdt *et al.* 2004) implies that there is something emerging at the distinct places where such differing mobilities—bodies, objects, imaginations—become articulated with each other. The concept of 'intersecting mobilities' transcends the binary thinking of tourist destinations as inhabited by locals and visited by tourists. To overcome this burden of (applied) tourism studies, Sheller and Urry (2004, p. 6) have described what happens at tourist places as "hosts-guests-time-space-culture[s]". The revealing aspect of time-space cultures underlines the stable but not static character of tourism-related urban places like the Admiralbrücke. To speak of such places in terms of contingently reproduced time-space cultures highlights the distinct interplay of people who bring places into being. The time-space aspect of the events can be highlighted in two aspects. With respect to the materiality of the bridge itself, in summer, it appears like a stage for a gathering every evening; in winter, more like a space of passage. Considering its atmosphere, we find a pulsating rhythm at the bridge regulated by the season and the time of day. The gatherings at the Admiralbrücke are not reproduced as exact copies every time—they are subject to a certain evolutionary contingency. This affects, for example, the types of people gathering there: for some urbanites, the bridge might be not 'cool' any longer; others are just getting into it. The distinctive potential ascribed to hanging out at the bridge presumably changes gradually over time.

Intersecting mobilities further means that the particular scene at the Admiralbrücke is constituted by several mobilities that operate in conjunction. Baerenholdt *et al.* (2004) distinguish between three types of mobilities: mobile objects, corporeal mobilities and imaginative mobilities (details are given in the next section). In order to specify NMP-informed thinking about tourism, some proponents draw on the notion of performance: "The NMP… understands tourism and travel as complex systems of people and places that come into existence *through performances*" (Mavrič and Urry 2009, p. 650, emphasis added).

Following this framework, it is possible to conceptualise the Admiralbrücke as a tourism-related place and gathering-like hang-out commons constituted by a multiplicity of intersecting mobilities. As such, it is surprisingly stable but not static. In the next step, we explain the diverse mobilities constituting the Admiralbrücke in more detail. Afterwards, we elaborate in greater detail how these unbounded gatherings are synthesised via *performances*.

The intersection of mobile objects, corporeal mobilities and imaginative mobilities

How can we understand the summertime evening social at the Admiralbrücke as produced through the intersection of diverse mobilities (and immobilities)? Drawing on our empirical work, we observe all three types of mobilities conceptualised by Baerenholdt *et al.* (2004). There are mobile objects, corporeal mobilities and imaginative mobilities involved in the reproduction of the gatherings at the Admiralbrücke. These mobilities do not necessarily need to be on site. Corporeal mobilities designate, e.g., locals, (new urban) tourists, cyclists, street peddlers, and so on. Some of them just pass by; others reside there. One could even add the swans and ducks passing on the channel underneath the bridge since they contribute to the set-up of the scene. A rather remote but definitely not irrelevant mobile object is the sun. As a mobile object, it produces the sunset people particularly enjoy at the bridge. To give an example of a more earthly mobile object, one could mention beer bottles: distributed mainly via Spätis[11] located near the bridge, the bottles reach the bridge.[12] They get clinked a few times, emptied and eventually leave the bridge, e.g., via shopping trollies used by people who collect them for the bottle deposit. Some of the bottle caps are indeed pushed into the tar gaps and remain as *immobile objects*. As such, the Yelp user we cited above memorialises them: "And still, somehow the bridge has charm. I think of the bottle caps driven and trampled into the cobblestone." As a memory of its author, or as a useful tip triggering anticipation of future visitors, this *imaginative mobility* informs the way the author and readers feel the attraction to go there (again) and to perform places like the Admiralbrücke.

These few examples reveal how diverse mobilities constitute the gatherings. The exemplary mobilities mentioned put into relief the far-reaching preconditions that make them possible. It needs photos and postings communicated via social media to promote the bridge as a *'this is so Berlin* place'. It needs supply chains to provide beer and beverages. It also needs street sweepers to come by regularly. These preconditions help to dissolve the boundaries of what happens at the Admiralbrücke. We record the gatherings as "not fixed or given.... It is more profitable to see them as 'in play' in relation to multiple mobilities and varied performances stretching in, through, over and under any apparently distinct locality" (Baerenholdt *et al.* 2004, p. 145). The bridge thus could be understood as a place "organising a multiplicity of intersecting mobilities" (Baerenholdt *et al.* 2004, p. 2).

As an interim result, we record that the evening socials represent sociomaterial hybrids. As such, the Admiralbrücke only contingently produces, reproduces and fixes itself as a place "fit to play" (Sheller and Urry 2004, p. 6). We aim to document the gatherings there as "hybrids bridging the realms of humans and nonhumans" (Baerenholdt *et al.* 2004, p. 2). Such "bridging is brought about by diverse mobilities and proximities, flows and anticipations, performances and memory as well as extensive socio-material networks stabilizing the sedimented practices that make tourist places" (ibid.). In order to detail how these assemblages emerge, we now turn to the question of how they are co-*performed*.

Co-performing socio-material gatherings at the Admiralbrücke

In a rather general sense, using the term 'performance' first highlights the fact that these evening socials need to be enacted to become a *new urban tourism* reality. This emphasis on the *eventfulness* of performances reveals the key role that time and space play for the enactment of the gatherings at the Admiralbrücke. This leads us to the capacity of performances to interlink all elements involved in the gatherings we approached as scenery organising intersecting mobilities. All these notions insinuate the relationality the involved elements are aligned with: "The scene is only produced, the setpieces and backcloth drawn together and inscribed with particular meanings, when *performed*" (Baerenholdt *et al.* 2004, p. 3, emphasis added). So, how can we detail the way the people on site co-perform what happens there?

Drawing on a relational understanding of space, it is important to look at two processes that mutually affect each other (Löw 2016). For one, we analytically assume the co-performers to make sense of the elements by relating them to each other.[13] Mobilities and immobilities are synthesised as space, in our case as hang-out scenery.[14] One could say that the spatiality of the scenery is emphatically experienced, affectively understood and physically incorporated and enacted (Helbrecht and Dirksmeier 2013). Equally, people arriving at the Admiralbrücke position themselves in a certain manner in relation to the encountered scenery. Hence, the co-performers on the bridge simultaneously act as spectators, actors and members of a temporary and anonymous ensemble. While co-performance is motivated by the existence of the hang-out commons, it is the act of co-performing that produces it.

The pivotal literature on tourism as a performed phenomenon (e.g., Edensor 2009, Coleman and Crang 2002, Urry and Larsen 2011) emphasises the "significance of materiality and objects" (Haldrup and Larsen 2006, p. 276) in the reproduction of tourism-related spaces. The gatherings at the Admiralbrücke are inconceivable without the distinct material qualities the co-performers refer to on site. Particular human actions result from and inform the social and material scenery on the bridge. These actions, especially those relating to co-dwellers and material objects, are relevant for such simple questions as "where do I want to sit down?" The material components of the gatherings at the Admiralbrücke—e.g., the bollards on the bridge—cannot be reduced to merely passive carriers of meanings and sign value. The bollards' affordance to lean on them is a striking example of this significance of materiality. More generally, the Admiralbrücke could be understood as space, which is "a concrete and sensuous concatenation of material forces" (Wylie 2002, cited in Edensor 2007, p. 206). As a space, it "possesses an agency to impact upon the sensibilities of those who dwell and move within" (ibid., pp. 206–207).

Concluding thoughts

The phenomenon of summertime hang-outs at the Admiralbrücke points to the constitutive potency of *new urban tourism* that was the starting point of our inquiry. We began by raising the question of what emerges where and when tourists and residents rub shoulders. Our case study at the Admiralbrücke provides one possible answer: an urban hang-out commons, co-performed by thousands of people every year. Similar cases of such rhythmic and informal evening gatherings can probably be found in most major metropolises in Europe and beyond. These gatherings reflect a quality of public social life in these cities. They are thought-provoking phenomena regarding contemporary modes of urban coexistence. Co-performed hang-outs represent specific public places of encounter which simultaneously offer the chance to stick with one's kind, to make new friends, to get to know people from different backgrounds or simply to enjoy a social scenery at no or low cost. Additionally, at least the case of the Admiralbrücke reveals how urban places originally used primarily as traffic areas may be transformed into temporary shared spaces. This is not guaranteed by official declarations, but the corporeal appropriation of such places.

Highlighting such aspects of urban hang-out venues is in no way intended to prejudge the conflicts that surround such places, the various competing claims, and practices or assessments about how they are to be negotiated. Following our abductive methodology, we thus started with a phenomenon that sparked our interest, in particular, to build a hypothesis by drawing on existing theories. More empirical research on participants of the Admiralbrücke and comparable hang-outs is necessary to test and possibly refine these hypotheses.

We proposed to conceptualise the gatherings as an urban commons in the form of a *rhythmic (re-)enactment of temporary socio-material gatherings*— co-produced and co-consumed by the people dwelling on site. In doing so, we addressed three pressing issues for urban and tourism studies dealing with *new urban tourism* phenomena. First, our case study empirically transcends clear-cut and mutually exclusive categories used to describe tourist places as geographically fixed entities, where certain types of people (e.g., locals/ tourists) are involved in a distinct manner (e.g., produce/consume). The hang-out commons at the Admiralbrücke are co-performed by 'residents' and, very likely, a broad variety of temporary 'city users' (Martinotti 1993, cited in Costa and Martinotti 2003, p. 60) such as tourists, expats, exchange students and interns hanging out at the bridge as well (Novy 2017, p. 430). Following Kaschuba (2014) or Lloyd and Clark (2001, p. 357), even those who believe themselves to be 'residents' have long started to approach their own city 'as if tourists'. Ultimately, defining types of people involved does not get us very far in trying to understand how this urban chill-out phenomenon comes into being. We take these diverse (temporary) urbanites conceptually into account as co-performers. Their gatherings are motivated by neither monetary interests nor by legal or policy decisions, but by the needs and creative involvement of participants. As such, it does not get us very far to ask who the ones who produce hang-out venues are, and who is represented as the consuming class. The gathering-like evening socials at the Admiralbrücke seem to be 'prosumed' as hang-out commons. In distinction to what is widely understood as commons, in the case of the Admiralbrücke, there is indeed no clearly bounded group, with its defined procedures of decision-making and engagement. Finally, our case study shows that temporary socio-material gatherings, like the ones at the Admiralbrücke, need to be understood not as fixed entities, but as unbounded. The types of mobilities intersecting on site indicate that the far-reaching movements taking place before and after the gatherings at hang-out venues like the Admiralbrücke emerge and fade away in a distinct rhythm.

Second, we highlighted the fact that the aforementioned mobilities intersecting at places like the Admiralbrücke need to be *performed*. The idea of 'intersecting mobilities' proves useful to elaborate on the ground how the hang-out commons at the Admiralbrücke emerges through encounters of highly mobile people, objects, imaginings and immoveable material components alike. This approach emphasises the significance of performance, as the activities that articulate these mobilities with each other need to be performed to set the scene and to put the gathering in play. As mentioned above, we thereby addressed a limitation of performance-centred accounts in urban tourism research, as recognised by Giovanardi *et al.* (2014). This limitation "relates to studies that consider the intersection between performances of tourists and locals within the frame of conflict... and opposition... thus offering only a limited account of the possible outcomes of these encounters" (Giovanardi *et al.* 2014, p. 104). Nonetheless, our case study should prompt further research detailing how exactly 'appropriate' or 'disturbing' performances (de)stabilise such outcomes like hang-outs/commons.

Third, the perspective that we propose highlights the idea of hang-out events as hybrid socio-material gatherings. Thus, in order to understand them, it is not sufficient to look at social actors alone, but also at their interaction with the materiality of the site. It is this materiality that makes the site pleasant, that shapes how people congregate and relate to each other. However, what still needs to be detailed empirically is how tourist performances *relate* to materiality in concrete terms (Sommer 2018). After all, this is a defining strength of the performance approach, which emphasises the fact that actions are not conceivable without taking into account stages, decor or set pieces.

All in all, urban hang-out sceneries, like the one at the Admiralbrücke, reveal the deep interconnectedness of urban everyday street life and tourism. The everydayness of places like the Admiralbrücke is of interest in terms of what we call *new urban tourism* and is simultaneously constituted by this form of city usage. The hang-out commons we outlined in this study is one possible outcome. Approaching the goings-on at the Admiralbrücke beyond mutually exclusive categories meant focusing on the interplay of intersecting mobilities, co-performing urbanites and the socio-materiality of the scenery. Generally speaking, it seems inevitable and promising to build on diverse approaches (mobility studies, assemblage thinking, tourism studies) in order to grasp the relationality of such urban tourism phenomena.

Notes

1   C. Sommer and M. Kip contributed equally to this work.
2   Such urban spaces of encounter, like Canal Saint-Martin, can also be approached as places of *Muße* (see Kramer, Winsky and Freytag, Chapter 9 in this volume).
3   Stock (Chapter 3 in this volume) shows how conflictive narratives on *new urban tourism* are based on opposing the right to the city to the right to mobility.
4   Similar case studies conducted in other cities are rare or have a different orientation. Freytag (2010), for example, analysed mobility patterns of repeat visitors to Paris who aim to participate in everyday life.
5   The *Oooh, Berlin!* website (www.ooohberlin.com), for example, promotes the place explicitly to locals and expats: "We are OOOH BERLIN and we lovingly create FREE 'cool maps' for Berlin locals, expats, and culture-hunting visitors!" (available at ooohberlin.com, accessed 30 January 2018).

6 Entry on Yelp by Yukie S. from 1 May 2014; accessed 28 August 2018; our translation from German into English. Available from: www.yelp.de/biz/admiralbrücke-berlin-2

7 Entry on Yelp from 13 March 2011; accessed 28 August 2018; our translation from German into English. Available from: www.yelp.de/biz/admiralbrücke-berlin-2

8 Entry on Yelp from 30 April 2010; accessed 28 August 2018; our translation from German into English. Available from: www.yelp.de/biz/admiralbrücke-berlin-2

9 See also Larsen's remarks on visting friends-and-family tourism, Chapter 2 in this volume.

10 Although some people might take advantage of the situation and make money during these events, they are not the driving force behind the organisation of the gatherings. It is because the events happen regularly that some small entrepreneurs have started to make some money—from vendors, street musicians to can and bottle collectors. State agents, such as police officers or sanitation employees, regulatory personnel or conflict mediators of the municipality, provide a certain framework, however contested, for the evening gatherings, but, obviously, they do not organise the events.

11 This term is used throughout Berlin to refer to the city's convenience stores, which are often open 24/7.

12 As we already noted in our field observation, (alcoholic) beverages are also sometimes sold by street vendors.

13 Of course, personal dispositions (e.g., mood, milieu, etc.) as well as hegemonic discourses (about, e.g., the 'right' way to 'really' experience Berlin) prefigure this way of performative placemaking.

14 Such processes of synthesisation could be easily imagined considering the way people 'understand' distinct settings. Think, for example, of an ensemble consisting of a computer, a printer, a telephone and a desk. This may be enough to make a room an office.

References

Baerenholdt, J.O. *et al.*, eds, 2004. *Performing Tourist Places*. Aldershot and Burlington, VT: Ashgate.

Cohen, S.A. and Cohen, E., 2017. New directions in the sociology of tourism. *Current Issues in Tourism*, published online: 8 July [accessed 10 August 2018].

Coleman, S. and Crang, M., 2002. Grounded tourists, travelling theory. *In*: S. Coleman and M. Crang, eds, *Tourism between Place and Performance*. New York and Oxford: Berghahn, 1–20.

Costa, N. and Martinotti, G., 2003. Sociological theories of tourism and regulation theory. *In*: L.M. Hoffman *et al.*, eds, *Cities and Visitors. Regulating People, Markets, and City Space*. Malden, MA: Blackwell, 53–71.

De Angelis, M., 2010. On the commons: a public interview with Massimo De Angelis and Stavros Stavrides. *An Architektur & e-flux journal*, 17 (August), 4–7.

Dirksmeier, P. and Helbrecht, I., 2015. Resident perceptions of new urban tourism: a neglected geography of prejudice. *Geography Compass*, 9 (5), 276–285.

Edensor, T., 2007. Mundane mobilities, performances and spaces of tourism. *Social & Cultural Geography*, 8 (2), 199–215.

Edensor, T., 2009. Tourism and performance. *In*: T. Jamal and M. Robinson, eds, *The Sage Handbook of Tourism Studies*. Thousand Oaks, CA: SAGE, 645–657.

Flick, U., 2014. *An Introduction to Qualitative Research*, 5th ed. London: SAGE.

Freytag, T., 2010. Déjà-vu: tourist practices of repeat visitors in the city of Paris. *Social Geography*, 5 (1), 49–58.

Giovanardi, M., Lucarelli, A. and L'Espoir Decosta, P., 2014. Co-performing tourism places: the "Pink Night" festival. *Annals of Tourism Research*, 44, 102–115.

Glaser, B.G. and Strauss, A.L., 1967. *The Discovery of Grounded Theory*. Chicago, IL: Aldine.

Haldrup, M. and Larsen, J., 2006. Material cultures of tourism. *Leisure Studies*, 25 (3), 275–289.

Holm, A. 2015. Welche Stadt sehen wir? Die Urbanisierung des Tourismus [online]. Available from: www.schader-stiftung.de/galerie/artikel/welche-stadt-sehen-wir-die-urbanisierung-des-tourismus-als-simulacrum-des-staedtischen/ [accessed 31 August 2018].

Helbrecht, I. and Dirksmeier, P., 2013. Stadt und Performanz. *In*: H. Mieg and C. Heyl, eds, *Stadt. Ein interdisziplinäres Handbuch*. Stuttgart: J.B. Metzler Verlag, 283–298.

Hess, C. and Ostrom, E., 2007. *Understanding Knowledge as a Commons*. Cambridge, MA: MIT Press.

Kaschuba, W., 2014. Kampfzone Stadtmitte: Wem gehört die City? *Forum Stadt*, 41 (4), 357–376.

Kip, M. *et al.*, 2015. Seizing the (every)day: welcome to the urban commons. *In*: M. Dellenbaugh *et al.*, eds, *Urban Commons. Moving Beyond State and Market*. Basel: Birkhäuser, 7–25.

Kleinen, D. and Kühn, C., 2016. Urbane Aushandlungen. Die Stadt als Aktionsraum. *In*: W. Kaschuba, D. Kleinen and C. Kühn, eds, *Urbane Aushandlungen. Die Stadt als Aktionsraum*. Berlin: Panama Verlag, 7–12.

Kornberger, M. and Borch, C., 2015. Introduction: urban commons. *In*: C. Borch and M. Kornberger, eds, *Urban Commons. Rethinking the City*. New York: Routledge, 1–21.

Lloyd, R. and Clark, T.N., 2001. The city as entertainment machine. *In*: K.F. Gotham, ed., *Critical Perspectives on Urban Redevelopment*. Amsterdam: Elsevier Science, 357–378.

Löw, M., 2016. *The Sociology of Space. Materiality, Social Structure, and Action*. London: Palgrave.

MacCannell, D., 1973. Staged authenticity: arrangements of social space in tourist settings. *American Journal of Sociology*, 79 (3), 589–603.

Maitland, R., 2008. Conviviality and everyday life: the appeal of new areas of London for visitors. *International Journal of Tourism Research*, 10 (1), 15–25.

Maitland, R., 2010. Everyday life as a creative experience in cities. *International Journal of Culture, Tourism and Hospitality Research*, 4 (3), 176–85.

Maitland, R. and Newman, P., 2004. Developing metropolitan tourism on the fringe of central London. *International Journal of Tourism Research*, 6 (5), 339–348.

Maitland, R. and Newman, P., 2009. Conclusions. *In*: R. Maitland and P. Newman, eds, *World Tourism Cities. Developing Tourism off the Beaten Track*. London: Routledge, 134–142.

Mavrič, M. and Urry, J., 2009. Tourism studies and the new mobilities paradigm. *In*: T. Jamal and M. Robinson, eds, *The Sage Handbook of Tourism Studies*. Thousand Oaks, CA: SAGE, 645–657.

Novy, J., 2011. Kreuzberg's multi- and intercultural realities. Are they assets? *In*: V. Aytar and J. Rath, eds, *Gateways to the Urban Economy: Ethnic Neighborhoods as Places of Leisure and Consumption*. New York: Routledge, 68–84.

Novy, J., 2017. 'Destination' Berlin revisited. From (new) tourism towards a pentagon of mobility and place consumption. *Tourism Geographies*, 20 (3), 418–442.

Novy, J. and Huning, S., 2009. New tourism (areas) in the 'New Berlin'. *In*: R. Maitland and P. Newman, eds, *World Tourism Cities. Developing Tourism Off the Beaten Track*. London: Routledge, 87–108.

Ostrom, E., 1990. *Governing the Commons: The Evolution of Institutions for Collective Action*. Cambridge: Cambridge University Press.

Paavola, S., 2004. Abduction as a logic and methodology of discovery: the importance of strategies. *Foundations of Science*, 9 (3), 267–283.

Pappalepore, I., Maitland, R. and Smith, A., 2010. Exploring urban creativity: visitor experiences of Spitalfields, London. *Tourism Culture & Communication*, 10 (3), 217–230.

Pappalepore, I., Maitland, R. and Smith, A., 2014. Prosuming creative urban areas. Evidence from east London. *Annals of Tourism Research*, 44, 227–240.

Peirce, C.S., 1903. Harvard lectures on pragmatism. Abduction and perceptual judgments. *In*: C. Hartshorne and P. Weiss, eds, *Collected Papers of Charles Sanders Peirce V. 5 & 6*. Boston, MA: Belknap, 113–120.

Salazar, N., 2017. Afterword. *In*: J. Rickly, K. Hannam and M. Mostafanezhad, eds, *Tourism and Leisure Mobilities. Politics, Work, and Play*. London: Routledge, 248–252.

Sheller, M. and Urry, J., 2004. Places to play, places in play. *In*: M. Sheller and J. Urry, eds, *Tourism Mobilities. Places to Play, Places in Play*. London: Routledge, 1–10.

Sheller, M. and Urry, J., 2006. The new mobilities paradigm. *Environment and Planning A: Economy and Space*, 38 (2), 207–226.

Smith, A. and Pappalepore, I., 2015. Exploring attitudes to edgy urban destinations: the case of Deptford, London. *Journal of Tourism and Cultural Change*, 13 (2), 97–114.

Sommer, C., 2018. What begins at the end of urban tourism as we know it? *Europe Now* [online], 3 (5). Available from: www.europenowjournal.org/2018/04/30/what-begins-at-the-end-of-urban-tourism-as-we-know-it/ [accessed 10 August 2018].

Streit Entknoten (= Azad und Wietfeldt GbR), 2011. *Abschlussbericht Mediationsverfahren Admrialbrücke*. Berlin: Streit Entknoten.

Urry, J. and Larsen, J., 2011. *The Tourist Gaze 3.0*. London: SAGE.

Wöhler, K.H., 2011. *Touristifizierung von Räumen. Kulturwissenschaftliche und soziologische Studien zur Konstruktion von Räumen*. Wiesbaden: VS Verlag für Sozialwissenschaften.

11 You are a tourist!

Exploring tourism conflicts by means of performative interventions

Nils Grube

Introduction

The 'tourist' often proves to be a controversial and extremely ambivalent figure across many different scientific and social discourses (Cohen 1974, McCabe 2005). In particular, it seems difficult to reconcile the idea of oneself being a tourist. This difficulty is surprising, however, given the fact that "tourism has become a significant aspect of contemporary social life" (Baerenholdt *et al.* 2004, p. 4). Indeed, since the emergence and expansion of mass tourism in the middle of the twentieth century, there has been a continuous increase in global travel movements (Ashworth and Page 2011, Law 2002, Selby 2004). Modern societies are characterised by a high degree of mobility and transient ways of living and working or, as Mimi Sheller and John Urry emphasised in 'The new mobilities paradigm', "all the world seems to be on the move"[1] (2006, p. 207). Travelling is, of course, part of this new dimension of mobility.

According to the definition of the United Nations World Tourism Organization (UNTWO), a tourist is someone "who travels to and stays in places outside the usual environment for not more than one consecutive year for leisure, business and other purposes" (UNTWO 1995, p. 1). This broad definition implies a wide range of different motives for and characteristics of tourism. Thus, tourism does not only subsume recreational or leisure trips. It also includes educational seminars, trainees and internships, exchange semesters, business and conference trips, transnational project work, multi-locational living, job-related commuting and proximate forms of travel-ling such as volunteer tourism (Wearing 2001) or forms of digital nomadic 'workation' (Klug 2018). This suggests that more people are taking on the role of a tourist more often than ever before, and tourist behaviour is occurring more frequently, as well as in more situations and places than previously assumed. With the great variety of different forms and facets constituting tourism, the complexity of the social figure of the tourist is also growing, thus challenging the traditional image and stereotype of the mass tourist.

While these new forms of mobility increasingly intermingle with everyday work and life (Larsen 2008, Chapter 2 in this volume), tourism itself has changed. Professionally organised services allow tourists to move 'off the beaten track'. Forms of 'temporary living' in cities, in privately rented apartments for example, make it possible for tourists to approach everyday urban life and thus achieve more 'authentic' experiences. These and other new forms of tourism, as illustrated by the research on *new urban tourism* (Maitland and Newman 2009 and in this anthology), blur the lines between tourism and everyday life as well as between the concepts 'tourist' and 'local'.

Alongside this development, criticism of tourism in cities is also on the rise (Colomb and Novy 2017). Discussions about the limits of tourism and 'overtourism' that began in certain coastal regions of Southern Europe during the 1990s (Boissevain 1996, Saarinen 2014) are reaching more and more cities and finding expression in relatively open forms of 'tourismphobia' (Milano 2017). Especially in 'new tourist areas' (Maitland 2008), inner-city residential districts in which *new urban tourism* 'has its home', locals are increasingly objecting to touristification processes within their residential areas (Novy 2017a, 2017b, Füller and Michel 2014; see also Sommer and Kip, Chapter 10 in this volume). The reactions range from simple amusement over naive and clumsy visitor behaviour in public spaces to an outright rejection of visitors who lack sensitivity for the neighbourhood structures and who destroy them through their mere presence.[2] In this context, anti-tourism activists view tourists as visible signs of social change and drivers of displacement processes in inner-city residential areas (Novy 2013). Overpriced offers are usually dismissively termed by locals as tourist traps into which visitors continuously step due to their lack of local knowledge. However, if these traps become prevalent, the potential for conflict increases because their emergence effectively crowds out amenities for the local population. Concerns about the destruction of everyday structures by tourist masses are indirectly discharged in 'micro-practices of resistance' (Novy 2017a, p. 5) such as graffiti with anti-tourism slogans or, in the most extreme case, directly in the form of squatting in holiday apartments or physical attacks on tourist buses and rental bikes.[3] This, in parts, massive uprise of resistance against processes of touristification underlines the emerging need for action, resulting from growing tourist activities in urban neighbourhoods.

This criticism of tourism and the ambivalent view on the tourist as a social figure both served as the starting point for a series of intervening field experiments initiated and conducted by the author and various groups in Berlin throughout the course of 2015 and 2016.[4] These field experiments were intended to not only investigate the manifestations, effects and perceptions of tourism in urban space, but also to analyse the extent to which performative interventions in urban space are useful for learning about existing modes of tourist practice. They are theoretically based on the performance metaphor put forth by American sociologist Erving Goffman (1959). Following this approach, the objective of the study was to learn more about the perception and impact of tourism by consciously assuming the role of a 'tourist'.[5] Using temporary 'performances of tourism' in urban space, the field experiments aimed to 'touristify' various locations by means of active intervention. The general goal of these interventions was twofold: first, to gain new insights into the external perception of tourism by analysing the openly expressed reactions to the socio-spatial environment through targeted provocation; second, to achieve a critical reflection of one's own (tourist) practices and the related modes of action.

This chapter highlights and discusses the method of intervening field experiments. It will examine the extent to which the specific approach can be utilised to learn more about tourism and its perception and modes of action by means of individual interventions in the research field. The research is based on the assumption that tourism has an impact on the socio-spatial environment, which can be produced and investigated at the same time by executing separate performative acts. The article begins with a brief scientific overview of the figure of 'the tourist' and the ambivalence associated with it. These considerations are then incorporated into Goffman's theory of performance and linked to performative approaches in tourism studies. The third section introduces the method and the experimental set-up of the field experiment. In the fourth section, various forms and moments of anti-tourism criticism in the Berlin district of Neukölln illustrate how the physical presence of 'the tourist' is put into context by ongoing change within the neighbourhood. The article continues with a presentation and discussion of the main results. It concludes with a critical reflection on the method, while discussing the general exploration of the effects of tourism in urban space.

Theoretical considerations: the 'tourist' in a performative world

In his critical review of Cohen's (1974) essay 'Who is a tourist?', Scott McCabe almost pityingly points out that "being a tourist must be a pretty miserable existence" (McCabe 2005, p. 85). Tourists are usually portrayed as second-class citizens who, from the point of view of many inhabitants at a visited destination, draw attention to themselves through their "fatuous, lazy and plain dumb" (ibid.) behaviours. Others such as David Bowen and Jackie Clarke have pointed out that the discomfort among tourists against forms of mass tourism has grown. "[T]he unenviable reputation of mass tourists built up over the last 50 years or so and the caricatures that abound—for example, the *ridiculous* tourist, the *naive* tourist or the *rich* tourist" (Bowen and Clarke 2009, p. 2, emphasis in original) lead many individuals to dissociate themselves from being tourists.

Furthermore, Scott McCabe criticises that tourism studies often reproduce these negative images. Empirical surveys of travellers' definitions and perceptions of tourists tend to reveal that many travellers differentiate between their own modes and evaluations of travel and that of others (e.g., O'Reilly 2005, Galani-Moutafi 2000). For example, a self-differentiation is often carried out in the form of a role distance, as Jacobsen (2000) emphasised in his description of the 'anti-tourist role'. This concept describes "individuals, who are attached and committed to a role but who wish to distance themselves from the identity that accompanies it" (ibid., p. 286). Laura Week (2012) provides a very illustrative example for this role distance by examining and analysing the demarcation tendencies of 'travellers'. By identifying themselves as travellers, individuals develop alternative types of travel behaviour in an attempt to counter the problems they associate with tourism. In this context, 'travelling' is conceived as much more positive and sustainable than tourism. McCabe (2005) also points to the significant differentiations between travellers and tourists within tourism studies. In an empirical survey, for instance, many travellers claimed to go on trips instead of going on vacation as tourists do, or expressed their desire to explore and experience foreign countries and cultures rather than merely taking a break from being at home.

This discrepancy points to a central conflict: why is it so difficult to come to terms with the role of 'the tourist' when, at the same time, people are increasingly adopting this role, both consciously and unconsciously? It is precisely this ambivalence about the role of the tourist between practice and delimitation that is to be examined in the interventions by means of field experiments. As urban and tourist spaces offer a suitable stage to assume a large variety of different roles (Helbrecht and Dirksmeier 2013), the theoretical approach of performance proposed by Erving Goffman is especially apt for the field experiments.

Goffman's and Butler's performance perspective on social life

In *The Presentation of Self in Everyday Life* (1959), Erving Goffman understands people and their interactions as actors in social roles. For Goffman, considering the nature of social life as a constant and ongoing drama means applying the rules of theatre: individuals take on different roles and perform them continuously and in constant interaction with their surroundings. This means that these theatrical performances are not only characterised by individual scenes, but also by how actors perform and interact with the ensemble or by their costumes, requisites and settings. The audience ultimately decides on the performance's success or failure. For the drama of social life, therefore, social status can only be secured by a successful performance in interaction with the audience (Goffman 1959, p. 75). In this sense, social roles are created through individual performances and performed in front of an audience. However, there is a lack of consensus within the debate about performance regarding the question of freedom in exercising roles. Goffman (1959) defines performance as "all the activity of a given participant on a given occasion which serves to influence in any way any of the other participants" (p. 15). Critics argue that such a notion would designate individuals "as strategy-making beings, always calculating how situations might best be engineered to their advantage" (Edensor 2009, p. 543).

In contrast, Judith Butler (1993) argues in favour of self-reflexivity and control over particular performative roles. Butler illustrates how existing role models are exercised as unreflective habits. In order to be perceived as female, she argues, a socially recognised form of femininity must be expressed. By using the example of gender, Butler replaces 'performance' with the term 'performativity' to emphasise the repetition and reproduction of actions. Playing with dolls or wearing dresses are seen as attributes assigned as feminine. By adopting these attributes, women or girls would continually perform gender "through a repetitive iteration which seems to produce unambiguously gendered bodies" (Edensor 2009, p. 544). According to Butler's understanding of the performativity of tourism, it is worth discussing whether tourists are not active and permanent performers of their own role but rather fall into a predefined role themselves and thus adapt their behaviour.

Despite its antinomies to Goffman's view, Butler's performativity approach proves to be very fruitful for the field experiments. Especially its emphasis on the reproduction and repetition of actions in the definition and internalisation of certain role models serves as a great theoretical starting point for examining existing ideas and clichés about the figure of the tourist empirically. In the context of the field experiments, Goffman's strategic reflexivity of performances does not pose any theoretical difficulties. In fact, it constitutes the centre of its research design as the field experiment performances are carried out in order to provoke certain reactions. Drawing on Goffman and Butler, the performativity of social roles implies that only by performing the roles of a tourist does one become a tourist. Therefore, performative interventions within field experiments present an adequate method for exploring the potential conflicts that are associated with 'tourists' in urban settings. In addition, it allows for a closer evaluation of different role models and tourist practices.

Performance perspectives in tourism studies

The performance metaphor in tourism studies can be traced back to the 1970s (Edensor 2009). Following Goffman's notion of the social theatre, Dean MacCannell (1976) concludes that tourists only experience authenticity in a staged manner. This 'staged authenticity' is developed and professionally performed front stage, while the 'true', authentic everyday life of local cultures remains backstage, inaccessible to tourists (MacCannell 1976). This early reference to Goffman's concept of social theatre illustrates how closely tourism is linked to the performatively produced staging it is set in. However, academic focus was mainly placed on professionalising the production of tourist experiences. In the 1990s, John Urry developed an influential approach, placing the perception of tourists at the centre of his reflections and concentrating on the emergence of the tourist experience. He identifies visual impressions as the main component of tourist experiences. With the notion of the 'tourist gaze', Urry emphasises how these experiences are dependent on their surroundings: "When we 'go away' we look at the environment with interest and curiosity [...] we gaze at what we encounter. And this gaze is socially organised and systemized" (Urry 1990, p. 1).

Although Urry takes into account the significance of (social) settings, his representational approach was criticised by the 'performance turn' in tourism theory from the late 1990s and early 2000s (Edensor 2000, 2001, Coleman and Crang 2002, Baerenholdt *et al.* 2004). This turn—in contrast to privileging the visual—argues that tourism "demands metaphors based on being, doing touching *and* seeing rather than just seeing" (Cloke and Perkins 1998, p. 189, emphasis in original). Authors such as cultural geographer Tim Edensor also questioned the fixture of typologies of tourists put forward by others (e.g., Cohen 1974) because they seem to be useful in identifying regularities based on varieties of practice rather than certain types of people. In contrast, the metaphor of performance favours the understanding of tourism as a "process which involves the ongoing (re)construction of praxis" (Edensor 2000, pp. 322–323). Following Goffman's understanding of everyday performances, these new approaches "highlighted the corporeality of tourist bodies… [and] shifts methodological attention from meanings and discourses to embodied, multisensuous, collaborative and technologized *doings* and *enactments*" (Larsen 2008, p. 26, emphasis in original). With regard to tourists and performing tourism, cultural geographer Pau Obrador Pons also emphasises this importance: "It is because we are doing something in a particular way that we are tourists and we adopt tourist consciousness" (Obrador Pons 2003, p. 52). From this perspective, the specific link between tourism, social life and performance becomes evident. While Baerenholdt *et al.* (2004) stress that tourism has become a significant aspect of social life today, Edensor (2000, p. 323) underlines that "the whole of social life can be considered as performative".

Today the emergence of *new urban tourism* supports research informed by a performative approach (Stors *et al.*, Chapter 1 in this volume). This type of tourism is characterised by tourists who increasingly move beyond the beaten track in order to experience and co-creating authentic urban everyday life (Maitland 2013). It indicates that the concept of staged authenticity produced inside equally constructed 'tourist bubbles' (Judd 1999) has to be studied more carefully and include paying much more attention to its constitutive performances and performers. In other words, 'urban tourists' should be seen as "performers that can be characterised by temporarily varying practices of a tourist nature" (Dirksmeier and Helbrecht 2015, p. 278). Tourism thus appears as a transient performance on a stage. These tourist practices of 'doing something in a particular way' should be examined with the help of field experiments.

Methodological references: how to perform a 'tourist'?

The initial consideration for developing the field experiments involved a critical perspective on 'being in field'. These deliberations focus on the role of the researcher and his or her influence on the field in question. On the one hand, the external researcher intervenes in the field as part of his or her own research activities. On the other hand, the subjects to be investigated may perceive the external researcher, which might change their behaviour. In order to investigate the conflicting nature of tourism in local urban neighbourhoods, a method was sought that incorporates exactly this awareness of direct influence in the field while allowing it to be applied.

Social research by means of field experiments

Social experiments can be divided into two different categories: laboratory and field experiments. Laboratory experiments take place in a closed setting that is specially equipped to conduct the experiment. The laboratory makes it possible to exclude external influences in order to achieve and prove the expected result. Both types are characterised by a staging of events, but whereas the staging in a laboratory takes place in an artificial setting, field experiments occur in a more 'natural' environment, which is familiar to the researched subjects (Singleton 1988, p. 192). By actively intervening in the non-experimental environment, researchers aim to reveal common activities (Eifler 2014). However, this method has both advantages and disadvantages. On the one hand, it is more difficult to establish internal validity using this method because the test conditions are more difficult to control and can rarely be repeated with the same result. But on the other hand, a potential advantage is that people in the field do not know about the ongoing experiment. This proves especially useful if their behaviour is to be made the subject of the scientific investigation (ibid., p. 206).

Despite the disadvantage of reproducibility, a test arrangement in the natural environment of the test subjects proves to be appropriate for investigating tourism by means of targeted interventions and the resulting reactions and behavioural patterns of residents. As described at the beginning of this chapter, tourism is often assumed to be conflictive and is presented as a serious threat to a neighbourhood. In contrast, this study aims to challenge such biased assumptions with the help of performative interventions. By this means, it unfolds some of the multifaceted reactions of residents to tourist performances. Furthermore, the natural environment makes it possible to experience the quality of one's own performance in field experiments and to test the performance based on provoked reactions. However, a significant risk in conducting field experiments is the unpredictability of reactions. In addition, other external influences can impair the experiments, making it impossible to verify the correlations between action and reaction. In order to counter the risks and to expand the classical setting within the field experiment method, further approaches from artistic spatial research were included during the methodological design process.

Spatial and performative interventions during field experiments

In addition to the social field experiment method described above, the dramaturgical approach inherent in street theatre provides another valuable basis for designing performative interventions. In this form of theatrical performances, smaller scenes are performed in public spaces in order to temporarily break up everyday urban routines in a playful and subtle way. The US-american performance art group *Improv Everywhere* provides a comedic example of this method. In their project *Human Mirror*, pairs of twins were dressed alike and positioned opposite each other in a New York metro. By doing so, the performative intervention created a deliberate irritation and surprise for other passengers (Improv Everywhere 2008). A similar approach to active intervention in public space was pursued in the work *White Spots* by the architect collective *Raumlabor Berlin*. As part of an intervening installation, several white cars were parked in a Munich suburb in varying numbers and arrangements. The intervention aimed to investigate the acceptance of difference and tolerance towards the foreign. The specific formation of the parked cars represents an intervention in the street scene that simultaneously appears unusual and organised, thus creating a kind of artificial 'threat backdrop' (Raumlabor Berlin 2006).

Both examples of the spatial intervention method employ the act of intervention rather than relying on pure observation and evaluating reactions to it: there was no comprehensive investigation into the perception of the intervention. The focus here was placed on the visual-artistic act. Nevertheless, the two approaches provide interesting ideas on how to challenge and provoke everyday structures in a playful and spatially effective way.

Another relevant reference is the 'detournement method' developed by the French artist group Situationist International (SI) (Debord and Wolman 1956). This method was born out of a critique of the capitalist paralysis in artistic practice and the weakening of art's revolutionary potential. It argues that artistic acts can only succeed if existing structures are consciously selected, broken down and placed in a modified context (ibid.). Only by reproducing existing elements in an altered context (misappropriation) is it possible to capture interrelations and reveal them in an indirect and subtle fashion. In the case of exploring anti-tourist tendencies in a residential neighbourhood, this requires reflection on common stereotypes associated with tourists.

The presented forms of intervention, especially in combination with the notion of foreignness, that lead to an irritation of everyday structures and the provocation of reactions were of primary interest for the methodological design process of the field experiments in Neukölln.

Touristification of urban neighbourhoods: the case of Neukölln, Berlin

To gain a deeper understanding of the antinomies when dealing with 'tourists', it seems pertinent to examine the socio-spatial context in which this ambivalence is most evident. Inner-urban residential areas present an excellent field, as in such areas the resident population's everyday life directly collides with tourists' desire to explore. As such, the neighbourhood of Neukölln in Berlin was selected as a field. For decades, Neukölln was considered a socially problematic area. Especially after the fall of the Berlin Wall in 1989, living conditions in the northern part of Neukölln were some of the worst in the city. Because the housing stock was in bad condition and rents were low, the area attracted poorer households, immigrant workers and students. Rates of unemployment, dependency on social welfare, and the proportion of poor residents of non-German ethnic background were statistically high (Huning and Schuster 2015). However, while many Berliners avoided the run-down neighbourhood, rising rents in the gentrified areas in other parts of Berlin began driving creatives, young urbanites and art scenes to Neukölln during the mid-2000s. As a result, the street scene began to change: vintage shops, record and book stores, art galleries, student cafés and hip bars started to pop up, creating a new image of the neighbourhood (ibid.). This socio-cultural change has ultimately contributed to a highly dynamic 'rental gentrification', which today affects the area enormously (Holm 2013). The increased attractiveness of the quarter is also reflected in a growing touristic interest in Neukölln.[6] Especially for younger tourists, visitors and other urban explorers, "Neukölln is now very much on the map as one of Berlin's most exciting neighbourhoods" (Ayres 2016). Diversity is precisely what draws many visitors as an online travel guide states: "Neukölln can be as gritty as it is charming and calls out to be explored" (ibid.).

However, resistance and protest have emerged among parts of the population of Neukölln. These parts see a direct relationship between the increased tourist attractiveness and dynamic changes in the neighbourhood. Anti-tourism graffiti can be seen scrawled across the walls of buildings, or as this example on an electrical terminal shows: "No more hipster party pack! Holiday apartments for refugees and homeless people. Airbnb is destroying our neighbourhood" (translation by the author, Figure 11.1). This claim does not address tourists in general but rather a specific type of tourist: the young, urban-lifestyle-oriented, 'off-the-beaten-track' tourist who uses short-term rental apartments instead of traditional forms of accommodation. This 'hipster party tourist' is attracted by the specific neighbourhood's reputation or its manifold nightlife opportunities. The ruthless partying in holiday apartments privately rented through touristic online platforms is one of many examples of how conflicts surrounding tourism are marked by an interrelationship between negative impacts on the neighbourhoods and the different or new forms of consumption or lifestyles, which are attributed to consumers from abroad.

Individuals perceived as 'foreign' are criticised not only for their physical presence, but also for their appearance. A poster spotted in Neukölln in the summer of 2011 poses the question "Are you a KIEZKILLER too?". The term KIEZKILLER refers to 'Kiez', which is a Berlin-specific name given to certain, mostly inner-urban residential areas, comparable to neighbourhoods. Since Kiez also describes the direct living environment, it is often of great significance for the residents in terms of identity and community. In this context, a KIEZKILLER appears to be a serious threat to the neighbourhood. The poster suggests, a KIEZKILLER can be identified by a wide range of indications: woollen hats worn even during the summer,

Figure 11.1 "No more hipster party pack!", anti-tourism protest in Berlin-Neukölln, 2016.

Source: Nils Grube.

big headphones, mirrored sunglasses, takeaway cups containing soy-based chai lattes, sneakers, an iPhone for tweeting every ten minutes, and a messenger bag with a MacBook inside. This poster serves as an excellent example of how the visible display of certain objects, attributes and practices could lead to conflicts in the neighbourhood. By using the word 'killer', the critic addresses in a very provocative way people who have a certain style of dressing or behaving that corrupts the environment. This representation is, of course, a very strong exaggeration of the situation as well as of the socio-spatial impact of individuals. It can even serve, to a lesser extent, as a serious warning that provides educational guidance on how to dress or behave properly in the respective neighbourhood. Nevertheless, the poster bears witness to a more far-reaching normative interpretation, which very often takes place in media discussions about gentrification. In short, during the course of the displacement process, high-income gentrifiers—the so-called young urban professionals ('Yuppies')—are invaders who contribute to the transformation of urban districts through higher purchasing power and targeted demand for higher-priced goods. The KIEZKILLER depicted here has a very high degree of ascribed status symbols and lifestyle-related possessions, thus fitting into the prevailing image of the 'yuppie'.

Although these critiques have been on the rise, counter-movements that question this virulent anti-tourism and the 'tourist bashing' have also emerged.

In the summer of 2012, for example, the Neukölln-based leftwing activist group *AZE*[7] held a neighbourhood discussion entitled "Spot the Touri!". The word 'Touri' is a common abbreviation for tourist, which is used by Berlin residents as well as in the media in a mocking or derogatory manner. In the invitation to the discussion, the group denounced the limited connection between tourism and neighbourhood change as well as the discursive construction of the 'Touri', which stems from racial and xenophobic resentments. They wrote: "Spot the touri! We are on the lookout for the official scapegoat for high rents, noisy partying, and lack of German-ness. And how can we define the Touri? Touri is the special Berlin name for a tourist. Definition of the Touri: 'foreign looks, foreign language, foreign habitus, foreign-ness'."[8] The group addresses the xenophobic criticism of tourists, according to which this single (foreign) group of people is blamed for rising rents or conflicts about nocturnal noise disturbances. These neighbourhood destroyers (see KIEZKILLER-Campaign) become identifiable through an apparent 'non-German-ness' behaviour or appearance. In this example, too, certain forms of looks and behaviour are associated with an identifiable foreignness and otherness, which seems to be anchored in the criticism of tourism in Neukölln.

Because of these rising tensions, Neukölln proves to be a predestined field to approach the conflicting nature of the tourist as a social figure. Similar to the unknown authors of the KIEZKILLER-Poster, the AZE activist group exaggerates the image of the tourist among critics. But in the case of the AZE group, the example shows more clearly how tourists (a) are pushed into the role of a scapegoat for everything negative, and (b) can be identified as 'non-Germans'. AZE could be seen as a counter-movement opposing the xenophobic tendencies of the ongoing tourism critic in Neukölln. These examples prove that Neukölln is a particularly appropriate field for the planned experiments, whose implementation and results are presented in the following section.

Performing tourism: intervening field experiments in Berlin-Neukölln

In order to conduct the field experiments and intervene in the field, a number of organisational preparations and conceptual considerations were necessary. As a supervisor not only interested in the intervention itself, but also in the role of the 'tourist' and its ambivalent perception and a critical evaluation of the chosen method, the greatest challenge was finding people to carry out the field experiments. Therefore, participating people had to be thoroughly instructed about the research project and thus get closely involved in the whole research process. What also proved to be difficult was that there was no budget available for the remuneration of any research assistants or professional performers. This problem was solved by integrating the project into a critical urban walk, which the author was able to implement as part of his own activist work with the Berlin Critical Geography Group.[9] However, these conditions were expected to yield a rather heterogeneous and indeterminable group of participants. This factor was also considered and used product-ively: the urban walks were conceptualised so as to comprehensively prepare participants for carrying out the intended field experiments. The way in which the field experiments were conducted is explained in detail in the following section on the experimental set-up.

Set-up of the intervening field experiments

A total of five urban walks were organised in 2015 and 2016 to conduct the field experiments. At the forefront of these walks, the author informed the participants about the upcoming tasks. Basic information was provided in the invitation text, announcing the walks via newsletters, websites or direct emails. Fundamental considerations on the ambivalent figure of the tourist and the theoretical frame of the performance were mentioned as well as direct references to the intended active exploration of tourism in the neighbourhood of Neukölln:

'I am a traveller, not a tourist!'—Why does no one want to be a tourist? What does it even mean to be a tourist? According to the perform-ance theory approach, being a tourist implies a role adoption. Tourism needs to be performed to obtain social reality. That's why tourism practices are central to examining tourism and its general rejection. We want to perform tourism in urban spaces with all its iridescent shapes and facets. Not only would we like to focus on self-awareness, but also on the outer perceptions: we adjust the way we gaze upon things and we exceed limits of common usual experiences. At the same time, we challenge local structures of everyday life and touristify them by our own appearance. We are annoying, we collect affects, we even provoke conflicts and drive them close to an escalation. In the end, we will know more about us and the effects of our actions as well as urban tourism and its increasing impacts on Berlin's neighbourhoods. Please bring touristic accessories like cameras, umbrellas, and rolling suitcases to promote our experiment!

This invitation was also written so as to motivate the participants to sharpen their consciousness about being in the field and to inform them that during the walk they would probably be perceived as tourists anyway. By asking the participants to bring touristic items such as cameras or umbrellas, the author also hinted at certain items or attributes that could be used in order to perform tourism in a 'right' way. At the beginning of each walking tour, the author assumed the role of the instructor of the experimental walking tour and read the invitation aloud again.

Before the field experiments started, further preparations were neces-sary. These were divided into two steps: a short field inspection and a joint workshop in which Goffman's theory and the methodological approaches of performative intervention were presented and illustrated. During the first step, it was important to ensure that all participants had a general understanding of the field prior to the interventions. For this reason, a brief inspection of the quarter was carried out. By walking through several streets of the neighbourhood guided by the author, the participants were instructed to pay attention to possible signs of tourism or tourism-related conflicts. Initial impressions such as foreign-language speaking guests in cafés, signs that kindly ask guests to be quiet in front of bars, or a notably high density of eateries and restaurants were collected and shared in a brief group discussion. In addition, the author provided basic facts about the district and its latest developments.

The brief inspection of the field and the sharpening of the focus on tourist moments in the neighbourhood made it possible to prepare the group's participants for exploring tourism. This was followed in the second step by an introduction to the special research methodology. As "the notion of performance suggests that particular enactions need to be learned so as to achieve a degree of competence" (Edensor 2000, p. 326), another important step in preparing the field experiments was the theoretical introduction through which the participants of the walking tour were enabled to intervene as tourist performers. To this end, the participants were asked four trivial questions about general visible features and characteristics of tourism in the city:

(1) What do tourists do?
(2) What do tourists wear and/or how do we identify tourists?
(3) Where do we find or encounter tourists?
(4) And how do locals react to tourists?

These questions reflect the main theoretical considerations explained earlier. They aim to shed light on some of the common associations and stereotypes attached to tourists. While the first three questions try to uncover images of what a tourist is and how he or she can be visually identified, the fourth question focuses on the perception of encounters between locals and visitors.

Within the context of a joint workshop the answers from the groups were written on cards and collected on a wall. Based on the answers, a rather classic, clichéd image of a 'tourist' emerged in most of the workshops: city maps, photo cameras and day packs reveal tourists, as do questions about directions or slow strolls. Suitable places to meet tourists would be sights, the city centre, hotels, restaurants or metro stations. The reactions to tourists were diverse: the answers to this question ranged from positive reactions, such as helpfulness, to clear rejection and ignorance. At this point, it is necessary to emphasise that the answers given in this query and the resulting images are of utmost importance for the subsequent experiments. Only the tourist attributes and aspects mentioned allow the group of participants to take on the role of the 'tourist' or to carry it out in a convincing manner. Therefore, the author has refrained from adding additional aspects that might differentiate various forms of the 'tourist' figure.

Afterwards, Goffman's performance metaphor on social life was presented. With the help of this theoretical perspective, the collected answers could easily be translated and transformed into theatrical elements. The tourist practices listed under question one became actions and scenes on the stage. The answers to the second and third question were used to identify requisites (2) and sceneries (3) to support the performative acts. Using answers to the fourth question, the workshop highlighted possible audience reactions to the performances. With this reversal of questions in the individual components of the performance, it was possible to go beyond quickly conveying Goffman's theoretical metaphor and making it comprehensible. At the same time, the first ideas of potential tourist performances became apparent, which could then be elaborated and trialled as interventions in the subsequent field experiments.

In order to conduct the field experiments, the participants formed small groups and developed ideas for performative interventions. The answers to the audience reactions mentioned above served as a starting point: just as in the theatre, the question of the extent to which the audience would be involved was left to the discretion of the performers. Since tourism and its conflicting nature in public space was to be investigated, performers were instructed to deliberately provoke conflicts.[10] The majority of the performative interventions undertaken by the groups were primarily oriented towards the image of the mass tourist: pavements were blocked by suitcases or standing in the way, and passing pedestrians were repeatedly asked the same silly questions. In order to verify whether the results of the interventions were satisfying, the experiments were repeatedly interrupted, analysed and modified by relocation, changed requisites or varied performances.

Main results of the intervening field experiments

As an excerpt from the various field experiments, three examples are presented and considered in more detail here. In the first example, one group dealt with a variation of the performance of a guided tour (Figure 11.2). With such a performance, a clearly recognisable form or element of organised tourism needed to be installed in the public space of the neighbourhood. In order to call more attention to themselves, the group wore matching hats and carried city maps. The group then moved through the neighbourhood, suddenly changing direction at a loud command from the guide in a way that was incomprehensible and unexpected for unknowing bystanders. A remote observer noted the reactions of the locals and examined whether the intervention had any effect on the surroundings. The intervention was probably perceived as touristic, but not particularly noticed or even critically mentioned. However, after modifying the experimental set-up, the group was able to provoke one critical reaction: the group spread out, taking over the cycling path as well as the pavement, and caused negative reactions by an annoyed cyclist, who shouted at the group that it should move out of the way.

Figure 11.2 Experimental group with unexpected turns, Berlin-Neukölln, summer 2015.

Source: Nils Grube.

In the second example, another group played with the dichotomy of antipathy and empathy in their field experiment. For this purpose, they used rolling suitcases. With the increase of privately rented holiday apartments in the residential areas, rolling suitcases are generally regarded as a visible sign of tourism and are notorious as an everyday source of conflict because of the noises they make when rolling over cobblestone streets. At the same time, rolling suitcases are shaping the debate about incompatibility and conflicts over touristification processes. The slogan 'No more rolling suitcases', sprayed on a wall in Neukölln in 2011, has gained city-wide popularity and serves as a frequently quoted symbol for tourism criticism in Berlin (Novy 2017b). With the rolling suitcases, the group staged a rolling suitcase accident on a street corner (Figure 11.3). They hoped that after the accident, a derogatory reaction due to the noise and the mere number of 'trolley tourists' could initially be reversed, so that bystanders of the group would rush to help. However, the intended reaction did not occur; one reason might be that the street was relatively empty at the time of the experiment. In a second attempt, the group tried changing the scenery: in the outside area of a well-filled cafe, a meeting of three tourists was staged. The tourists came from

Figure 11.3 Performative intervention of an artificial rolling suitcase accident, Berlin-Neukölln, summer 2015.

Source: Nils Grube.

different directions with their rolling suitcases and greeted each other demonstratively, then parking their rolling suitcases in front of the cafe in a clearly visible position. After having a cup of coffee together, they said goodbye and left in different directions—but with the wrong suitcase. Here, too, reactions of both antipathy (visible tourist practices and items in front of the cafe) and empathy (comments from cafe visitors or staff that the suitcases were accidentally swapped) were hoped for. Despite the new scenery, the intended reactions largely failed to materialise.

In the last example, one group addressed 'party tourism'. As previously mentioned, the behaviour of younger 'tourists' at night is a predominant area of conflict in Neukölln. In addition to noise disturbances and littering, residents often criticise the ignorant and self-centred behaviour of so-called 'party tourists', predominantly young visitors who travel to the city only for its night life. Taking up this conflict, the group asked passers-by in English and in a very polite manner how to reach a nearby park. This park is famous as a place where illegal drugs can easily be purchased, which makes it a popular destination for many party tourists. For some locals, tourists are seen as a main contributor to the demand for drugs in that park (Viil 2018). When the respondent gave the necessary information, the group became rowdy, throwing confetti in the air and cheering loudly that the party is about to start. In one attempt of this experiment, an unexpectedly unpleasant situation arose for the group. After the interaction, the respondent, an older woman, rushed angrily behind the performers and confronted them. She was very annoyed by the group's reaction. In her view, she had helped by giving friendly directions and had received a rather ignorant and self-centred response. In order to de-escalate the situation and calm her down, the group explained the experiment. The woman then asked if the group members live in Berlin and when they confirmed this, she surprisingly replied that in this case everything would be fine. Knowing that the group members are Berlin based, seemed to appease the woman in a profound way and she simply left.

This result reflects a certain explosiveness with regard to the apparently differentiated evaluation of behaviour based on the knowledge of the geographical origin of the performers. 'Berliners' apparently are less easily accused of conflict-inducing behaviour than people from abroad. Hence, the result also provides further insights into the ambivalent perception of and judgement on 'tourists' in the neighbourhood. The occurrence of certain behaviours or characteristics, such as speaking in a foreign language, creates stereotypes and clichés in the perception of the subject. In this case, there was an aversion to the ignorant, complacent behaviour of the 'party tourists'. The way in which the annoyance of the elderly lady vanished after clarifying the set-up of the experiment, however, also reveals how quickly these role assignments can change again. This strengthens those theoretical approaches which understand tourism as performatively produced.

Reflexions on the method of performative intervention

In a final round, participants shared and discussed the experiences gained during their performative interventions. First, they reflected on how much they themselves had learned about the role of tourism and tourist practices in an urban residential area. Almost all of the participants reported a deeper understanding of social interactions in public space, the assumption of social roles, and the effects of performed acts on the surrounding area. Second, participants discussed whether the field experiments provided insight into the external perception of tourism in the neighbourhood. In this sense, the undertaken effort was only partially successful. Outsiders often reacted unexpectedly positively to the tourist performances. Only in a few instances were grievances openly expressed or negative reactions provoked. This result cannot be clearly explained. On the one hand, it allows assumptions to be made that conflicts about touristification are not as far-reaching as presumed. On the other hand, the method may also be viewed critically. It may prove to be unsuitable for grasping these conflicts, as residents may not react spontaneously to the interventions or express their criticism only among themselves.

Above all, non-local participants reported that they tended to avoid provoking negative reactions and conflicts during their experiments. In their reflections, they perceived the task of intervening local everyday structures as difficult, because they could not directly grasp what these structures entailed. Similarly, they were less familiar with the subtleties of tourist conflicts in Neukölln. Another possible explanation for the lack of more profound results may be that the interventions were developed and carried out within a short period of three hours in one afternoon. Over a longer period, it may be possible to modify and refine the interventions and optimise them in order to achieve more direct reactions and conflictive situations.

Furthermore, recording external perceptions proved difficult. Perception itself is hardly measurable, so that the observations could only be based on recognisable reactions or behavioural changes in the audience. Although individual observers were set up, they often felt recognised as such by the 'audience'. Technical tools such as hidden cameras could contribute to making performative interventions appear 'more real'. The aspect of credibility was also discussed in connection with the performance itself. As a result, the participants concluded that it is important to avoid reflecting on one's own acting during the performance, as this can cause the performance to lose its effect on the audience. However, only a few groups succeeded in doing this. The example of the rolling suitcase accident showed that the performance appeared to be too 'unnatural' to achieve the desired effect. This experiment could be improved by recruiting a higher level of acting talent. In the specific urban context, Georg Simmel's 'blasé attitude' of city dwellers should also be considered. According to Simmel, city dwellers become more blasé because of the constant barrage of external influences on the human senses that they experience in the urban environment (Simmel 1903). The public spaces and streets in the highly heterogeneous experimental field of Neukölln offer spectators many unusual scenes and conspicuous 'actors'. Thus, the performed interventions were not even noticed or recognised as such. Here, too, the performances could benefit from clearer and more precise articulation.

In a final step, the groups discussed whether their interventions have the potential to affect the neighbourhood and to disrupt existing resentments towards tourists. It was noted that the scope and number of interventions were too limited to challenge prejudices against tourists. Due to the low intensity and number of interventions, only rudimentary reactions were achieved. The absence of strong negative reactions can be explained by a tendency to avoid publicly expressing their anger due to existing social norms.

Nevertheless, the approach presented here has proven to be promising. The ongoing debate about touristification in Neukölln can be described as a very passionate, emotional conflict. Actively intervening and provoking reactions with performative interventions was therefore a suitable means for examining veritable manifestations of these conflicts. This is precisely why the method provides a useful approach to acquiring knowledge and insights on the impacts of tourist practices or conflict-inducing practices. During the field experiments, it became clear that certain tourist practices could have different effects, not only because of the number of people, but also because of the kind of performance. This result was one of the most significant findings of the performative interventions.

Conclusion

In this chapter, the method of performative interventions as part of social field experiments was presented and discussed. These field experiments were intended to examine both manifestations, effects and perceptions of tourism in urban space, as well as the extent to which performative interventions in urban space could serve as a useful method for challenging existing understandings of tourist practices. Following the assumption that tourism has an impact on the socio-spatial environment, which can be produced and investigated at the same time, consciously assuming the role of a 'tourist' should make it possible to learn more about the perception and impact of tourism. For that purpose, various scenic performances of tourism were developed and carried out through temporary interventions in the neighbourhood of Berlin-Neukölln.

Two objectives were pursued. On the one hand, the experiments were meant to address the effects and perceptions of tourism and how tourism can lead to conflict in urban spaces. On the other hand, the experiments aimed to provoke the public into revealing potential resentment and negative attitudes towards tourists. Although only a few negative reactions were observed, the method proved very effective in demonstrating the complexities of tourist performances within field experiments. This ultimately facilitates a deeper understanding of the role of the 'tourist'. Consciously assuming the role of the 'tourist' is not enough to create social reality. In order to attain this status, it is necessary to perform in front of an audience. Perception falls between the act itself and the resulting reaction.

With the emphasis on the procedure's experimental character, the methodology provides an innovative research approach. By means of targeted and active intervention, the field is manipulated in such a way so as to allow any exposed fundamental interactions to be investigated. As a consequence, the method poses a high risk in terms of calculating and forecasting results. This risk of an unpredictable outcome is deliberately included in the process using a conscious trial-and-error research approach. It underlines that exploratory testing and acting is more important in this method than the precise execution of a scientific study to prove previous assumptions. Performative interventions and field experiments thus make an important contribution to the research on tourism conflicts and ambivalence in connection with the role of the 'tourist' between practice and delimitation.

The Neukölln case study highlights two final findings in particular. First, Neukölln has proven to be a complex stage for performing tourism in such a way as to evoke differentiated public reactions. Due to its socio-spatial heterogeneity and diversity of use, the neighbourhood is a good example of those new tourist areas in which touristic, recreational and everyday practices are intertwined, thus making categorical attributions such as 'tourists' virtually impossible. The assignment of the conscious execution of the role of the tourist in the Neukölln field proved equally complex. Goffman's understanding of performance as a reflexive instrument that can be used to influence others led to difficulties with regard to the exposure of tourism-critical reactions. Even if John Urry once unmistakably and simply stated that we are all tourists all of the time (Urry 1995), this circumstance remained a challenge in the experimental handling of a conscious use and execution of this role. In this respect, the initial statement 'You are a tourist!' seems as simple as it is difficult.

Notes

1 In their paradigm, Sheller and Urry include movements of people for leisure or tourist travel along with movements as a result of flight and migration, as well as movements of material and immaterial objects such as ships, data or places (Sheller and Urry 2006).
2 This phrase refers to Hans M. Enzensberger's often-quoted assertion that the tourist destroys exactly what he or she is looking for by finding it. In fact, Enzensberger wrote in his text on the *Theory of Tourism*: "By [the goal] being reached, it has already been destroyed" (Enzensberger 1962, p. 192).
3 In May 2016 activists squatted in an Airbnb flat in the Berlin district of Neukölln to protest against the professionalisation of renting out of former residential flats to tourists (Jacobs 2016). In Barcelona anti-tourism protesters have launched numerous, partly violent actions in recent years. In 2017 tyres on sightseeing buses and rental bikes were slashed. In summer 2018 members of a leftist Catalonian youth organisation hijacked a tourist bus and hung out posters to demonstrate against mass tourism (Sobot 2018, Landbeater 2017).
4 The implementation of the field experiments emerged from the author's reflections on how tourism and conflicts around it can be experienced through artistic, intervening, participating or activist methods within the framework of urban walks. The author used various walks to instruct its participants on intervening performances of tourism in space and to evaluate the results of the field experiments with them. This chapter will present its major results and learnings.
5 Within the context of the conflicts around tourism in the neighbourhoods and the tendencies of many travellers to distinguish themselves from tourists, the 'tourist' is treated primarily as the image or metaphor constructed by negative associations.
6 See Parish (Chapter 5 in this volume) for a critical examination of 'new wellness industries' as a signifier for ongoing gentrification and emerging *new urban tourism* in the Toronto neighbourhood of Roncesvalles.
7 AZE is short for *Andere Zustände ermöglichen* which can be translated as *enable alternative conditions*.
8 The whole invitation can be found online: http://aze.blogsport.de/touristen/.
9 The Critical Geography Berlin is a loose association of critical geographical scholars and operates between academia and activism. In addition to hosting workshops, participating in discussions and publishing joint research results, the group organises monthly urban walks to different places in Berlin and on topics of critical geography (www.kritische-geographie-berlin.de).

10 However, in order to prevent an over-escalation of the situation, performers were instructed to resolve the intervention in a playful manner.

References

Ashworth, G. and Page, S.J., 2011. Urban tourism research: recent progress and current paradoxes. *Tourism Management*, 32 (1), 1–15.

Ayres, D., 2016. Neukölln like a local. *Travelmag.com* [online]. Available from: www.travelmag.com/articles/neukolln-like-a-local/ [accessed 9 May 2018].

Baerenholdt, J. *et al.*, 2004. *Performing Tourist Places*. Aldershot: Ashgate.

Boissevain, J., 1996, *Coping with Tourists: European Reactions to Mass Tourism*. Providence, RI: Berghahn Books.

Bowen, D. and Clarke, J., 2009, *Contemporary Tourist Behaviour: Yourself and Others and Tourists*. Wallingford: CABI.

Butler, J., 1993. *Bodies that Matter. The Discursive Limits of Sex*. London: Routledge.

Cloke, P. and Perkins, H.C., 1998. 'Cracking the canyon with the awesome foursome': presentations of adventure tourism in New Zealand. *Environment and Planning D: Society and Space*, 16 (3), 185–218.

Cohen, E., 1974. Who is a tourist? A conceptual review. *Sociological Review*, 22, 27–35.

Coleman, S. and Crang, M., 2002. *Tourism: Between Place and Performance*. New York: Berghahn Books.

Colomb, C. and Novy, J., 2017. *Protest and Resistance in the Tourist City*. London: Routledge.

Debord, G. and Wolman, G.J., 1956. Mode d'emploi du détournement. *Les Lèvres Nues*, 8.

Dirksmeier, P. and Helbrecht, I., 2015. Resident perceptions of new urban tourism: a neglected geography of prejudice. *Geography Compass*, 9 (5), 276–286.

Edensor, T., 2009. Tourism and performance. *In*: T. Jamal and M. Robinson, eds, *The Sage Handbook of Tourism Studies*. London: SAGE, 543–557.

Edensor, T., 2001. Performing tourism, staging tourism: (re)producing tourist space and practice. *Tourist Studies*, 1, 59–81.

Edensor, T., 2000. Staging tourism. *Annals of Tourism Research*, 27, 322–344.

Enzensberger, H.-M., 1962. Eine Theorie des Tourismus. *In*: H.-M. Enzensberger, ed., *Einzelheiten I Bewusstseins-Industrie*. Frankfurt: Suhrkamp, 147–168.

Eifler, S., 2014. Experiment. *In*: N. Baur and J. Blasius, eds, *Handbuch Methoden der empirischen Sozialforschung*. Wiesbaden: Springer, 195–209.

Füller, H. and Michel, B., 2014. 'Stop being a tourist!' New dynamics of urban tourism in Berlin-Kreuzberg. *International Journal of Urban and Regional Research*, 38 (4), 1304–1318.

Galani-Moutafi, V., 2000. The self and the other: traveller, ethnographer, tourist. *Annals of Tourism Research*, 27 (1), 203–24.

Goffman, E., 1959. *The Presentation of Self in Everyday Life*. New York: Doubleday & Company.

Helbrecht, I. and Dirksmeier, P., 2013. Stadt und Performanz. *In*: H. Mieg and C. Heyl, eds, *Stadt. Ein interdisziplinäres Handbuch*. Stuttgart: J.B. Metzler, 283–298.

Holm, A., 2013. Berlin's gentrification mainstream. *In*: C. Bernt, A. Holm and B. Grell, eds, *The Berlin Reader. A Compendium on Urban Change and Activism*. Bielefeld: Transcript, 171–187.

Huning, S. and Schuster, N., 2015. 'Social mixing' or 'gentrification'? Contradictory perspectives on urban change in the Berlin district of Neukölln. *International Journal of Urban and Regional Research*, 39 (4), 738–755.

Improv Everywhere, 2008. Human Mirror [online]. Available from: https://improveverywhere.com/2008/07/06/human-mirror/ [accessed 9 May 2018].

Jacobs, L., 2016. Erst belegt, dann besetzt. *Die Zeit*, 4 May [online]. Available from: www.zeit.de/gesellschaft/2016-05/berlin-hausbesetzung-ferienwohnungen-airbnb-polizei [accessed 19 July 2018].

Jacobsen, J.K.S., 2000. Anti-tourist attitudes: Mediterranean charter tourism. *Annals of Tourism Research*, 27 (2), 284–300.

Judd, D.R., 1999. Constructing the tourist bubble. *In*: D.R. Judd and S.S. Fainstein, eds, *The Tourist City*. New Haven, CT: Yale University Press.

Klug, K., 2018. Neo-nomadismus: digital – multilingual – global. *In*: K. Klug, ed., *Vom Nischentrend zum Lebensstil*. Wiesbaden: Springer, 17–26.

Landbeater, C., 2017. Anti-tourism protesters in Barcelona slash tyres on sightseeing buses and rental bikes. *The Telegraph*, 2 August [online]. Available from: www.telegraph.co.uk/travel/news/bus-attack-in-barcelona-adds-to-fears-as-tourism-protests-grow/ [accessed 19 July 2018].

Larsen, J., 2008. De-exoticizing tourist travel: everyday life and sociality on the move. *Leisure Studies*, 27 (1), 21–34.

Law, C.M., 2002. *Urban Tourism: The Visitor Economy and the Growth of Large Cities*. London: Cengage Learning EMEA.

Maitland, R. and Newman P., 2009. *World Tourism Cities. Developing Tourism Off the Beaten Track*. London: Routledge.

Maitland, R., 2013. Backstage behaviour in the global city: tourists and the search for the 'real London'. *Procedia: Social and Behavioral Sciences*, 105, 12–19.

Maitland, R., 2008. Conviviality and everyday life: the appeal of new areas of London for visitors. *International Journal of Tourism Research*, 10 (1), 15–25.

McCabe, S., 2005. 'Who is a tourist?' A critical review. *Tourist Studies*, 5 (1), 85–106.

MacCannell, D., 1976. *The Tourist*. London: Macmillan.

Milano, C., 2017. *Overtourism y Turismofobia. Tendencias globales y contextos locales*. Barcelona: Ostelea School of Tourism & Hospitality.

Novy, J., 2017a. 'Destination' Berlin revisited. From (new) tourism towards a pentagon of mobility and place consumption. *Tourism Geographies*, 1–25.

Novy, J., 2017b. The selling (out) of Berlin and the de- and re-politication of urban tourism in Europe's 'capital of cool'. *In*: C. Colomb and J. Novy, eds, *Protest and Resistance in the Tourist City*. London: Routledge.

Novy, J., 2013. Berlin doesn't love you. Notes on Berlin's 'tourism controversy' and its discontents. *In*: C, Bernt, A. Holm and B. Grell, eds, *The Berlin Reader. A Compendium on Urban Change and Activism*. Bielefeld: Transcript, 223–237.

Obrador Pons, P., 2003. Being-on-holiday: tourist dwelling, bodies and place. *Tourist Studies*, 3 (3), 47–66.

O'Reilly, C.C., 2005. Tourist or traveler? Narrating backpacker identity. *In*: A. Jaworski and A. Pritchard, eds, *Discourse, Communication and Tourism*. Clevedon: Channel View Publications, 150–169.

Raumlabor Berlin, 2006. White spots – Toleranztopographien [online]. Available from: http://raumlabor.net/white-spots/ [accessed 24 January 2019].

Saarinen, J., 2014. Critical sustainability: setting the limits to growth and responsibility in tourism. *Sustainability*, 6 (1), 1–17.

Selby, M., 2004. *Understanding Urban Tourism: Image, Culture and Experience.* London: I.B. Tauris.

Sheller, M. and Urry, J., 2006. The new mobilities paradigm. *Environment and Planning A*, 38, 207–226.

Simmel, G., 1903. Die Grossstädte und das Geistesleben *In*: K. Bücher and T. Petermann, eds, *Die Grossstadt. Vorträge und Aufsätze zur Städteausstellung.* Dresden: Gehe Stiftung zu Dresden, 185–206.

Singleton, R., ed., 1988. *Approaches to Social Research.* New York: Oxford University Press.

Sobot, R., 2018. Barcelona tourist bus stormed by protesters as they launch summer of chaos. *Express*, 9 July [online]. Available from: www.express.co.uk/news/world/986064/barcelona-holiday-protest-tourist-backlash-arran [accessed 19 July 2018].

Urry, J., 1995. *Consuming Places.* London: Routledge.

Urry, J., 1990. *The Tourist Gaze: Leisure and Travel in Contemporary Societies.* London: SAGE.

UNTWO, 1995. *Technical Manual: Collection of Tourism Expenditure Statistics* [online]. Available from: www.e-unwto.org/doi/pdf/10.18111/9789284401062 [accessed 19 July 2018].

Viil, L., 2018. A communal balancing act: everyday struggles of local activists in the context of Görlitzer Park. *In*: Autor*innenkollektiv Gras and Beton, eds, *Gefährliche Orte. Unterwegs in Kreuzberg.* Berlin: Assoziationen A, 163–172.

Wearing, S.L., 2001. *Volunteer Tourism: Seeking Experiences That Make a Difference.* Wallingford: CABI.

Week, L., 2012. I am not a tourist: aims and implications of 'traveling'. *Tourist Studies*, 12 (2), 186–203.

Index

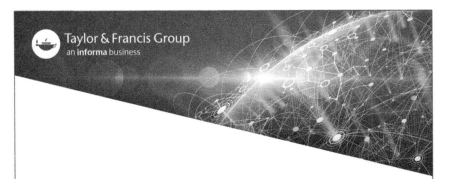

Printed and bound by CPI Group (UK) Ltd, Croydon, CR0 4YY

01/05/2025

01858420-0001